FISHER
ANNOTATED TRAVEL GUIDES

Sandra Hart

Edited and Annotated by
Robert C. Fisher

Contributing Editors
Susan Irwin-Wiener
Nancy Henzel-Clarke
Claire E. Devener

Best of the
Caribbean
1984

Fisher Travel Guides
New York / Easton, Maryland / Champaign, Illinois

DEDICATION
For Michael Burke and the way we were. For Dena Kaye
and Sy Grossman and the way we are. For Nancy
Henzel-Clarke, Susan Irwin-Wiener and Claire Devener,
each of whom did much, much more than friendship
ever required. Thank you each for existing.

Library of Congress Cataloging in Publication Data

Hart, Sandra.
  Best of the Caribbean, 1984.

  (Fisher annotated travel guides)
  Includes index.
  1. West Indies—Description and travel—1981–
—Guide-books. I. Fisher, Robert C. II. Title.
III. Series
F1609.H33   1983   917.29'0452   83–16290
ISBN 0–8116–0057–2

Maps and city plans by Pictograph.

Text and cover design by Parallelogram/Marsha Cohen

Editorial production services by Cobb/Dunlop Publisher Services, Inc.

The Fisher travel guides include:

Bahamas	**France**
Bermuda	**Germany**
Best of the Caribbean	**Greece**
Britain	**Italy**
California and the West	**Japan**
Canada	**Mexico**
Europe	**Spain and Portugal**
Florida and the Southeast	**Texas and the Southwest**

Distributed in the U.S.A. and Canada by
New American Library, 1633 Broadway, New York, N.Y. 10019

Distributed worldwide by
**New American Library, Inc., International Department
1633 Broadway, New York, N.Y. 10019**

Printed in the United States of America

Contents

Foreword   ix

List of Maps   xi

The Private Islands   1

    Mustique   1

    PSV   2

    Peter Island   2

    Young Island   3

    Palm Island   4

Anguilla   6

    The Hard Facts   6

      Planning Ahead, Getting There

    Anguilla Today   7

    Touring Anguilla   9

    Inside Information   10

      Hotels and Guesthouses, Restaurants, Nightlife, Shopping, Sports

Antigua   16

    The Hard Facts   16

      Planning Ahead, Getting There, Formalities on Arrival, Settling Down, Getting Around

    Antigua Today   20

    Touring   21

    Inside Information   25

      Hotels, Restaurants, Nightlife, Shopping, Sports

Barbados   41

The Hard Facts   41
Planning Ahead, Getting There, Formalities on Arrival, Settling Down, Getting Around

Touring   46
Inside Information   49
Hotels, Restaurants, Nightlife, Shopping, Sports

Bonaire   60

The Hard Facts   60
Planning Ahead, Getting There

Bonaire Today   62
Touring   63
North Bonaire, South Bonaire

Inside Information   65
Hotels, Restaurants, Nightlife, Shopping, Sports

Dominican Republic   72

The Hard Facts   72
Planning Ahead, Getting There, Formalities on Arrival, Settling Down

The Dominican Republic Today   74
Touring   74
Santo Domingo, Elsewhere on the Island

Inside Information   79
Hotels, Restaurants, Nightlife, Shopping, Sports

Grenada   88

The Hard Facts   88
Planning Ahead, Getting There, Formalities on Arrival, Settling Down, Getting Around

Grenada Today   91
Touring   92
Outside St. George's

Inside Information   94
Hotels, Restaurants, Nightlife, Shopping, Sports

Guadeloupe 101

The Hard Facts 101
*Planning Ahead, Getting There, Formalities on Arrival,
Settling Down, Getting Around*

Guadeloupe Today 106
Touring 107
Inside Information 112
Hotels, Restaurants, Nightlife, Shopping, Sports

Haiti 129

The Hard Facts 129
*Planning Ahead, Getting There, Formalities on Arrival,
Settling Down*

Haiti Today 131
Touring 132
Inside Information 134
Hotels, Restaurants, Nightlife, Shopping, Sports

Jamaica 144

The Hard Facts 144
*Planning Ahead, Getting There, Formalities on Arrival,
Settling Down, Getting Around*

Touring 148
Inside Information 151
Hotels, Restaurants, Nightlife, Shopping, Sports

Martinique 165

The Hard Facts 165
*Planning Ahead, Getting There, Formalities on Arrival,
Settling Down, Getting Around*

Martinique Today 169
Touring 171
Inside Information 174
Hotels, Restaurants, Nightlife, Shopping, Sports

Nevis   185

The Hard Facts   185
Planning Ahead, Getting There, Formalities on Arrival

Nevis Today   187
Touring   188
Inside Information   192
Hotels, Restaurants, Nightlife, Shopping, Sports

Saba   201

The Hard Facts   201
Planning Ahead, Getting There

Saba Today   202
Inside Information   204
Hotels, Restaurants, Nightlife, Shopping, Sports

St. Barts   207

The Hard Facts   207
Planning Ahead, Getting There, Formalities on Arrival, Settling Down

St. Barts Today   210
Touring   211
Inside Information   212
Hotels, Restaurants, Nightlife, Shopping, Sports

St. Eustatius   219

The Hard Facts   219
Planning Ahead, Getting There, Formalities on Arrival, Settling Down

St. Eustatius Today   221
Touring   222
Inside Information   224
Hotels, Restaurants, Nightlife, Shopping, Sports

St. Kitts   228

The Hard Facts   228
Planning Ahead, Getting There

St. Kitts Today   **230**

Touring   **231**

Basseterre, The Philatelic Bureau, The Chateau of M. de Poincy, Bloody Point, Carib Indian Remains, Old Road Town, Middle Island Village, Halfway Tree Village, Brimstone Hill Fortress, Mt. Misery, Black Rocks, Estridge Research Station, Frigate Bay

Inside Information   **234**

Hotels, Restaurants, Nightlife, Shopping, Sports

St. Martin   **242**

The Hard Facts   **242**

Planning Ahead, Getting There, Formalities on Arrival, Settling Down, Getting Around

St. Martin/Sint Maarten Today   **246**

Touring   **246**

Inside Information   **248**

Hotels, Restaurants, Nightlife, Shopping, Sports

Index   **261**

"The traveler should not take the journey. The journey should take the traveler. . . ." Words that belonged to John Steinbeck.

But what better way could there be than as a sojourner to approach the scattered 7,000-some smorgasbord of islands that make up the Caribbean . . . many admittedly just uninhabited rocks and reefs. The traveler (a different breed than the tourist) arrives on any of the thirty-plus major islands of the Caribbean with an open mind, heart and willingness for whatever comes his way.

You will be on your own journey. We've just passed the same way a little ahead of you and would like to pave the not-always-paved roads. We'd like to show you some of the special places you might want to search out on your own.

We know that not everyone will agree with our choices, and we've been very selective. But we too have paid our dues—shaking sand out of suitcases, hauling sail on many of the large yachts that sail in these waters, watching the dolphin come to play at our bowsprit, counting stars at midnight, then arriving at a new port-of-call early each morning for a new Caribbean day.

Caribbean days include bantering with the kids who dive off the island of Dominica, asking the inevitable, "Hey Cap, you want coconut? We get you one for $5 beewee." Inflation, it's everywhere. The compromise comes at $2 beewee.

Caribbean days are dancing barefoot at the Admiral's Inn in Antigua to a twelve-member steel band, the instruments made from cut-off oil drums, certain that the ghost of Lord Nelson who once fought the French from this English naval base is dancing with us.

Days in the Caribbean mean taking to the heart of Haiti, the first black republic, perhaps poor in material goods, but with an inner sense of pride and self, and an outer display of spirit in her paintings, passion and perseverance.

These sun-streaked days include galloping polo ponies in the north of the Dominican Republic, led by an Indian maharaja who oversees some 3,000 working horses and polo ponies.

They include wandering topless on the relaxed beaches of St. Barts, the perfect French island of cuisine, private beaches, beauty and the total power to cast a spell.

Caribbean days mean discovering Saba, a 3,000-mile high volcano that shoots straight out of the sea, sharp and steep, where there are no beaches. The women weave lace and the men go to sea, as they have done for generations. It feels like Atlantis.

Many of these ports are just now being "discovered" by the traveling public in America and Europe. But Christopher Columbus came before us all. He made four journeys to this still-New World for their Spanish majesties, Isabella and Ferdinand. His final thanks was very lonely—an isolated death on European shores. But in his will, he asked to be buried in Santo Domingo. Eventually, his wish was granted.

But now it's your journey, traveler. May it treat you well.

(S.H.)

About the Book

This book tries to provide precise information for the experienced traveler. We include ratings for hotels and restaurants, ranging from 5 Stars (best) to 1 Star (Good). Ours is the first guidebook to attempt this kind of classification on the Caribbean, and we can't for a moment imagine that everyone will agree with the author and the editor in their choices. On the other hand, we believe Sandra Hart and Robert C. Fisher are as qualified as any other observers of the Caribbean scene to make these selections, and to rate the tourist establishments honestly and fairly. They have been assisted by an informal committee of experts who have been guaranteed anonymity, but we hasten to add that all decisions are the responsibility of the author and editor.

About the Author

Sandra Hart, author of this experienced travelers' guide to The Best of the Caribbean, is a long-established expert on these islands in the sun, having written about them for many publications, including *Vogue* and *Town and Country*. In her capacity as author, she has visited all the populated islands of the Caribbean, and in her years spent with Windjammer Cruises, has sailed to most of the area's harbors and ports. An accomplished sailor, she has skippered every kind of vessel including the world's largest commercial sailing ship, the *Fantome*. Ms. Hart, between bouts of writing and the many days spent investigating every corner of the Caribbean, is writing a novel in which the island and her love of sailing feature prominently.

About the Editor

The editor and annotator of a new series of guidebooks, including *Best of the Caribbean,* Robert C. Fisher, says his qualifications include more than 20 years of work with the Fodor guide organization, where he was selected by Eugene Fodor to succeed him as editor-in-chief of the series and president of the company. During his time with that firm, he helped create more than 62 titles, including one on the Caribbean, and was responsible for the rewriting and revising of all 75 books in the series, covering 120 countries. The work necessitated constant travel and continuous study, he says, and the frequent trips to the Caribbean were the best part of it. His formal education also prepared him to be a judge of travel standards, he feels, as he concentrated on international relations at Harvard College, on international law at Columbia University Law School and on the social sciences at Tokyo University Graduate School and Poona University in India.

On the professional side of things, Fisher is a former president of the New York Travel Writers' Association and is now president of the Society of American Travel Writers. He is also director of a charitable foundation, the International Association for Medical Assistance to Travelers (IAMAT), whose services he recommends highly.

If you have read this far, you must be a friend or a relative of the author or editor, possibly a reviewer, or as many of us, a hopeless addict of travel books and guidebooks. We thank you in any case, and hope this guide will be useful to you.

List of Maps

	Page
1. The Caribbean Area	5
2. St. Martin, St. Barts, Antigua	23
3. Grenada, Barbados	45
4. Haiti and Dominican Republic	75
5. Guadeloupe, Martinique	103
6. Jamaica	148
7. Saba, St. Eustatius, St. Kitts and Nevis	203

IMPORTANT NOTE ON PRICES, ETC.

Prices mentioned in this book were accurate at time of writing, but as all experienced travelers know, nothing in life is forever, particularly costs, hours and days of closing, and the ambience of a hotel or restaurant. Please phone ahead to obtain reservations, confirm price ranges, or check closing times in order to avoid being disappointed. We will be delighted to hear from you, whether it be a recommendation, complaint or both at: **Fisher Travel Guides, Suite 2300, 401 Broadway, New York, N.Y. 10013.**

STAR RATING SYSTEM

Hotels

★★★★★ 5 Stars. Super deluxe establishment, BEST of the best.

★★★★ 4 Stars. Deluxe. As comfortable as your own home, with better service.

★★★ 3 Stars. Superior. Has qualities that make it stand out.

★★ 2 Stars. Excellent. Nothing at all to complain about.

★ 1 Star. Good. One or two things may be missing, but an O.K. place.
Recommended.

Restaurants

★★★★★ 5 Stars. Best.

★★★★ 4 Stars. Excellent.

★★★ 3 Stars. Very Good.

★★ 2 Stars. Good.

★ 1 Star. Simple, but tasty food.
Recommended.

IMPORTANT NOTE: The Star Ratings for each country's hotels, restaurants and points of interest are based on each country's merits alone, and are not to be compared with ratings given to places in any other country. Standards and attitudes in each country vary, and so, therefore, must our ratings.

Best of the Caribbean

The Private Islands

A smattering, scattering dash of five islands that have been independently purchased by international consortiums. In some places, villas scattered over the island provide accommodation. In other places, visitors may stay in a true Main House. In no case will accommodations be inexpensive. ($200 double, U.S., *off*-season, is about the average.)

★★★★★ Mustique

nearest major airport: St. Vincent

When Koo "kooed" here with Prince Andrew, it made international headlines. Almost forgotten (for the moment) was that Mustique has been the traditional Caribbean hideaway of Princess Margaret who keeps a house here, and where the Prince stayed. Another luminary who keeps smaller quarters is Mick Jagger, in one of the 26 villa-homes it's possible to rent. Houses on the island total 42 and range from two to six bedrooms; rents are from $1,375 to over $5,000 a week, each with maid, cook and gardeners. It's possible to rent Princess Margaret's own house (four bedrooms), Les Jolies Eaux, with swimming pool and a few royal touches. Far more sumptuous is Sir Colin Tennant's compound, a Moorish-style mansion rising by the sea, all of white Barbudian coral and turquoise trim, Vincentian parrots on the wing outside, several pianos and a solid silver bed inside.

The future of Cotton House, a sprawl of villas that weave their way around manicured grounds and a swimming pool, is unknown. Opened by Sir Colin and other homeowners, it was sold to French owner, Guy de la Houscaye, and has had a succession of managers (He resides in Martinique where he owns the Bakoua Hotel.) Hopefully, it will reopen for the 1984 season since the villas are a bit of English perfection. The main house is usually a meeting place for backgammon, lunch, dinner, high tea or a discrete nightcap.

Two new tennis courts opened this season, along with a foliage-hidden outdoor bar, and some twenty riding horses are new "guests" who are expected to earn their keep. On some nights, there's a jazz band imported from neighboring Barbados, and Mustique now has its own steel band.

But the island mainstay remains Basil's Beachbar, managed by Basil Charles. The bar is open for lunch, dinner, drinks, gossip-swapping and down-and-out lie-telling (an island sport). If it's happening in Mustique, it's either happening at Basil's or he knows all about it. The food gets an A+ too!

1

Cost: Cotton House: $210–$275 per double, MAP, in-season. Villa rentals range from a high of $5,000 a week (six bedrooms), to a low of $1,375 a week. All villas come with maid, cook, island gardeners, and personal mini-moke. Contact: Holiday Homes and Yachts, 183 Madison Avenue, New York City, NY 10016.

★★★★★ PSV

PSV (officially, Petit St. Vincent) is a true refuge . . . for the rich and famous who crave a period of privacy, for executives who need to disconnect from their offices, and for all who wish to disappear into a realm ruled by graciousness.

Hayes Richardson helped create the perfection of PSV and is part-owner. He and his wife, Jennifer, manage the 22-cottage PSV Resort, with the help of a very good staff, and an amiable yellow Labrador foursome. (One of the dogs, Alexander, tends to adopt guests. With any encouragement, he'll drop by for a visit and stay for tea. Another, Samson, sleeps in the office telephone booth. He leaves room for callers, but be warned: he snores loudly!)

Ten of the cottages are scattered amidst flowering beachside foliage and four more are tucked away on hillsides. The remaining eight, perched atop cliffs, offer views that astound, day or night. Each is a private world of double-bed rooms, living room, dressing room, with red tile floors, straw mat rugs, walls of bluebitch stone (quarried on the island), brightly colored fabrics, woven wall hangings, greenery and fresh flowers. And here the closets are not bare. You'll find large golf umbrellas, beach towels, beach chairs, and other amenities. Outside is a wooden deck, a hemp hammock big enough for two, and a mailbox.

PSV is famous for its mailboxes. Just leave a message or food or drink order in the mailbox and hoist a yellow flag. One of the island's squad of roving mini-mokes will soon be by and your request fulfilled. You don't wish to be disturbed? Hoist the red flag.

For daytime activities PSV offers sunning, windsurfing, croquet, tennis, swimming, boutique browsing, strolling or jogging along a winding "nature path," and day sails—in a 38-foot trimarran, "Piragua." If you are so inclined, a picnic lunch and snorkling gear can be whisked by launch to nearby Petit St. Richardson, a tiny sand stage set with a palm tree, thatched roof hut, and one picturesque piece of bleached driftwood. Your very own private island.

At night most guests wander up to the main house, known as the Pavillion, to sip drinks on the terrace while the sun sets over the harbor; later there's dinner by candlelight. Most Wednesday nights a band, imported from neighboring Union Island, provides lively "jump-up" entertainment for guests and the Grenadine yachting crowd. On Friday nights, tables, chairs, linen, silver, and sometimes even a piano, are transported to a torch-lit stretch of sand for a beach barbeque. Here the heavens entertain. Stars lighting and breaking, a few falling into eternity. Peace prevails.

Cost: $163–$193 per person double occupancy (in season). Full American Plan.

★★★★ Peter Island

The Peter Island Hotel and Yacht Harbour Club in the British Virgin Islands is secluded and very private. Norwegian ship owner, Peider Smedwig, had the A-frame chalets prefabed in Norway in the early 1970s and sent over on his own ships. But don't let "prefab" scare you. Managers David and Gae Benson give personal attention to every manicured nook and ship-shape cranny, under the corporate eye of present owners, the Amway Corporation of Michigan.

Five new cottages of wood and island stone construction are underway; several additional tennis courts and a rondelle restaurant will open during the 1984–85 season. Each of the present ocean view duplex cottages are newly decorated in powder blue or coral decor with shell motif against modern Scandinavian wood, and each has a small refrigerator for stocking goodies.

There are tennis courts (one for night play), sailing on windsurfers, sunfish, 19-foot Squibs, snorkeling with equipment provided, and several horses for gentle trots along the beach (the horses aren't that fast). The Bensons will also arrange for a scuba boat to pick up certified guests—or sign uncertified ones for a resort course—to explore the HMS *Rhone,* a famous British ship sunk in the 17th century. The ship was used for filming *The Deep,* but more important to divers, it's now the home for many of the myriad fish in these tranquil, tropical waters. Deep sea fishing can also be arranged.

Peter Island also offers day boating trips to Virgin Gorda for picnics and snorkeling at the rock-hewn Baths and there are sunset cocktail sails throughout the week.

Music of some sort livens every winter evening. Bands are often imported from the neighboring island of Tortola, some 20 minutes away by water taxi.

For sensational solitude, with others of your choosing in a hilltop four-bedroom villa, the Crow's Nest earns its name, and comes with maid and cook service. Someone has to use that soccerlength living room! A mini-moke is provided for the Nest's guests; others walk the few minutes to their oceanside chalet where visiting yachts are their nearest companions.

Cost: $325 per double, MAP, in season; 10% service charge; 5% government tax. The Crow's Nest; $1,500 daily for eight guests.

★★★★★ Young Island

Young Island nests some 200 yards off St. Vincent's shores (connected by turn-around ferry). Manicured gardens housing one of the Caribbean's largest collections of plants and fruits—hibiscus, bougainvillea, ginger, flamboyant, pineapple, almond, mango, breadfruit, banana—is just a smattering of what's grown and what's apt to turn up on lavish breakfast or lunch plates. Here, too, is the largest species of the St. Vincent parrot . . . some in cages . . . some flying free. The unquestioned maestro, Cyrano de Bergerac, "works" the cottages for handouts of crackers or preferably the kitchen-baked banana bread. You will definitely know when he's in your neighborhood.

Far more discrete are partners Vidal Browne, who manages as well, with his lovely Marlon, and Dr. Fred Ballentyne (who occasionally windsurfs over at lunch). There's also a 44-foot ketch for day and sunset sails; a tennis court for night play; sunfish and snorkel equipment for guests.

Besides the thirty cottages where birds and bougainvillea play, Young Island has other "theirs-alone" touches: a separate offshore island called the Rock Fort (originally Ft. Duvernette). Here you can climb rocky steps to see the remains of one of the Caribbean's many forts, cannons, the supply storeroom, and a few bedding chambers. Once a week, there's a cocktail party at the base of the Rock Fort, with drinks and tid-bits brought over by the staff (many of whom proudly average 12 years of service), all night-lit by flaming torches.

Daytime you can lunch on the beach under thatched-roof gazebos, then recover in hammocks built for two. Nights, you rendezvous in the Longhouse bar, then dine in the split-level dining room where huge boulders form one wall and a string band serenades softly. In winter, conversations are likely to be in English; summers, they're more likely to be in French or Spanish, due to the heavy requests from European and South American guests.

But just so there's no mistake on the island ambience . . . The only time shoes are worn are on the tennis courts, although you might wear a Dior or a Givenchy to dinner.

Cost: $230–$260, MAP, double, in season. Off season, $145–$160, double, MAP.

★★★★ Palm Island

Technically and politically connected to St. Vincent, Palm Island is its own special place. It's owned and managed by John Caldwell (originally from Texas) and his wife, Mary. Mary designed the Palm Island Beach Club; John built it. Barefoot informality reigns.

The resort is a scattering of single-story stone cottages designed to welcome a maximum of 48 guests. The rooms are airily decorated with quilted green bedspreads, straw floor mats, wooden shutters, Mexican artwork; in some cottages draped mosquito netting adds a further tropical touch; other rooms offer open-to-the-sky showers, reached directly from the beach or via a connecting bathroom door. On each of the cottages' private patios are freshly-painted green wooden chaises, for sunning or sipping afternoon tea, delivered each day on request. Dining on a covered terrace consists of Continental cuisine and a lot of fresh fish from the sea. Steps away, the covered bar, with white metal, blue-cushioned furniture faces Casuarina Beach (dotted with white wooden, blue-cushioned chaises from which drinks or even lunch can be ordered) and a yacht-filled harbor. During the winter season, Saturday night is jump-up time. A steel band comes over from Union Island, just ten minutes away by boat.

There's a small boutique here, with Sea Island cotton dresses for women and shirts for men, along with some imports from other Caribbean islands and copies of a fascinating book, *Desperate Voyage,* written by John and describing his incredible post World War II single-handed voyage across the Pacific in a 29-foot sailboat.

Once a week the Sun Princess drops anchor here so you'll share the long stretch of Casuarina Beach with some 600-plus of the cruise crowd and the visiting yachting set. But since Palm Island has five of its own beaches, all shaded by coconut palms (hence the name), you can always opt for a more secluded beach to call your own. Sports are very Caribbean-casual: snorkeling, scuba diving (although spear fishing is not allowed), deep sea fishing, wind surfing and hobie cats are offered. Or you can take a special day sail to the Tobago Cays or charter a Palm Island yacht and visit other Grenadine islands.

Cost: $185–$195 double in season, Full American Plan.

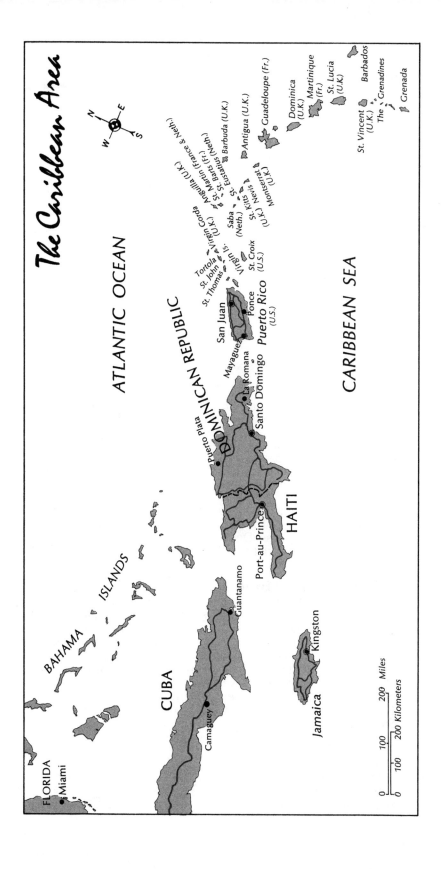

The Caribbean Area

N

W — E

S

ATLANTIC OCEAN

FLORIDA
Miami

BAHAMA ISLANDS

CUBA

Camaguey

Guantanamo

Jamaica
Kingston

Puerto Plata

DOMINICAN REPUBLIC

Santo Domingo

La Romana

Mayaguez

HAITI

Port-au-Prince

San Juan

Ponce

Puerto Rico
(U.S.)

St. Thomas
St. John
Tortola
Virgin Is.
(U.K.)
Virgin Gorda (U.K.)
Anguilla (U.K.)
St. Martin (France & Neth.)
St. Barts (Fr.)
St. Eustatius (Neth.)
St. Croix
(U.S.)
Saba
(Neth.)
St. Kitts
Nevis
(U.K.)
Montserrat
(U.K.)
Barbuda (U.K.)
Antigua (U.K.)

Guadeloupe (Fr.)

Dominica
(U.K.)

Martinique
(Fr.)

St. Lucia
(U.K.)

Barbados

St. Vincent
(U.K.)

The Grenadines

Grenada

CARIBBEAN SEA

0   100   200 Miles
0   100   200 Kilometers

THE HARD FACTS
Planning Ahead
Costs
The price of your Anguillian visit will depend on where you stay. Book into one of the luxurious hotel resorts and you're talking at least $100 a day without meals. Choose a guesthouse or rental apartment (all with kitchenettes) and costs will be well under that, even in-season. Most restaurants are extremely reasonable, and there's really not much in the way of shopping. Days are usually free since nature doesn't charge.

Climate
This is an island with too little rainfall for local citizens, but that makes it just perfect for vacationers. The warmest months are from July to October, and the coolest period is between December to February. The traditional trade winds blow from the east, and there's little talk of "how's the weather?" It's usually weather-perfect in paradise.

Holidays and Special Events
The most unusual days are only-in-Anguilla days: February 10 is Constitution Day; May 30 marks the commencement of the Anguillian Revolution and secession from the Associated State of St. Christopher-Nevis-Anguilla in 1967; December 19, Separation Day, marks the formal separation of Anguilla from the Associated State. Other holidays are: January 1, New Year's Day; May 23, Whit Monday; the Queen's Official Birthday in mid-June; Carnival Week, the first week in August, with August 1, 4, and 5 as official holidays . . . lots of boat races, dancing, and partying; Christmas Day and Boxing Day (December 26); Good Friday and Easter Monday (as well as Sunday).

Sources of Information
Stateside, contact the Anguilla Tourist Information Office, 25 West 39th Street, New York City, NY 10018; or the Caribbean Tourism Association, 20 East 46th Street (Room 1201), New York City, NY 10017. Once on the island, stop by the Anguilla Tourist Office, the Secretariat, The Valley.

Packing

With the exception of a few pharmacy items (toothpaste, sun-tan lotion, etc.), pack what you need for a casual island stay. All clothing should be washable or expendable, since dry cleaning doesn't exist. Women may want a long skirt or caftan; men rely on slacks and lightweight shirts. A sports jacket (for men) and sweater (for women) is also a good idea for nights when the temperature dips. As on all the islands, don't wear bathing suits into town or at lunch tables without coverups. Pack film . . . it's expensive when available.

Documentation

A valid passport is always best, although a birth certificate or voter's registration card is accepted for U.S.-born citizens, as well as U.K. and Canadian citizens. All visitors must have a return or on-going ticket.

Getting There

Getting there is half the fun if you take the ferry (three times daily) from St. Martin (French side). Two ferries, *Cheers* and *Treasure Spot* take a little over half hour, and the new hydrofoil, *Arawak II* is a bit faster. Cost about $7. There's also daily air service from St. Martin on Windward Island Airways (WINAIR), Air Anguilla, and Carib Air, all scheduled carriers. Charter flights are also easy to arrange, but they can be expensive unless there's a small group traveling. There's no direct jet service from anywhere. You have to work just a bit to deserve Anguilla.

Money

Officially, the Eastern Caribbean dollar is the currency, although we've never seen the U.S. dollar turned away. There are four banks on the island who will change your money if you insist. Present rate of exchange is $1 U.S. to $2.65 E.C. (subject to currency fluctuation).

Tipping

Most hotels add a standard 10% service charge to hotel and restaurant bills, but double check to be sure. An extra tip is always appreciated for friendly (if island slow) service, and what's your hurry anyhow?

Learning to Cope

Shopping.   Shop hours are bankers hours, and both are the same: 8 AM to noon and from 3 PM to 5 PM, Mondays through Fridays. Saturday is catch as catch can, and boutiques at the hotel-resorts will open if you ask at the reception desk.

Electricity.   It's 230 volts almost everywhere except the resort hotels, where it's probably 110 AC. Confused? So is the system. Ask at your hotel.

Communications.   Cable and wireless is the answer to all telephone calls (as it is in most of the Caribbean), as well as telex and cables, both locally and internationally. However, during unspecified hours, the cable and wireless operator may not be operating at which time one makes a "special booked call." This can be time consuming and expensive. Example: a telephone call to San Juan that didn't go through, $47 U.S. dollars from a hotel! Anguilla's stamps are good take-home finds for collectors, since they're unusual and very attractive.

Language.   Strictly English, sometimes with a slight lilt.

ANGUILLA TODAY

It's possible Donald Westlake capsuled the spunk and spirit of this special island just 16 miles long and 3 miles wide, tucked off the north coast of St.

Martin, in his book, *Under An English Heaven.* The book is subtitled, "Being a true recital of the events leading up to and down from the British invasion of Anguilla on March 19th, 1969, in which nobody was killed but many people were embarrassed." It was an "invasion" that made international headlines, but most readers were unaware that headlines of another sort would be made in the mid to late 1980s.

This may be the mating call of the last hideaway in the Caribbean . . . the Caribbean the way it was meant to be: without plastic or flown-in anything; lots of secluded nooks and niches for private picnics; enough hotels and housekeeping cottages to go around; slightly inconvenient so that a 10-minute plane connection is required from St. Martin or better yet, the 35-minute ferry that loads kids, cats, groceries, engine parts, folk who live there, and you (if you'll fit). Some sort of organized "nightlife" is arranged weekends at the handful of very spiffy hotels that have mostly grown just this year, but a true Anguillian evening is still spent at *Smitty's* dancing barefoot on the beach while the scratch band plays on, eating barbecued chicken or fish with your fingers and talking to the leading citizens of the island, almost all of whom—probably including the entire government—are here.

Fortunately, most of the world doesn't know about Anguilla yet, and we were literally threatened by good friends from London who tried to bribe us not to write about their favorite get-away spot. It's with mixed feelings that we're letting you in on the news.

Anguilla is the island that hosted the British invasion, basically held by mistake, in 1969. The reasons are truly Caribbean and complicated, but Britain didn't seem to understand that the Anguillians wanted to remain British, and not be separated into a state with St. Kitts and Nevis, a good 70 miles southeast. They had nothing against the good people of Nevis and St. Kitts; it's just that they also had nothing in common with them. Somehow, Whitehall never quite got the message the jungle drums had intended delivering. England sent paratroopers in full battle dress . . . the paratroopers landed and dug trenches in the Caribbean sun . . . the cows and goats were mystified . . . the kids were hysterical . . . and the adults waved British Union Jacks in welcome. After a while, the soldiers stuck their rifles in the sand, shed their battle fatigues and went swimming while everyone cheered.

Now, Anguilla is again a British Dependent Territory, which is just dandy with everyone, and the only unhappy people are the British soldiers who now have to pay to visit like other vacationers. It's this independent spirit for which the Anguillians are known. In fact, the first known inhabitants, the Carib Indians, named the island "Mallaiuhana." But they ate visitors. Today Anguillians welcome visitors, even British paratroopers.

A view of Anguilla today comes each Sunday when the boat races are held at Sandy Point. These unique 25-foot sailboats are made lovingly, carefully, and expertly on the island. They all have a triangular mainsail, and a bow that prefers to ride almost underwater. These sailboats are fast and the races bring out the entire island to watch. Bet on and cheer *Eagle I* against the *Concorde* or better yet, the *Eagle II.*

If you are here in March or April, you might see humpback and sperm whales on their annual migration to Greenland and Iceland. If you miss them on their route north, come around in September and October, when they're on their way home (they "winter" near St. Vincent and Bequia). Since these slow-moving whales, traveling in schools, tend to hug the shoreline, their 50-foot-plus bulks are quite a show.

While the word spreads like bush fire when the whales pass, chances are you'd see them anyhow, since most days are spent at one of the more than 30 beaches or on a day sail to one of the islands offshore. Adventure one day (it's only possible twice a month) to Sombrero Island (38 miles northwest of

Anguilla and only ¾ths of a mile long), a barren, treeless rock, except for the lone lighthouse that's been operating since 1869. Your only "invitation" is aboard the schooner *Warspite,* perhaps the most famous of Anguilla's famous boats that was built in 1909. *Warspite* travels out with supplies and mail to the men who man the lighthouse on the 4-hour, predawn sail. Don't wear your designer jeans!

With such perfect beaches right on Anguilla, the only reason to visit these offshore islands is to add the spice of a day sail, perhaps just as far as nearby Sandy Ground where there are picnic tables for the occasional pic-nickers (you, with the help of your hotel or a local grocery store, provide the picnic). There was a bit of a scandal here recently when a local entrepreneur decided to set up a drink stand. We expect he's been convinced to take his pops and beers back to the mainland. Beach selection is totally individual just like the island itself; a swing in the hammocks at Rendezvous Bay or a picnic with lobster caught that day at Shoal Bay Beach and a bottle of white wine and crunchy fresh-baked bread. The choice is yours.

We expect the island's only traffic light is still blinking in vain at the four-way intersection of the "Valley," the main town on the island. It is consistently ignored by the 6,500-some Anguillians, not to mention visitors, donkeys, goats, and chickens.

Cattle graze, goats munch the scrub bush, village elders take tea under the tamarind trees, and a visitor is the occasion to wave hello. Welcome to the Caribbean the way it was meant to be.

TOURING ANGUILLA

The northernmost of the Leeward Islands of the Caribbean, Anguilla's 35-square miles are scalloped and sculpted with inlets, forming private coves and bays, which is where most visitors spend their days, either on, in or around the water.

With an island so small, eel-shaped in its sprawl, it's an easy matter to take a taxi or rent a car to the settlements outside The Valley (the capital town), of Long Bay Village, South Hill Village and Blowing Point Village, all rural communities where cattle graze and farmers go about their work-a-day business.

Several old plantation houses have been newly painted and freshened, and most residents of these stone and wood houses are pleased to have visitors. The walls as well as the roofs have been brightly shingled and they're easy to spot. You may stop off at the caves at the Fountain, where pirates and smugglers are thought to have stored their goods. Today the caves are a source of fresh water and receive an occasional curious visitor.

Stop by Sandy Hill where Anguilla won its first battle with outsiders, the French, who left licking their wounds in 1796. At Rendezvous Bay Hotel, some of the cannons used by the French are now part of the landscape.

During salt harvest time, the gathering, grinding, and packing of the salt is fascinating. When the harvest is ready, the salt ponds glisten pink and silver in the bright sunlight. The reapers begin work at the first rays of light, hauling their grey wooden flats into the ponds and lifting the salt into wicker baskets to drain before placing the crystals into the barges.

There's not really much to "tour" as such, although the tourism depart-ment has set up a small display of handicrafts, and you should stop by anyhow if only to say hello and get a free map.

Most visitors pause at the tomb of Governor Richardson at Sandy Hill. The Governor left his sloop, the *Sea Flower,* to heirs who became the first settlers on the Virgin Islands. Another battle took place here at Sandy Hill where the French invaded again in 1796, and again left in a hurry when the enterprising Anguillians used lead weights from their fishing nets as cannon shot (they'd run short of the real thing).

The famous Anguillian fishing boats are lined up at Island Harbour, if they're in from the day's catch (lobster is the mainstay). This is also the boarding place for a sail to Scrub Island just offshore. Do as you're told en route, and bow low to the Serpent Mouth, a cave at the eastern tip of the island. Every Anguillian knows the serpent is all-powerful, and arranges sudden changes in the weather when not properly acknowledged.

"Touring" really comes as new happenings each day, discovering new twists and turns in the eel-shaped, beach-rimmed island of Anguilla.

Inside Information

Hotels and Guesthouses

Accommodations on Anguilla range from guesthouses and efficiency apartments to resort-hotels that can hold their own anywhere for style and standards. All of these accommodations add a 10% service charge and 5% government tax; and all are run with the personalized stamp of their on-duty AM to PM managers.

★★★★★ CUL DE SAC

The "house" that British managers Robin and Sue Ricketts built, of six rooms in seaside villas, nestled around Shaddick Point. All apartments have bedroom-sitting room with kitchenette, maid service, and a spectacularly simple but sophisticated decor. Interiors are by Larry Peabody and his Haitian-brilliant cotton bedspreads, heaps of pillows, and paintings of a single flower. Exterior, strictly by nature, with waves crashing against the rocks, sea spray, and sunsets with evening cocktails served on your private patio. While the beach is a true "cul de sac," there's a full range of water sports. Meals are in the main house with salon setting chic, unless you prefer to hide away in your private villa. Entertainment by the best groups on the island on Tuesday, Thursday, and Saturday PM. *Cost:* $80 to $100 per double, EP.

★★★★★ MALLIOUHANA HOTEL

Opening like a flower, the first petals of the Orchid and Tamarind villas unfolded their designer doors in 1983, followed by some of the 20-room hotel spectacular in 1984. A total of seven villas will complete the setting on the western end of Anguilla by 1985. Managers Robin and Sue Ricketts have put planning, education, and experience into their partnership with a British magnate. The setting couldn't be more sensational on a bluff with the ocean below, and free-form swimming pool and tennis courts above. M. Jo Rostang, owner of *La Bonne Auberge* in Antibes (one of France's top restaurants), oversees the kitchen. The swimming pool is a forecast of the luxury of these Moorish-styled villas with fresh water cascading from the pool into the sea below. The interior of each villa, designed by Larry Peabody, carries out the individual floral theme that includes canopied beds and bathrooms (roughly the size of your average suite—12' × 12' to be exact) done in Italian marble with mirrors. Plants and flowers to match your villa, inside and out. *Cost:* Villa: $600, CB; three bedrooms with three baths, plus terraces and fully-equipped kitchen. Suite: $300, CB; double, $150, CB.

★★★ CINNAMON REEF
Fourteen chalets spread out over 26-acres, all nicely landscaped, opened in 1983. Owner Jack Hauser and son, Scott, have handled everything personally from conception to on-site management. All villas have a raised bedroom, separate sitting area, Spanish-Caribbean decor, and a private patio with a view of the sea. There's a restaurant featuring continental food, tennis courts, 12-foot sailboats, and an almost Olympic-size swimming pool; British hosts, William and Christine Bamford, presiding. *Cost:* $200 per double, MAP.

★★★ SKIFFLES VILLAS
Five pink stucco villas stretch out along a bluff on Lower South Hill, overlooking the sea, sunrises and sunsets in an isolated splendor. Each villa is done in rainbow colors—greens, blues, peach, orange—with rattan furniture, sisal rugs, and floor-to-ceiling windows. Each comes with a fully-equipped kitchenette, maid service, and a large fresh water swimming pool. *Cost:* $100–$150 per double, EP.

★★ BAYVIEW APARTMENTS
Mostly for long-term rentals. Well-respected resident Rupert Carty has three apartments for rent (if you can get in), and a few houses. The apartments are on Sandy Ground, with the beach on the doorstep, and several simple but sufficient restaurants nearby. Mr. Carty and family have a long line of requests and heavy repeat business. *Cost:* $35–$45 for one bedroom apartments; CP.

★★ CORITO BEACH COTTAGES
A clustering of ten do-it-yourself cottages on a sliver of beach on the southern coast, spaced with lots of seagrape trees (great for shade). Hammocks hang among them and you have your choice of sun, sea or a siesta. Cottages are comfortable (all with maid service), light and bright in Caribbean colors, and it's good family fare especially when you consider the adjoining restaurant, *La Bonne Table,* simple, honest food for nights when cooking-in isn't your style. *Cost:* $45 to $140, EP; one to three bedrooms; all with kitchenette.

★★ RENDEZVOUS BAY HOTEL
It's all in the family. The Gumbs family patriarch Jeremiah, wife Lydia, and lawyer-manager son, Allan, give this 20 room hotel on a superb beach its personality. Jeremiah Gumbs has been a minister in the government like others in his extended family. (A relative, Metropolitan police officer Gumbs of Anguilla, was the first black policeman in England.) These family facts and the family atmosphere more than make up for rooms that are somewhat spartan and grounds that could use pruning. There's a tennis court surrounded by lots of tropical foliage, but it's that pristine white beach that tempts visitors—like lemmings to the sea. *Cost:* $95 per double, MAP; $65 per double, EP.

ANGUILLA HOLIDAY SPA
The same English ownership, Jack Nicolian, and his son, Manuk, who started the successful Inglewood Health Hydro in Berkshire, England, have decided Anguilla makes the perfect hideaway spa of 40 bungalows centered around a health club. Decor is utilitarian with saunas, impulse showers, massage, underwater massage, steam bath, mud bath, seaweed bath, physiotherapy, ultrasonic treatment, wax bath, short-wave diathermy, and even more "fun" things like tennis and pool sports. There's an English pub in the main building with lots of slim statuary showing you the way you're suppose to look.

MERRYWING RESORTS

One, two, and three bedroom condominiums had trouble getting their doors open, but rooms are large and airy in Mediterranean style white stucco villas. Villas are duplex with the second story the favorite "living" area, bright patterned sofas, spreads and drapes, and a wraparound view of the ocean with balcony. Managers are Mr. and Mrs. John Batson who attend to all with a personal touch. All villas have large kitchens and come with maid service. *Cost:* $275–$280 for two and three bedroom villas, EP.

Restaurants

On this small island, restaurants range from sumptuous and sophisticated to small and special in home-style fare. Everywhere, the accent is on fresh fish and locally grown fruits and vegetables. And everywhere, reach for the crisp bread, baked in brick ovens just hours before. Cost averages $20 for dinner without wine, but can dip lower at a beach bar with beer, band, and barefoot dancing!

★★★★★ SMITTY'S

Euton Watkins Smith, a member of the island assembly, opened a beach bar . . . a simple honest beach bar (not bistro) that barbecues fish and chicken on weekends. Everyone on the island comes to drip barbecue sauce on their whites, dance barefoot in the sand, and have a whale of an evening. Daytime other members of the island government may gather for a game of "huff," a variation of draughts and dominos played *very* loudly. On weekends, Catherine Strauss formerly of Florida may be there with her polaroid taking snaps that she sells for a few dollars in cardboard frames. Smitty's truck proclaims it's "A Place Worth Finding." And it is. *Inexpensive.*

★★★★ CUL DE SAC

(Tel. 2461). The restaurant within the hotel of the same name. Reservations required. Ambience is relaxed sophistication and the menu runs the gamut from soups of pumpkin, conch and cucumber, to christophene salad and escargot. Entrées might be snapper in *pappillote* or a light curry sauce; grilled lobster with butter sauce; or the fish of the day cooked Anguillian style with tomatoes and onions. Some nights, there's *terrine de legumes* in a sauce aurora; *blanquette de langouste;* prime ribs of beef. A definite is their *mousse au chocolat* which has won the raves of *Gourmet,* or you could vote for the *nougat glace* with raspberry sauce. *Expensive.*

★★★ BARREL STAY

This beachside bistro took its name from the barrels, shined and polished into tables, with fish net on the walls and other suitably nautical atmosphere. The menu too reflects the sea and there's always a catch of the day, along with lobster in every form (it's the main catch in Anguilla). This is a place to lunch, beach and stay . . . maybe until dinner. *Moderate.*

★★★ THE FISH TRAP

Open for lunch and dinner, this spot at Island Harbour gives you a view of the slim fishing boats with fanciful names—*LIAT, Snapeedo, MASH*—that brought your main dish only hours earlier. For openers, a *crab farcis,* escargots, or *jambon papaye,* followed by snapper filet *au vin blanc, papillotte* or *au poivre vert.* This might be the place for a large and luscious lobster, or *fondue bouguignonne* for two. Owners Thierry and Patricia Van Dyck are originally from Belgium and their pristine table settings reflect their homeland, along with taped music, small bunches of flowers and the sounds of the sea. *Moderate.*

★★★ RIVIERA

This combination of beachside restaurant and small boutique makes an afternoon of it, as you order first, shop while waiting, and return to your table along with the first course. Owners Sylvaine and Didier Van have made a delightful combination on an open patio-restaurant in Sandy Ground. And they're more than happy to have you take a swim or take a turn at the dartboard after dining. Hanging plants and nautical flags add to the friendly atmosphere and the menu is local-delicious—fish soup, hearts of palm salad, lobster and lobster salad, conch creole, and always a fresh fish of the day. *Moderate.*

★★ THE AQUARIUM RESTAURANT

The accent here is on local folk enjoying both food and chatter, with stewed lobster, fresh fish, turtle, welks and conch (stewed, frittered or fried), mutton or a chicken curry . . . your choice, started off with turtle soup or conch chowder. It's island folk and food surrounded by the sounds of the sea. *Inexpensive.*

★★ HARBOUR VIEW

First-rate home cooking by Lucy Halley, the matriarch of her establishment. Meals are served on a raised porch overlooking Sandy Ground and the Salt Ponds (luminous in the light). Each dish is prepared one at a time, no matter how many there are in your party. The menu might feature steamed grouper, snapper cooked in its own juices, grilled lobster or chicken with all the "fixin's." Don't forget the special brick oven baked bread. On Friday and Sunday there's a buffet and scratch and string band. *Moderate.*

MALLIOUHANA

(Tel. 4972–741). Sounds sensational, but the "main man," chef Jo Rostang, still holds court at his own establishment, *La Bonne Auberge* in Antibes, France, and flies in only for the 1984 winter opening season. Since his restaurant there gets rave reviews from the toughest of critics, this restaurant perched on a hilltop sounds as superb as the star-spangled view. Cuisine will be French with local food used. Reservations a must. *Expensive.*

Nightlife

An island without steel bands? What can this mean in the Caribbean? It means there are string and scratch bands, where the instruments are not the heralded steel drums but instruments that are all string or scratch pieces.

Probably best known is Bankie BanX and his backup group of eight, Roots and Herbs, who give concerts on many parts of the island, and as of this year, will hold forth in their own club at *The Fountain.* Ask anyone, even your record store back home. The group has released two albums, *Sooth Your Soul* and *The Battle's On.* Bankie himself plays every instrument *except* drums. Anguilla and Anguillians do the unexpected!

Cul de Sac features the Mayoumba Folkloric Group, really a scratch band of ten men and women, who sing and perform different African songs now transplanted to Anguillian shores. The group was named for a town on the west coast of Africa and they perform on Tuesdays, Thursdays and Saturdays. In *Justina,* a woman dances and shuffles as she sings "Dry Weather House," a song about a house that was good only when the weather was good. There's a romantic duo, "Under the Coconut Tree" (using a palm borrowed from the Cul de Sac decor). It's plain fun to look and listen and join in at the musicians' request. Claude, formerly known as the waiter, becomes an accomplished performer and dances with Kathy, the gracious hostess. And everyone dances with everyone in proper Anguillian style.

On Saturday, the "Missing Brothers" usually perform. Their name is not without reason since they have a tendency to "go missing."

On Thursday and Saturday nights the *Mariner's* on the beach at Sandy Ground has more than its usual gathering of the yachting crowd (whoever's in port). These are nights for a scratch and string band and inexpensive but tasty food.

Harbour View where Lucy Halley cooks up a storm every night has healthy helpings of a special buffet, and a scratch and string band on Friday and Sunday nights. Lucy never lacks for an audience, either for the food or the music.

And "if it's Saturday night, it must be Smitty's" isn't a requirement, but almost is. His truck backs up to the beach bar and Smitty himself presides over the barbecued chicken and fish. You open the beer or soda yourself while the dancing goes on, barefoot and becalmed Anguillian style.

Shopping

The shopping pleasures on Anguilla are shopping treasures, not big buys, but small finds as befits this island 16 miles long and 3 miles wide.

If she's in residence, give a call to Judy Henderson (tel. 2149). Her watercolors of the island and its residents are among the best finds here. Also stop by the small shop at The Corner to see the shell work of Benny Fenton.

Several small shops in the Valley (the main town) have limited selections of beach wear—Clothesline, the Olive Branch, and Raps. The Sunshine Boutique, attached to the Riviera restaurant, has some surprisingly French-looking beach designs . . . surprising, until you see the "Club Med" labels. Owner Sylvaine Van has a Club Med connection!

The boutiques attached to the hotel-resorts all have their own offerings. At Cul de Sac the accent (this season at least) is on goods from Haiti— embroidered pillow covers and light clothing of Haitian cotton. Both Cinnamon Reef and the Anguilla Holiday Spa have small boutiques of casual clothes and small take-home gifts.

But one of the most unusual gifts might be a small packet of something natural from the Rasta's "natural foods" stand. Here the practitioners of this sect must be Anguillian-born, so they're true, gentle believers.

Sports

There wasn't much in the way of official snorkeling or scuba diving until Cul de Sac took the lead and christened Tamarianin Watersports, the name combining that of organizer Iain Grummitt and his daughter, Tamarisk. Iain runs the diving, offering a PADI certification course for $225 or a resort course for $50. For those already certified, Iain leads you through the submerged, silent, special world of Anguilla's coastline, exploring sunken coral gardens and cave formations. Here in the underwater world, sea ferns and feathers beckon with waving tentacles. There are great branches of golden elkhorn coral, rounded mountains of star coral, flower coral, and leaf coral. And around, about, and in between dart stripped squirrel fish, torpedo-headed wrasse, butterfly and angel fish, sergent majors and damselfish, trumpetfish and garfish, and shimmering metallic squids. At the ocean's bottom look for clusters of sand dollars . . . tempting. Anguilla asks that you don't take any of the precious, living coral reef and we repeat their request.

Tamarianin Watersports also has two 16-foot catamarans, sunfishes, Windsurfers (they give lessons on these as well), a 15-foot day-sailer, and an 18-foot power craft that's used mostly for the divers. There is also a 32-foot flattop for transportation to the dive sites.

Fishing for local gruntfish, snapper, parrotfish, grouper or chub is easy to arrange through any local fisherman, and an added benefit is the ride in his sturdy, hand-built, fast-moving Anguillian boat. Ask your hotel to pack a lunch or make one up yourself from the small markets about town. If you feel like getting up early and going along as the guest of a fisherman as he inspects his lobster pots, there probably won't be any charge, but it would be nice (for both of you) if you brought the beer.

Tennis is available at Rendezvous Bay Hotel, the Malliouhana, the Cinnamon Reef, the Anguilla Holiday Spa, and several of the apartment complexes.

There are scattered putting-greens, but no golf course at present. The sport that is uniquely Anguillian are the boat races held on Sundays with major contests on Easter Monday, Anguilla Day, and all of Carnival Week in August. This is when *everyone* on the island heads down to the beach to watch the racing (just a few feet from shore within easy view), snack on the sizzling barbecued chicken, lobster and fish, and cheer in time to the string bands who add to the air of high hilarity. (There is serious betting going on behind the scenes.)

There are no blueprints for the Anguillian racing boat. It's built from tradition, experience, and personal judgment; a skill handed from father to son. The deep hulls are filled with hundreds of pounds of ballast which is shifted during the race, according to sea and wind conditions and in dire straits, hurled overboard! To the winner go the bets and beers.

THE HARD FACTS
Planning Ahead
Costs

Antigua's prices are not quite as inflated as those on some of the other islands of the Caribbean. You will get your money's worth here . . . spacious beachside accommodations, every conceivable sport facility, nonstop entertainment, and attentive service. This island offers excellent value.

Most of the resort hotels are now back to MAP (two meals, usually breakfast and dinner). The 1984 *in*-season (Dec. 15–April 15) average is about $165 for a double room, MAP. But Antigua is also an island that offers many small hotels, each with its own particular charm. These are usually on the beach and do have their own smaller scale water-sports operations and evening diversions as well. These prices run about $55–$75 for a double room, *in*-season EP (no meals). A 6% government tax and a 10% service charge will be added to your bill.

Rates are reduced as much as 40% after April 15, and there are many package tours in both summer and winter that combine flight, hotel room, meals and special extra features for additional savings. Check your travel agent, airline or hotel representative for the most up-to-date information on these.

Not too long ago visitors were pretty much limited to hotel dining rooms. Recently many good little restaurants have popped up in and around St. John's. Even though you may be on a MAP plan, arrangements can usually be made for a dinner or two "out" by asking to substitute lunch for your hotel's evening meal. Experiencing the congeniality and good local food in any of the dozen or so restaurants is something you should not miss.

Two people can spend about $12 to sample one of *Brother B's* delicious daily West Indian specials; up to $65—for dinner, cocktails, a glass of wine, service and tax—for the elegance of Curtain Bluff's restaurant.

Our restaurant selections are classified as inexpensive ($12–$15 per person); moderate ($15–$25); and expensive ($25 and up per person).

As it seems to be all over the Caribbean, film is more costly than it is at home. There are good duty-free prices on liquor, especially rum, jewelry, perfume and other luxury items in Antigua's shops.

16

Climate

Temperatures range from 75°F. in January and February to 85°F. in August and September. Nights are pleasantly cool because of constant northeast trade winds. Humidity is relatively low, and rainfall averages about 40 inches per year.

*and remem-
ber: The
summer
season is
very pleasant
and costs
less*

Holidays and Special Events

Public holidays include: New Year's Day; Good Friday; Easter Monday; Labour Day (1st Monday in May); Whit Monday; (Early June), Queen Elizabeth's Official Birthday; Carnival Weekend (1st Monday and Tuesday in August); Independence Day (November 1); Christmas Day and Boxing Day (December 26).

Special events are:

Tennis Week—First week in January: international tournaments, clinics and friendly matches that draw top-seeded players from the United States and Europe. Although the action is now shared between Curtain Bluff and the Half Moon Bay hotels, all this volley madness began when Curtain Bluff's team (consisting of owner Howard Hulford and Ed Sheerin, right hand) discovered small boys hiding in the brush to watch, wait and glean a very out-of-bounds tennis ball. They decided to invite the wide-eyed youngsters in for out-of-season play and teaching on the courts when they were empty. Now several talented boy and girl players are sent to serious tennis camps in the United States at Curtain Bluff's expense.

Sailing Week—End of April–early May: This annual regatta, the number-one race week in the Caribbean, attracts almost 300 yachts from all over the area, Europe, North and South America. It's both midday madness and midnight madness, with *very* serious racing by day and very serious partying by night. It's actually a survival contest, for "the" major racing yachts come from all over the world to participate. The daily races are sailed on "legs" that vary according to each day's program (one or two days for recuperation), all of which are "around Antigua" races. It begins, however, with an Antigua-to-Guadeloupe sail and a battle-to-the-death return race. The extended week (eight or nine days) ends in one day of frivolity—small boat sailing and make-it-yourself contraptions that either sink or succeed in English Harbour. The last night is the formal Lord Nelson's Ball at the Admiral's Inn in English Harbour, when manager Ethelyn Phillip swears (each year for some 16 years) "never again!"

Carnival—Late July–early August: A ten-day festival of street parades featuring floats, colorful costumes and much merriment. There are Carnival Queen and calypso and steel-band contests, talent shows and nonstop entertainment. The climax is "J'ouvert," a jump-up that starts at 4 A.M., when street dancers and steel bands wind their way through St. John's.

Tour Operators

Major U.S. tour operators include: Adventure Tours; Caribbean Holidays; Flyfaire; GoGo Tours; Liberty and Travel Impressions. In Canada: Carnival; Fairways; Fiesta; Holiday House; Kuoni and Sun Tours.

Sources of Information

In the U.S., contact: *The Antigua and Barbuda Department of Tourism,* 610 Fifth Avenue, Suite 311, New York, NY 10020 or Eastern Caribbean Tourism Association, R. 411, 220 East 42nd Street, New York, NY 10017; in Canada: 60 St. Clair Avenue, East, Suite 205, Toronto, Ontario MYT1N5. In Antigua, the local *Tourist Office* in St. John's is at the corner of High Street and Corn Alley (Tel. 20029).

Packing

As you would for most of the Caribbean, pack lightweight clothing, the same as you'd wear at home in the summer. Some of Antigua's deluxe hotels do require a jacket and tie for dinner; but generally dress is Caribbean-casual—long skirts or dresses for the ladies; sportshirts and slacks for the men. In town, neither shorts nor beach attire should be worn; a skirt or slacks will be much more appropriate. There are some lovely, handprinted fabric designs and locally made, ready-to-wear garments that can be bought in Antigua, so don't overpack. You'll probably be adding to your wardrobe here.

Documentation

No visa is necessary for U.S. or Canadian citizens. Proof of citizenship or residency and an onward or return ticket are the only requirements.

Getting There

Pan Am, American, BWIA, and Eastern serve Antigua from major U.S. cities. Air Canada and BWIA have flights from Canada and BA from London.

Formalities on Arrival

Customs officers are courteous and efficient, and usually showing your U.S. or Canadian passport will get you through quickly with just a question or two. Items for personal use allowed duty-free entry include: 200 cigarettes or 50 cigars or 1/2 pound tobacco; 1 quart liquor and 6 oz. perfume. On departure, there is a $8 EC tax levied on passengers traveling to Anguilla, Dominica, Grenada, Montserrat, Nevis, St. Lucia, St. Kitts and St. Vincent; it's $10 EC for all other destinations.

Money

Antigua's currency is the East Caribbean Dollar ($EC); around $2.70 EC is approximately the equivalent of $1 U.S. American currency is accepted everywhere. Even though you may get a better exchange rate at banks than in shops and hotels, remember there's a 1% government tax added, and lines are always long.

Getting into Town

We don't recommend the bus from airport to town

The hotels of Antigua are spread out all over the island. Your choice of transportation is to take a taxi or rent a car at the airport. Taxis do not have meters, but fares are set by the government. Pick up the official taxi-fare pamphlet, which lists in both EC$ and US$ fares to each hotel and other popular destinations.

Settling Down

Choosing a Hotel

Most of Antigua's hotels are medium sized—50 rooms or so—but charming 14-room inns and 400-room, self-contained resorts are found as well. Selecting a place to stay depends on your personal needs and tastes. . . . Tennis enthusiast? Half Moon Bay and Curtain Bluff have some of the island's best facilities. A full resort with every water sport at your doorstep? Code's Halcyon Cove, Halcyon Reef at Marmora Bay or Blue Waters are your best bets. History and a lively boating crowd appeal to you? The Admiral's Inn in historic Nelson's Dockyard has both. Want to be close to town but have a pool and fine dining facilities? Barrymore should fit the bill. The roll of the dice from morning till night? Castle Harbour, Antigua's original casino, and Code's Halcyon Cove, Antigua's newest casino, have one-armed bandits that get going some days before noon.

For those who insist on a swimming pool, check carefully because only nine of the major hotels offer this facility.

There are also many cottages, apartments and villas to be rented. At Dickenson Bay alone, three complexes offer over 50 self-contained units right on one of Antigua's best beaches. Villas are available by the week or month. Some include cook, laundress, gardener and chauffeur in the price. The Tourist Office has a list of properties and real-estate agents, or contact Antigua Villas Ltd., P.O. Box 719, St. John's (Tel. 22924 or 20485).

There are now time-sharing resorts on Antigua. . . . The latest on the scene was the Copper and Lumber Store, with 14 apartments; the Capstan House with eight two-story apartments and the Canvas and Cordage Store apartments. Galleon Beach's 19 cottages have been operating as part hotel, part time sharing for over three years; The Inn at English Harbour converted its 30 rooms to time-sharing apartments; and Code's Halcyon Cove has added 25 beachfront rooms that work under this system. All are members of R.C.I. (Resort Condominiums International), whose reciprocal-exchange programs entitle owners to holidays virtually anywhere around the world.

Choosing a Restaurant

Do try to eat out a few times during your stay . . . it's a way to get to know the island, the people and other hotels for future reference. Although the choice of restaurants in Antigua is not large, it is interesting. The selection includes West Indian, Continental, French, Chinese, English, Italian, Swiss and, of course, seafood. Lunch hours are noon–2 or 2:30; dinner from 7:30–9:30 or 10. Reservations should be made when visiting other hotels and the smaller eating spots in season; but, whatever the season, it's always a good idea to call first, just to be sure the place you've chosen is open at the time you arrive.

Tipping

A 10% service charge is added to all hotel and restaurant bills. It's always nice, however, to show your appreciation for extra service with an extra tip. Taxi drivers generally expect a tip that is 10% of the fare.

Learning to Cope

Business Hours. Most *shops* are open Monday–Friday from 8:30–noon and 1–4. Some stores follow the Thursday custom of closing at noon; most observe this half day on Saturday. There is no hard-and-fast rule, however, and some shops stay open all day, every day. *Banking hours* are Monday–Thursday from 8–1 P.M.; Fridays from 1 P.M. to 3 or 5 P.M.

Electricity. 110 volts, 60 cycles. U.S. style plugs are used, so adapters are not needed. Double check, because a few hotels use 220 volts.

Water and Drink. Water is desalinated and purified. It's not terribly tasty. However, looking at it another way, maybe it's just too tasty!

more impor-tant, the water is safe to drink

Communications. To call Antigua directly from the United States, dial 809 + 46 and the local number. On the island, making overseas telephone calls requires a lot of patience; connections can take hours and then are often bad. For overseas assistance, dial 890; 0 for local assistance. The best place to *send cables and make phone calls* if you are *in town* is from the St. John's Cable and Wireless Office on St. Mary's Street. *Postage rates* for an air-mail letter to the United States and Canada are 60¢ EC for 1/2 oz.; postcards—30¢ EC. Offical *delivery time* is 3 to 5 days, but it's usually more like a week.

Language. English is the language of the island. It may take a while to attune your ear to the Antiguan's special lilt, but you'll soon find yourself picking up the many colorful local expressions.

Medical Assistance.   The main hospital is Holberton on Queen Elizabeth Highway (Tel. 20251). Most hotels have their own doctors on call.

Getting Around
By Car
Rental cars may be reserved through Antigua Car Rentals (Avis); Carib Car Rentals; Dollar Rent-A-Car; Budget and Ramco (Hertz). Before hiring you must obtain a temporary *visitor's driving permit*—accomplished by showing a valid driving license at Police Headquarters and paying $10 U.S. Cars, available with automatic or stick shifts, include mini-mokes, Jeeps, English and Japanese makes. Airport and hotel delivery can be arranged. Prices average $30–$35 U.S. per day with unlimited mileage; $190 U.S. up per week. Don't forget, keep to the left at all times!

By Bus
Not recommended as schedules, if they exist, are very erratic.

By Taxi
Taxis can easily be found at all hotels, in St. John's and at Deep Water Harbour. Rates are approved by the Antiguan government and published in an official taxi-fare pamphlet available at hotels and the Tourist Office. A three-hour tour is about $15 per passenger (four to a car), but from the airport and St. John's, individual fares have been set for all destinations.

ANTIGUA TODAY
Nelson's Dockyard, the center of the Caribbean sailing world, is filled in winter and increasingly in summer with the finest ships in the world. You may see the stretched-out beauty of *La Belle Simone* at anchor, *Lac II* with its helicopter on deck for quick arrivals and departures or an Arab oil-rich plaything, *Mohamedia.* Those yachts are strictly private, but some other beauties aren't, and they charter out for week-long or month-long sails through the Caribbean. You may meet Canadian Prime Minister Pierre Trudeau or Diane Von Furstenburg, not together, jumping from the decks of *Ticonderoga, Jaeder, Mistress Quickly, Panda* or *Gitana IV,* just a handful of the superyachts that accept guests until late April, when all the sailing madness ends in a week called Antigua Race Week. Close to 300 yachts battle it out by day on the race course, and their crews contest all night to see who can party the longest and still be able to race the next day.

This renaissance dates back to 1948, when the Vernon Nicholson family sailed into English Harbour. The Nicholsons are irrevocably sketched into Antigua's past and present. Their irresistible, captivating patriarch and his now-deceased wife, Emma, had stopped off aboard their 70-foot schooner, *The Mollihawk,* en route to Australia from their Irish homeland. Aboard ship were their two sons Desmond and Rodney, and a cat and a rocking chair that were the only items Emma had been permitted to bring with her. Commander Nicholson recalls that "the entire scene was one of desolation. A ghost town when we entered, with cobwebs, banging shutters, falling steps, mice and lizards running about." But cannon, iron cauldrons, and pieces of history remained, creating their own lure. Pillars were still standing, even if the walls and roofs weren't. Since the Nicholsons needed to refit *the Mollihawk* for the still-intended journey to Australia, the family moved into one of the more complete brick buildings while work was in progress on their schooner.

As always when fate meets chance, the Nicholsons unintentionally developed a sailing business when some of the winter visitors, who were staying at the island's expensive beach resorts, wanted to see other islands as well and asked to charter their ship. They intended to leave, but somehow, some way, it never happened.

Today, as you wander the buildings that have been restored, you may meet a hurrying, slightly disheveled man in his 50s, Rodney Nicholson, who is now the owner of the island's major yacht-chartering business. His brother, Desmond, can sometimes be found at Carib Marine, where he sells items needed by yachtsmen.

In the early 1950s, the organization called the Friends of English Harbour was formed under the patronage of Queen Elizabeth II and Prince Phillip, Princess Margaret (who honeymooned here with Lord Snowdon), Lady Churchill, several members of the superprivate Mill Reef Club and, somewhat later, George Morrill, helped restore the Admiral's Inn and other Dockyard buildings that could be saved.

Today, as you stroll around the flower-dotted, partly restored Dockyard that's actually the original English Harbour creation of the mid-1700s, you're not in a dusty museum. Far from it. You're wandering around a living, used dockyard, as it was intended to be. Only the names and the ships at anchor have been changed to protect the guilty. Sitting under a tree outside the Admiral's Inn (both an inn and a restaurant), you may see Richard Burton lunching at a table under another tree.

Antigua is attempting to rejuvenate its floundered pineapple and sugar production, but the island remains almost totally dependent on the flux of tourists from North America and Europe. The present government, headed by a prime minister (on November 1, 1981, when full independence from Great Britain became effective, the title changed from premier), the Honorable Vere Cornwall Bird, has reopened the sugar mills. While tourism is an enterprise of increasingly hot competition among all the islands of the Caribbean, it seems to be Antigua's present focus, possibly because it doesn't have Jamaica's bauxite, Trinidad's overflow of offshore oil, or the French West Indies' security as part (not colonies) of France, with a steady flow of francs from Paris. Antiguans are cautious. They hope Mr. Bird is right and that a balanced economy can be achieved.

Meanwhile they wait and wonder, perhaps over a game of warri, the complicated arithmetical, brain-storming game played with island seeds moved around a carved wooden board. Like many of the people of Antigua, the game can be traced to Africa.

TOURING

There are no regularly scheduled sightseeing excursions here. Local taxi drivers are Antigua's unofficial tour guides. They know and love all 108 square miles of their island and are always eager to share their information, amusing anecdotes and favorite spots with visitors. Taxis can be hired by the hour, by the day or by the tour, and rates are set down in the fare pamphlet put out by the Tourist Office.

Antigua is only 15 miles across

For those who have time or prefer to drive themselves, renting a car is a good way to explore at your leisure. Most roads are smoothly paved and people are friendly. Once you're accustomed to driving on the left, you'll have no problem discovering hidden coves, interesting villages, and out-of-the-way tropical sights. Here are some of the highlights, both historic and visual, that you can see during your stay.

In the capital, St. John's Cathedral sits on a hill between Long and Newgate streets. The original church, built in 1683, was replaced by a stone building in 1745, which lasted until the great earthquake of 1843. The present structure was dedicated as a cathedral in 1847, and the parish church was completed the following year. The interior is completely encased in pitch pine, a construction method resistant to earthquakes and storms. The iron entrance gates were erected by the vestry in 1789, and the figures of St. John the Baptist and St. John the Divine at the southern entry were supposedly taken from one of Napoleon's ships and brought to Antigua by a British man-of-war.

Farther up the hill is Government House, the offices and official residence of the governor, guarded by white-coated, shiny-helmeted sentries. This building was originally comprised of two houses standing side by side with a street between. The early structures are wooden 17th-century colonial architecture, but concrete extensions have been added in recent years.

The public market, at the foot of Market Street, is especially lively on Friday and Saturday mornings. Vendors come from all over the island to display their colorful fruits and vegetables in the open air, and the haggling is loud and fun. If you're lucky, you'll be able to pick up an Antiguan black pineapple; it's said to be "the sweetest in the world."

The Rum Distillery, located next to Deep Water Harbour, is where Cavalier and Old Mill rums are made. Visits can be arranged if you give notice. Call 21072 or 21012 for further information, or contact the Tourist Office.

Fort James, a half mile from the city, is built on St. John's Point, which faces the harbor entrance. This was the main lookout station for St. John's, and many cannons still secure the fortification.

The capital itself is a neat, well-laid-out little city. There are a lot of interesting old buildings, shops and restaurants to discover, and much restoration is going on now. Redcliffe Quay, on Redcliffe Street just below the U.S. consulate, will take up almost an entire block when renovation is completed. This new gallery will have boutiques, restaurants, gourmet food shops and apartments within its old stone walls.

After getting to know the capital, get out and explore the rest of the island. At the top of a "things-to-see" list is historic Nelson's Dockyard. (Do your utmost to schedule your visit on a day when no cruise ship is in port in St. John's on the opposite end of the island.) This naval base was commissioned by Britain in 1755 to protect its Caribbean colonies from the French, Spanish and Dutch, who were vying for control of the rich "sugar and spice islands." Landlocked, natural English Harbour is one of the safest in the world. It provided protection for the British fleet during the Napoleonic Wars. Admiral Horatio Nelson had his headquarters here from 1784 to 1787, while he commanded the Royal Navy in the Leeward Islands.

Today the Dockyard is a memorial to 18th-century British sea prowess as well as a working, used dockyard. It's not just a dusty museum but a mecca for yachtsmen from all over the Caribbean. Several of the buildings in the complex have been restored through the efforts of "The Friends of English Harbour," and entrance fees help defray the costs of their work.

Inside the gate is the Admiral's Inn, a small, 200-year-old hostelry with a lot of nautical atmosphere, good food and a large terrace overlooking the harbor. The ground floor was once used for the storage of pitch, turpentine and lead, and the upstairs rooms were the offices of the Dockyard's engineers. The Admiral's House, built much later in 1855, is now a museum housing bits and pieces from the long conflicts between the British and the French, Dockyard documents and historic Antiguan memorablia, including a canopied, four-poster that is said to have been Nelson's own.

Those interested in archaeology should check here to see if Desmond Nicholson is still conducting Thursday-afternoon guided tours of the Indian Creek diggings. The ancient Arawak artifacts from excavations made by the

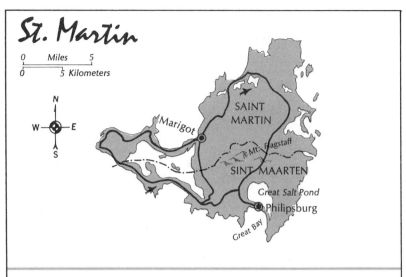

St. Martin

0 Miles 5
0 5 Kilometers

N
W E
S

SAINT MARTIN

Mt. Flagstaff

SINT MAARTEN

Marigot

Great Salt Pond

Philipsburg

Great Bay

N
W E
S

Gustavia

Lorient

Corossol

0 Miles 2
0 2 Kilometers

St. Barts

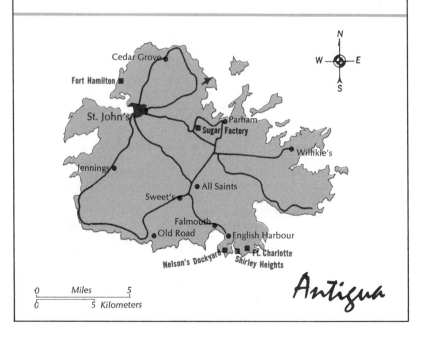

N
W E
S

Cedar Grove

Fort Hamilton

St. John's

Parham

Sugar Factory

Willikie's

Jennings

All Saints

Sweet's

Falmouth

Old Road

English Harbour

Ft. Charlotte

Nelson's Dockyard

Shirley Heights

0 Miles 5
0 5 Kilometers

Antigua

Antigua Archaeological Society and Yale University may be seen at nearby Dow's Hill, a former NASA Apollo Station. Desmond's impromptu tours and lectures are not only informative, they're downright fun!

Farther into the Dockyard is the Copper and Lumber Store, a beautiful, weathered-brick, Georgian-style building that has recently been converted into 12 unusual apartments. The Officers' Quarters are still under reconstruction; and the Galley Boutique houses a small clothing shop and a very informal restaurant right next to the docks. Rena de Bruyn, who set sail from South Africa on a Caribbean yachting adventure that ended up at English Harbour, has set up the only working sail loft in the Caribbean owned and operated by a female sailmaker. It's in the original 18th-century building once used by Nelson's sailmakers. There's much more of interest here, but pick up a copy of *The Romance of English Harbour,* a complete guide to the Dockyard, to appreciate fully what went on in the past and what is going on today. The booklet is available in the small shop on the ground floor just left of the Copper and Lumber Store.

Take the footpath at the entrance to the Dockyard up to Fort Berkeley. It's an uphill, 15-minute walk to one of the first fortifications built to guard the entrance to English Harbour. From here a device consisting of a huge chain and a timber boom was drawn across the narrow entrance to keep out unwanted visitors.

On the way up to Shirley Heights is Clarence House. This mansion, on a low hill overlooking the Dockyard, was built for Prince William Henry (who later became the Duke of Clarence and then King William IV), while he was the commander of *The HMS Pegasus* in 1787. The stone building has interesting period furnishings, mostly on loan from the National Trust; maps and charts of the area and a splendid view. The present governor uses Clarence House as his country home, but when he is not in residence, the caretaker will let you visit. Princess Margaret and Lord Snowdon spent part of their honeymoon here, and a luncheon was held here for Queen Elizabeth and Prince Phillip when they were on the island in 1977.

Above the Dockyard is Shirley Heights, the army counterpart of the navy's installation below. Named after Sir Thomas Shirley, who was responsible for the stronghold when he was the governor of the former Leeward Island in 1781, the fortifications are mostly ruins now. Arches from the old barracks, the Block House and the military cemetery containing an obelisk to the officers and the men of the 54th Regiment can still be seen. The view from Shirley Heights is spectacular at sunset, and on a clear day you can see Montserrat, some days even Guadeloupe.

Other points of interest around the island include Devil's Bridge at Indian Town near Long Bay on the east coast. This natural bridge, with its surf-spouting blowholes, was formed over the centuries by the pounding of the Atlantic on the rocks. For hikers Greencastle Hill, with its controversial megaliths, is an interesting excursion. There is some question whether these formations were set up by the Arawaks as shrines to the Sun God and Moon Goddess or are unusual geological phenomena. Whatever their source, they are well worth the climb.

Devil's Bridge is best on a windy day

Then there are the churches: some very old and historic, some partial ruins and many built overlooking the sea. St. Mary's, the oldest, is at Old Road Village and has a memorial to the first European child born on Antigua. St. George's at Fitches Creek has a beautiful ocean view and an interesting cemetery. St. Peter's in Parham, an irregular, octagonal-shaped building, is considered a "masterpiece of ecclesiastical Georgian architecture." Just outside Liberta, the island's largest village, is a Catholic church on a hill where the road forks off to Fig Tree Drive. There is no signpost indicating this picturesque route, but you can't miss the large, bright pink church. Fig Tree

Drive has no fig trees (this is the Antiguan name for banana trees), but the narrow, winding road climbs up through rain forest thick with flowers, giant ferns, fruit trees and pineapple plantations. There is a fine view of Boggy Peak, the highest point on the island, and the road passes several little fishing villages as it skirts the sharply indented coastline. From here it's just a short drive into St. John's.

The best way to get to know the island is not touring per se but getting to know its people. This can be arranged through the Tourist Office's official "Meet the People Program," which will try to put you in touch with Antiguans who share your profession as well as your interests.

Shell collectors, bird watchers, divers, lovers of long, empty expanses of sand or those with plenty of time should fit in a visit to Barbuda. Part of the State of Antigua and just 30 miles to the north of the island, this small, flat coral atoll has a population of just over 1,000. By boat it's a long, often rough trip, but small planes service the island twice a week, and a day trip can be arranged through one of the local travel agencies in St. John's or the local flying club at the airport. Beaches go on forever, and many are deserted; there are numerous wrecks scattered on the offshore reefs for scuba diving; and the bird sanctuary across the lagoon is the nesting place for thousands of frigate birds. There's just one hotel here, 27-room Coco Point. This very exclusive, expensive enclave caters to big business moguls and celebrities who value their privacy.

Inside Information

Hotels

Antigua has 33 hotels, 32 apartment properties and 14 guesthouses—a wide variety of accommodations that should please everyone. The largest concentration of guest facilities is at Dickenson Bay, which contains three cottage and apartment complexes, two hotels, several restaurants, shops and other amenities. The rest of the resort hotels are scattered all around the coast. We've chosen what we feel are Antigua's best hotels . . . large (127 rooms), medium (50 rooms) and small (14 rooms); expensive, moderate and modest; the most complete resorts and guesthouses offering charm and convenience. Summer visitors would do well to verify whether the hotel of their choice is open year round. Some, though not all, have adopted the practice of shutting down for a month or two during the slow season to refurbish and spruce up for the big *in*-season crowds. September is the usual time for this, but each hotel chooses the dates.

There's scheduled to be a "mini-boom" in hostelries when the rebuilt Capstan House and the Cordage and Canvas Store open their Georgian colonial doors in 1984. Along with the Copper and Lumber Store, this triumvirate will form the Prince William Careenage conglomerate of over 40 luxury condominiums for rent at luxury prices. And they promise to welcome guests at the airport in "one" of their chauffeured Rolls-Royce Silver Clouds.

Smaller Hotels

★★★★ ADMIRAL'S INN
Nelson's Dockyard, English Harbour. Just inside the gate of historic Nelson's Dockyard, this friendly, informal inn has nine rooms upstairs and five more

Heaven for those oriented to the sea and the sea and fun-lovers

across the pillared courtyard. Some are air-conditioned; some have quiet ceiling fans; each is different in size, shape and decor. Room #1 is a favorite. It's spacious, has a king-size canopy bed, a blue and white print bedspread, a beamed ceiling, cross ventilation, so the fan is barely needed, and a view of the terrace and of the yachts at anchor. The annex rooms, with big baths and a patio, are the largest; the one closest to the bay is the best.

There's no beach here, but the hotel's boat will take you to Freeman's Bay in three minutes flat and will pick you up whenever you request, for access to this beach is best by sea. There's also a car that will run you down to Falmouth Apartments' Pigeon Point Beach. *Cost:* $60 to $65 per double, EP, in season; MAP is add. $25 per person per day. No credit cards accepted.

★★★ GALLEY BAY SURF CLUB
Five Islands. A 28-room hotel just three miles from St. John's but with the feeling of an exotic South Seas island a hundred miles from anywhere. That's the kind of secluded tropical paradise Edee Holbert and Liz Mellor have created and seek to maintain. Twelve large beach rooms "3 seconds from bed to sea" have king or twin beds, sunken tubs in the bath-dressing room, a patio for breakfast; four even larger executive beach rooms have all of the above plus a lanai lounge and bar. Farther back in a coconut grove on the property is the Gauguin Village—12 rustic accommodations, each with two thatched-roofed cottages connected by a breezeway; one for sleeping, the second a large bath and dressing room. "Family Gauguins," with two bedrooms, are also available. All have high-peaked roofs of woven palm mats, ceiling fans, and white-washed walls hung with colorful art and island objects. The beach here is a superlative half-mile stretch of white sand with fine shelling and snorkeling. There's a tennis court and horses for beginners as well as more advanced riders; sailing and deep-sea fishing can also be arranged. Food is highly praised—paper thin crepes, fish chowder, lobster Cardinale, roast duckling with banana stuffing and flaming desserts. So many guests have asked for recipes of these and other specialties of the house that management has printed a special recipe pamphlet to take home. *Cost:* $114 to $124 per day, double EP, in season. Family Gauguin, $170. Add $30 per person for MAP. No credit cards accepted. There's a 10-day minimum stay during the Christmas holidays and the month of February; 3 days other times of the year.

★★★ BLUE WATERS BEACH
Soldier Bay. Osmund Kelsick's 48-room hotel has the atmosphere of a small, refined inn where time passes slowly, in fact almost stops. Spread over 12 acres of property on the northwest tip of the island, this place is designed from and around nature. Several rocky breakwaters form a natural, perfect cove; and there's a rambling Botanical Garden whose walkways are lined with conch shells and where the shrubs, trees and plants are neatly posted. Each room in the two double-story, soft blue stucco wings has its own balcony or patio, air conditioning and beach view. Two additional luxury two-bedroom garden suites are hidden among the tropical foliage. The main building houses the open reception area that blends around a free-form, freshwater swimming pool. A West Indian-style bar and dining room overlook the pool and the 1,000-foot stretch of white sand beach below. Cuisine is international and noteworthy, and weekly beach barbecues and a lavish Sunday brunch are among the features. Things seem so relaxed and slow, with double hammocks scattered under the trees, but in actuality there's a lot going on. Sports are stressed—tennis, deep-sea fishing, scuba and snorkeling, water-skiing, archery, paddle boats, windsurfing, even para-sailing; Hobie Cat sailing and outdoor shuffleboard. Indoors, there's pool, table tennis and darts in the Poinciana Game Room. A very proper British high tea is served on the

patio every afternoon from 4:00 to 5:00, and the evening brings rum-punch parties, crab racing, fashion shows and dancing under the stars. *Cost:* $94–$132, per day, double EP, in season. $28 per person, per day additional, MAP.

★★★ COPPER AND LUMBER STORE

Nelson's Dockyard, English Harbour. This 18th-century, gabled building has been completely restored and converted into 14 comfortable, well-appointed apartments for two to four persons. The largest are duplexes, with a double bedroom and decorative washstand upstairs; the bed-sitting-dining room, bath and fully-equipped kitchen are below. Beamed ceilings, exposed brick and white wood walls, individually printed spreads and drapes, ceiling fans, shutters and antique furniture retain the old colonial atmosphere. Manager Patsy Hodge once worked for the Antigua Tourist Board in Canada, so her experience in dealing with visitors and her knowledge of the island are a definite plus; and she goes out of her way to be of assistance to guests. A new restaurant opened on the ground floor last year with colonial accents and continental cuisine. *Cost:* $500–$700 per week, double, $800 for four, in season.

★★★ THE INN BEACH CLUB AT ENGLISH HARBOUR

Freeman's Bay. Ann and Peter Deeth recently converted their hotel, and renamed it the Inn Beach Club, into time-sharing studio and two-room apartments. In the meantime, the only change for the winter season is that there will be a choice of completely redecorated, newly-furnished suites, standard and bed-sitting rooms, and studios. Some of the accommodations have kitchenettes. The terrace restaurant with its sweeping view, and the beach restaurant will both serve breakfast, lunch and afternoon tea; candle-light dinner will be served up on the hill under the stars. Food is excellent here, and the Old English Bar, with its low beams and stone walls, is always a popular gathering place. Formal in winter, it swings in summer when son Paul is in charge. Sports facilities include waterskiing, Sunfish sailing, snorkel gear, glass panel floats and Windsurfers that are complimentary. Day sailing, deep-sea fishing and scuba can also be arranged. *Cost:* $160–$265 per day, double EP, in season. MAP is a $27 per person supplement. No credit cards accepted.

★★★ LONG BAY HOTEL

Northeast Coast. An intimate, informal resort out on a point, with the Atlantic on one side and a lagoon on the other. This is *the* place for scuba enthusiasts. Complete instruction facilities and special diving packages are available year round. Owner Jacques Lafaurie, an experienced diver himself, has been in Antigua 18 years, so he knows all the best spots. Sailfish, a 14' sloop, Boston Whalers, a 31' deep-sea fishing boat, a Trimaran for day trips to outislands, Windsurfers and a 47' ketch are all docked in the lagoon to keep snorkelers, waterskiers, sailors and fishermen busy as well. Twenty large double rooms, with verandas fronting the lagoon, are comfortably and colorfully furnished. Each has its own individualized island collage created by Jackie Lafaurie, Jacques' American-born wife. There are also four very unusual cottages, all differently shaped, of different sizes and decor—Cliff House, Hill House, Beach House and Round House; all have kitchenettes and range from rustic to elegant. Food here is Continental spiced with island specialties, and the wine selection is excellent. M. Lafaurie was born in France. Lunch is served at the Beach House. Breakfast and dinner can be taken in the attractive dining room decorated with Jackie's drawings and pink tablecloths covered with a gray and white striped fabric. Evening activities include a barbecue and steel band at the Beach House; a combo for dancing in the main building and

modified american plan (2 meals included) only

calypso singer every week. Fashion shows and underwater slide presentations are also frequent events. A small shop in the reception area has some unusually nice crafts, small drawings by Jackie, local pottery, clothing and gift items. *Cost:* $155 per day, double MAP, in season. Cottages: rates available on request. No credit cards accepted.

★★ ANTIGUA BEACH HOTEL

Hodges Bay. A 33-room hotel owned and operated by Brian Gonsalves, a fascinating man who is also the current president of the Antigua Hotel Association. Up on a hill but just a three-minute walk from a beach in the quiet, residential area of Hodges Bay, Antigua's oldest hotel, built in 1939, has been modernized. Enormous, almost suitelike, air-conditioned accommodations all have wall-to-wall carpeting and spacious terraces overlooking the sea or the greens of Gamble's Golf Course. For those who prefer to be on their own yet close to every convenience, there are seven efficiency apartments in the flower-filled garden.

The dining room has a view of the sea and is airy and spacious. Food is focused on West Indian and Continental specialties. There's also a coffee shop that is always open for snacks. One tennis court is lighted for night play, and every water sport is nearby. Weekly rum-punch parties. The feeling here is casual and relaxed, but the professional staff provides anything you want exactly when you want it. *Cost:* $90 to $120 per day, double EP, in season. MAP is an additional $25 per person. No credit cards accepted.

★★ FALMOUTH HARBOUR BEACH APARTMENTS

Falmouth Bay. Twenty-five double studio apartments—nine right on the beach, 16 on the hill—each with its own very large patio or terrace for lounging and dining. This quiet, secluded spot is strictly informal, but the apartments are attractively decorated and fully equipped. The maid comes daily to do dishes and straighten up, so there's really nothing to do here except enjoy the small but nice white sand beach; go waterskiing or take the Sunfish out; go shopping for fruit and vegetables in the village of English Harbour or bring home major supplies from the market in the Dockyard. *Cost:* $65–$70 per day, double, in season.

★ BARRYMORE HOTEL

Fort Road. The LaBarrie family's 36-room mini-resort is a terrific bargain. This relaxed alternative to a big hotel is built on three acres of land just outside St. John's. Eight blocks of blue and white single-story buildings are spread among the multiflowered gardens; one double-story structure, with the best rooms, is down by the pool. Accommodations are large, modern and comfortable, the majority with air conditioning and wrought-iron-trimmed terraces and patios that are almost as large as the rooms themselves. This is the kind of friendly, well-run place that really grows on you; most guests can be found sunning, lunching and lounging by the large freshwater pool. For those who prefer to move around, Antigua Car Rental (Avis), operated by Martin La Barrie, is right on the premises; riding, tennis and golf are nearby; and there's a courtesy car to run guests over to the nearest beach, just a five-minute drive. The popular bar is known for its island camaraderie and the Continental cuisine and island specialties of the DuBarry Restaurant live up to their good reputation. *Cost:* $44–$50 per day, double EP, in season.

NEW ANTIGUA HORIZONS

Northeast Coast. This 36-room hotel has just undergone a complete overhaul and should be mentioned because of the dedication, enthusiasm and excellent plans of the new English owners—Marie and John Stringer and Pamela Wood. Among the new facilities are two grass tennis courts and an improved hard-surface one; a swimming pool; a beauty salon; a complete face-lifting of the rooms, restaurant, lounge, bar area and a new chef and menu. The setting here is Long Bay Beach, fine for snorkeling and sailing. There are Sunfish to take out and a motorboat for fishing and picnics on nearby deserted Green Island. All this adds up to a potentially fine spot for "easy living and seclusion in style," which the owners are seeking. Entertainment includes a Friday-night steel band; Saturday calypso music and a Sunday jazz-buffet lunch. No stars due to renovation. *Cost:* $130 to $150 per day, double MAP.

SPANISH MAIN INN
East Street, St. John's. A relaxed, intimate inn in the heart of town. There are 14 good-size rooms on the second floor of this wonderful old, restored mansion with shutters, balconies and gables. Hospitality is traditional here, and owners Janice and Bob Branker welcome their guests warmly. The rooms are spic and span and have an eclectic mix of simple, comfortable and colorful furnishings. There's no air conditioning, but fans provide enough of a breeze. You can't beat the convenience of being able to walk to town and down the stairs to one of the better restaurants in St. John's. *Cost:* $35 per day, double EP, in season.

Special Hotels

★★★★★ CURTAIN BLUFF
Old Road, Morris Bay. To its long list of repeat guests this individual resort is *the* place to be in Antigua. With an occupancy rate of 90%–100% year round, real planning is required if you want to stay here. There are 50 spacious, well-decorated rooms (many with 2 double beds), cooled by ceiling fans and constant breezes from private terraces opening onto the Caribbean. Bluff Villa, at the tip of the peninsula, is a secluded cluster of multilevel buildings connected by breezeways and porches. There's a kitchen, living room, dining area and three bedrooms that can accommodate up to six persons in this self-sufficient suite.

Managing director Howard Hulford and his wife, Michelle, have put their personal touch into every aspect of this deluxe property . . . Howard, in his unfailing attention to detail and his desire to achieve perfection (a greenhouse growing orchids and an exotic plant nursery) and Michelle in beautifying the hotel's decor and adding artistic touches. Associates Ed and Anne Sheerin assist the Hulfords in every effort that's very much a team success. Facilities include some of the island's best tennis (4 courts and a teaching lane); a putting green; free scuba for certified divers; snorkeling; waterskiing; sailing on Sunfish or on the Hulford's own 48-foot ketch, *Salmaat;* and deep-sea fishing. Each evening there's different entertainment, and it's always refined and in good taste. The taste in the dining room (jacket and tie after 7:00), centers on a Swiss chef who's been with the hotel since 1964 and Hulford's wine cellar—10,000 bottles in a newly-expanded cave that guests are encouraged to visit. There's a cozy, circular bar that's a replica of a sugar mill—high conical roof, thick stone walls—and a beach bar that's set in the middle of palm trees. Service is perfection; somehow just the right things seem to appear at just the right moment. What more could one ask? *Cost:* $270–$280, per day, double MAP in season. Bluff Villa—$940 per day, MAP, for up to six guests. No credit cards accepted.

Larger Hotels

★★★ HALF MOON BAY HOTEL
Seventeen miles from St. John's on the Atlantic coast. One hundred rooms and two suites are set in four wings among a 150-acre tropical garden. This is a rather reserved, genteel country-club atmosphere with a lot of emphasis on sports. All accommodations face the sea, are decorated in cool white and bright blue and have their own balconies or patios. Top-notch facilities

[handwritten margin note:] modified american Plan (2 meals included) only

include five all-weather Laykold tennis courts; a nine-hole golf course; a kidney-shaped, freshwater pool overlooking the Atlantic; Windsurfers and Sunfish; snorkeling; a reef-protected 3/4 mile crescent beach; two tropical hiking trails; a beauty salon and a small shopping arcade.

Cuisine is international and stresses reliably good fresh fish, local specialties and baked goods. For variety there are special weekly steak barbecues. Nightly entertainment—steel bands or dance combos, calypso music, crab races—rounds out the list of possibilities available at this beautifully-run, well-equipped hotel. *Cost:* $190–$220 double MAP, in season. The oceanfront suites, on request only, are suite rate double MAP, in season.

★★ ANCHORAGE HOTEL
Dickenson Bay. This 99-room hotel unfolds as you walk through an open front door to a reception area, with trees and hanging ferns growing through wooden slats open to the sky, to the open dining room and bar and then to a long stretch of open beach. Twelve tropically manicured acres hide 83 turquoise and sea-green stucco villas in architectural clusters two stories high; 17 additional Tahitian-type breeze-conditioned, thatch-roof "Rondavels" are scattered among flowering shrubs. This is a restfully Caribbean, uniquely Antiguan atmosphere very conducive to unwinding. But there is activity for those who want it—shuffleboard right on the beach court, Ping Pong, putting greens, croquet and water sports shared with Code's Halcyon Cove next door and three Grasstex tennis courts (one lighted for night play). Food is excellent and abundant, and even special-diet menus can be arranged. Nightly entertainment includes dancing under the stars to different rhythms each evening. This hotel is well managed, and everything always works—a real plus! *Cost:* $180–$215 per day, double MAP, in season. No credit cards accepted. Children under six not encouraged.

(handwritten margin note: The rondavel originated in Africa)

★★ HALCYON COVE BEACH RESORT AND CASINO
Dickenson Bay. Activity is the key word at this lively, action-packed resort. Built in tiers, the hotel extends from the Warri Pier restaurant on stilts out over the Caribbean to the long, wide beach up to the hilltop Panorama restaurant—with the 126 rooms located by the beach, around the pool or in the garden. Some of Antigua's most complete water sports facilities and four tennis courts were merged with a new reception area; a third restaurant with indoor or terrace tables; an elegant, chandeliered, big-city-style nightclub; a casino; ice-cream parlor and shopping gallery. Even the ladies who hung their colorful dresses on a beachfront clothesline for guests to peruse have been taken care of—there's a special new display area just for them! No one—single traveler, couples or families—could possibly get bored here. But just in case you need some advice or assistance, Fay, the hotel's hostess, is one of the most helpful, charming ladies on the island. *Cost:* $160 per day, double MAP, in season; $130 per day, double, EP.

CASTLE HARBOUR CLUB AND CASINO
Michael's Mount, St. John's. Best for those who find games of chance irresistible and businessmen needing quick access to the capital, St. John's. This is actually a medium-size hotel with the conveniences of a large hotel. Fifty good-size double rooms and suites are all air-conditioned, have telephones, fresh flowers every day and a balcony overlooking the capital, just a two-minute taxi ride away.

Breakfast and lunch are served on the poolside terrace, where daytime activities are centered except when cruise ships are in port. The casino opens before noon for the whole afternoon! Most guests come here to gamble, often on special tours tailored to both individual and group needs, which include free or reduced air fare, room, food and booze when gambling interest is assured by the prior purchase of chips. Food here is Continental, and Antiguan, French and Italian specialties are served in the air-conditioned Beef and Bottle adjoining the casino. Other entertainment includes nightly movies, live bands, fashion and floor shows, steel bands, limbo contests and barbecues—more than enough to ensure that guests generally stay put, most to play or pay in the casino. *Cost:* $65–$70 per day, double; MAP is an additional $25 per person. Dinner plan is $18 per person, per day additional.

HALCYON REEF RESORT

Marmora Bay. The approach is spectacular . . . the road winds down to Marmora Bay and down and around to this sprawling place on an eastern peninsula, surrounded on three sides by the Atlantic. One hundred rooms, built to the international standards of Holiday Inn, Inc., the former owner of this property. The resort now offers two double beds in each room, telephone, air conditioning and private patio or terrace overlooking the sea. Three pale pink stucco, two-story buildings are decorated in Caribbean modern with a kaleidoscope of color schemes.

One of the most spectacular settings hotel on antigua

The Olympic-size, freshwater pool is protected from wind by a glass wall on the ocean side, and so lunch, late afternoon drinks and evening barbecues are always comfortable. There's a beach bar for snacks, the Fiesta Room, an air-conditioned dining salon serving Continental and West Indian cuisine, and the Caricabana coffee shop for meals. Regular nightly entertainment features steel bands, calypso music, fashion shows and floor shows with top performing artists.

Rounding out the facilities are two tennis courts and two beaches—one for swimming and the second, on the lagoon side, for water sports.

Because of its excellent meeting facilities, the Halcyon Reef does get a good number of conventions; but the grounds are so large and there is such a choice of restaurants and activities that individuals who prefer to get away from it all can easily do so. In fact, most guests find it difficult to escape from this rather splendid isolation with sunrise-to-sunset wraparound views; but then few try! *Cost:* $136 per day, double EP, in season; for MAP plan, add $35 per person daily.

Restaurants

Antigua's restaurants are small in number but big in variety. West Indian, Continental, seafood, Chinese, Italian, Swiss, and French cuisine are all available, and that's not even taking into consideration the elaborate buffets, brunches and barbecues offered by the major resort hotels.

There's real value here, and our price categories—*inexpensive* (under $15); *moderate* ($15–$25); *expensive* ($25 and up)—fall quite a bit below those of other islands. We're offering you a good sampling of both lunch and dinner places in every price range. Because most of these places are rather small, it's a good idea to reserve during the high season; and do check opening hours and days open. They fluctuate frequently.

★★★★★ CURTAIN BLUFF

Old Road, Morris Bay (Tel. 31115 or 31116). This is probably the most formal and formidable of Antigua's restaurants housed in the hotel of the same name. Owners Howard and Michelle Hulford are justifiably proud of their Swiss chef, Rudie Portmann, who has been with them since 1964, and their wine cellar in an underground cave that is kept at the proper temperature for the 10,000 bottles (give or take a few) that it houses. Chef Portmann won an award a few years ago from Craig Claiborne for his West Indian bouillabaisse.

The menu varies with 27 hot soups (among them, the local spicy pumpkin) and 17 cold soups that includes the humble banana. Desserts varies, but deep fried ice cream is a very special "special." The menu is continental with some Antiguan specialties and the *de rigueur* jacket and tie for men are required for the sophisticated atmosphere. *Expensive.*

★★★ THE ADMIRAL'S INN
Nelson's Dockyard, English Harbour (Tel. 31027). The yachtsmen's gathering place for breakfast, lunch, drinks and dinner. The menu is Continental and the food is consistently good—salads and sandwiches at noon; pumpkin soup, shrimp cocktail, lobster, lamb chops, kingfish, steaks at dinner. Desserts are excellent—the coconut custard is at the top of the list. The menu is on a blackboard that is carried around the large terrace and the timbered, stone-walled dining room—both locations equally atmospheric any time of day. *Expensive.*

Landlubbers are warmly welcomed, too!

★★★ COCKLESHELL INN
Fort Road, just outside St. John's (Tel. 20371). A bit out of the way but worth finding for some of Antigua's best seafood is served at this West Indian tavern (open for dinner only). The nine wooden tables (five on the porch, four inside) are set with simple straw mats and oil lamps and are often filled with regulars from the superprivate Mill Reef—discerning diners whose steady patronage is a fine recommendation in itself. The porch is airy; soft mood music plays in the background; and charming, soft-spoken Winston Derrick is the owner, host, chef and sometimes waiter. The fresh-fruit daiquiri is a perfect way to begin the evening meal—one is a fantastic mixture of melon, banana, pineapple and paw-paw frothed up in a blender with rum. Then there's Winston's delicate seafood gumbo, cockles in a tangy garlic sauce, lobster "Cockleshell style" (steamed, then removed from the shell, cubed and baked with egg and garlic butter) and the fish—king, dolphin, tuna, turtle, snapper, even barracuda—depending on what his sources have caught that day. Every ingredient is of the highest quality, freshness and 100% Antiguan, the only exception being the flour used in the home-baked bread and rolls. Desserts include flaming bananas, exotic fruit and ice cream; and the wine list is well-priced and simple—half a dozen dry, white French vintages, three Italian whites, a Beaujolais for those who insist on red wine and champagne (Dom Perignon when it's available). *Moderate* to *Expensive.*

★★★ COLOMBO'S
(Tel. 463–1024). Not only is the name and cuisine Italian, the three owners flew in their ideas and pasta makers from Sardinia. Located at the Galleon Beach Club, the food and entertainment brings rave reviews and visitor's curiosity. Try to imagine belly dancers from the Middle East (good!) accompanied by a Rasta band! When you get over your surprise, you'll happily get into the homemade pasta and seafood with pasta specialties. *Expensive.*

★★★ LOOK OUT
On top of Shirley Heights, this spectacular "look out" is open day and night. No matter what the time of day you couldn't ask for more in limitless horizons. There's always fresh lobster, fresh local fish, and a casual lunch menu that turns more formal at night with candles on the tables, lanterns nearby, and the sky above. *Moderate.*

★★★ PAPILLON BAR AND DINING ROOM
In a cul de sac off Redcliffe Quay, St. John's. The jungle mood of this restaurant conjures up the movie of the same name, and that's just what owner Fred Bill intended. A former warehouse with stone arches and ceiling fans, the steamy tropical atmosphere is carried out in high-back peacock chairs and 1902 photographs of Antiguan soldiers going off to war. The cuisine is a lunchtime mixture of standard deli-style sandwiches and salads to a Middle

East dinner drama of Syrian, Lebanese, and Israeli specials. A piano in the corner completes the "Casablanca" feeling, even if there are more jazz notes than Woody Carmichael tones. Drinks include the standard mai-tai's and champagne cocktails along with more interesting fare that need several days to ferment (the Antigua Smile or Papillon Special). *Moderate.*

★★★ THE RED SNAPPER
Outside the gates of English Harbour. Originally this building was a dispensary in Nelsonian days; now it has been updated by Bermudian-born Derek Pedro and his wife, Allison. Their mutual love of yachts and all things related to the sea is shown in the racing photographs on the walls that include the famous *Ticonderoga* (which Allison crewed on), and a beached boat from Bequia that decorates the lawn. It's the newest place to gather for lots of sailing talk, and English-Continental dishes that feature steaks, chops, stews, and fresh fish. *Moderate.*

★★★ THE VICTORY RESTAURANT AND BAR
3 Redcliffe Quay, St. John's. (Tel. 24317). For breakfast, lunch or dinner this restaurant receives and revives the tradespeople as well as the visitors in the newly rebuilt Redcliffe Quay arsenal of shops. You'll hear bits of local gossip from the long wooden bar, somewhat dimmed by the whirling wooden ceiling fans. This may well be the most ambitious menu in Antigua . . . lentil soup, grilled prawns, smoked salmon, beef pie, breaded grouper, grilled snapper, fresh lobster plate, and four avocado dishes. *Moderate.*

★★ DUBARRY'S
Barrymore Hotel, Fort Road, just outside St. John's (Tel. 21055). Only a year old, this restaurant's reputation keeps getting better and better. Conrad La Barrie runs everything beautifully, and his wife is your gracious hostess. The varied Continental menu changes monthly, but the lobster (3 ways); steak (au poivre, strip loin or filet) and chef's daily specials are always dependably delicious. A lot of time, thought and effort have gone into every detail of food and decor. Dining is indoors in a rather formal room or out on the veranda overlooking the lighted pool (our preference). Here the white walls with backlighted batiks, highly-polished wooden floors, peaked roof and bright orange and green napkins on crisp white tablecloths complement the flamboyant hibiscus and bougainvillea below to create an ambience of casual Caribbean elegance. There's a spacious bar and lounge area in a separate section, where you'll find yourself spending some time if you don't have a reservation for one of the terrace tables. Open and very popular for both lunch and dinner. *Expensive.*

★★ LE BISTRO
Hodges Bay (Tel. 23881). You're in France as soon as you enter the door . . . a cordial "Bon soir" from owners Yves and Chantal Robert; small candelit tables with red-and-white checkered tablecloths; French posters on the wall, Charles Aznavour on taped stereo. Thirteen tables can accommodate 54 people in this intimate dining spot. Chef Jean Michel is from Orléans. He came to Antigua with 18 years' experience in several well-known hotels and restaurants in Montreal and St. Martin. His menu is varied. It begins with onion soup, snails, a classic bouillabaisse, terrine, smoked salmon, crab or lobster cocktail. Main courses range from steak, done five different ways, to a rich Civet de Lapin in wine sauce. In between are Dover sole, three kinds of lobster, grilled duck with cherry sauce, seafood crepes with mushrooms and a light cream sauce, and the fish-of-the-day. Portions are copious, perhaps too much so, but everything is well prepared and nicely seasoned. The choice for dessert could be a simple crème caramel or cherries jubilee. Three after-dinner coffees with Kahlua and rum (Caraibes); Tia Maria and cognac

(Espagnol) or Irish whisky (Irlandais) are available; and if you can still move after such a feast, the house digestif is a diabolical mixture of Calvados, Kirsch, cognac, Poire William and apricot brandy. The bill (but perhaps not the amount) is quite amusing—clever drawings representing the different courses and beverages. Open for dinner only. *Expensive.*

★★ OFFICERS' QUARTERS REFRESHMENTS
Nelson's Dockyard in English Harbour on the second-story veranda of the original Officer's Ward Room for Nelson's staff. This is a sunrise to sunset spectacular for "pick-thee-ups." The menu covers the range of Nelson fare (ask first, not everything on the menu is in the kitchen). Forenoon and it's a cup of Antiguan bush tea or percolated coffee with a pastry. At Eight Bells (high noon), a bowl of thick Antiguan soup is recommended along with thick sandwiches. First Dog (named for the watch of the day and is also called Tea Time), what else but a cup of herbal tea grown in the adjacent garden with hot buns, scones or cake. The menu lists herbal teas with the ailments they are said to cure: "nunu and balsam for old age; mauby for increased appetite; guma for baby gripes; mint leaf as a nightcap." The toddies appear for Last Dog (or sunset retreat). Fruit punches feature the local pawpaw, guava, soursop, tamarind, and sugarapple. *Inexpensive.*

★ BROTHER B'S
Long Street, St. John's (Tel. 20616). Host Hilson Baptiste is quite a character whose informal, open patio draws a faithful crowd. A place for lunch at wrought-iron tables shaded by umbrellas; very local in ambience, food and folk. Fine, hearty, old-fashioned Antiguan recipes are featured daily—dumplings and mackerel; pepper pot and funghi (corn meal); ducana (sweet potato dumplings) and salted fish; curried conch or pellau (seasoned rice)—should be tried at least once. Fresh fish, baked or fried chicken usually eaten with a very, very hot sauce; breaded pork chops and lobster, accompanied by delicious locally grown vegetables, are also on the menu. *Inexpensive.*

★ SPANISH MAIN INN
East Street, St. John's (Tel. 20660). Janice and Bob Branker, ex-New Yorkers, run their small, sparkling guest house-restaurant with pride. Janice's "roots" are Barbudian, and some of the secrets of her success in the kitchen are her mother's recipes for such creative cookery as shark puffs, conch vinaigrette, cockles, lobster and in-season guinea fowl and venison Barbuda style. All are highly sought by Antiguans and visitors alike: but her hamburgers and omelets (nine listed on the menu, but any combination you might crave can be made up) are island famous, as is the knockwurst with sauerkraut, a rather unlikely offering on a predominantly West Indian menu but a very popular one. *Moderate* (at lunch) to *expensive* (for a full-course dinner).

★ THE YARD
Upper Long Street, St. John's (Tel. 21856). A little garden restaurant with just 12 tables under a galvanized tin roof. On the left is a pretty, old beige house with brown shutters; on the right a busy luncheonette; and banana trees and flowering plants are everywhere. The setting is simple, but the food is very well prepared. Among the interesting choices could be coconut soup, spicy meat patties or steamed cockles for starters. A good steak and a vegetarian dish are always on the menu along with such West Indian dishes as cockle and rice salad; fish with breadfruit or potato chips; stuffed crab; lobster and lobster salad; even a bacon cheeseburger or a club sandwich at lunch. Desserts are delicious and homemade. Open for lunch, dinner and Sunday brunch from 10:00 to 2:30. *Moderate.*

BACH LIEN
Hodges Bay, reservations required. We weren't able to find out a thing more about this newest, hottest, most expensive Vietnamese restaurant that just opened its doors.

18 CARAT
Lower Church Street, St. John's. Light lunches, especially healthy, exotic salads, are served in the courtyard in front of this little white house with yellow shutters that is a lively discotheque in the evening. A popular meeting place on Fridays from 4:00–5:00, when it's Happy Hour. *Inexpensive.*

CHINA GARDENS
Newgate Street, St. John's (Tel. 21298). Bobby Margetson's second-floor, indoor dining room in an old West Indian house is a favorite for good, change-of-pace Chinese cuisine. *Inexpensive.*

DARCY'S AT KENSINGTON COURT
St. Mary's Street, St. John's (Tel. 21323). Josephine Williams's friendly, flower-filled courtyard restaurant is surrounded by shops. Darcy's Rising Sun Steel Band plays here at noon every day but Sunday and then sells their record. Lunch can be very local, pleasant and relaxed except when a cruise ship is in town; then count on it being crowded. Lobster salad sandwiches; an Antiguan special-of-the-day—funghi with stewed conch, curried chicken with rice, potato dumplings; fresh fish; grilled lobster and a variety of rum concoctions, including pineapple and banana daiquiris, are among the offerings. *Inexpensive.*

LE GOURMET
(Tel. 22977). An Antiguan colonial-style restaurant located on Fort Road in St. John's. Started by Swiss-born partners Kurt Schollenberger and Heinz Witschi, the accent is on French cuisine and European service. Lobster is often on the menu—fresh from seawater holding tanks; local fish, and many spicy sauces. *Moderate* to *expensive.*

MAURICE'S
Market Street, St. John's (Tel. 20660). Enter the local life through a long corridor into an open garden with tables, chairs and "the boys" sipping rum at the long bar. Maurice Martin has been in business 12 years, and his West Indian specialties—lobster thermidor; cold plates accompanied by breadfruit and salad; and fresh filet of fish in lime butter—are very popular with local businesspeople during the week. *Inexpensive.*

PIZZAS IN PARADISE
Falmouth Bay. A boating crowd "hangout" for lunch and late night snacks. This informal, roadside pizzaria al fresco has a large, covered, outside terrace away from the heat of the enormous ovens. There's an interesting choice of toppings, some quite tropical, as well as the traditional cheese and sausage. *Inexpensive.*

SHORTY'S
Dickenson Bay. A bit wild, quite wacky and wonderful. It's strictly for a barefoot, shorts, slacks or bikini lunch and swim-stop. Many of the boat people and the local residents head here. But you won't be treated like an outsider; you'll be considered one of the Antiguan family. At this famous calypsonian's beachside bistro, which serves basic sandwiches and a lot of local drinks (beer and rum predominate), a warm inner feeling convinces you that you've found a bit of the heart of Antigua. *Inexpensive.*

THE VILLAGE
(Tel. 24158) Dickenson Bay (Tel. 22930). On the beach next door to Antigua

Village, everything is open, and so the terrace, bar and even the inside tables are always cooled by sea breezes. This is an attractive new place that gives cordial and very efficient service. Wednesday night is jazz night, with a 4:30 to 6 PM happy hour every night. The French chef's forté is fish at lunch and Continental specialties served (with entertainment) in the evening. The buffet spread, enlivened by calypso music, has become very popular. *Moderate.*

Nightlife

Nightlife centers on the resort hotels, and every evening offers such diverse attractions as limbo dancers, fancy floorshows, dance combos, jazz, calypso singers and some of the Caribbean's best steel bands.

There are now two air-conditioned *casinos* on Antigua. The original, at the *Castle Harbour Hotel* on Michael's Mount in St. John's, has blackjack, craps, roulette, baccarat, chemin de fer and 50 slot machines. The bells start ringing at 11:00 A.M. when cruise ships are in town, but the normal hours are 9:00 P.M.—4:00 A.M. *Code's Halcyon Cove* in Dickenson Bay has just opened the island's second gambling center, which includes every form of betting game and entertainment as well.

St. John's has several good local nightspots. Two discothèques, *18 Carat* and Tameka right next door to one another on Church Street, alternate in popularity and are best on Saturday nights. But *Maurice's* on Market Street has long been number one for entertainment with both Antiguans and visitors. Owner Maurice Martin books top acts from all over the Caribbean and the States into his "anything goes" garden club. There's a good house combo, and this is the place to hear the best in calypso, both the old, traditional Trinidadian variety, such as the multitalented Lord Melody, and up and coming youngsters. The action here gets under way at 10:30 P.M., and there's a $5 EC admission charge.

Bandit's on Old Parham Road is the newest "in" dance spot. It's a dark disco up front with flashing black lights; "double your image, double your fun" is the motto here! In back there's a quiet lounge bar where you can escape the upbeat music and frenetic dancers. The ambitious plans of soft-spoken owner Anderson O'Marde include late supper in the garden of his old house, which he calls "a relic"; talent shows; Thursday night open house with free admission; ladies' night on Friday; and half price at the gate and for mixed drinks on Sunday.

Chips, at the Halcyon Reef, is a nightclub with ever-changing entertainment, some imported from stateside.

Those staying out toward English Harbour have *The Floating Disco,* a houseboat moored in Falmouth Bay. This could have been moved by now because of residents' complaints about the noise or it could have been air-conditioned, as promised by the owners, because its location made it very popular with yachtsmen. The music here is the latest from everywhere, and the dancing is animated; there's an upstairs deck for those in need of a breath of fresh air. Another place in this area is *The Hideaway,* a very local disco on the road to the Halcyon Reef Hotel. It's air-conditioned and has taped, upbeat Caribbean music that starts to jump after midnight on weekends.

Shopping

Shoppers in Antigua will turn up many excellent luxury labels as well as attractive, locally made products. Even though the selection may not be quite as mind boggling as on some of the Caribbean's more highly touted "paradises for bargain hunters," shopping here is relaxed and much less hard sell, and prices *are* comparable to many other islands.

In the capital, St. John's, on High Street, *Y DeLima Ltd.* is best for watches, jewelry, cameras and binoculars and *The Scent Shop's* focus is on fragrance. On St. Mary's Street, *The Specialty Shoppe Ltd.* specializes in Waterford and other fine, handcut lead crystal, jewelry and bone china from over a dozen manufacturers. In the liquor department, *Manuel Dias* and *Quin Farara's,* both old, established merchants on Long Street, have the widest selection of spirits. Rum, especially Cavalier, distilled in Antigua and aged in oak casks, is one of the most popular items visitors carry home.

Resort wear, from West Indian fashions on hand-blocked, Sea-Island cottons to original haute couture by Heike Peterson, is also of interest. This talented, German-born designer who settled in Antigua in 1964 has her workshop and showroom, *The Studio,* in a tastefully restored old townhouse on Cross Street, just opposite Government House. Here she takes a variety of fabrics from all over the world—silk, chiffon, voile, jersey, lace and cotton— and turns them into elegant, custom-order gowns and cocktail dresses, one-of-a-kind and limited production fashions for the beach, day, at home and evening wear. The workmanship is impeccable; a lot of attention is paid to detail and finishing. Downtown on St. Mary's Street, her *Bay Boutique* carries slightly less expensive ready-to-wear.

The very special handmade jewelry, bags and belts of *Taylor Designs* are carried here and at several other boutiques. For a visit to the workshop to see the complete collection, call Mrs. Neville Iken (22061). Her designs consist of some unusually attractive combinations of shells, macramé and coral made up in combs and necklaces.

Other fashion stops worth making include *Lady Hamilton* on Church Street; *Nubia, Cornelia's* and the *Pink Mongoose,* on St. Mary's Street, for locally-made shirts, skirts, dresses, beach cover-ups and swimsuits as well as bags and hats, jewelry and other gifts. Also on St. Mary's Street, in a weathered, brown, two-story house, is the main branch of *The Coco Shop* (also at Code's Halcyon Cove, Blue Waters Hotel, Deep Water Harbour and the airport). Their large collection of men's, women's and children's clothing in their own original design Sea-Island cottons as well as Liberty of London fabrics; French perfume; ceramics and other Antiguan specialties have long made this shop a favorite with visitors (including Jacqueline Onassis). Next door *The West Indian Sea Island Shop,* in another pretty, shuttered building, carries the Caribelle line of clothing, dress lengths and wall hangings with tropical motifs. They are made at Romney Manor on St. Kitts using the ancient Indonesian dye-resistant process of batik and tie-dye and some hand painting. Farther up St. Mary's Street is *Kel-Print,* Antiguan artist George Kelsick's main outlet for his original, hand-printed fabrics, shirts, skirts, children's wear and T-shirts.

Over on Redcliffe Street are some of St. John's newest and prettiest shops. *A Thousand Flowers* sells Indonesian "Java wraps," batiks by the yard or made up in high-style clothing that is hard to resist. The designs and colors are magnificent, and there are not only cotton beachwear and daytime wear but some smashing evening outfits in silk as well. Sonia, the manager, is an expert at tying those two-yard sarong lengths in a variety of ways, and just to be sure you don't forget how to wrap, fold and knot, ask her for the diagrammed brochure to take home. There's also a *Java Wraps Boutique,* on the beach at Buccaneer's Cove, that is under the same management. Some exclusive silk-screened creations by *Dominic*—bikinis with matching pareos, scarves and men's shirts done in lightweight materials in striking color combinations—are carried at these two stores, but his atelier, in an old plantation house on Marble Hill near Dickenson Bay, is definitely worth a side trip.

The cool Redcliffe Quay complex includes a long-time favorite, the *Galley Boutique* (the original is at Nelson's Dockyard), where owner Janie Easton has taken on a smiling, savy partner from Jamaica, Mrs. Janet Roberts.

Hung hem-to-hanger with sophisticated styles, Janie keeps the accent on fabrics from Antigua, which she has sewn into international designs. Right now, the "in" look is safari hats that come in white or natural straw and are the rage in London, Paris, Palm Beach or Antigua! (You can also spot brunette Janie by the one she usually wears.) *The Goldsmitty,* owned by Hans and Nancy Smit, is the place to drop into for a bauble to take back home . . . a one-of-a-kind bauble made from gems and gold that the Smits make from South American and European stones and metals. Their display window, deceptively simple, à la Tiffany's, gives you fair warning. (Summers, the Smits can be found at their other shop in Marblehead, Massachusetts.) A find here won't be cheap, but you won't be sorry you made the investment.

Well-made straw work—mats, baskets, hats, even chairs—may be purchased at the *Industrial School for the Blind* on Market Street. Other souvenirs are available at *Shells 'N Things, Treasure Cove Ltd., Shipwreck Shop, Arawak Craft,* the *Ark* and *Daniels.* A few of the things to look for in these centrally-located stores are warri boards, shell items, fine pottery, leathercraft, woodwork, and ceramics. The *Ceramic Factory* near the airport has those lovely pottery figurines, lamps and vases you often see decorating hotels and restaurants as well as homes around the island. *Trade Winds Pottery,* in an old laundry on the hill behind Code's Halcyon Cove Hotel, has handmade straw, wood and pottery work, and you'll often see local artisans practicing their crafts.

In English Harbour (also known simply as The Dockyard), *Galley Boutique* is headquartered in an 18th-century building that fits part and parcel into the still-working dockyard once used by Admiral Horatio Nelson. Inside her boutique, hewn with rough stone blocks and wooden crossbeams, the limited space is chockablock with Janie's own designs and some imports. She does many of her own batiks in her hilltop home and then has local ladies sew them into bikini and long-skirt sets; deceptively simple dresses (long and short) that are both right for the island and right on the patio back home; Antigua "me come from" T-shirts; a smattering of shirts and trunks for men; and, fleetingly during the annual Race Week, a number of those changing designs, which are quickly snapped up. On the import list are the sensational hand-screened prints of Jean-Yves Froment.

Froment is the leading fabric designer of the Caribbean

Last but not least, when visiting The Dockyard be sure to stop by *The Restoration Fund Gift Store,* a retail shop opened by the Friends of English Harbour. Proceeds from articles sold here are used for further restoration and to promote educational maritime and historical activities in the Dockyard. Prints, charts, souvenirs, books and a lot of nautical items are displayed, and future plans include on-the-spot design and execution of crafts and confections with both a historic and an Antiguan touch. These will be produced in the Blacksmith's Forge, the Admiral's Kitchen, the Shipwright's Shop, the Mast Shed and the Officers' Quarters; they are sure to be high-quality items, and the cause couldn't be more worthwhile.

Sports

Beaches

For variety and number, Antigua is tops for beaches: "365 uncrowded, unspoiled beaches all around the island," that's what every brochure says; but the truth is no one has ever made an official count, and so there could be even more. Most are protected by offshore reefs and thus have little or no surf; some of the best, Green Island, for example, are accessible only by boat. Most hotels are on the sea; those that are not generally offer free transportation to nearby beaches. One word of caution: Keep your distance from the manchineel, a pretty little tree that bears yellow flowers and then green apples. Even brief contact can burn and blister the skin! A nibble of an apple causes *extreme* illness.

Deep-Sea Fishing

Marlin, sailfish, tuna, wahoo, dolphin, king mackerel, barracuda, bone fish and tarpon are just a few of the sport species that abound in Antigua's coastal waters. To arrange fishing charters: See your hotel's activity desk; go down to Nelson's Dockyard at English Harbour; or contact one of the following— Catamaran Hotel (Falmouth Harbour, Tel. 31036); Code's Halcyon Cove Hotel Water Sports at Dickenson Bay (Tel. 20256, ext. 268); or Ken Malone (through the Red Snapper restaurant in English Harbour). Malone's cruiser, *Caramel,* has been awarded several trophies, including "largest tuna caught" and "most overall poundage." Rates average about $200 for half a day; $300 full day. Open bar and all equipment are included; and half the catch usually stays with the skipper.

Golf

Antigua has two courses. *Cedar Valley* (Tel. 20161) is a par 70, 18-hole, professional course three miles outside St. John's. Gas carts, caddies, a small clubhouse for refreshments and a pro shop are available. There are nine holes at *Half Moon Bay Golf Course* (Half Moon Bay Hotel, Tel. 22726 or 22728). The par is 34; resident pro Wentworth Brodie gives lessons; caddies and rental clubs are available.

Horseback Riding

Horses may be rented at *Galley Bay Surf Club* and at the stand adjacent to *Code's Halcyon Cove Hotel.* The government does discourage beach riding, however.

Sailing

Just about anything that floats can be rented at *Buccaneer Cove* or *Code's Halcyon Cove Water Sports.* Most hotels provide Sailfish, Sunfish and Wind-surfs free of charge for guests. Two reliably good daylong sailing excursions are: The *Jolly Roger* and *The Servabo,* a 95-foot gaff-rigged Brixham Trawler, which sail almost every day on picnics to offshore islands. Since space is limited for both boats ask your hotel to make reservations.

Week- or month-long *interisland cruises* are best arranged through *Nicholson Yacht Charters* (Tel. 31093) at English Harbour. This is the Caribbean's oldest established yacht broker, handling a complete range of charter boats from 40 feet to 120 feet, all with professional crews.

Scuba Diving and Snorkeling

Scuba courses are offered by *Code's Halcyon Water Sports Center.* There's an introductory *"Resort Course,"* a three-hour lesson ($20) or a lesson and guided reef dive on the same day ($35). A 30-hour full *"Certification Course"* provides three reef dives and all equipment for $200. Diving charters may also be arranged at about $100 for two, $140 for three or $180 for four divers, including all equipment. *Long Bay Hotel* and *Curtain Bluff* both have their own *complete scuba facilities*—free for guests of the latter who are certified divers.

Popular dives around Antigua include *The Jetias,* an English freighter that sank in 1917 while leaving St. John's Harbour; a sunken square-rigger in Deep Bay; Salt Fish Tail Reef that contains an abundance of sea life, and Horseshoe Reef, a U-shaped reef that protects the diving area from waves— clear and calm, ideal for beginners.

Barbuda, Antigua's sister island, has a coral reef with over 50 sunken wrecks to explore.

All beach hotels offer masks, snorkels and fins free of charge for guests. Snorkeling time is included on the cruises made by *Cavalier* and *Servabo* (see Sailing, above). Shorty's Glass Bottom Boat Cruises (Dickenson Bay) take snorkelers to a two-mile coral reef that has been designated a protected area; Miguel's Water Sports (across from the White Sands Hotel in Hodges Bay) has a glass-bottom boat trip to Prickly Pear Island.

Spectator Sports

Cricket is the national sport here. During the season, January–May, daily matches take place among Antigua's leading teams, and there are frequent inter-island skirmishes. *Netball* season in St. John's is also from January through May. Fall is *soccer* time, and *horse racing* at the Cassada Garden Turf Club may be enjoyed on public holidays.

netball =
volleyball

Tennis

Tennis is complimentary for hotel guests, but there is a nominal charge for night play on floodlit courts. Nonguests may play at most hotels, but guests have time preferences, and courts should be reserved in advance. The best facilities are at Curtain Bluff (four courts and a teaching lane); Half Moon Bay (five courts); and Code's Halcyon Cove (four courts). The first two hotels host several professional and amateur tournaments throughout the year. The following hotels also have courts: New Antigua Horizons (two recently built grass courts) and the Anchorage each has a total of three courts; the Cedar Valley Golf Club and Halcyon Reef each has two; and there's one each at the Antigua Beach Hotel, Galley Bay and Blue Waters.

Other Water Sports

Waterskiing is available at Dickenson Bay—Anchorage, Buccaneer's Cove, Blue Waters and Code's Halcyon Cove; Hodges Bay—White Sands Hotel; the Catamaran at Falmouth Bay; Curtain Bluff; Half Moon Bay; Halcyon Reef on Marmora Bay; Long Bay; and Galleon Beach at English Harbour.

Barbados

THE HARD FACTS
Planning Ahead
Costs

The average price for stylish serenity here hovers around $120 per day for a double room in season without meals. MAP plans (breakfast and dinner), available at most major hotels, will add anywhere from $16–$35 a day per person. There's an astounding variety of accommodations—almost 5,000 rooms—on this small but touristically well-equipped island.

Looking for a posh penthouse for two? Sandy Lane, one of the Caribbean's costliest resorts, has them for $800 a day with two meals. A nice double room with private bath in a small, immaculate oceanside guesthouse? No problem, there are plenty of these around for as little as $30 a night, EP. How about a villa for eight golfers or tennis enthusiasts? There's a fabulous one built right on the best golf course that rents for $504 per day and has its own figure eight-shaped pool, tennis court, cook, maid, laundress, and car with unlimited mileage. A roomy apartment on fashionable St. James Beach? You'll find one for $665 for the entire week including breakfast. That's Barbados—something suitable for every taste and budget.

All hotels and restaurants add a 10% service charge and 8% government tax to bills; a few properties tack on a surcharge during the Christmas/New Year holidays.

Off-season (April 16–December 15) reductions of as much as 45% and special 5- or 8-day packages such as the *Best of Barbados* provide even more savings by including airport transfers, gifts, discounts on car rentals, entertainment, shopping, tours, sports activities, and other surprises in the low, all-inclusive price.

Climate

Said to be one of the healthiest climates in the Caribbean. Tropical and cooled by gentle, easterly trade winds that keep humidity at a comfortable level all year round. Temperature averages 75° to 85°F., but seldom falls

Bridgetown is considered a very expensive place to live, so bring money!

41

below 68°F. or rises above 88°F. Rainfall for the entire island averages 60 inches a year. February and March are the driest months; September and October are the wettest.

Holidays and Special Events

New Year's Day; Good Friday (April 20, 1984); Easter Monday (April 23, 1984); May Day (May 1); Whit Monday; Kadooment Day (first Monday in July); Caricom Day (August 1); United Nations Day (first Monday in October); Independence Day (November 30); Christmas Day; Boxing Day (December 26).

Special events include the *Holetown Festival,* a February celebration commemorating the first settlement on Barbados in 1627. Cultural events, handicraft displays and a variety of continuous entertainment that include concerts, water and land sports, and religious services. In April, the *Oistins Fish Festival* is centered around this quaint town's main occupation. Fish-related competitions—boat and crab racing, the largest flying fish catch, and boning contest; entertainment and open-air bazaars are just a few of this historic community's events. The island's annual national folk festival, *Crop Over,* celebrates the end of the sugarcane harvest all over the countryside. The finale is *Kadooment,* a carnival-like celebration on the First Monday in July when colorful costumed bands parade in Bridgetown. There are Calypso competitions, the election of the King and Queen of the Crop (those who have cut the most sugarcane), a King and Queen of the costume bands, with arts and crafts events among the highlights.

Tour Operators

In the United States try Adventure Tours; Barbados Holidays International; Caribbean Holidays; FlyFare; GoGo Tours; Hill Tours; and Travel Center Tours.

Sources of Information

In the United States contact—the *Barbados Board of Tourism,* 800 Second Avenue, New York, N.Y. 10017 or 3440 Wilshire Blvd., Suite 1215, Los Angeles, Cal. 90010. *In Canada*—20 Queen Street West, Suite 1508, Toronto, Ontario M5H 3R3; Suite 1105, 666 Sherbrooke Street West, Montreal, Quebec H3A1E7 or Macleod Place 1, Suite 307, 5920 Macleod Trail South, Calgary, Alberta. Once *in Barbados* you can check at the *Board of Tourism's* information offices at either Grantley Adams International Airport or at Prescod Boulevard and Harbour Road, Bridgetown.

Packing

Keep in mind that you're visiting a country with a British heritage—and think conservatively. For daytime touring or walking around Bridgetown, slacks and skirts are appropriate. (Short shorts or a beach cover-up is inappropriate and unappreciated.) At night a simple cotton dress or a pretty skirt/slacks outfit is "right" for women. Men may wish to wear a sports jacket, but at most restaurants, jackets are optional. (Only a few hotels insist on jacket and tie and only on a few nights.) Women may wish to bring along a wrap for evening, but restaurants are not air-conditioned; they depend instead on the soft evening breezes to keep everyone cool and comfortable (and they do). Otherwise, you'll want to pack whatever sportswear you'll need to indulge in the sports of your choice.

Film is available in Bridgetown and at the resort hotels, but it's more expensive than at your local drugstore. Prescriptions can be filled in Bridgetown, but it would be wiser to plan ahead and bring with you whatever medical supplies you think you'll need.

Documentation

Proof of citizenship—a passport, birth certificate or voter's registration card—and a return or on-going ticket are required for stays up to six months by American, Canadian and British citizens.

Getting There

Airline service to Barbados is frequent. American Airlines flies direct from New York; BWIA from New York, Miami and San Juan; Eastern from Miami; and Pan Am from New York and Boston. Air Canada serves the island from Montreal and Toronto; BWIA from Toronto and Air Martinique, British Airways, BWIA, Cubana and Guyana Airways all provide Caribbean connections.

Major cruise lines from New York, Port Everglades and Puerto Rico all call in Barbados.

Formalities on Arrival

Customs

Formalities are generally efficently and speedily handled, though the lines can seem a bit long. If the lines seem too awesome, you can spend some time changing money at the airport bank. By the time you finish, the lines may have shortened to more tolerable lengths. No meat—cooked or uncooked—may be imported without a permit from the Ministry of Agriculture. 26 oz. alcohol, ½ lb. tobacco or 50 cigars and 200 cigarettes are allowed duty free entry.

you won't need a visa if you are american, British or Canadian

Money

The official currency is the Barbados dollar, $1 U.S. = $1.99 BDS, $1 Canadian = $1.67 BDS. By law, prices must be quoted in Barbados dollars. It's easier to convert your dollars to theirs, but U.S. and Canadian currency are accepted everywhere; change is usually given in local currency.

Getting into Town

Taxis are available at the airport, and though they're unmetered, fares to most destinations are prominently posted near the taxi stand. The taxis are fairly expensive, but until you get a feel for the island (roads are not very clearly marked), you'll probably be better off riding with someone who knows the way.

Settling Down

Choosing a Hotel

Barbados' hotels range from large (306 rooms in 5 hotels and 2 apartels in the brand new Heywood's Holiday Village complex) to tiny (8 room guesthouses). In between are small, medium and medium-large properties, condominiums, time-sharing units, cottages, and apartments. Most of these accommodations are on a beach or within walking distance of one. Luxury properties are centered on the West Coast in St. James Parish; more moderate-ly-priced accommodations and the majority of the housekeeping facilities are clustered in the well developed and very lively parish of Christ Church on the South Coast.

Many fully-staffed villas and private homes are available for rent by the week or longer. A reliable source of information on these is Villa Leisure, 411 Park Avenue, Scotch Plains, New Jersey 07076; tel. (800) 526–4244. They operate packages in conjunction with American Airlines and BWIA that include a self-drive car with unlimited mileage. Villa Leisure can furnish color photos and specifications on all properties they represent and they take the time and effort to review each one every year to be sure that all is as it should be.

Since accommodations on Barbados are so varied and numerous, read the brochures carefully and be sure to get advice from a travel agent who has been there.

Choosing a Restaurant

Restaurants in Barbados offer primarily seafood and Bajan/West Indian fare—though you'll find Continental entrées and a scattering of Italian eateries. Of the options, the first two are far superior (though the ubiquitous flying fish does get tiresome after a few days).

Tipping

10% is the going rate for taxis and restaurants that don't add on a service charge to these bills. At the airport 1 BDS is standard per bag.

Learning to Cope

Business Hours.   *Shops* are generally open from 8:00 to 4:00 during the week, from 8:00 to noon on Saturdays. *Banking hours* are 8 AM–1 PM Monday–Thursday; 8 AM–1 PM and 3 PM–5:30 PM on Fridays.

Electricity.   Conventional 110-volt, 50-cycle alternating current permits the use of standard American appliances.

Water and Drink.   Tap water is safe to drink throughout the island. Fine Barbados rum is famous—Mt. Gay, one of the best—and is very, very inexpensive here. Banks is the light, refreshing local beer.

Communications.   To *telephone direct* from North America, dial 809 + 42 + the local number. From Barbados, overseas calls to the U. S. and Canada may be placed by dialing 1 + the area code + the local number. Both internal and international telephone service are excellent. The local information number is 119. The main post office in Bridgetown is open Monday through Friday 8 AM–4:30 PM; rural branches close for lunch between noon and 1 PM, then remain open until 3 PM on Monday and from 3:15 PM Tuesday through Friday. Air mail postage rates to the United States and Canada are BDS 55¢ per ½ oz. for letters; BDS 40¢ for postcards. Average delivery time is 3 to 6 days in both directions.

Language.   The official and only language of Barbados is English, though Bajans speak it with a native inflection.

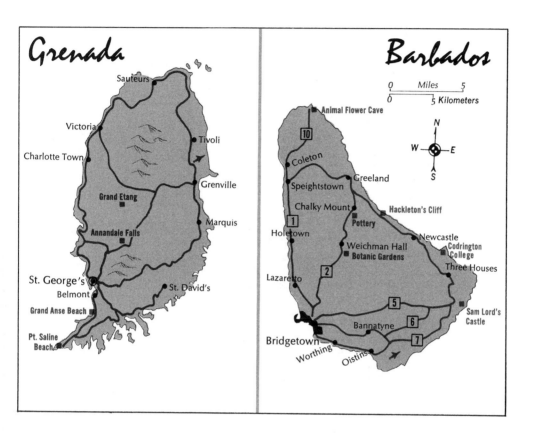

Medical Assistance.   The 600-bed Queen Elizabeth Hospital is located in Bridgetown; St. Joseph Hospital is in the parish of St. Peter. In addition, there are private hospitals and clinics throughout the island.

Getting Around

By Car

Open sided mokes and closed sedans may be rented in or near major hotels and in Bridgetown. If you plan to hire a car, you must register at a local police station and pay a BDS $10 fee. This procedure can be rapidly accomplished at the airport upon arrival. A convenient police desk is located in the customs and immigration area. In case you don't register here, be prepared to wait at local stations while more urgent matters are handled. Keep to the left; distances are posted in kilometers and the speed limit is 30 mph (20 mph in Bridgetown).

By Bus

Good service connects Bridgetown to the rest of the island on scheduled routes and at scheduled times (from 5AM to midnight) via modern, enclosed vehicles or quaint, open sided ones. *BDS* 60¢ is the set fare for any destination. Avoid taking these buses during rush hours. There are also mini-buses that ply the south and west coast roads. They are identified by a blue and white license tag with a B before the numbers and fares vary according to distance traveled.

By Taxi

There are nearly 1,000 on the island. Fares must be pre-set with the driver as meters are non-existent. If no taxi is waiting at your hotel entrance, ask the desk to call a driver who lives nearby. Recommended fares for island tours, certain popular destinations, and by the hour may be obtained from your hotel desk.

TOURING

"Barbados" is Portuguese for "beards", after the bearded fig trees growing here

We're assuming that you've rented a car and are touring on your own. However, if your navigational abilities are suspect, we suggest that you hire a car and a driver. Road signs are, in places, somewhat mysterious. Also, though we've covering the island in one fell swoop, you will probably wish to spend part of one day in Bridgetown, dividing your stay between touring and shopping, and then hit the around-the-island circuit on another day . . . or on two days. Though the island is small, roads don't run in straight lines, and so touring takes time.

Your first stop should be at the Barbados Tourist Office near the *Bridgetown Harbour* to pick up a very handy map called *Welcome to Barbados.* It contains an exhaustive list of the sights to be seen and marks their locations. The deep water harbor deserves a second look if for no other reason than that the decision to create it was made after almost 100 years of debate. It officially opened on May 6, 1961.

Next stop is *Trafalgar Square* in the center of Bridgetown. Park the car anywhere you can find a spot. From here all attractions are within walking distance. Trafalgar Square was once called Egginton's Green and as such contained the whipping post, the pillory, a horsepond and a dunking stool that, an offical account states, was used to "cool the ardour of certain females." It was renamed Trafalgar Square in 1806 to commemorate the Battle of Trafalgar and the death of Lord Nelson. Seven years later a statue honoring Lord Nelson, executed by Sir Richard Westmacott, was unveiled. The Bajan tribute, which predates London's version by 30 years, was in thanks for the part Nelson had played in protecting the island from pirates. The green has since disappeared, having been steadily eroded by vehicular traffic; now the island's tribute to Nelson is a lonely sentinal, hounded by the honk of horns. Near the statue is a tiered dolphin fountain, containing an outer basin of local coral stone, erected in 1865 to commemorate the debut of piped water to Bridgetown.

Barbados' legislature is the second-oldest (after Bermuda) in the western hemisphere

On the north side of the square are the *Public Buildings* that house the House of Assembly (on the right), notable for its series of stained-glass windows depicting English sovereigns from James I to Queen Victoria as well as Oliver Cromwell, whom Bajans so honored for his part in establishing their self-government. To the left is the towered Legislative Council Building.

South of the square is an inlet called the *Careenage* where ships were careened (tipped on their sides) and scraped, caulked and painted. Chamberlain Bridge, which spans the Careenage, is a replacement for a bridge, called simply The Bridge, from which Bridgetown got its name.

St. Michael's Cathedral is located east of the square, just behind the modern Financial Building. Originally constructed in 1665, it was destroyed by the hurricane of 1780, then rebuilt, then badly damaged by the hurricane of 1831. It has since survived unscathed. George Washington is said to have worshipped here when he visited the island in 1751 with his half-brother Lawrence who came seeking a cure for consumption. Lawrence never found the hoped for cure and George came down with smallpox, which scarred him for life. Nevertheless, both left the island with warm feelings for the country and its inhabitants. There is a house in Bridgetown that is pointed out as the one George Washington slept in, but like many of its stateside counterparts, there is no evidence that George ever laid head to pillow here.

Just south of Bridgetown is the *Barbados Museum,* with its collection of antique furniture, West Indian prints, Indian relics, glassware, maps and artifacts ($1.00 U.S. entry fee) and the *Garrison Savannah,* a 50-acre site that once served as the parade grounds for British troops and now is a recreational park, hosting frequent, spirited and very-well-attended cricket matches and infrequent horse races (five times a year). Garrison Savannah is situated off the main road. When trying to locate it, look for its neighbor, the faded red tower clock of *St. Ann's Fort,* a miraculous survivor of the 1831 hurricane that wiped out all in its path.

From here head down the Coast Road (number 7) into *Hastings,* named after the family who once owned a plantation on this site; *Rockley,* where the Rockley Park public beach is located; *Worthington; St. Lawrence,* where three of the island's best restaurants are located: Pisces, Witch Doctor and the Plantation House, as well as one of the island's liveliest nightspots, the *Caribbean Pepper Pot; Maxwell;* and into *Oisten,* where the Charter of Barbados was signed in 1652. You'll then pass *Christ Church* (Anglican), home of the famous "Mystery Vault of Barbados." As the story goes, coffins of Colonel Chase's family had at various times rearranged themselves within their vault, a phenomenon Bajans found disquieting. Finally, in 1820 the coffins were ordered removed from the vault and buried in different graves in the churchyard.

Your next landmark will be *Grantley Adams International Airport,* followed by *Crane Beach* (off the main road). A stop at the latter, just to gaze at the spectacular view from the hotel terrace and experience the soothing sea breeze that has beckoned travelers to this spot for two centuries, is well worthwhile.

Next stop: *Sam Lord's Castle,* which can be visited between 8:00 and 6:00 ($1.50 entry fee). Be sure to ask at the desk for a copy of Marriott's brief description of the Castle and its contents. If you become intrigued enough to want to find out more about Sam, *A Guide to Sam Lord's Castle,* written by one of his descendents, is available at the activities desk ($1.50).

Villa Nova, one of the finest examples of a great house built on a sugar plantation, was finished in 1834 and is filled with fine mahogany antiques. The late Earl of Avon, Sir Anthony Eden, former prime minister of Great Britain, and his wife, Clarissa Churchill, owned it for many years until his failing health prompted him to sell it. In 1971 it was purchased by Mr. and Mrs. Ernest Hunte, who live there today. Parts of the house and the gardens are open to the public (from 10:00 to 4:00, Mondays through Fridays, $1.50 entry).

About three miles outside Bathsheba is *St. John's Church,* set in a cool spot on the edge of a cliff. Wandering back into the graveyard, you will notice the stone of Ferdinando Paleologus who, the intriguing inscription proclaims,

[handwritten margin note:] Sam was a wrecker, luring ships onto the reef, killing survivors and looting the broken ships

was descended "from ye Imperial Lyne of ye last Chrisitan Emperors of Greece"; dates: 1655–1678. There is a variety of stones, some above ground and some with steps leading down into the ground, some marble, some coral rock. Near the sundial at the farthest end of the grounds, is the main attraction, a sweeping view of the valley and Atlantic coastline.

From St. John's you'll wind down a steep, twisting road to Martins Bay and on to Bathsheba. Here, if you're horticulturally inclined, you'll find *Andromeda Gardens,* containing in only a few acres almost every species of tropical plant, those found on the island as well as specimens from around the world ($1.50 entry).

Pressing onward, you'll travel up the sensibly-named East Coast Road. It was officially opened by Queen Elizabeth when she visited the island in 1966. (There's a plaque to that effect set in a boulder at the side of the road.) The landscape all along the east coast is exhilarating wild and picturesque. It's been compared to the raw and rugged beauty of the coast of Maine. Turning inland you'll pass through a series of blind S-curves bordered by sugarcane towering above your car. (A few strategically-timed honks of the horn are in order here to warn drivers zipping toward you.) You'll spot dairy and sheep farms, hear the crowing of cocks, pass little pink schoolhouses and homes painted in soft colonial colors.

Independence also came in 1966

If you're intent on seeing all the sights, *Cherry Tree Hill* will be your next stop. Once, so Bajans believe, there were cherry trees here that were swept away in a landslide. No matter, mahogany trees line the entrance to this very pretty spot, and there is a splendid vista of the rolling hills of the Scotland District located in the parish of St. Andrew, named for the patron saint of Scotland.

Near here is *St. Nicholas Abbey,* a 17th-century Jacobean-style plantation house filled with European antiques and native mahogany pieces and surrounded by lovely grounds. If the present owner, Lt. Col. Stephen Cave, a retired British Army officer, is here when you visit, you're in luck. He's charming and a font of information. (Open 10:00–3:30, Monday through Friday, $2.50 entry.)

South and east of St. Nicholas Abbey is *Farley Hill.* Here, in the late 1800s, Thomas Graham Briggs's palatial plantation house, with its exquisite furnishings and magnificent gardens, provided a perfect backdrop for the frequent and lavish entertainment of royalty, writers and the neighboring gentry. No expense was spared; no amenity was overlooked. All that remains now is a shell . . . though if you linger awhile on the terrace, once a kaleidoscope of brightly-colored stones, you should be able to envision the gaiety and the grandeur of its past. The government now owns Farley Hill and is carefully restoring the gardens. It hopes to raise funds to restore Farley Hall.

From here head to *Speightstown,* once known as "Little Bristol" (because William Speight was sent here by a firm located in Bristol, England). From this port was shipped all the sugar manufactured in the Leeward parishes of Barbados. On the outskirts of Speightstown is the government's 306-room $17 million Heywoods Holiday Village project, which was under construction when we were last there. It is slated to be open for business by the time you arrive. Heywoods Holiday Village is composed of seven small hotels/ apartels, each with its own manager; an administration building; shopping area; bar; restaurant; discotheque; meeting hall; market; laundry; sports center; 3 swimming pools; 5 tennis courts; and a 9-hole golf course. Much building is going on in Speightstown, with the result that what had been a lovely old town is now an architectural hodgepode, though the town conveys a prosperous air. On the way out of town, you'll notice remnants of Speightstown's gracious style—big stately houses, including one owned by Claudette Colbert, set back from the road.

From here down the "Platinum Coast" you'll find one luxury hotel after another. When you get to the Coral Reef Club, slow down. Its next-door neighbor is *Folkstone Park,* a marine reserve and museum. The reserve is divided into zones: The Scientific Zone is the province of those doing research on coral reefs and marine organisms; the Water Sport Zones are for waterskiing, boating, para sailing, and other water sports; the Recreational Zone, the most protected area, is set aside for snorkelers who can follow its underwater trail around an inshore reef. Scuba divers can head for Dottin's Reef, a seven-mile stretch about a quarter of a mile offshore, or dive around the sunken *Stavronikita,* a 356-foot freighter that has attracted all manner of marine life. (Diving at the latter site is recommended for experienced divers only). A note of caution: Barbados law prohibits the removal of any marine object, including coral, and forbids any fishing within the reserve.

Just south of here is *Holetown,* site of the first settlement in Barbados. English sailors gave the town its name because the river entrance reminded them of the "hole" in the River Thames at Limehouse—and although some diplomatic settlers tried to change the name to Jamestown, as a tribute to King James, Holetown stuck and eventually became official.

The colonists settled in 1627, not 1605 as the town's marker indicates

Due east of Holetown is Barbados's newest offering: *Harrison's Cave* (small fee). A tram takes visitors downward into the Great Hall, filled with thousands of gleaming stalagmites and stalactites, and then to the cascading Twin Falls, the very still Mirror Lake, and, near the lowest point in the cave, a dramatic 40-foot waterfall that plunges into a turquoise lake. Here visitors can get out, wander around and walk under the falls. The final stop is the Rotunda Room, with its dazzling display of pure alabaster formations.

Practically next door to the cave is *Welchman's Hall Gully,* a cool garden of fruit and spice trees and representative specimens of native flowers and plants, owned and carefully tended by the Barbados National Trust (small fee).

Inside Information

Hotels

Hotels here are snug, civilized havens where guests are encouraged to shed worldly worries and relax. There's no flash—just wonderful beach and sea vistas, comfortable accommodations and embracing tropical gardens. A comprehensive list of Barbados hotels would pass the 100 mark; we've included some we think are special, in alphabetical order.

★★★★ COLONY CLUB (ST. JAMES PARISH)
Young people, especially those who have to keep an eye on cash flow, might be better off in another hotel. However, this is one of the very best hotels in Barbados. It has a deserved reputation for courteous, efficient service, low-key elegance and attention to details. There's a Britishness about the place that manifests itself in the care taken with the floral arrangements and the assumption that proper dress will be (and is) worn for dinner (except on beach barbecue nights). It has a wonderfully-tranquil seaside terrace, 76 comfortable, tasteful rooms or villas—some almost on top of the pool—and a coral-rock main house that is open to the sea and the strand of sand. *Cost:* $190–$235, double MAP in season.

★★★★ GLITTER BAY (ST. JAMES PARISH)

One of Barbados' most attractive accommodations is in an idyllic setting—a 10½ acre estate that formerly belonged to Sir Edward Cunard. Registration is soothed by a glass of champagne in the separate reception building that is a 1930s mini-replica of Cunard's Venetian palace. Then it's just a short walk past shimmering fountains, glorious flowers, and towering royal palms to the spacious, tastefully appointed apartments (studios, single, double bedrooms and penthouses) housed in three-story white stucco buildings with elevators. Sleeping areas are carpeted and air-conditioned while living rooms are cooled by trade winds and wooden ceiling fans; terraces look out over the pool, the sea, and the refreshing gardens. Kitchens are well-equipped with Syracuse china, stemware and cutlery for eight and everything from cutting boards to electric blenders. The guest list and the owner's roster is very international and the facilities are superb—room service, an inviting bar and lounge area, nightly entertainment, an excellent restaurant, every water sport imaginable, a large pool, and new this year are two tennis courts. Bajan born and British-trained Theo Williams capably oversees the management of this new 89-room condominium complex that works like a small hotel. This very special corner of paradise hopes to complete its third and final building phase next year that will bring the total room count up to 125 which should rank it among the top ten resorts in the Caribbean. *Cost:* Studio $135; one bedroom suite $180–$240, double; two bedroom suite $310–$370; two bedroom penthouse $440, EP in season.

★★★★ SANDY LANE (ST. JAMES PARISH)

Plenty of rum drinks are served here on a lazy sunny afternoon, but martinis also adorn the courtyard tables facing the beach and the sea. This is a place for people who want to get away from it all . . . but not leave the amenities and the customs of their home country clubs entirely behind. The tariff here is high, the highest on the island and one of the highest in the Caribbean. Is it worth it? Most of those who stay here will tell you it is. It's a pretty place in a lovely setting, right on a sweep of beach dotted but not crowded with the hotel's blue and white umbrellas. Everything is peaceful and snug; there's a quiet elegance as well as attractive people to share it with. Sandy Lane's rooms are also soothing: Set off from soft, pastel-colored walls, the comfortable furnishings are usually replaced at the first sign of wear. Guests' wishes are taken very seriously. As long as something is available on the island, the hotel can and will obtain it on request. Five tennis courts, water sports and the golf course (across the street at the Sandy Lane Golf Club) are first rate. There's also a secluded pool area at the upper edge of the expanse of terraced lawn. At night soft lights illuminate the graceful lines of this former great house, now expanded to 124 rooms and suites. Those who've stayed in the world's best hotels will be aware of the absence of some of the subtle niceties of service and attention to details that make a hotel truly great. But the many faithful who come here year after year seem content to overlook any imperfection. *Cost:* $335–$385, double; $575–$950, suites. MAP in season.

★★★ COBBLERS COVE (ST. PETER PARISH)

Occupying the northernmost position in the string of luxury hotels that line Barbados's west coast, the pretty main house was once a private home. Not too many two-story, balconied guest appendages, with 39 suites, have been added, preserving this hotel as an intimate place to be shared with no more than 78 other guests. A pool is poised on the edge of the crescent beach, dining is open-air, and features Continental food with a Bajan flavor. Shopping in nearby, bustling Speightstown is varied and good. Water sports are free and include unlimited use of water skis, sunfish and windsurfers. *Cost:* $250, double MAP in season.

★★★ CORAL REEF CLUB (ST. JAMES PARISH)
Gracious club style, accents of fresh floral displays, an airy, uncluttered decor and quietly attentive service are four of the attributes that make this hotel a favorite for many. Other inducements include its secluded beachside location, water sports and tennis options, pool and candlelight dining with the setting sun as a backdrop. Exchange privileges with two other resorts add variety. (By the way, bring a tie: this is one of the few hotels in Barbados that makes a point of requesting them during the winter season.) *Cost:* $220–$308, double AP (3 meals) in season.

Built around a private mansion which is now the hotel's main building

★★★ CRANE BEACH (ST. PHILIP PARISH)
If you close your eyes as you stand on the cantilevered terrace just outside the bar area, you'll imagine that you're on the bow of a ship. Gentle trade winds blow with dreamlike softness over you, into the bar and into the restaurant beyond. Beneath you the surf pounds. Open your eyes, and you'll likely be mesmerized by one of the most spectacular and bewitching views in the Caribbean. You're atop a high, rocky cliff beneath which a staircase spirals to pink coral sand; powerful rolls of water hit the beach, sending spray flying; farther out, hues of turquoise and aquamarine dazzle under the intensity of the sun. Crane Beach is an old hotel from another era. And it has an old-world feel. Built in the 18th century as a retreat for travelers seeking the medicinal effects of fresh sea air, it commands 1,000 feet of unspoiled ocean footage and offers 25 rooms, many with antiques, newly and elegantly redone, some with four-posters. There are 4 tennis courts and two pools—the upper one is on the edge of the cliff and is set off by Roman columns; the other, in a tropical garden setting. There are two bars and a good restaurant in a striped-tented, candle-lit pavilion room. Nearby there's golf and horseback riding. *Cost:* $70–$150, double; $200–$250 suites. EP in season.

★★★ MARRIOTT'S SAM LORD'S CASTLE (ST. PHILIP PARISH)
Beneath a beautiful, domed, plasterwork ceiling (a copy of one at Windsor Castle) near a curved mahogany staircase, the ghost of Sam Lord still roams—at least according to guests who've so sworn; certainly Sam's spirit is still felt. Those who would like to stay in Sam's room, sleep in his massive four-poster, ponder the mystery of a hollow hiding place in the three steps that lead to his bed (some say he hid his rum here; Bajans speculate that he stored ammunition) and try to imagine life at the castle in the mid-1800s need only plan ahead and send Marriott a special request. One caveat: Marriott has restored the antiques and modernized the baths in the ten rooms of the castle; even though all have wonderful four-posters and most have a lot of atmosphere, those who prefer modern accommodations would be advised to select one of Marriott's 259 comfortable, more conventional rooms, suites and cottages. Sam's big, square, seemingly-indestructible castle, with its crenellated battlements, is the visual focal point of this resort, but the grounds ramble over some 72 acres that are so well designed and landscaped that one never has a feeling of being crowded. The wide beaches are perfect for lazing or walking, although the Atlantic surf is a bit rough. Swimmers who prefer tamer waters can slip into any of the three pools. There is a health spa, a game room and seven lighted tennis courts. Two pretty restaurants and two snack bars, one by the ocean, the other by a pool, provide sustenance. A long list of daily activities (from goat races to group jogging to sea cruises) and entertainment every night offer diversion. *Cost:* $122–$142 double; cottages $200; suites $264–$500 EP in season.

The castle is one of Barbados' touristic highlights

★★★ SANDY BEACH (CHRIST CHURCH PARISH)
39 one-bedroom and 50 two-bedroom suites with fully-equipped kitchens, private patios or balconies. This carefully designed hotel has consistently maintained one of the island's highest occupancy rates since its 1980 open-

ing. Innovative general manager, Alfred Taylor, has a flair for detail and seems to have anticipated every possible tourist need. Complimentary in-house facilities include extensive water sports (Boggie boards, air mattresses, windsurfs, pedal and sail boats, snorkeling equipment, a 3-hour cruise, and scuba lessons), and a self-service laundromat. Continental breakfast trays are set up in the rooms of businessmen and early departing guests. There are four specially-equipped suites for physically disabled vacationers; an MAP plan including unlimited choice from the à la carte menu as well as dinner shows and dinner-cruise options, sophisticated office equipment, and secretarial service available. Free, unlimited use of the nearby Universal Health Club; personalized, laminated luggage tags; toiletry kits for those arriving minus baggage; a bi-monthly newsletter; champagne for honeymooners and bed-side "Tia Maria Welcome" miniatures are just a few of the little extra touches. *Cost:* One bedroom suite $145: two bedrooms $215, EP in season.

★★★ SETTLERS BEACH (ST. JAMES PARISH)

Located just on the outskirts of Holetown, on 4 acres. This hotel offers 22 handsome, two-bedroom villa apartments with sitting rooms and kitchens set on well-tended lawns that converge on the beach and the sea. Open-air dining is provided under pyramid roofs overlooking the sea or at the Coral Reef and Sandpiper hotels with which it has exchange privileges. There's a pool on the grounds; water sports are just up the beach. *Cost:* $193–$204, double EP in season.

★★★ TREASURE BEACH HOTEL (ST. JAMES PARISH)

A luxurious little oasis well-situated along a nice 150-foot stretch of beach in the Payne Bay area. Owned and beautifully managed by Mary and Charles Ward (she's American, he's Bajan), who live on the premises to assure constant attention. The atmosphere is casual and relaxed, the service warm and caring. Mary's talented green thumb is obvious in the lush gardens. 24 spacious, cheery one-bedroom suites have cathedral ceiling, living room, air-conditioned bedroom, an enormous balcony and a dressing room. These rooms are clustered around the pleasant pool and patio bar. Three smaller studios are set back amidst the flowers. The outdoor dining room is popular with outsiders as well as hotel guests and there is music twice a week. Water sports of every variety are just outside the front door. This is the kind of place that brings back a lot of repeat customers and the place boasts of one of the highest occupancy rates on the island. But it's first come, first accommodated (Sir Lawrence Olivier regrettably had to be turned away last year), so make reservations early year round. No children under 12 during February. *Cost:* $90 studio; $130 standard suite; $150 superior suite, double or single EP in season.

★★ COCONUT CREEK CLUB (ST. JAMES PARISH)

A younger crowd tends to gravitate to this informal, friendly spot, now part of the St. James Hotel Group. Cottages horseshoe around a busy pool by which a stepping-stone walkway circles to a stone stairway that takes one to a narrow beach . . . one that gets very much narrower at high tide. No matter. The beach is usually used for strolling, while the pool, rocky perches and the English pub (complete with dart board and cricket bats) are the congregating areas. 49 rooms are poolside or beachfront, all air-conditioned, all with balconies or patios. *Cost:* $170–$200, double MAP in season.

★★ EASTRY HOUSE (ST. PETER PARISH)

Gordon Carlstrom, president and manager of Eastry House, estimates that 70% of his guests have been coming here for the past ten years for an average stay of three to four weeks. It's that kind of place. Pink and homey and surrounded by gardens tended and worried over by Carlstrom and his wife, it

Maid service is included in the room price

offers comfortable rooms, stocked with books for an afternoon retreat from the sun, that are furnished with an assortment of antiques and modern pieces. Each of the 34 rooms in this hilltop perch has a balcony from which guests can gaze down to the sea (450 yards away), and, on request, special arrangements can be made for such things as a refrigerator kept stocked with champagne. There's a tennis court and large pool on the grounds as well as a cool, natural grotto some 70 stone steps down into the earth. The entrance to the grotto is circled by a profusion of orchids, Trumpet Flowers, Queen of the Night, and special hybrid poinsettas, 27 kinds of hibiscus as well as other flowers. Down by the sea are the hotel's beach club and an informal al fresco dining area. Evening dining and dancing take place on the hotel's terrace. Queen Ingrid has stayed here, and so have Princess Anne and Peter Ustinov. *Cost:* $100–$150, double CP; $140 one-bedroom apartments with kitchen, EP in season.

[handwritten: Eastry is a former plantation house]

★★ SANDPIPER INN (ST. JAMES PARISH)
The decor of this small, 32-room inn is a West Indian rustic mix, with vaulted, wood-beam dining areas, colorful prints and wall hangings and, all about, lush flower growth and shrubbery. Over half the rooms are suites with kitchens; all have air conditioning and balconies or patios. The one- and two-story cottages are grouped around a small, free-form pool. Dining is open-air or at two sister resorts, the Coral Reef Club or Settlers Beach, and one of the three usually has entertainment. There are two tennis courts; shopping is nearby; golf, and water sports can be arranged. No children under 12 January 15–March 15. *Cost:* $194–$232 double, $244–$388 ocean view suites, MAP in season.

★★ SOUTHERN PALMS BEACH CLUB (CHRIST CHURCH PARISH)
A fun, lively place with lots of activities and facilities geared to a definitely under 50 crowd. The architecture is as varied as the guests—a good cross section of Americans, Canadians, Europeans, business travelers, and vacationers. Spread out like a maze over six acres and 1,000 feet of beach, multi-buildings of all shapes, sizes, and heights house 121 rooms, also of varying shapes and sizes. This hotel grew sideways by taking over less successful neighboring properties. These acquisitions were painted pink and white and numerous pathways were constructed to the original structure. You might need a guide to find your room a second time, especially if you arrive after dark. Happy hours, Bajan cooking lessons, drink-making demonstrations, arts and crafts classes, a wide variety of evening entertainment, boutiques, a good restaurant, two pools, unlimited water sports, and a late-going disco round out the well-rounded list of things to do.

★★ ST. JAMES BEACH CLUB (ST. JAMES PARISH)
A recent condominium development that doubles as a 131-room hotel. There are 54 studios, 55 one-bedroom and 14 two-bedroom suites, and 8 penthouses that can be expanded to three bedrooms. All but the studios have complete kitchens, and there is a radio, telephone and wall safe in each unit. Fine facilities here include room service, shops, a meeting and conference center, catering and babysitting, free sauna, gym and air-conditioned squash court (open 24 hours—rackets and balls are gratis); two new tennis courts, a large pool with swim up bar, coffee shop, and one of the island's better restaurants—*The Sand Dollar.* Live entertainment or music is provided every evening. The beach nearly eroded away here last year but a great deal of time, money, and effort was expended to bring back the sand which with Mother Nature's cooperation should be in place when you get there. *Cost:* Double room $120–$135; suites $160–$315; penthouses $320–$360, EP in season.

★ BARBADOS BEACH VILLAGE (ST. JAMES PARISH)

Though there's only a small beach, there's a lot happening on it: a full array of water sports and a hundred or so guests strolling, jogging or basking. The complex is a swirl of pastel structures nestling amid landscaped greenery. All rooms and suites have balconies, some overlooking the pool, the sea and the gardens; some have kitchenettes. Two new tennis courts were added last year. The accent is on informality for dining—in the octagonal restaurant—and dancing—in the Hippo disco. During season there's usually entertainment of some sort every night. *Cost:* $80–$140 EP in season.

a lively place

★ GREENSLEEVES (ST. PETER PARISH)

A gothic *G* marks the entrance to this elegant apartel, where each of the 12 hotel rooms is actually an apartment, with kitchen, one or two bedrooms and patio. The arched white walls, tapestries and Spanish accents of the spacious main house evoke the impression of Morocco. The wonderful food, served by the pool in an open, pavilion-style restaurant lined by Roman columns, is Continental with West Indian touches. The pool and most of the buildings are on the inland side of the road, but bar, beach and informal dining facilities are maintained across the street, right on Caribbean sands. *Cost:* $154–$268, EP in season.

Restaurants

Dining in Barbados is a slow, relaxed affair. It often proceeds on a veranda or on a terrace by the sea where soft, caressing trade winds make air conditioning unnecessary. Some spots are chic and romantic, others down-home and informal. Though you'll find Continental entrées on many menus, the best bet is to stick with West Indian offerings and the fruits of the nearby seas.

Flying fish is one of the island's specialties—you can order it baked, fried, broiled and, occasionally, stuffed. Other specialties are langouste (a clawless Caribbean lobster), sauteed sea eggs, dolphin, kingfish, and turtle soup. Blood pudding, callaloo soup (thick and spicy, made of okra, salt pork, crab meat and a spinachlike vegetable called callaloo), coconut-milk sherbet and goat (which, when properly prepared, tastes astonishingly like lamb) are also favorites; other meats are imported and not very special. Carrots, beets and cabbage are served as side dishes, for these are the island's newest crops. Sample the local hot sauce sparingly, it is said to "roast the tongue"!

At all but the strictly Bajan restaurants, *Expensive* means around $25 per person without drinks; *moderate* around $18 and *inexpensive* under that figure, at Bajan spots figure around $10 per person, making all Bajan places strictly *inexpensive*.

"Sea eggs" are sea urchin or oursin

Try your goat curried

★★★ LA CAGE AUX FOLLES (PAYNE BAY, ST. JAMES)

Nick Hudson, always an innovator (Bagatelle Great House and The Gourmet Shop are two of his creations), has done it again. Book well in advance as there are just 22 places in this intimate new dinner spot which instantly became the preferred place for both local and visiting gourmets when it opened last year. The atmosphere is tropical French—a cage of colorful macaws and parrots in the small bar (Pernod is a specialty); lots of flowers, soft background music by Charles Aznavour, and a teeny tiny dance floor where frequent shows are staged by fashion designer Simon whose super-chic boutique is next door. Menus are simple but everything is fresh and well prepared—filet of beef with bearnaise sauce, live Canadian lobster prepared in a variety of ways, an Oriental specialty or two (Peking duck is one of the best), French cheeses, unusual homemade desserts, and a very nice wine list. *Expensive.*

★★★ PIPERADE (ST. JAMES)

Tel. 24111. Located in Glitter Bay Hotel, this charming pink, green, and white terrace restaurant has careful, though sometimes a bit slow, service and a very interesting menu. The shrimp dishes—à la gingembre (marinated in ginger, white wine, lime, herbs, then deep fried in a beer batter and served with tomato mayonnaise) and à la Barbade (covered with coconut, sautéed with herbs and onions then flambéed with rum and lime juice) are very special. For those who are tired of just plain steak, the *filet de boeuf Pecheur*—steak filet pan-fried with mushrooms, onion, brandy, red wine, cream, and topped with curried shrimp—is highly recommended. The wine list here is extensive and expensive with a choice of fine vintages from France, Italy, Spain, California, Germany, and Portugal. There's entertainment almost every evening that varies from calypso singers to soft guitar melodies. *Expensive.*

★★★ PISCES (ST. LAWRENCE GAP)

Tel. 86558. In a small, graceful house set in a lovely, little blue-green cove just off the main road. Drinks are served in a plant-filled, white-latticework area facing the cove and the reef. To dine one goes down the stairs to a terrace only feet above gently lapping waters. Candles romantically illuminate the tables. Its soft, intimate atmosphere is complemented by good food, including Bajan bouillabaisse, callaloo soup, flying fish, poached dolphin, shrimp, kingfish and langouste. Reservations are a must. *Expensive.*

Fine view combined with some of island's best cuisine

★★★ THE SAND DOLLAR (ST. JAMES)

Tel. 21707. This elegant seaside restaurant is in the St. James Beach Hotel and is very popular with local residents. The chef's paté—flavored with Tia Maria, brandy and cream; broiled dolphin served with almond slivers; snapper fillet poached in a sauce of tomato, garlic, bayleaf, thyme, diced pineapple, and lightly-curried coconut milk, and the deviled rock lobster are as tasty as they are unusual. Service is friendly and no one tries to rush; so long, leisurely dinners are the thing here. The setting is so pleasant you'll probably want to linger on to enjoy the music and dancing as well. *Expensive.*

★★ BAGATELLE GREAT HOUSE (ST. THOMAS)

Tel. 50666. The grande dame of Barbados's restaurants since the cellars of an imposing, 1600s plantation house (once the home of Lord Willoughby) were transformed into a series of intimate, lantern-lit chambers, separated by graceful archways. This is the place to head for romantic, patrician dining, which is more satisfying if one sticks to such island favorites as callaloo soup, stuffed flying fish or frogs legs. *Expensive.*

★★ BROWN SUGAR (BRIDGETOWN, NEAR THE ISLAND INN)

Tel. 067684/60057. Offers delicious West Indian fare, including one of our favorites, Solomon Grundy, described as HOT and it is. The decor here is similar to Pisces (no surprise because the same hand, that of Martin Donowa, molded both) but on a more informal scale. Upstairs dining is beneath a latticework ceiling and whirring fans; downstairs tables are arranged in a little garden area. Candle light, a lot of healthy hanging plants, and Barbadian wall hangings soften the rustic edges. Lunch is buffet style, tandoori chicken (good, though not cooked in a tandoori pot), lobster and a crabmeat Carlisle are three dinner specialties. Try their mystery dessert. *Moderate* to *expensive.*

★★ CRANE BEACH RESTAURANT (ST. PHILIP)

Tel. 36220. In a striped-tented pavilion, a few steps up from the cliff-hanging bar area and directly in line with whispering sea breezes. (One almost wishes a storm would form and lightning would flash over the cliffs; this would be such a cozy, romantic place from which to watch.) Seafood accompanied by fresh vegetables is the main attraction here, with turtle soup, curried shrimp, grilled lobster and Crane chubb meunière on the recommended list. Madras-skirted-and-scarfed waitresses are attentive and pleasant. *Moderate* to *expensive.*

★★ GREENSLEEVES (ST. PETER)

Tel. 22275. This is probably the island's most ambitious menu—15 hors d'oeuvres, 10 soups, 21 main courses, 8 desserts, and 5 different kinds of coffee! Smoked scotch salmon, frogs legs, coquille St. Jacques prepared not only with scallops but flying fish and kingfish as well, Steak Diane, duck à l'orange, *steak au poivre,* and *scampi au ricotta* are just a few of the house specialties. The setting is poolside and couldn't be more romantic —candle light, fresh flowers, soft music and stars twinkling above. *Very expensive.*

★★ WITCH DOCTOR (ST. LAWRENCE GAP)

Tel. 87856. Owned by the same family who started Pisces across the street. A huge mask of a witch doctor greets one at the door; inside the mask forms a motif, which is repeated throughout the network of small dining rooms—interspersed with other African and Bajan carvings. As one would expect, the menu is an African–West Indian mix with interesting and un-usual offerings. Recommended are the split-pea and pumpkin soup, African ground-nut stew, soul stew, missionary curry and kingfish Carib. *Moderate.*

★ GREENHOUSE (CHRIST CHURCH)

Tel. 89033 ext. 266. Sandy Beach Hotel's attractive open-air restaurant is housed under a seaside, wood shingled palapa. The regular à la carte menu is continental, specializing in steak and seafood with Bajan touches. Their Friday night "Bajan Cohoblopot" is a fantastic array of authentic local dishes such as codfish cakes, sea eggs, coucou, curries, stews, black pudding and souse, and jug jug. A detailed description of each dish is given to each guest. This is a perfect introduction to Bajan cuisine at its best. *Moderate.*

★ FOOLISH FISH (LAND'S END, ST. MICHAEL)

Tel. 76295. This popular seafood restaurant moved last year to a pretty little gingerbread house on the new road facing the harbor. The menu focuses on just about anything that swims—clams, dolphin, fish cakes, garlic shrimp, flying fish, kingfish, lobster, red snapper, scallops—plus a good sirloin for die-hard meat lovers. Open lunch and dinner. *Moderate.*

★ THE PLANTATION (ST. LAWRENCE)

Tel. 85048. This has the spacious, cool rooms and pillared-portico entrance so characteristic of stately Barbadian great houses. Whether seated in the inside drawing room or outside on the verandah overlooking wooded hills, you will be delighted by the lantern light, soft breezes and gentle, night rustle of leaves and palms that seem to promise gracious dining. What follows is friendly service and good, though not outstanding, food. Most interesting is the duck in the chef's special pineapple sauce; also dependable is the Bajan seafood platter. (An added attraction of The Plantation is that it's right next door to the Stables disco/pub and just up the road from the Caribbean Pepper Pot—for one taxi ride you've an evening's worth of dining and nightlife.) *Moderate* to *expensive.*

THE CAPTAIN'S CARVERY (ST. LAWRENCE GAP)

Tel. 89605. At The Ship Inn a nightly "Master Table" buffet features three main roasts—beef, Canadian smoked ham, local pork, Norfolk turkey or leg of lamb, carved to your liking; pepper pot soup; coldcuts with special house piccalilli sauce; baked potato; homemade whole wheat rolls with sesame seeds and a scrumptuous coconut pie. One of the few places on the south coast where good late night snacks—fish and chips, shepherds pie, etc.—are available in the lively bar. *Moderate.*

ATLANTIS HOTEL (ST. JOSEPH)

Tel. 33445. Located in Bathsheba, with spectacular views of the crashing Atlantic surf; an excellent place to fall into if your around-the-island tour lands you in the area around lunchtime. The Sunday buffet is famous with an emphasis on local dishes and seafood. Reservations are obligatory, especially for terrace tables. *Inexpensive.*

Nightlife

Find out where "The Merrymen" are playing (check the local paper) and do head over. A veritable Barbados institution, this group has an incredible repertoire of Caribbean, Latin, and Country and Western songs that radiate good fun and generally pack the dance floor with visitors and Bajans of all ages. For a different kind of show there are now three "Dinner Theaters" on the island. The original *1627 and All That* takes place in the Barbados Museum and is a full evening's entertainment ($29U.S.) which includes leisure time to tour the museum, drinks, and hor d'oeuvres served in the courtyard to the accompaniment of a strolling guitarist. There is a buffet dinner and an inventive, well-produced dance show that explores the Bajan heritage from its African beginnings to the present. *Barbados, Barbados* is a fun musical comedy based on the life of colorful Rachel Pringle whose misadventures are depicted in the historic Boiling House at Balls Plantation. For $30U.S. you get transportation (it's quite far from the St. James hotels), hors d'oeuvres, wine, unlimited drinks, a copious Bajan buffet, and plenty of laughs. The *Plantation Tropical Spectacular* ($25U.S.) is held on Wednesdays in the garden of *The Plantation* restaurant. This is also a full evening of song, dance, folklore, and island music. For dinner try the *Planter's Punch* and treat yourself to the free after-show at the Stables Disco Pub. Each month the Band of the Royal Barbados Police Force provides open-air concerts around the island, events that always attract a large audience. Traditional shows with limbo dancers, fire-eaters, and steel bands are held nightly at one of the hotels. (Again check the paper for places and times.) Also many of the hotels have lively entertainment of the pop variety or offer quiet dancing beneath the stars. Jazz fans should not miss *Belair* on Bay Street, a rather seedy but very popular upstairs club in Bridgetown's "red light district." Music here usually goes on all night with musicians stopping by at all hours for impromptu jam sessions. The island's discos tend to be tame by stateside standards, however, you might try out the *HideAway* if dining at Bagatelle Great House; *The Stables* near The Plantation restaurant is western-style and draws a young crowd that tries its skills on the mechanical bull. *The Hippo* at Barbados Beach Village; the *Flambeau* in the Hilton and the *Unicorn* in the Southern Palms Beach Club are slightly more sophisticated with recorded music that ranges from reggae to rock. Singles should definitely check out the scene at *The Carlisle,* supposedly a membership club but guest admissions are available at the door. This place swings both inside and out with live bands that often perform for barefoot dancing on the beach as well as on an elevated, partly-covered platform. Then if you still have some energy left, visit Baxters Road, "the street that never sleeps" where small, very lively sidewalk eateries serve fish and chips, pork, liver and Bajan-style fried chicken from smoldering coal pots.

Shopping

Barbados offers duty-free, also called in-bond, shopping for crystal, china, figurines, perfumes, cosmetics, sweaters, tobacco, liquor, watches and jewelry. However, depending on where you live, you may or may not realize substantial savings. Generally, sweaters, liquor and tobacco are good buys, but if you plan to make an investment in crystal, for instance, you should be aware of the prices in your local stores. You should also plan to do your shopping at least 24 hours before departure to allow time for purchases to be delivered to the airport or to your ship.

Broad Street is the main shopping street in Bridgetown. Here you'll find *Harrison's,* a department store that has obtained exclusive import rights for Dunhill, Guerlain, Lancome, Patek Philippe, Rosenthal and Les Must de Cartier products. Other major stores include *Da Costa's, Cave Shepherd; Y. de Lima* and, on a slightly smaller scale, *India House.* All have branches, with less selection but correspondingly smaller crowds, elsewhere on the island. Jewelry specialists include *J. Baldini, Correias, Bayley's,* and *Chattel House.*

For Bajan-made items, try the *Best of Barbados* shops, which feature prints, watercolors and designs created by Jill Walker. Or wander around *Pelican Village,* a thatched-roof, 3-acre complex near the harbor where Bajan artisans offer everything from dolls to wood sculpture to sundresses. On the subject of things Bajan, this is probably a good spot to mention that Barbados's best rum is Cockspur VSOP, a 14-year-old sipping rum; next best is Cockspur Special Reserve.

There are several art galleries where local artist's work may be purchased. The best include *Bay Gallery* in Bridgetown; *Devonish* and the *Arts Council Gallery* in Pelican Village; *Garrison Gallery* and the *Hilton Art Gallery* in St. Michael; *Dayrells Art Gallery* in St. George and *Talma's Mill* in Christ Church.

Antiquaria on St. Michaels Row in Bridgetown has many fine examples of antique furniture, early maps and engravings, tea caddies, china, silver, glass, water colors and oil paintings, old bottles, brassware, and other bibelots.

Chic little shops, many carrying high-ticket creations, are scattered along the west and south coasts. A few to check out include *Batik Caribe* at the Hilton, Sam Lord's Castle, Paradise Beach and Southern Palms hotels; *Gearbox* in Hastings; *Hibiscus, Origins* and *Gaye Boutique* in Holetown; *Frangipani* at the St. James Beach Club; *Dotto* and *Quest Collections* at the Sandy Lane Hotel; and *Petticoat Lane* at the Hilton, which carries Carol Cadogan's unusual clothing fashioned from patchwork, laces, old and new fabrics. *Simon,* whose flounced, frilled and handpainted day and evening wear is very popular with the international set has relocated from Holetown to a charming little white cottage in Payne Bay. Educated at London's Royal College, Simon has a marvelous knack for making clothes that are colorful, comfortable, very feminine, and extremely elegant. Most of his designs are one of a kind or few of a kind, and he makes up special orders.

Those in accommodations with kitchens should not miss *The Gourmet Shop* just next door to Simon's (opposite the Treasure Beach Hotel in St. James). Nick Hudson flies in fresh delicacies from Canada and Martinique such as live lobsters, Grade A-1 beef, French patés, cheeses, wines, champagnes, croissants, and breads. He also stocks imported tinned goodies as well as homemade lime pie, cheesecake, and coffee-cream pie.

Sports

Beaches are best on the sheltered west coast where the Caribbean is warm and placid; the Atlantic side has long, magnificent, windswept stretches of sand as well, but strong waves and undercurrent often make bathing dangerous here. Water sports abound; you won't have to look far to find waterskiing,

Don't buy tortoise shell products, as they cannot be imported into the USA — endangered species

jet skis, parasailing, windsurfing or the newest craze—bumper boats. Two major reefs off the island offer an abundance of interesting marine life for snorkeling, for scuba fans there's the Berwyn wreck in the shallow waters of Carlisle Bay. More experienced divers can visit the S.S. *Stavronikita,* a Greek freighter that was severely damaged by fire in 1976 and was purchased by the government and sunk ¼ mile offshore as an artificial reef that is now part of the Folkstone Underwater Park. The wreck lies in about 130 feet of water; the shallowest cabin at around 80 feet. Good water sports operators for scuba include Les Wotton at the Coral Reef Club; Willie's Watersports at the Paradise Beach Hotel; The Dive Shop at the Holiday Inn; Scuba Safari near the Hilton; Sandy Beach Hotel Water Sports and Marine Dive Tours in Christ Church. The average price for a dive with equipment included is $25 US; other diving packages are also available. Deep sea fishing for barracuda, blue marlin, bonito, dolphin, grouper, kingfish, mackerel, snapper, snook, tarpon, tuna, wahoo, and yellow tail can easily be organized through most of the above operators. The average half-day charter rate which includes drinks and tackle is about $300 BDS. Sailing possibilities range from sailfish, cat and trimaran up to the schooners *Jolly Roger* and *Captain Patch.* These "pirate ships," along with the *Shady Lady* and *Irish Mist,* make half-day sailing excursions that include entertainment, lunch, drinks, and snorkeling. Cocktail cruises and evening sails are also available. Horseback riding may be arranged through Sharon Hill Riding Stables in St. Thomas. For golf, Sandy Lane's superb 18-hole course is on the site of an old sugarcane plantation that offers panoramas of the Caribbean and the surrounding countryside at almost every hole. Here there's a nice clubhouse, pro shop, driving range, and a putting and practice green as well. Fees range from $34 BDS off-season to $42 BDS in season for outside guests. Tennis courts are available at most major hotels and the government maintains courts at Garrison in St. Michael (grass court, $3 BDS per hour) and Folkstone, St. James (hard surface $1 BDS per hour). Telephone 75238 for information on these. The soccer season runs from January through June; polo is played at the Barbados Polo Club in St. James; cricket, the national sport, is played from June through December, though formal and informal matches can be found year round. The former are played at the historic Garrison Savannah, also the location of the Barbados Turf Club where horse racing is held on various Saturdays during the year and big purse events, such as the Cockspur Gold Cup Race, attract international entries.

The west coast is called the Leeward side (pron. loo-word)

THE HARD FACTS
Planning Ahead
Costs
We're almost afraid to put this in print, but Bonaire's costs are low—about $100 for the best possible accommodations. Air fare, however, does have to be taken into consideration and this cost can be high. Check out latest package and bonus programs from the airlines. As the saying goes, "good things come in small packages" and tiny Bonaire more than repays what you pay to get to these sunny, sea-filled shores.

Climate
Needless to say, it's warm all year (averaging about 75°F.), but it can be breezy, as the divi-divi trees prove. This is the "national" tree of the A.B.C. islands, whose sharply bent branches point northeast, the direction of the wind.

Holidays and Special Events
New Year's Day; February is Carnival month with dancing and parades; Good Friday; Easter Monday; Coronation Day on April 30; Labor Day is on May 1; Ascension Day; Celebration of Dia de San Juan is on June 24 when folkloric dances are held throughout the villages and at the Celebration of Dia de San Pedro, on June 28; also look for folkloric dances and songs in North Salina and Rincon during late June. Big doings at the annual Sailing Regatta in mid-October; Kingdom Day is December 15; Christmas is celebrated on December 25 and 26. And only in Bonaire, does Santa Claus arrive by boat or airplane to be greeted by government officials as well as the children!

Tour Operators
In the New York area contact Caribbean Holidays; FlyFare; Cavalcade Tours; and GoGo Tours. In Chicagoland: Underwater Adventure Tours; Sport Trek; and Butler Travels. In the New Jersey area try Ocean Quest; and in Maryland Adventure Tours is a best bet.

Sources of Information
Bonaire Tourist Office, 1466 Broadway, Suite 903, New York, NY, 10036; in Canada, the Bonaire Tourist Office, 815-A Queen St. East, Toronto, Ontario,

Canada, M4M 1H8. In Bonaire, the tourist office is at 1 Breedestraat, in the capital Kralendijk (Tel. 8322 or 8649). Most valuable for visitors is the free "Bonaire Holiday" that's updated quarterly and is offered free by the tourist office and at hotels or the airport. It's as pink and easy to spot as the Bonaire flamingos.

Packing

The Flamingo Beach Hotel's phrase said it best . . . "toes are in, ties are out." Pack anything comfortable and casual with emphasis on sunwear, both in, on, and around the water because that's where you'll spend almost all of your day. Nightlife is equally casual, with the possible addition of a sweater or one long sleeved something for an unexpected breeze. *Always* pack double the film you think you'll use; film is not always available and it's more than twice the price you'd pay at home.

Documentation

Even cruise visitors need proof of identity for a 24-hour stay. Visitors from the USA should always travel with a passport, a birth certificate, an affidavit of birth or a naturalization of citizenship certificate. An alien registration card or a voter's registration card will also serve as proof of citizenship.

Getting There

The only direct service is once a week from Miami on ALM Antillean Airlines. Other than that, it's American Airlines from New York, to either Aruba or Curaçao, where it's an easy connection to Bonaire on ALM. Eastern Airlines offers daily connecting service to Curaçao and Aruba from approximately 30 U.S. cities via Miami. There's also daily service from New York with a Miami connection to either Aruba or Curaçao. Among the A.B.C. islands, ALM Antillean Airlines offers the only inter-island service.

Money

U.S. \$1 = NAF 1.77, the official currency. The Netherland Antilles florin or guilder is accepted everywhere, but so is the U.S. dollar. Since almost all the prices are quoted in the official currency, plan on doing a bit of division.

Tipping

There's a standard 10% service charge added to all hotel and restaurant bills (with the exception of the Flamingo Beach which adds 15%). That's not an increase, it's just that other hotels also include a separate 5% tax. It all equals out. For exceptionally good service an additional small tip is always appreciated.

Learning to Cope

Business Hours.   Mondays through Saturdays, 8 AM to 12 noon; then from 2 PM to 6 PM. When a rarely seen cruise ship is in port anything goes!
Electricity.   127 volts AC on 50 cycles, on which U.S. made appliances work.
Communications.   The telephone system from the United States is direct dial. Call 011–599–7 plus the number. Within Bonaire telephones are at the hotel desk or go to the telephone company in Kralendijk and be prepared to wait.

Airmail letters to the United States are NAF .75; postcards are NAF .45. Letters to Canada are NAF .80; postcards are NAF .50.

Language.   The official language is Dutch, but you'd have a hard time proving it since Papiamento is the language of the people. English and Spanish are spoken with equal ease.

BONAIRE TODAY

It's only a small corner of the globe, some 50 miles north of Venezuela, 24 miles long and from three to seven miles wide, and shaped like a boomerang. This small, special corner of the Antillian islands was the first to declare a tenth of its territory a national park. Bonaire is a special island that long ago became the first Caribbean island to prohibit spearfishing and coral taking. It is a special island, for here one of the major industries, a large salt company that bought some 5,000 acres and set about gearing up the salt industry, constructed a sanctuary for thousands of flamingos that live here.

Bonaire is also known for its unsurpassed diving, snorkeling, bird-watching, and lively people—here everyone is an individual. Oh yes, it's also an island where the garbage cans are handpainted works of art.

Bonaire offers nature's best, above and below the seas. The land is flat and cactus-strewn with occasional divi-divi trees interspersed by a lonely palm tree. Shopping isn't a reason to come here, nor is there much in the way of "nightlife;" there's only one mini-casino.

There is the unrivaled show each sunset between 5:18 and 5:22 P.M. when flocks of the flamingos rise over the mangroves, skim the trees, then head north over the open sea. No one knows why or even where they fly for certain. It's thought they head to Venezuela; long necks stretched out, feet flattened behind, and wings in constant motion. What is known is that they return again each morning. The best place to see this phenomenon is between the two sets of slave huts (anyone will give you directions, and besides, there's only one road going in that direction).

This is also an island chosen by Dee Scarr, Captain Don Stewart, and several other well-known sea experts as home.

Dee Scarr is a relatively new resident (having lived here about five years), but she's already making a bit of island history with her "Touch the Sea" program that includes very "individualized" dive programs where you're introduced to Popcorn, Adele Davis or One-Eyed Jack; all three are friendly moray eels, at least friendly to Dee and her diving companions. Tamer divers might prefer meeting Oliver Twist, a peacock flounder; Friday, the file fish; and Sir Timothy, a trunk fish. They're all Dee's friends that she feeds and in her own way "touches."

Only in Bonaire is the leading hotel, the Flamingo Beach, a former prison camp—that is, it was a detention center during World War II when the Americans had a communications base here. Now one of the most powerful radio stations in the world is here, Trans-World Radio, which beams out its missionary message to born-again Christians throughout the Western Hemisphere, into northern Africa, and even behind the Iron Curtain.

The island first entered the history books when Amerigo Vespucci sailed by in 1499, and named the island after the Arawak name, Bo-nah. The Arawak word meant "low country," and is still applicable for a landscape with great salt flats and a terrain of cactus and scrub. The original, highly valuable, Brazil wood was taken by the Dutch who laid claim to the islands in the 1630s. Then the only settlement was the town of Rincon, famed today for Sunday excursions for homemade ice cream!

The Dutch concentrated on harassing the Spanish from the A.B.C.'s—Bonaire being the "B"—much as the English and French played war games farther north in the Windward and Leeward islands.

Officially the Dutch became the landlords in 1636, and the aggressive Dutch West India Company was in charge until 1792. Some 100 slaves were imported from Africa, but they mixed and married with the Dutch (as did the Indians who survived).

Since World War II, word of Bonaire has spread, and today with Bonaire the smallest in population of the six Dutch-administered islands (Aruba,

Bonaire, Curaçao, Sint Maarten, Saba, Sint Eustatius), genuine travelers return year after year, much as the flamingos who spread their wings and return at the start of each new day.

TOURING BONAIRE

Kralendijk, the capital of Bonaire, is the midway point for excursions to the northern and southern halves of the island. A tour of Kralendijk itself can be accomplished in a stroll of an hour or less.

We suggest that you begin your walk near the piers, at a plaza called Wilhelminaplein—named for Queen Wilhelmina (1880–1962) of The Netherlands. In the center of the plaza is a simple monument, with the dates 1634–1934, erected as a tribute to 300 years of Bonaire-Dutch friendship. At one corner of the plaza is a small Protestant church (small, because 95% of the island's inhabitants are Catholic); across the street is the government office building. Close by is an old fort affording a sweeping view of the island. It was used by the British during their brief early 19th-century occupancy of the island; today it functions as Bonaire's Institute of Folklore and houses an eclectic collection of early island artifacts.

Down by the water you'll find a tiny Aegean-inspired (and Caribbean-colored) columned building where a Bonaire couple sells fresh fish caught in local waters by one of the fishing boats nudging the nearby dock. (Plan to arrive early in the morning to get the best of the catch.) Also in the area is a fresh vegetable and fruit market; on the piers children play and in the water look for schools of fish. On the water are tugs waiting to assist oil tankers into BOPEC. From water's edge you might make a circle through the town; a ramble where one is free to make one's own small and personal discoveries. (You might see how many painted eye symbols you can find; they're supposed to ward off evil spirits.)

North Bonaire

Park Pleasures.   There are two northbound excursion possibilities. The first, and longer one, will take you to and through Bonaire's National Park and will involve a full day of wandering. So plan to leave early, pack a picnic lunch and a bathing suit.

As you head along the shoreline road heading north you'll find places where you can stop and park. From coral-walled perches look down over crystal clear waters punctuated with intriguing coral formations. At one such stop-and-look spot you'll find the *One Thousand Steps* that lead down to one of Bonaire's best scuba areas. Actually, there's a bit of hyperbole here; there are only 67 steps—the trip back up from the water (especially to those laden with diving gear) just seems much longer than the scamper downward.

Proceeding on you'll see caves etched in the coral on the inland side of the road centuries ago by the ocean's long reach. Farther along, just before the road curves away from the sea, you'll spot the *Bonaire Petroleum Company* (BOPEC) storage tanks. BOPEC is a U.S.-Dutch consortium set up to handle the storage and transfer of crude oil brought via supertankers from Nigeria, Venezuela, and other oil producing nations and destined for United States and South American markets. (By the way, BOPEC gets high marks from local environmentalists for its careful no-spill handling of oil operations.)

Farther on is *Goto Meer,* a salty primordially beautiful inland lake where a hugh flock of vibrant pink flamingos has found sanctuary. You'll not soon forget the sight of these flamingos preparing for take-off by "walking" on the water—then lifting off, black undersides shining, wings outstretched. You'll see young flamingos in the group, as well as fully grown goddesses with eight-foot wingspans.

From here head north to the *Washington/Slagbaai National Park,* its entrance guarded by goats, cactus and divi-divi trees. Admittance is $1.50 for adults, children under 15 enter free. Once inside, you'll find a museum with a curious collection of artifacts including a resplendent antique hearse. Also here is Karpata, a mustard-colored, remodeled great house with wet and dry laboratories for the study of marine life by visiting biologists. There are also exhibits, like a diarama of reef life, for the edification of visitors.

Of more interest are the coves and paths and birdlife and the untouched wildness of the preserve's 13,500 acres. The park is supervised by a Dutch environmental group, STINAPA, who has done a splendid job of protecting it. You'll find no garish refreshment stands or camping sites or superhighways in the interior. Just nature. Visit one of the observatories and watch for the green and yellow parrots that always fly in pairs. (And if you're ornithologically inclined, see how many of Bonaire's other 135 bird species you can spot and name.) Stop, swim, and picnic along the shoreline of broken coral bits thrown landward by the sea. Follow a footpath to Mt. Brandias, the park's highest point. Or pick out a cove for sunbathing. You might also make a stop at one of the Park's most dramatic spots, Boca Cocolishi, a bay on the windward side where waves sweep in some 300 yards through a high coral cutout. The Park is open seven days a week, from 8 AM to 5 PM.

Sunday Serendipity.   Another worthwhile northern jaunt, best saved for a Sunday, involves a loop through Rincon, Boca Onima, and Seroe Largu. If you set off in the early afternoon you'll arrive in Rincon just in time to join what seems to be a Sunday Bonaire tradition: the tending to one's sweet tooth at Rincon's little ice-cream shop. It's located next to the Amstel Bar in the center of town, and since there's usually a slew of citizens waiting for a scoop, you'll have time to settle upon an appropriate flavor. There are 15 homemade varieties from which to choose including pistachio, sour-sop, banana, and pineapple.

Rincon itself is a splash of ice-cream colors. Your first sight of the town, located in a valley in the center of Bonaire's northern arm, will be of little mango, tangerine, lime, and lemon colored houses. Rincon, the island's oldest village, was once home to the slaves who mined the salt flats some 17 miles to the south.

As you head east, out of Rincon and towards Boca Onima, you'll see groups of horned goats and cactus fences that keep them from straying into and destroying yards and gardens. You may see a piglet or two on the road or catch an impromptu roadside soccer game.

The lure of *Boca Onima* is its stalactite and stalagmite caves and more specifically, the inscrutable Arawak inscriptions painted on the cave ceilings. There's an eerie, almost Stonehenge feeling in the caves where the silence is broken only by the sound of slow dripping water.

Another rewarding Bonaire site and worth a special trip is the observation point at *Seroe Largu.* During daylight you'll have a clear view of Kralendijk, the western shoreline, and Klein Bonaire. At dusk, or under the spell of moonlight, the view becomes softer, enchanting and romantic.

South Bonaire

Flamingo Flights.   To watch the nightly sunset exodus of Bonaire's flamingo flock, plan to leave Kralendijk in late afternoon and head south along the coast road. Your first landmark will be the *Trans World Radio* towers which belong to one of the world's most powerful radio stations. From here Christian missionaries are able to beam messages throughout the Western Hemisphere and into the Middle East and Africa.

Farther on look for the sparkling mountains of salt belonging to the

Antilles International Salt Company. These solar salt flats, harvested twice a year, are a major contributor to Bonaire's economy. They also serve as a feeding and breeding ground for flamingos.

You may be able to catch a glimpse of the flamingos feeding at one of the pans, though you won't be able to see or gain access to the Pekel Meer breeding sanctuary itself (because the birds need privacy and quiet). It's here that every one of the southern Caribbean's 10,000 flamingos was born. No one knows how long the birds have used this area for a breeding ground. But there is one recorded defection: In 1943 the birds were frightened away from this spot by the noise of war planes and ships. They didn't return until World War II ended and they didn't start breeding here again until 1950.

Near the salt company's white pan, in a rock-strewn, desolate area, are two groups of slave huts, a matter of minutes apart. Each hut is big enough to allow two men to sit and chat together, but not tall enough for standing room. In fact, they were designed for sleeping only during the salt-mining slaves five-days-a-week stays. The stone huts, topped with sugarcane reed roofs, have been restored to their original 1800s state, as have a nearby overseers house and a drying shed.

Go about a hundred yards past the second cluster of slave huts, through a clump of bushes, for the best view of the famed flamingo flight. (Yes, you also can view the flight through telescopes from the Flamingo Tower Observatory, but you won't need magnification to see the birds and it's just more fun to watch the departure from the ground.)

Lac Bay Trip.   For another south of Kralendijk trip, pack up a bathing suit and head for Lac Bay. Here you'll find mangrove swamps, piles of conch shells, and Cai—a little fishing village. There are picnic areas in the hills near Cai's white sand beaches and the bay water is wonderful for swimming and snorkling.

If you'd like to "go native" come to Cai on a Sunday. You'll see lots of Bonaire families being serenaded by Radio Caracas (courtesy of dozens of car radios set to the same station). There's an exceedingly informal restaurant here that serves cold beer, Tortuga sate (braised turtle meat), fresh fish, and fish soup. Enjoy. It's a friendly crowd.

For less cameraderie, visit Cai on a weekday—or discover your own southern coast beach. There are lots of private, pretty places to play.

Inside Information

Hotels

★★★★ FLAMINGO BEACH HOTEL
This was the former "prison camp" in World War II, once named the Hotel Zeebad, where the prisoners, like today's guests, saw no reason to leave. Some of the original quarters have been kept—expanded, spruced up—and now there are more than 100 rooms. A jacuzzi is the midnight focus of many an impromptu party. There are two restaurants: one slightly Caribbean dressed-up, the *Chibi Chibi* which is open to sea and night air for dinner; and a casual seaside restaurant where both the guests and the chibi chibi birds take breakfast and lunch. At oceanside, there's a slim beach, full snorkel and diver center, plus a hotel-based yacht for half-day, full-day or sunset sails. *Cost:* $65–$125 per double, EP, in-season. $28 additional per person, MAP. Off-season: $45–$75 per double, EP; MAP still $28 per person (import taxes; shipping, etc.)

★★ HOTEL BONAIRE AND CASINO
This is the problem child, and the largest hotel on the island, with 134 modern rooms, four suites, and the island's only casino. The "problem" is that the hotel is owned by the government, and contracted out to hotel management groups, who seem to change as fast as the spin of a roulette wheel. But it's where there's nightlife action, a small putting green for mini-golf and two excellent boutiques. In the hands of the right hotel management group, their problems may be soon solved, since all the facilities for a first-rate hotel are here. *Cost:* $69–$79 per double, EP; suites $140; $28 additional, per person MAP. Children under 12 free with parents.

★ CARIB INN
The brochure says "all rooms overlook our private swimming pool . . . two rooms which form an upstairs unit overlook the sea." And they do, all five rooms. But they're five neat-as-a-pin, Caribbean sunny rooms, run with the personalized attention of Bruce and Liz Bowker. While there's no restaurant attached, and only a small beach, Mrs. Morris runs a small grocery store across the way, and all rooms have a refrigerator and electric kettle. About 80% of the guests are divers as is Bruce Bowker, the owner, who also manages the dive center. *Cost:* $35–$45 per double or single, EP, in season.

★ HABITAT
This is a 51-bed hotel run by, for, and around divers. Captain Don Stewart is owner and major domo, and the hotel completely reflects his personality and the concept of a totally self-sufficient environment, drawing on, but never taking from, nature. The concept is in the very name of the hotel . . . habitat. Accommodations range from basic cottages to "monk's cells" for singles, and almost all clientele are divers in the beginning, intermediate, or advanced stage. Cap'n Don probably has the most thoroughly equipped diving center on the island, committed personnel, a photo lab for the development of underwater (and some above water) photos. Hammocks hang in the trees, there are quiet resting if rustic places, and the entire feeling is that of a natural "habitat." *Cost:* $60 for double cottages; $80 for two bedroom cottages; dormitory-style "monk's cell" quarters also available. Children under 12 not encouraged.

Restaurants

We've rated expensive in the $25 to $30 range; moderate about $15 to $18; inexpensive, $12 and under.

★★★★ BEEFEATER
(Tel. 8081/8193). Brothers Richard and David Dove brought over a bit of old England when they expatriated themselves. The decor is very upscale English pub in a true Bonairean townhouse with London scenes and ship renderings on the walls, crisp linen, fine crockery and glassware on the tables along with candles and small sprigs of flowers. The menu is perhaps the most refined in town and offers caviar with a cream cheese and onion starter, and homemade fish paté. The main course always suggests a fresh local fish, broiled à la meunière; creole or oven-baked beef bourguignon and a spicy beef kabob. *Expensive.*

★★★ BISTRO DES AMIS
(Tel. 8003). Meat dishes are particularly good here, since owners Lucille and Jan Von Tilberg also own the business that imports meat for the entire island. It's obvious that choice cuts appear on their menu which is French inspired. For starters order escargot with garlic bread or a gratineed onion soup; main

courses might be coquille St. Jacques in thick cream sauce; boeuf bourguignon; steak au poivre; langouste, boiled, broiled or à la thermador; or a
fresh local fish in a white wine sauce. Toulouse Lautrec motifs are inside and
out. The dining room itself is done in beige and chocolate brown decor,
lighting is dim, and there's a long, richly-appointed wooden bar framed by a
wine rack with some 100 bottles of the finest French wine. There's usually
dancing on weekends. *Expensive.*

★★★ CHIBI CHIBI TERRACE—CALABAS TERRACE

(Tel. 8285). Both restaurants, one for lunch and one for dinner, are at the
Flamingo Beach Hotel and both are open to sea and sky. The casual Calabas
Terrace is for lounging and looking at the snorkelers, windsurfers, and divers
offshore or the tiny and insistent chibi chibi birds trying to share your lunch or
a simple sandwich. Try the stuffed avocado with lobster or the diver's plate
that usually features tuna fish and fruit. But sample the thick soups first.
They're superb. Some nights dinners are served here informally—Indonesian
style on Tuesdays; Antillean dishes each Thursday PM; American-style barbecues on Saturday. Dinner in the Chibi Chibi Terrace is somewhat more
formal; dishes are based on Continental cuisine—filet mignon, fresh local
fish of the day, amandine chicken or the very special Keshiyena (chicken and
rice, baked and served in a carved out, gently cooked, gouda cheese). There's
some form of local entertainment each night along with the genuinely friendly
atmosphere throughout this hotel. *Expensive.*

★★★ DEN LAMAN

(Tel. 8955). The food is good and the atmosphere great! It's really not fair to
judge the temperature of dishes delivered, since diners keep jumping up to
watch the antics of the finny residents of ceiling to floor, wall to wall,
9,000-gallon aquariums that cover two of the walls. A moray eel that seems a
good five feet long snakes by, sand sharks glance at your dinner plate, less
imposing sea cucumbers, anemones, Hawaiian shrimp, crayfish, blowfish,
sea urchins, octopus, and huge turtles move at their own pace in this control-
led environment. The owner, Max Rijna, insists nothing on the menu occupied his tanks! For starters try fish cerviche, conch "Kralendyk," home-
smoked fish followed by a whole red snapper, broiled or fried conch or the
special, conch à la Lac (from that region), chateaubriand Strasbourg, filet
mignon à la champignon. The help-yourself salad bar is dished from a small
wooden boat. Weekends, there's dancing to a local band on an open terrace.
Expensive.

★★★ HABITAT

(Tel. 8290). The dinner mood is set in the casual inside bar with taped music
or a local combo that then merges onto the open deck for dining. And deck is
the proper term here, for all is nautical following owner Cap'n Don Stewart's
love of the sea. (He'll personally supervise fish dishes, but doesn't eat them.)
The seaside dining room has a thatched roof, red tablecloths, candles on each
table, and the surf pounding on rocks below. It's very atmospheric. Both
Continental and Mexican cuisine are featured, and the spicy tacos are some
of the best, followed by Don's own recipe for chili. There's also a good filet
mignon some nights and always a local fish. Cap'n Don even promises not to
frown as you eat it. *Moderate.*

★★★ MONA LISA

(Tel. 8308). The bar is the place to meet the in-town local set around sunset,
very casual with an adjoining dining room that's well attended by new
owners. Lunch can be as simple as grilled ham and cheese sandwiches, a
salad nicoise, mushrooms on toast or the ever-changing Mona Lisa special.
Dinner always has a "diver's menu" at $10 providing a hearty soup and fish

dish. Entrées are tasty shrimp in garlic, king crab legs, broiled lobster tail, frogs legs, tournedos with sauce bernaise, imported sirloin, wiener schnitzel or pork chops, Bonairean style. Homemade pastries are their pride along with strong Dutch coffee. *Moderate.*

★★★ ZEEZICHT

(Tel. 8434). While waits can be long between courses, no one seems to mind at this seaside restaurant whose name means almost that—sea vista in Papiamento. There are two floors in this restaurant and an open terrace which is also used for lunch or dinner. A rather different menu features Chinese, local, and Dutch dishes, with some Italian specialties! Fried fish creole, goat curry, conch cooked at least three different ways (a Creole prize). Wor Hip Har; sweet and sour shrimp or fish; conch chop suey (!) are the Chinese entrées. From Europe, red snapper fried in butter with mushrooms and capers; a king crab à la française; fondu homard à la thermador; Lobster à la Zeezicht; or the Zeezicht special of conch, fish, lobster, oyster sauce with an unusual Rijsttaffl. Lunch is *moderate;* dinner *expensive.*

★★ HOTEL BONAIRE AND CASINO

(Tel. 8448). Since this is Bonaire's largest hotel, complete with casino, there's a lot of PM action here. The Neptune dining room hosts dinner most nights from a continental menu and on Tuesday night there's a Bonairean menu and folkloric show. On Thursday evening it's Indonesian night. Saturday is a traditional barbecue with all the sauces and spices, and Sunday there is an eye-opening champagne brunch. Visit the casino after you've paid your dinner check! *Expensive.*

BORINQUE SNACK

As the name implies, a snack shop that's simple, plain, and honest. Drop in for lunch or in the evening. Drippy hamburgers with big, fat homemade french fries or the local curried goat. This place runs to its own beat with weird and changeable hours. *Inexpensive.*

Nightlife

The flashy, flashing lights on the corner of Breedestraat and Kerkweg are flashing no more. The E WoWo Disco (Eye, in Papiamento) has gone "up-town." Not geographically, but in tone. The new owner, Tom Spee, has completely redone the interior of E WoWo nightclub with oatmeal sectional sink-in sofas and natural wood tables, with wall murals done by Bert Keller. Drinks and light snacks are served until the early morning, and the taped music is European and mellow in note and mood. A reggae or true disco tape slips in occasionally.

The spin of the roulette wheel, the slap of blackjack cards or the tinkle of quarters in the one-arm bandits are heard nightly at the Hotel Bonaire's casino, the only one on the island.

The two major hotels—The Flamingo Beach and the Hotel Bonaire—both have shows or entertainment of some sort almost every night in season. At the Flamingo Beach Hotel, there's only one rule, "nothing should be plugged in" . . . meaning no electrified, amplified-anything. Instead, they feature island-renowned Cai-Cai and his fellow guitarists. Other nights there's a group that does folkloric dances and a trio of vocalists has been popular here. Each night features some form of low-key, unique entertainment.

For concerts, call the Cultural Center (Tel. 8558).

Besides the nightly games of chance at the Hotel Bonaire and Casino, they also have live entertainment: one night it might be the folkloric dancers who spin out bits of island legend and lore and other nights it might be some "imported" talent from Aruba, Curaçao or South America.

The Habitat hotel concentrates on individual conversations and dancing in its darkened bar is the nightly habit of the diving set, no matter where they're staying. If you think fishermen have tales "of the ones who got away," wait till you eavesdrop on the divers' tales of, "you'll never believe what we saw today!"

At all the fully-equipped dive centers on the island—and for certified divers only—the most spectacular nighttime activity is a "night dive," never alone and always with underwater lanterns to view the activity below. Those fish tales you can believe!

Shopping

The boutique at the Hotel Bonaire is devoted to clothing that has some designer names mixed in among interesting Indian cottons, casual jeans, T-shirts, and cool tops. Unexpectedly, you'll come on a dress by Gloria Vanderbilt or Diane Von Furstenberg, a Halston or Donald Brooks number or a Rudi Gernreich design; and prices for these names are quite reasonable. There are also men's shirts, swimsuits, and some Bonaire-weight slacks. Mixed among all are a sampling of "sparkle-plenty" evening dresses and jump suits that you may pass up. Additionally there's a small selection of needle-point that's fun to do on the beach.

The Ki Bo Ke Pakus Boutique at the Flamingo Beach Hotel (meaning— What Do You Want Boutique) tries to give you what you want in caftans, many in handscreened fabrics; pareus to tie any one of 50-some ways (a printed sheet shows you how); tops for both men and women; scarves; a good and ever-changing selection of T-shirts that proclaim in print and picture the glories of Bonaire; and always, some really good Dutch chocolate.

A small branch of Spritzer and Fuhrmann is here, unquestionably the most Caribbean-known name for jewelry, crystal and china. But this is a branch of its big sisters in Curaçao, Aruba and St. Martin, and the selection isn't as big as there. What they do have is of the highest quality—14", 18-karat gold chains for $152; Swiss watches with their gold-clad guarantee; French perfumes; and an occasional find such as silver plated picture frames that display three to six favorite shots at $26 or $46.

Littman Jewelers is one of our favorites. The owners, Steven and his wife Esther, are both gemologists and sometimes do their own designs. They import emeralds from Colombia; sapphires from Sri Lanka and Thailand; and ivory from the Far East. This is truly a family business, since the patriarch, Marshall Littman, has the original shop in Philadelphia (the Bonaire branch opened in 1981). Here a 16" gold chain of 18-karat gold might be $280; a 24" chain about $495; a ruby and diamond ring in 18-karat gold a mere $725. But it's truly unusual pieces you'll remember (if not buy)—such as the one-of-a-kind Indian head opal pin for $1,600 made from an Australian boulder opal. There are also Rolex, Seiko, and Ebel watches at 30% to 35% under stateside prices or an Élysée pen set for $50.

Another daytime haunt is Natasja and Alexander (named for the owners', the Gerharts, children), in a cul-de-sac off the main street, whose last find were some 47 different designs of really unusual high quality beach towels. (We know they're hard to pack.) They also have handcrafted items from Peru—wooden dishes, objets d'art, basketware along with skimpy, shapely designed bathing suits for men and women; and combs for the hair that you'll actually use.

Things Bonaire has reasonable items at reasonable prices. Manager Jean Meiss is also an artist and paints some of the unglazed pottery pieces and encourages other local artists. She also has dresses for under $25; pareus for about $15; unisex shirts at $10; tote bags, and of course, entrants in the unofficial Bonaire T-shirt design contest.

Ayllu, an Inca word meaning "cooperative" divides both its display of crafts and the proceeds between the artist and the tiny shop. The artist gets the higher percentage of whatever is sold. Items are a mixture of Latin American samplings—molas from Panama; paintings from Ecuador; straw work from Surinam; woven hangings from Peru; and locally-made crafts.

A must stop is the Fundashon Arte Industria Bonariano, backed by the United Nations, the Netherlands Antilles Government and the unions. Their efforts provide craft training and sales in a showroom off J. A. Abraham Blvd. in Kralendijk. At very low prices, you'll find jewelry made from black coral with sterling silver inlay; leather purses and wallets; stained-glass pieces; handscreened fabrics.

Some of the techniques are truly interesting to watch. The stained glass, made mostly by young people who have been provided with sheets of colored glass, is then designed and cut with touches of silver added. These are then made into lamps, jewelry, boxes, and candleholders. The woodworking shop produces picture frames, inlaid boxes, and ashtrays. The only other items shown are from the other five Netherlands Antilles islands that have similar U.N.-sponsored programs.

There are no art galleries as such, but there's certainly an "underworld" of artists when you can track them down. There's Bert Keller (of garbage-can fame) who also does serious and impressive murals (at the Flamingo Beach Hotel and E WoWo). Papa Melaan works in oils and acrylics. Adi Figeroa shows her acrylic paintings on driftwood and paper. Nina Gauche from the United States does washes in pastels and vibrant hues. Allie Hollywood does murals on buildings as has Roy Wanga (his can be seen at the Fitness, Body Building and Boxing Center in Bonaire).

Also you can contact the Central Cultural Council for Bonaire CCCB. There just may be that art show they've been promising to hold when you're there. At some point in the mid-1980s a cultural museum is planned at Ft. Oranje. Keep asking!

Sports

Daylife and even some sports nightlife is lived in, around, and on the sea. The sea is why most visitors come to Bonaire (the island itself is a coral reef, surrounded by more coral reefs). Some come to swim. Others to snorkel. Many, many more come to scuba dive. The beaches are mostly small slices of private sand cut from the ocean's grasp. The beaches along the southern coast (where the hotels aren't) are some of the best and most private, and this is the place to make a day trip with a picnic basket packed by your hotel.

For snorkeling, reefs are close to shore, and visibility ranges from 70 to 140 feet. There are so many dive locations they're impossible to number, but an educated guess by the well-known professional divers approaches 100 sites in waters they know well.

Dee Scarr is one former Miamian who provides an excellent dive adventure. Her "Touch the Sea" program personally "introduces" you to Dee's finny friends at $25 a dive. (Tel. 8288). Cap'n Don Stewart, a sailor with a sense of storytelling, runs a first-rate dive program at his Habitat hotel where he even has a lab set up for the processing of underwater photos, equipment rental, and a young, dedicated diving staff. Bruce Bowker at the Carib Inn does a similar program on a smaller scale, but with his own dive secrets and lots of youth and enthusiasm.

Both the big hotels house separate underwater programs—Peter Hughes runs "Dive Bonaire" (Tel. 8285) at the Flamingo Beach Hotel with scuba programs that range from the basic resort course to a full certification program, and of course, dives for those already certified by day and by night. The Hotel Bonaire and Casino (Tel. 8448) features a "learn to dive vacation" from their Bonaire Scuba Center, and while all the island programs are independent of each other, each has a first-rate reputation among the diving set.

The hotels also offer windsurfing (about $10 per hourly rental, or a five day hourly "how to" program for $60); sun or sail fish sailing ($10 an hour, $15 with instruction); waterskiing ($25 for a half-hour skim over the surf and $30 for a beginner's course); and daylong fishing trips. Each hotel also has its own yacht for half-day, full-day, sunset, and moonlight sails. (Cost varies on length of trip, but averages about $20; drinks are "on the house.")

There's a special shuttle service to the deserted island offshore of Klein Bonaire for $10, where you're shuttled and forgotten (until pick-up time) for a day of shelling, sunning, and snorkeling. A "guided" snorkel trip can be arranged, but few guests opt for extra company.

For true, really true Caribbean sailors, the annual October sailing regatta is one where "anything goes." Boats range from small to medium in size, and multi-hulls or mono-hulls are welcome. In fact, if it floats, it qualifies.

Bird-watching, particularly for the Bonarian-born breed of flamingo (there are some 8,000 in Bonaire alone) is an island tradition. There's even some 5,000 acres set aside for a flamingo reserve shared with other feathery flocks. One of the best flamingo-watching spots is at Goto Meer on the northwest coast. The birds appear literally to "walk on water" for takeoff, soaring overhead with wing spans that are up to eight feet across. They're a brilliant pink, due to a natural diet of brine shrimp, and to watch them take flight is a view of the world that was when the world began, as the birds soar amid surrounding scruff and cactus that stand silent sentinels.

If you look fast, you may see signs of the even faster Lora bird—a large, stubby, green and yellow parrot with a wing spread about 18 inches. These birds always travel in pairs, and are usually spotted in the 13,500 acre Washington-Slagbaai National Park where there are bird observation posts throughout. But these birds aren't so fast that there doesn't exist the possibility of their extinction, and only about 2,000 remain in the wild. A few others just "happen" to have their wings on the mend in homes in Bonaire.

Out of the capital, on the main road to the slave huts, there's a Flamingo Tower Observatory that is a simple raised wood platform. It's supposed to be manned weekends from 4 to 6 P.M. and has a magnifying coin-operated telescope. But won't your own eyes, aided by binoculars, do just as well from the road?

One of the best beaches for snorkeling or scuba is Pink Beach, about 20 minutes from town. Here, hundreds of bone fish tempt the true fisherman who knows the spirit of these fish. Ask your hotel personnel; they'll probably steer you to a boat and driver for fishing the easier-to-tackle mackerel, king tuna, wahoo, barracuda, and swordfish since fishing bone fish is difficult to arrange. (Cost runs about $300 for an all-day fishing charter, with fishing gear, tackle, bait, drinks, and lunch guaranteed. The only thing not guaranteed is the fish!)

There are two tennis courts at the Hotel Bonaire and Casino, and several more in town. The hotel also has a putting green for "let's pretend" golf. Serious golfers will choose another island.

Both the Flamingo Beach Hotel and the Hotel Bonaire and Casino have the newest "in" sport—that is, if you can do it—called windsurfing. With fairly strong offshore winds, this isn't the easiest place to learn. The Flamingo Beach has also recently added bicycles to their sports possibilities, and you can cycle in late afternoon for bird or people-watching.

Dominican Republic

HARD FACTS

Planning Ahead

The Dominican Republic is a 24-hour-a-day country. While the sun shines, there are sports aplenty—and a lot of interesting sightseeing possibilities. Activity ceases around twilight—only to pick up again around 9:00 (dinner time) and then continue through the night—at nightclubs, discos and casinos.

Holidays and Special Events

New Year's Day (January 1), Our Lady of La Altagracia (January 21), Duarte's Birthday, honoring the Dominican Republic's founding father (January 26), National Independence Day (February 27), Good Friday, Easter, Labor Day (May 1), Corpus Christi (celebrated 60 days after Easter), Restoration Day (August 16), Our Lady of Las Mercedes (September 24), Christmas Day (December 25).

Sources of Information

For questions that need answers before your departure for the Dominican Republic, contact in the United States either the *Dominican Tourist Information Center*, 485 Madison Avenue, New York, NY 10022, or the *Dominican Republic Tourist Office*, 100 N. Biscayne Blvd., Miami, FL 33132. Once you arrive in the Dominican Republic, the *Dominican Tourst Information Center*, Arzobispo Merino 156, in *Santo Domingo* provides help and advice.

Packing

In the resort areas the accent is firmly on informality. However, if you are planning evenings on the town, when trips to the theater or fine restaurants are contemplated, gentlemen should pack lightweight suits, sports jackets and ties. Women should bring summer dresses and wraps to ward off the effects of air conditioning and perhaps long skirts for special occasions. During the day, casual wear—including slacks, jeans and T-shirts—is appropriate. (Shorts are generally less accepted and not acceptable at all if you wish to enter the cathedral.) If you plan to do any horseback riding, you may want to bring along some low-heeled boots. Do pack a lightweight sweater for late-night strolls, for temperatures occasionally dip slightly below 70°F. in the evening.

Film is available but at prices higher than those in the States. It's best to come prepared. You can buy *drugs* with a prescription, but if at all possible, you should fill prescriptions before you leave for vacation.

Getting There

Airline Services: Daily air service is available from New York, Miami, Dallas, San Juan and Port-au-Prince (Haiti). Several charters and specially-scheduled flights depart from points throughout the United States and Canada. American and Dominicana fly from New York to Santo Domingo; Dominicana and Capitol fly between New York and Puerto Plata. From Miami, Dominicana, Eastern, and American fly to Santo Domingo; Air Florida goes to Santo Domingo and Puerto Plata. American flies to Santo Domingo from Dallas via Miami. Eastern, Dominicana, PrinAir fly from San Juan to Santo Domingo; Dominicana and Air Florida make a Port-au-Prince (Haiti) to Santo Domingo hop.

Cruise ships make regularly-scheduled calls on the small natural harbor of Puerto Plata on the north coast.

Formalities on Arrival

Customs

Informal. On arriving you'll be issued a tourist card ($5.00) after presenting proper identification—proof of birth (a passport, voter's registration card or birth certificate). Before leaving you'll be charged a 10 peso departure tax. (Notice: Drug laws are strictly enforced.)

Money

The official currency is the Dominican peso. While the peso is officially equal to one U.S. dollar, the value of the peso is considerably lower (sometimes one-third lower) on what is known as the "parallel market." A number of Dominican commercial banks exchange dollars for pesos legally at the parallel rate. Street moneychangers also offer better than official rates, but be prepared to bargain. Also, plan carefully. It is difficult to convert pesos to dollars and the peso has no value outside the country. Tip: Travelers can save money by paying restaurant and hotel bills with cash or travelers checks rather than credit cards since credit card transactions are billed at the official one dollar to one peso rate.

Getting into Town

Rental cars are available at Las Americas Airport in Santo Domingo and at La Romana. (Gas stations are open from 6:00 to 6:00.) Taxis are available in all major cities and can be hired for day trips. Also, Santo Domingo has a metropolitan bus system.

Avis, Hertz, National and Budget have airport offices

Settling Down

Chinese, Italian, German, French, Continental and Dominican fare can be obtained; some restaurants have informal atmospheres, others are elegant. The base for many of the finest dishes is seafood, fresh from surrounding waters.

Learning to Cope

Business Hours. Shops generally open at 8:30 AM, close at noon and reopen from 3:00 until 6:30 or 7:00 PM.

Electricity. Conventional 110-volt, 60-cycle alternating current permits the use of standard American appliances.

Language. The official language of the Dominican Republic is Spanish; however, most who regularly come in contact with tourists speak some English.

THE DOMINICAN REPUBLIC TODAY

Occupying roughly two-thirds of the island of Hispaniola—an island it shares with Haiti—the Dominican Republic is a collection of disparate elements: towering mountain chains, supporting grassy ridges, forestlands, wide, fertile sugarcane-planted plains, and, in the north, long stretches of unspoiled beaches and, in the south, rocky shores and crashing surf. Christopher Colombus asked to be buried in this, his favorite and "most beautiful" land in the new world, and so he probably was—"probably," because Seville, Spain, also claims possession of his mortal remains.

"True" independence is usually dated to 1844

Nickel, gold, silver and amber are mined in the mountains. Sugarcane is the country's number one industry, thanks to the Gulf and Western conglomerate. You'll see herds of cattle and horses; every house seems to have at least one pig—and sheep graze on hilly slopes. Tourism today ranks third as a source of income for the island, but the number of incoming travelers climbs steadily each year. With more and more resort facilities being built, the Dominican Republic is well on its way to becoming discovered anew.

Santo Domingo, the capital, has traditionally been the main draw for travelers because of its Colonial City, good restaurants, and lively nightlife. Farther out on the eastern coast are Gulf and Western's ultraelegant Casa de Campo resort and the newly-created Altos de Chavon. Gulf and Western has made a major contribution to this country partly because of its expansive sugar industry and partly because of a genuine commitment.

The northern coast, boasting the island's best beaches, is only now beginning to offer resort facilities. But beaches such as Playa Grande and those close to Sosua, a town settled by Jewish refugees who fled from Europe in the 1940s, are still pristine. The rugged peninsula of Samana, where runaway slaves from the United States settled in the 1800s, is a haven for sports fishermen and hunters. Santiago, in the interior of the island, surrounded by luxuriant farmland, is the center for the tobacco and rum industries.

The Dominican Republic may one day lose its freshness, but for now it warmly offers the traveler its rich heritage and infinite variety.

TOURING

Santo Domingo

Ask your taxi driver to take you to *Columbus Park* (Parque Colon). Once here amble your way through the black marketeers, the free-lance amber merchants and the little boys selling peanuts as well as plaster ashtrays that they solemnly swear are solid mahogany. Before you stands the imposing bronze statue of Christopher Columbus, set in the center of a brick courtyard surrounded by green, iron benches. Columbus's arm points north to the point where he first landed.

To the south is the *Cathedral of Santa Maria la Menor,* the new world's oldest cathedral (open 3:30 to 5:30; proper dress is required; guides speak English, Spanish, Italian; no fee; tips accepted). A splendid coral-lime, Roman-style structure, it was built between 1514 and 1540. Though time and wars have taken their toll, its 14 palm-forest pillars, intricate four-way domes, its series of graceful arches (displaying the motif of a spear in tribute to Queen

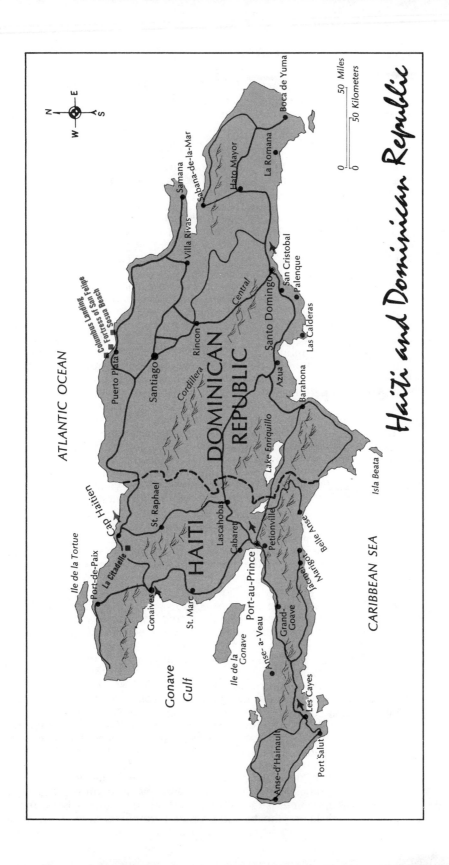

ATLANTIC OCEAN

Ile de la Tortue

Port-de-Paix

La Citadelle

Cap Haitien

St. Raphael

HAITI

Lascahoba

Cabaret

Petionville

Port-au-Prince

Grand-Goave

Anse-a-Veau

Ile de la Gonave

Gonave Gulf

Gonaïves

St. Marc

Les Cayes

Port Salut

Anse-d'Hainault

Jacmel

Belle Anse

Marigot

CARIBBEAN SEA

Isla Beata

Lake Enriquillo

Barahona

Azua

Las Calderas

Palenque

San Cristobal

Santo Domingo

Cordillera Central

Rincon

Santiago

Puerto Plata

Columbus Landing
Fortress of San Felipe
Sosua Beach

Villa Rivas

Samana

Sabana-de-la-Mar

Hato Mayor

La Romana

Boca de Yuma

DOMINICAN REPUBLIC

N
W   E
S

50 Miles
50 Kilometers
0
0

Haiti and Dominican Republic

Isabella) and the symmetry of its 14 chapels (seven to the south, seven to the north) embody grandeur. And there are fascinating details that you'll need a guide's help to find: for example, the three crosses on one of the arches that provided sanctuary to any prisoner who could reach and touch the spot. One of the most elaborate of the chapels is the "Sixteena," with its Dominican silver and mahogany detail work and its 14 paintings, 12 depicting the apostles, two the evangelists. Sadly, many of the cathedral's silver and gold embellishments are now gone, stripped and carried away by various occupiers of the city.

Murillo's madonna is the cathedral's best painting

The most famous of the looters was Sir Francis Drake who, for 24 days in 1586, commandeered one of the chapels as his headquarters, slung and secured himself in a hammock, surrounded himself with appropriated gold and silver and issued orders to terrorize and eventually burn the city. One night out of drunkenness or pique, he chopped off the hands and the nose of a statue of a bishop. The statue remains as he left it, a silent rebuke to a discourteous guest. A pulpit, also destroyed by Sir Francis Drake, is, however, being restored. (Sir Francis left untouched the bishop's seat, the oldest piece of mahogany in the new world.)

At the west entrance to the cathedral an eternal flame burns in a Byzantine lamp of silver and semiprecious stones near the elaborate tomb of Christopher Columbus. Formed of Italian marble, onyx, bronze and gold, it is topped by a statue symbolizing liberty and guarded by lions representing Spain. On October 12, the date Columbus reached the new world, three caskets—bronze, crystal and lead, nestled one inside another—are ceremoniously and symbolically unlocked by the bishop. (Is Columbus *really* buried here? In his diary, he expressed the wish to be buried in this "land he loved best," and on the cathedral's monument is the testament of Charles I of Spain and Maria de Toledo that they complied with his request. Yet Seville, Spain, also claims to have his bones, and each city has an array of experts who attest to the veracity of its claim. It is doubtful that any claim will ever be substantiated to such an extent that one city will yield.)

Pope Jean Paul II visited here in 1979

Beneath the cathedral are catacombs and tunnels leading from the palace to the cathedral to the fortress. Trujillo used to walk through here to get to mass but ordered the area sealed when it was discovered that revolutionaries were also moving about down here. (Trujillo was assassinated in 1961.)

On the corner is *The Tostado House,* built in the 16th century and boasting the only geminated window in America. Restored in 1970, it now houses the Museum of the Dominican Family (or more precisely, it holds the accoutrements of a wealthy, Victorian-era Dominican family).

Head down Padre Billini Street toward the river and you'll spot the *Ozama Fortress* and the massive *Tower of Homage.* Now they form the focal point of a gentle park, but once the tower was the watchpoint from which Spanish guards kept a vigilant eye on the river entrance. In later years they gained infamy as a repository for political opponents of Trujillo.

You're now on the first street of the new world (1502), *Calle de las Damas,* where the ladies of the court of the viceroy, Diego Columbus, were housed. (At one time it was the custom for a woman to toss an orange from her balcony to an admirer below as a way of saying "I like you.")

On this street is the colonial, 16th-century *Bastidas House,* once the home of Rodrigo de Bastidas, a mayor of Santo Domingo. It is now a museum holding workshops and exhibits of treasure retrieved from sunken ships. Also here is the house of Knight Commander Nicolar de Ovando, first governor of Santo Domingo. The house has undergone careful restoration to its 16th-century beginnings. Now it is a hotel owned by the Dominican government.

Across the street is the *National Pantheon,* a former Jesuit monastery built in 1714, later a theater, now a burial ground for fallen national heroes and martyrs. Trujillo had wanted to be buried here, but presumably the government felt he fit neither category and so buried him elsewhere. Some of the tombs hold famous people, but many are empty. The enormous chandelier was a gift from Spain's Francisco Franco.

Just up the street is *Our Lady of Remedies Church,* which conducted mass before the cathedral was built; a bit farther on is the *Museum of Cases Reales* (Royal Houses), a restoration of the former headquarters of the colonial government. It contains a map from the Columbus era, furniture of the 17th century, implements, artifacts and a coin room. On the other side of the street is an ancient sun clock.

Farther on is Diego Columbus's palace, the *Alcazar* (open 9:00–12:00, 2:30–5:30; admission 75¢). When you enter, you'll be greeted by fierce gargoyle faces, a protection for the house against evil spirits. On the ceiling are recreations of 17th-century-style animal faces. Many of the furnishings are skillful recreations; some are gifts from Spain; others are original. Some of the treasures you'll come on include Columbus's plates bearing the inscription "To Castile and Leon, Columbus gave a new world," the *Four Whole Parts of the Chronicle of Spain* (dated 1604) and three valuable tapestries— one from the 17th century, which was donated by the Duke of Veragua, took more than 25 years to finish. Above its battle representation is woven the Columbus coat of arms. In the entrance room is a replica of the *Santa Maria* that was donated by Trujillo. In the music room is an illuminated manuscript of Gregorian chants (dated 1597). There's also a large 15th-century carving with gold overleaf, which was created from one piece of wood. It depicts the death of Mary. After it was shattered into 41 pieces by the revolutionaries of 1965, it took ten years to restore.

In the kitchen, with its waist-high copper water jugs and pottery displays (some original), sun streams across a Roman stone window seat. If you lean on the ledge for a moment and peer down at the street carts and the Ozama River, you may find yourself speculating on what Columbus saw from this vantage point some 400 years ago. The centerpiece of the kitchen is the tiled fireplace and the huge copper pot in which all the household's food was prepared. Once this pot was kept bubbling at all times. Because of its nonstop use, it served as the unwitting culprit in a number of poisoning deaths. Don Diego Columbus wisely had food sent first to the adjacent servants' dining room for tasting. If the servants survived, he indulged.

A stone ship's stairway, which was traversed by such adventurers as the conquistadors Ponce de Leon, Francisco Pizarro and Hernando Cortez, leads to the second floor. First stop: the bedroom of Dona Maria, Diego's wife. Her room (and others you'll see) has a prayer stand and a small closet for two saints. The closet was always kept locked so that no one could learn the identity of another's patron saint.

The view from the balconied anteroom, which overlooks shacks across the river, presents a sharp contrast to the substance of the Alcazar. This chamber leads to Diego's regal bedroom. The massive headboard bears the Columbus coat of arms, and over the bed is his 16th-century ivory crucifix. Bars cover the windows, presumably for protection. You'll also see a wooden secretary inlaid with ivory and fitted with secret drawers in which state documents were kept.

Nearby there is a sitting room that overlooks Calle de las Damas, the Ozama River and, just below, the gate to the palace. Today you may see a powerboat whiz by on the river or cranes unloading cargo, but centuries ago it was here, on the window seat, that Dona Maria sat patiently waiting for Diego to return from his voyages. Sometimes, one imagines, she whispered prayers for his safe return; other times she must have been filled with loneliness and despair. Her last vigil ended in grief. Diego died aboard a ship bound for Spain; it took years before news of his death reached her.

After you leave the Alcazar, head to the *Atarazana,* the new world's first

[handwritten margin notes: Diego was Christopher's son; Built in 1509, The Alcazar lay in ruins from 1850 to 1957, when Trujillo began its restoration; Maria was the niece of King Ferdinand]

trading center and arsenal as well as a training ground for troops. Its cluster of Spanish patios and eight colonial buildings, dating from the early 1500s, now houses a network of shops, art galleries and restaurants.

Southward, on the corner of Emiliano Tejera, is *Casa del Cordon* with a replica of the belt of the order of St. Francis carved over its door. Built in 1503, it is remarkable for being the new world's first stone house and for having served as the temporary residence of Don Diego Columbus and his wife while the Alcazar was being built. Like so many of the Colonial City structures, it has been faithfully restored. Today it is a bank that has carefully adapted its 20th-century functions to the desire to preserve the integrity of its 16th-century headquarters. Guides will show you around the offices and board-room.

Farther west are the ruins of *St. Francis,* a church and a monastery built in 1544. Two blocks south of here (on Hostos Street) stands another ruin: that of the 1508 *St. Nicholás de Bari Hospital,* the first hospital of the new world.

At the westernmost point of the Colonial City is *El Conde Gate,* the main entrance to this historic sector of the capital. Guarded at all times, it is the place where the independence of the Dominican Republic was declared in 1844 and the site of an eternal flame that burns near a mausoleum where the remains of the country's three founding fathers (Duarte, Sanchez and Mella) are entombed. Today you'll most likely see children playing a game of stickball near the gate while the sun shines golden and timeless on this symbolic linking of the old and the new.

Elsewhere in Santo Domingo is the *Cultural Plaza* (at Maximo Gomez Avenue, corner of Cesar Nicolas Penson Street), a cluster of good-looking, modern buildings that stand on the site of the Trujillo mansion and house the excellent pre-Columbian displays of the *Museum of the Dominican Man,* the *National Library,* the *Museum of Natural History* and the *Gallery of Modern Art.* Also on the grounds is the *National Theater,* the fourth largest national theater in the world, at which Dominican artists and guests such as the New York Philharmonic regularly perform. (Tickets for most concerts are very reasonable.)

The Presidential Palace (on Moises Garcia Street) is worth a glance while riding by, but it's only open to visitors with a special permit that's difficult to obtain.

A variety of parks is scattered about town. In the *Eugenio Maria de Hostos Park* vendors transform balloons into all kinds of shapes, including rabbits, dogs, space helmets . . . name an object, and they'll probably be able to come up with something close. Day and night it's a popular (and safe) place to stroll. Sometimes folkloric dancers perform. On special holidays festivals are held here.

There are also beautifully-landscaped parks that meander east along the waterfront from the Hotel Santo Domingo to the Caribbean Sea. The *Zoologi-co Nacional Park* offers a children's zoo as well as one of the largest aviaries in the world, a cool lake for aquatic birds and an African plain where animals roam free. Nearby is *Dr. Rafael Moscoso National Botanical Gardens* (Jardin Botanico Nacional) covering almost two million square meters and featuring 200 varieties of palms, a Japanese garden and an enormous floral clock. Horse-drawn carriages are provided for touring the grounds.

Just outside town, off Las Americas Highway on the way to the airport, is the *Parque Los Tres Ojos de Agua* (Park of Three Eyes of Water), so named because of three sunken, circular pools set at different levels in a stalactite-and stalagmite-filled cave 50 feet underground.

Elsewhere on the Island

A day trip out to *La Romana* is well worthwhile both to get a feel for the sugarcane-filled countryside and to stop at the magnificent Casa de Campo complex and nearby *Altos de Chavon,* a recreation of a 16th-century village where artists live and work.

The North Coast, once called the *Amber Coast* (because of the amber deposits in the nearby hills), is best known for the beauty of its wide, sweeping beaches, its protected palm-fringed coves and its backdrop of rich, lush vegetation. Once undeveloped, this area is now sprouting an array of resort complexes and condominiums.

In Puerto Plata a cable-car trip to the top of *Isabel de Torres* peak offers a spectacular view of hill and dale and the ocean beyond. Not so worthwhile is a trip to the old (1540) but souvenir-selling *Fort of San Felipe* surrounding the peak.

As yet, the resorts are still not really ready

Inside Information

Hotels

Santo Domingo

★★★★ ALTOS DE CHAVON

This is as "authentic" a 16th-century village, Spanish style, as Roberto Coppa and the Bludhorn family could make it. Coppa is a set designer who worked in conjunction with Fellini, and the Bludhorn family have contributed some of their Gulf and Western fortune to the creation of this village that was opened in January 1980.

A lot is going on behind the peaceful stucco and limestone facades shimmering in the Dominican sun. There's a small inn, La Posada, for guests who don't care for the fancier sprawl of Casa de Campo (a step-sister of the Gulf & Western patriarchy). There are also some 35 efficency apartments (more are planned), built "casita" (or country house) style. These apartments are usually taken by the handful of artists in residence who remain here for three months at a time. Others are occupied by some of the 100 students in a new arts education program begun just last year in conjunction with the Parsons School of Design in New York.

★★★★ LA POSADA

Only 10 rooms which opened in 1981, but many prefer their special sense of privacy, perched high on a cliff over the Chavon River amid greenery and nature's gifts. You can be as alone or together as you wish with other residents, most of them students in the new arts program or resident artists on a three-month stay. Each room in the two story posada has a small refrigerator for drinks and snacks and there are restaurants on the property. Decor is sophisticated sleek to stark and features Italian prints and Caribbean-colored fabrics. Then there's that knock-out view of the river flowing past your wooden shutters. *Cost:* $125 per double, EP.

★★★★ SHERATON HOTEL AND CASINO

Spacious, attractive and lively, this hotel has 260 air-conditioned, balconied rooms with a sea view, a collection of interesting Dominican paintings, and a very helpful well-trained staff. For wanderers, it's within strolling distance of the Colonial City; for guests who don't like to wander, there's tennis, a pool, a health club and shops. (The hotel also has a collection of special amenities, like babysitters, tour and translation services, and rooms designed for the

The most active hotel in the country

handicapped.) The elegant Antoine is a good dining spot; El Yarey is a favorite piano bar—for listening and quiet dancing; the Omni disco, one of the best on the island, starts to jump around midnight; there is also a casino; and for those who don't want to call it a night, there's La Canasta, which offers Dominican food 24 hours a day. *Cost:* $95 per double EP, in season.

★★★ HOTEL SANTO DOMINGO
There's a fresh, breezy feel in the Hotel Santo Domingo's Oscar de la Renta-designed lobby and patios, where an artful melange of light-wood latticework, tiles, plants, mirrors, Dominican marble and restored Dominican antiques produces a cosmopolitan, inviting ambience. Most of the 220 large, air-conditioned rooms face either the landscaped grounds or look out over the craggy Caribbean coastline. (Another more modest, less expensive 165 rooms are located across the street.) There are two large pools, three tennis courts (one lighted for night play), a sauna, and shops in an inner courtyard. Cocktails are offered in the comfortable La Cabuya Bar; dining is either an informal affair in the muraled El Vivero restaurant or quite formal in the opulently-appointed El Alcazar, one of the island's best restaurants. Nightlife is offered by the chic Neon 2002 discotheque, and sophisticated nightclub entertainment can be found at Las Palmas (Thursday, Friday and Saturday). Those staying here have guest privileges at Gulf and Western's other Dominican resort—Casa de Campo. *Cost:* $55–$110 per double EP, in season.

★★ HOSTAL NICOLAS DE OVANDO
Located in the colonial section on Calle de las Damas, the oldest street in the new world, the 60-room Hostal Nicolas de Ovando can trace its origins to the 16th century when it consisted of two adjoining houses, one the residence of Knight Commander Ovando, the governor of Hispaniola from 1502 to 1509, the other the fortified home of conquistador Francisco Davila. Before restoring the buildings, much research was done. Then centuries of hodge-podge architectural additions were stripped away. What emerged was a handsome, colonial manor house. Much of the interior, including the enchanting inner courtyard and the graceful gallery, private chapel and vestibule, reflects efforts to preserve the hotel's heritage. Here and there are antique tapestries; rooms are furnished with reproductions of Spanish antiques and are being spruced up a room at a time. The bar and the fine restaurant are both furnished in styles consistent with the building's 16th-century origins. This is not a hotel for sports enthusiasts, but there is a pool on the grounds and a lot of possibilities for exploration afforded by the surrounding historic neighborhood. *Cost:* $50, double EP, in season.

a bit of Old Spain (the King and Queen stayed here) but the elegance is tarnished

La Romana

★★★★★ CASA DE CAMPO
This may well be the perfect resort. It's secluded but has its own private jet strip for easy international accessibility. It's elegant in a quietly understated way. The grounds are physically beautiful, all 7,000 acres of them. Its accommodations and cuisine are first class, and it offers an exhaustive array of excellent sports facilities.

Owned by Gulf and Western, Casa de Campo is nestled on the southeastern coast of the Dominican Republic near the sugar town of La Romana. It was designed by Dominican-born Oscar de la Renta (who has a house on the grounds) in rambling thatched-roof style, using indigenous woods, Dominican tiles, warm fabrics and impeccable taste. The 450 airy rooms, casitas and villas are grouped around beautifully-landscaped golf courses and tennis courts or poised on the Caribbean shore. There are a handful of restaurants— Tropicana, where most dining is open-air overlooking the Caribbean; Les

manager anthony Bayarri runs this special place with a special hand

Canaris, a country-style French restaurant in a plantation-house setting; El Lago, off the 18th hole golf course; and a coffee shop, El Patio.

To challenge even the best golfers, there are two Peter Dye championship 18-hole courses (entirely built by 300 Dominicans armed with machetes, shovels and wheelbarrows). There's a 15-court tennis complex; five swimming pools; a marina offering cruising, sailing, fishing and skin-diving outings and a weekly regatta; trap and skeet shooting ranges; a dude ranch and a polo club run by the nephew of the Maharajah of Jodphur, Maharaj Jabar Singh, a former 8 goal player who has won championships all over the world. (Polo matches are held here three times a week; they draw players and ponies from North and South America. The maharaj also presides over adjacent stables where there are about 3,000 thorough-bred horses.) *Cost:* $170–$195 double EP, in season.

★★★ JACK TAR VILLAGE
Ideal for those who want the self-contained, all inclusive resort. This lush, landscaped, 3-story, 208-room complex offers something for every-one. Guests can join scheduled activities from 9:00 A.M. till 10:00 P.M. in everything from donkey races to merengue lessons. For non-joiners or the in-dolent there's sunning by an enormous pool or combing two miles of im-maculate beach. The hotel's 18-hole Robert Trent Jones golf course is deceptively palm-fringed and peaceful, masking the challenge. Golf clubs can be rented. *Cost:* From $875 per person per week all inclusive, in season. From $1,400 per double per week all inclusive, in season. Individual non-package rates are available for off season.

★★★ SOSUAMAR
This new, full-service, villa-type hotel is set back one mile from the beach and offers a panoramic view of the Atlantic Ocean. Frequent shuttle service is available to both town and beach. There are 40 villa units ready and another 40 planned for completion in 1983. Pool, tennis, reciprocal golf privileges, and local entertainment are just a few of the attractions at this well-run property. All units have full balconies, most with ocean views and kaleido-scope sunsets. *Cost:* $800 per person per week in season, all inclusive. From $120 per double per night in season, all inclusive.

★★ CLUB NAUTICO LOS CHARAMÍCOS
Privately owned condos are occasionally available for rent by pre-arrangement with management. Exclusive, secluded, directly on water, lo-cated on the outskirts of town. Outside visitors aren't encouraged. *Cost:* From $650 per week, in season.

★★ LAS BRISAS
Quiet and casual, eight private, double-occupancy cabanas are a five-minute walk to beach, restaurants or La Roca disco. Rooms are super-clean, air-conditioned, and are located in a rural setting. Hotel Sosuamar's pool and tennis courts are available to guests free of charge. Owner Sylvie Papernik makes you feel that her casa is su casa. *Cost:* $25 per double, in season.

Samana
★★ BAHIA BEACH RESORT
Formerly Cayocoa Hotel, this hotel overlooks the tiny fishing village of Samana and the beautiful Samana Bay. Good beach, spectacular sunrises and sunsets, set on 121 acres of national park land. There's snorkeling, tennis, boating, and one of the finest amber shops on the North Shore, owned by American Dan McAuley and his Dominican-born wife, Alexia. Dinner is

usually served under the stars. The scene is informal. *Cost:* $80 per person for double occupancy, in season.

★★ OUT ISLAND VILLAS
Operated by the Bahia Beach Resort property, these are 11 rooms and 9 two-bedroom villas on an island off Samana. Ideal for those whose desire is absolute tranquility. Boat service connects the Villas with the Bahia Beach and mainland. Bridges also connect the villas to the mainland. There are side paths and seats along the way to stop and rest or picnic in solitude. *Cost:* $65 per person for double occupancy, in season, EP.

★ EL PORTILLO
A must for serious beach lovers, this cabana-style complex offers accommodations directly on Las Terrenas beach, a glorious expanse of white sand. Local boys will climb the nearest palm tree to fetch you your own private coconut. Otherwise, the scene is absolute tranquility and there's maximum privacy. Informal, but comfortable rooms with ceiling fans. Hotel has a private air strip. *Cost:* From $60 per night per double, in season.

MELIÁ DOMINICANA
To date, this is the only Caribbean hotel owned by the chain of Madrid-based Meliá International Hotels. Although its location is somewhat out of the mainstream, the Colonial City is only a fifteen-minute or so drive away and just outside the hotel's gates is the Paseo de los Indios Park where one can take a relaxing stroll or a strenuous jog by the sea. On the grounds are eight tennis courts, a health club, and a pool containing a sunken bar. La Casa restaurant, a re-creation of an old colonial house, offers well-executed Continental fare; gambling is welcomed at the Meliá Casino, open from 4 PM to the wee hours; L'Azotea, the hotel's rooftoop nightclub, is open for dancing at 9 PM, with weekend shows at 11:30 PM. *Cost:* $85 per double EP.

Punta Cana

★★★ CLUB MEDITERRANEE
Its 600-bed village in Punta Cana was opened in April 1981. A $10-million complex, it covers 70 acres on an exquisite, unspoiled stretch of beach. Each of the three stucco bungalows is air-conditioned and contains a double room. In the center of the village is a plant-filled, vaulted dining area that later functions as a disco, bar, pool, outdoor theater and a thatched-roof center for arts and crafts. Sports facilities include ten tennis courts (four lighted), a baseball and a soccer field; also deep-sea fishing, windsurfing, sailing and snorkeling are available. Excursions into the countryside and overnight trips to Santo Domingo can be arranged. *Cost:* $690 up, single, per week, all inclusive, off season, including air fare from USA.

Puerta Plata and the North Shore

Major projects slated for 1983/84 completion are: *Hyatt; Holiday Inn; Melía; Euro Hotel; Village Caraibe; and Villas Doradas.*

Restaurants
Santo Domingo

★★★★ IL BUCO
Across from the cathedral in the Colonial City. Owned by Baron Giuseppe Storniolo di Margi, alias Pucci, a skeet shooter and a pilot who came to the Dominican Republic with Gulf and Western nine years ago to set up sports activities. He'd always enjoyed cooking, and so he decided to stay and open

a restaurant. On the menu is a reproduction of a sketch he found in an ancient cookbook in his home in southern Italy, but the contents of the menu are the real delight. He specializes in homemade pasta, veal and seafood dishes. In the Festival Gastronomico Dominicano 1980 his culinary expertise led to his capturing of first, second *and* third prizes. Green lasagna "garisenda" won first prize, his stuffed chicken breast "di Margi" (with prosciutto, homemade mozzarella cheese, chicken livers, cream, Marsala wine and fresh mushrooms) won second prize; white rice with four cheeses "Risotto" won third prize. *Moderate.*

★★★★ LINA
Has reigned as the best restaurant in Santo Domingo since it opened its doors. Some say it's one of the best in the world. Lina, once Trujillo's personal chef, is a master of Spanish paella and is equally and justifiably renowned for her zazuela (with shrimp, lobster and an accent of Pernod) and sea bass dishes. *Expensive.*

But it is noisy — come here for the food, not the atmosphere

★★★ EL ALCAZAR
At the Hotel Santo Domingo, this is one of the most enchanting spots in town thanks to the magic tenting, mirrors and latticework wrought by its designer, Oscar de la Renta. Known for its flambéed Continental dishes and its delicate handling of local fish, it's the place to head for when you're in the mood for grand and romantic dining in a hushed, subdued, formal atmosphere. *Expensive.*

★★★ EL CASTILLO DEL MAR
Dinner conversation here is punctuated by the sound of the Atlantic surf pounding onto nearby rocks and the strumming of beach-roving musicians. This is Santo Domingo's only oceanside restaurant, partly by default since hurricanes tend to topple the city's ocean hugging structures. The accent is appropriately on seafood. The fare is as good as the place is pretty. *Moderate.*

★★★ EXTREMADURA
Located in the Hostal Nicolás de Ovando on Calle de las Damas, it is furnished in a style harmonious with the building's handsome, 16th-century colonial origins. The menu is international with an accent on such Spanish dishes as paella and sea bass with orange sauce, a dish that lures people here from all over the world. *Moderate* to *expensive.*

The decor is that of Spain's Extremadura province

★★★ D'AGOSTINI
Offers Italian and international fare, a wine list of impeccable quality and lofty price and a handsome setting (once a private home) in which to indulge. *Expensive.*

★★★ JARDIN DE JADE (EMBAJADOR HOTEL)
Owned by Simon Yip, who also owns a nightclub and a restaurant in Hong Kong. It opened in 1978 with the owner vowing that he would serve authentic Chinese food. He does in spacious, graceful surroundings. Elaborate eight and ten-course dinners are the norm here. Peking Duckling, presented with great flourish is the pièce de résistance. *Expensive.*

★★★ LA BAHIA
A favorite of Dominicans who spill out of cars and pour in here by the eights and tens. The specialties are very fresh seafood, including "mero al coco" (sea bass in coconut sauce) and "chillo al coco" (local fish in coconut) as well as spaghetti and conch. Small, informal and reasonably priced, the restaurant opens at 9:00 and stays open until 2:00—or until everyone leaves, which can be 4:00 or 5:00 A.M. Dining is at formica-topped tables seating on cane

With meals here, try delicious local beer, El Presidente

chairs to the occasional accompaniment of street-vendors hawking. (When we were last there, a wicker salesman stood peering in at us halfheartedly trying to sell just one more item.) *Inexpensive* to *moderate.*

★★★ VESUVIO I
One of the oldest restaurants in the country and very social—a place to see and be seen. The best dining spot is on the veranda where soft evening breezes sweep and the splashing sounds of the Caribbean surf, just across the road soothe. Specialties are Italian food, including veal piccata, fettucine and manicotti as well as fresh seafood. *Expensive.*

★★ CHEZ FRANCOIS
Located in a pretty little antique-filled house in the colonial section, it offers fresh fish superbly prepared with French finesse under the watchful eye of its French owners. Soft European music wafts through the dining area; menus are in French, of course, and Spanish. *Moderate* to *expensive.*

★★ EL CASERIO
An old favorite of Dominicans, El Caserio offers huge portions of very good Spanish food from 10 AM to 3 AM. One of the specialties is sea bass Basque-style, another is Zarzuela de Marisos (seafood in pernod sauce). In the back of the restaurant is an amiable Spanish "taverna." *Inexpensive.*

★★ MAISON DE LA CAVA
Its setting is so special that the quality of the food . . . it's Continental and good . . . seems an extra, unexpected bonus. As the name suggests, dining is in a cave some 50 feet undergound reached via a narrow, iron, spiral staircase that circles guests down to tables strategically positioned around still-growing stalagmites and stalactites. It's popular for dinner and for late-night dancing to a live band. *Moderate* to *expensive.*

★★ MESON DE CASTILLA
Located near the National Palace (and a ten-minute walk from the Sheraton), Meson de Castilla serves wonderful Spanish food amidst typical Spanish decor. Among the specialties are grilled lamb, paella, and seafood (including large—for the Caribbean—lobster and fresh shrimp). *Inexpensive.*

★ VESUVIO II
A more informal version of its sire, it features pizza and pasta in a pleasant setting. It generally attracts a somewhat less moneyed crowd. *Inexpensive* to *moderate.*

CAFE AMERICUS
In the old city, this is not a place to go for atmosphere. It's small, almost cafeterialike, and the owner who is from the Basque part of Spain doesn't speak English . . . but he does go out of his way to please, even bringing musicians in off the street to serenade you. And the paella is delicious and downright cheap. An evening here can be a fun change of pace. *Inexpensive.*

EL BODEGON
Near the cathedral in the Colonial City is a cool and cozy place to take a lunch break between sights. Specialties here are the ceviche, "mero a la vasca" (bass), and "cassoulet a la Gascona" (lamb and pork stew with sausage); they also have a variety of good pasta dishes. *Inexpensive* to *moderate.*

Puerta Plata and the North Shore

Major projects slated for 1983/84 completion are: *Hyatt; Holiday Inn; Melía; Euro Hotel; Village Caraibe;* and *Villas Doradas.*

Elsewhere On The Island

★★★ LA PIAZZETTA

At Altos de Chavon is set an old country inn overlooking a river and surrounded by peaceful walkways and exotic flower displays. At night the nearby palms are spotlighted giving a dramatic and romantic effect. The fare here is Italian, with fresh fish, pasta and veal the highlights. *Expensive.*

★★★ LES CANARIS

Part of the Casa de Campo resort, this is a gracious French country restaurant with a veranda for pre- or apres-dinner drinks and a limited but excellent French menu. *Expensive.*

Nightlife

Santo Domingo is a city that stays up late, and there's plenty to keep one occupied. In the Jaragua Hotel is *La Fuente,* the Caribbean's best and most famous nightclub. Its show is replete with colorful, entertaining feathers and flash Vegas style (albeit the showgirls are shorter). In season international stars headline. (Reservations are a must.) Another nightclub is the *Maunaloa,* where Latin entertainment is featured, although they're starting to bring in international stars. The atmosphere is very dark and candlelit; between shows a Latin orchestra plays for dancing, merengue and otherwise. Both are reminiscent of nightlife in the "old" Havana.

de la Renta did Las Palmas' decor, too; there's a raised floor

Disco dancing can be had at the small and exclusive *Neon 2002* at the Hotel Santo Domingo or at the big (400-plus capacity) and pretty *Omni* at the Sheraton where sections of the dance floor rise to showcase the very good dancers and things start to jump around midnight. Other discos include *Waldo's I* and *Waldo's II* at the Jaragua. Waldo's II is about twice the size of the Omni. Here very good dancers are filmed, and the film is projected on one of the walls.

For non-hotel nightspots do include the *Village,* with a DJ who spins music for a young crowd, and *Raffles*—named for the famous Singapore hotel. Raffles, a trendy nightspot, has pretty people, subdued lighting and an eclectic decor, dominated by a collection of clown paintings. The music is a mix of American and European; there are light snacks of the peanuts and chili con carne variety. Just across the street is a backlit statue of Friar Anton de Montesinos, unveiled on October 12, 1982, honoring the Friar's outspoken opposition to slavery.

Quieter shows featuring sophisticated entertainment can be found at the Hotel Santo Domingo's *Las Palmas* on Thursday, Friday and Saturday nights (on other nights there's disco dancing) at the piano bar, *El Yarey* in the Sheraton and the *Embassy Club* at the Embajador.

When the gambling urge strikes, head for the casinos at the *Sheraton, the Meliá, Dóminicana, Embajador,* the *Jaragua,* the *Nacoa* or the *Maunaloa.*

Also, there are concerts and theater productions at the *National Theater;* theater and dance presentations at the *Palace of Fine Arts;* and occasionally folkloric dancers at the *Museum of the Dominican Man.* At evening's end you might hail a horse and carriage for a leisurely, airy trip back to your hotel.

Elsewhere on the island: Casa de Campo offers *La Cana Bar* for dancing after 8:00. And there's a disco called Genesis at *Altos de Chavón* featuring an ultrasophisticated sound system designed by Paramount Pictures.

Shopping

Although the Dominican Republic offers good buys on a variety of wicker and woven products, handicrafts, strong Dominican-blend coffee, art and hand-embroidered children's clothes, the main attractions are amber and, to a lesser extent, larimar stones.

Much of the amber is supplied by northern mountain people who travel under cover of night to mine their own secret veins and then return home before dawn with a cache available for sale to trusted middlemen who in turn supply the factories. Classified as a semiprecious stone, amber is fossilized resin, which, in the Dominican Republic, is often 30 million years old. Though one usually thinks of amber as a translucent honey color, its most common hue, you'll find it here in shades of red, blue, black, green and pure crystal (blue is most expensive, then red; yellow the least costly). Also affecting the cost is the presence or the absence of a fossilized insect and the kind of insect enclosed in the stone. A piece of yellow amber containing an ant, for instance, is more expensive than a clear stone; a top-quality stone containing a rare frog or long extinct lizard can go for $15,000.

One tip: Beware of the street amber vendors. Many offer plastic versions that to the naked eye look authentic. When buying amber, ask to see it under ultraviolet light. You'll find that real amber has a beautiful, fluorescent glow.

Larimar, also known as Dominican turquoise, is a cloudy, blue-green stone. It's found only in one spot on the southern part of the island.

If you'd like some nice amber at very reasonable prices (one third to one half off U.S. retail prices), head to the *Luperon Amber Factory* in the Colonial City (106 Calle Gral. Luperon), and meet owners Dan and Alexia McAuley. Dan and Alexia design many of the necklaces and bracelets, and you can watch some of their workmen creating them for you. Clear pendants and necklaces range from $10–$50; one-of-a-kind insect-entrapped pieces sell from $10 to $1,000 (for a 30 million year old amber entombed praying mantis)—and treasures like a gold and black amber chess set go for around $1,200. Also ask to see their special scorpion pieces. Alexia is a charming and interesting conversationalist on her native Dominican Republic. Dan is an American.

a visit here is highly recommended, if only to meet the McAuleys

Maria Ambar is well known for top-quality amber. They have an extensive collection ranging from gift to collector items. And it may be of interest that in the United States all these prices would be at least double.

For local Dominican items, try the *Bishop's Basket* run by the Episcopal Church, the *El Conde Gift Shop* and *El Mercado Modelo,* a kind of farmers' market filled with humanity where bargaining for goods is expected. Also, the government sponsored *Planarte* offers excellent pottery buys (for instance, a handsome tea service for six with sugar dish and creamer for about 20 pesos), as well as interesting goods of leather, papier mâché, and straw—all made by Dominicans.

The shops of *La Atarazana* are fun to walk through, though you're apt to find neither bargains nor really special merchandise. There are duty-free shops here as well as at the *Santo Domingo Hotel,* the *Sheraton,* the *Embajador, Las Americas Airport* and the *Centro de los Heroes* offering perfumes, cameras, jewelry and liquor. Liquor is generally a good buy, but savings on other things may be marginal. (Payment in duty-free shops is in U.S. dollars, Canadian currency, British pounds and other currencies.)

Sports

Unlike most Caribbean islands, baseball, not soccer, is the national *sport.* The winter (professional) season runs from late October through January; the summer season goes from April to September. Games are held at the Quisqueya Stadium in Santo Domingo. There's also a short basketball season (from mid-June through August) at the Olympic Center in Santo Domingo; polo matches are usually run three days a week at Casa de Campo; and there's cockfighting at Santo Domingo's Coliseo Gallistico.

There are tennis courts throughout the country and golf courses at Casa de Campo and in the Puerto Plata, Santiago and Jarabacoa areas. (The Santo

La Romana and Puerto Plata have the best beaches. Best near Santo Domingo is Boca Chica

Domingo Country Club is usually restricted to members only.) Arrangements for fishing and scuba expeditions can be made through your hotel, as can rentals of sailboats and appointments to parachute-jump or horseback-ride.

Though swimming in the rough surf of Santo Domingo is not advised, quiet coves farther eastward are perfect for quiet dips. The northern coast of the Dominican Republic has wide, lovely beaches, and, of course, most hotels have their own swimming pools.

Grenada

THE HARD FACTS
Planning Ahead
Costs

The name is pronounced Gruh-nay-dah, the accent on nay

Grenada offers excellent value year round. Deluxe properties average about $160 for two with breakfast and dinner in season (Dec. 15–April 15). Comfortable accommodations in inns, guesthouses, housekeeping cottages and apartments range from $34 to $112 per double, EP. Off-season rates fall about 30 to 35%. Promotions such as the "Spice Filled Holiday" offer discounts, gifts, special events, and other extras for even more savings. A 10% service charge and 7½% government tax is added to all hotel bills.

Write any Grenada Tourist Office (See Sources of Information) for their "50 Things, to Buy, See and Do for $1 U.S. or Less" flyer.

Climate

One of Grenada's main attractions is its average temperature which hovers around 80°F. Year round trade winds keep humidity low, and dining verandas and living quarters are designed to take advantage of this cooling effect. June to December is the rainy season, but showers are short and the tropical vegetation is at its best at this time.

Holidays and Special Events

Official holidays include: New Year's Day; Independence Day (Feb. 7); National Day, the Anniversary of the Revolution (March 13); Easter Weekend (April 20 to 23, 1984); Labor Day (May 1); Whitmonday, Corpus Christi; Carnival (August); Christmas Day; and Boxing Day (Dec. 26). Special annual, nautically oriented events are: *Around Grenada Yacht Race,* which draws international yachtsmen the first week in January; a *Game Fishing Tournament* in late January or early February; and the *Carriacou Regatta,* a 3-day nonstop celebration in August with music, races on land and sea, and a performance by the Big Drum Dancers.

Tour Operators

In the U.S. try Adventure Tours, Butler Travel, Caribbean Holidays, Catuvi, Cavalcade, Flyfaire, and Libgo. In Canada: Pleasure Tours.

Sources of Information

In the United States contact the Grenada Tourist Office, 141 E. 44th Street, New York, NY 10017; Tel. (212) 682–9554. In Canada, the Grenada High Commission, 280 Albert Street, Ottawa K1P5G8; Tel. (613) 236–9581 or Grenada National Tourist Office, 143 Yonge Street, Suite 102, Toronto M5C1W7; Tel. (416) 368–1332. Once in Grenada, stop by the Grenada Tourist Board on the Carenage for answers to any questions you may have.

Packing

Dress in Grenada is decidedly informal but in the capital of St. George's, shorts and other skimpy attire is not appropriate. Ladies should pack a sweater or shawl for evening and comfortable walking shoes, but leave room for the sundresses beach vendors sell in all patterns and colors at prices that can't be beat. For men, ties are rarely required. Lightweight sportswear and maybe a jacket for special occasions should be included.

Documentation

Proof of citizenship (passport, voter's registration card or birth certificate) and a return airline ticket are needed for entry by U.S. and Canadian citizens. A stay of 3 months is permitted without a visa.

Getting There

Airline service to Grenada is not yet direct, but the new international airport, expected to open at the beginning of 1984, should change this. Until that time, the best way to get to the island is via Barbados. Here an interline desk is set up in the airport to shepherd Grenada-bound passengers past customs and immigration and on to connecting 45-minute LIAT flight. Minimum connection time is two hours and passengers must have confirmed tickets to use this service. It is strongly advised that you choose the nonstop Barbados-Grenada flight whenever possible. American Airlines, BWIA and Pan Am serve Barbados from New York; BWIA and Eastern from Miami. Air Canada and BWIA leave from Toronto to Barbados; Air Canada from Montreal. For those who wish to fly via Trinidad, American, BWIA, and Pan Am depart from New York; Air France, ALM, and BWIA from Miami. From Trinidad, it's a 35-minute flight to Grenada.

Cruise ships (Costa, Chandris, Cunard, Home Lines) from Port Everglades and San Juan, make regular calls at the Carenage in St. George's.

Formalities on Arrival

Customs

U.S. and Canadian citizens are allowed to bring in 40 oz. of alcohol and one carton of cigarettes duty free. At departure, your immigration card and $5 EC are required.

Money

The official currency is the Eastern Caribbean dollar. Banks in St. George's and most hotels (at perhaps a slightly lower rate) will gladly convert U.S. or Canadian dollars. ($1 US = $2.65EC; $1 Canadian = $2.20EC with some slight fluctuation). Important note: Travelers checks are widely accepted but very few hotels, shops or restaurants honor credit cards.

Getting Into Town

The presently used airport, Pearl's, is a 45-minute roller coaster drive. Travel time will be cut to just 10 minutes, once the new international airport opens at Point Salines. Taxis are plentiful at the airport and prices are posted.

The local currency is called the Bee Wee, as in British West Indies, about 3 to a U.S. dollar

Settling Down

Choosing a Hotel

Grenada's small hotels, inns, and guesthouses range from four to thirty rooms. The Holiday Inn (still closed at press time) plans to reopen with 150 rooms and two more new 150-room hotels are on the drawing boards. Possible accommodations range from luxurious antique furnished suites with sunken bathtubs or private swimming pools, spacious villas and apartments complete with housekeeper to simple, immaculate guesthouses. We've rated only the best.

Villa rental information may be obtained from Bain & Bertrand, P.O. Box 262, St. George's, Grenada; Tel. 2848 or Grenada Property Management, Golf Course, St. George's, Grenada; Tel. 4529. In season, all-inclusive prices range from $600 a week for a two-bedroom home with pool, up to $3,650 for a luxurious villa on its own private beach that can sleep 12. All properties come with live-in housekeepers.

Choosing a Restaurant

Most hotels are on the MAP plan; little-known limited exchange dining does exist. It might also be possible to substitute lunch for dinner at your hotel. Check in advance with the front desk on both of these points. Small restaurants in St. George's and the resort areas have lots of local color and serve a wide variety of seafood, West Indian specialties as well as Chinese, English, and Continental fare.

Tipping

Brochures say "tipping is not encouraged" and there's no pressure to do so, but the final choice is left to each traveler's discretion. A 10% service charge is usually added to bills.

Learning to Cope

Business Hours.   Shops open Monday - Friday at 8 AM and close promptly at noon for a one hour lunch. They reopen from 1 PM to 4 PM. Saturday hours are 8 AM to noon. Shops in the Grand Anse Shopping Center are open 8 AM to 5 PM Tuesday through Saturday. *Banks* open 8 AM to noon, Monday through Friday with an extra two hours, from 3 PM to 5 PM on Friday afternoons.

Electricity.   AC transformers and adapters are needed because Grenada's electric current runs 220/240 volts and 50 cycles.

Water and Drink.   All water is safe to drink, but if you get tired of the same old thing, try malt to strengthen your muscles or mauby, a popular digestive made from tree bark.

Communications.   To telephone Grenada from the United States or Canada and visa versa you must go through an overseas operator.

Airmail postage rates to the United States and Canada are 30¢EC for postcards and 60¢EC for letters. The Post Office is open 8 AM to 11:45 AM and 1 PM to 3:30 PM Monday through Thursday. Friday closing is at 4:30 PM. Air mail takes 10 days to two weeks.

Language.   English is the spoken language. The Grenadian lilt is quite musical though a bit difficult to decipher at times.

Medical Assistance.   There is a *hospital* in St. George's, a U.S. medical school in Grand Anse and an ambulance service for emergencies.

Getting Around

By Car

Rental cars or mini-mokes will be delivered to your hotel on request. All rental agencies are local, no Hertz or Avis, etc. Remember when driving, keep left and blow your horn often when approaching curves in the road.

By Taxi

Taxis are numerous and inexpensive. Standard fares have been set as well as touring rates. These are available at the airport and the Tourist Office and you should familiarize yourself with them.

By Bus

Brightly-painted, wooden buses and more modern mini-buses ply all the roads between major towns. Fares depend on distance traveled. The minis are more comfortable but be prepared for crowds and accelerated speeds. Hail both by waving your hand at the side of the road or at a marked bus stop. To get off, just shout to the driver or money collector, or knock three times on the outside of the car if you are near a window. Buses operate from 6 AM to 8 PM.

GRENADA TODAY

If you've been reading the major newspapers closely . . . or the newspapers published elsewhere in the Caribbean . . . you probably know that Grenada's had a rather hard time of it in the last few years. A truly beautiful island—lush—filled with hills, dales, tropical fruits, rain forests, waterfalls, flora and fauna. What makes this difficult for Americans to understand is that under the (formerly British) parliamentary system, an election can be called at any time. The result or the bottom line is that no one in or out of Grenada knows what will happen politically. It is true that Cuba is giving major technical assistance and manpower for the construction of a second airport here.

Grenada was British from 1783 to 1974 - hence the strong English air [handwritten marginal note]

None of this affects the visitor, however. It is mentioned merely because it may be of interest. The people of Grenada are warm, welcoming and gentle to each other and to their guests. They want you to share the beauties of their island, and they are extremely proud of their nation.

A little-known fact: There's a group from Bay Shore, Long Island (New York), that funds a medical-training center. The first students graduated in the spring of 1981; almost all were accepted for residencies in the United States. (Many, in fact 95%, came from the United States.) Working in some of the local hospitals and clinics are some excellent doctors from Cuba. And education is now free for school children.

Should you go to Grenada? Yes, an unqualified yes. The people are warm, gentle and loving. The island itself is a geographic delight . . . high hills covered with deep, deep foliage matched only in Dominica or in Guadeloupe's Natural Park . . . fruit fresh for the picking or for the buying at low prices . . . really small (mainly 20-room) hotels, with the exception of the 200-room Holiday Inn (and even that's built lower than a palm tree and provides thatched-roof villas). Then perhaps there's the very nicest thing of all . . . a genuine smile of welcome and, later, recognition, on the face of just about every Grenadian you'll meet. If your time permits, you'll also have the chance to dash off for some very secluded days in Petit Martinique, Carriacou—or Grenada's even more deserted, dependency islands (they're politically associated) of Ronde Island, Kick-em-Jenny, Green Bird and Conference. What more could you ask?

TOURING

Grenada is only 21 miles long and 12 miles wide, but there's a lot of spectacular scenery packed into this ever-changing island, the most southern in the Windward chain. It has a central mountain range that towers about 2,000 feet above sea level. There are banana, sugar and spice plantations . . . rivers that roam . . . waterfalls cascading and welcoming for a picnic . . . and perfect beaches.

Grenada is the only spice island in the Caribbean—nutmeg and mace the chief products

Most of Grenada's intimate, Caribbean-special hotels are in the south along the beaches of Grand Anse and L'ance aux Epines, but when the mood finally moves you from beaching to seeing, start in St. George's, the capital city. The center of the city is called the Carenage. It contains pastel-colored West Indian commercial buildings and shops fronting the harbor. Behind them small, neat houses made of brick (wood is no longer used, for it contributed to the spreading of a number of serious fires), topped with red fish-scale tile roofs. This is a busy port that provides facilities for private or chartered schooners and ketches and yawls anchored offshore along with commercial vessels loading and unloading foodstuffs from everywhere. The Grenada Tourist Board is here (a good place to stop for the latest information) along with the post office, public library, cable and wireless office, overseas telephone office, LIAT, and many small shops where you can pick up the spice baskets for which Grenada, "the spice island," is famous. Nutmeg, mace, bay leaf, cinnamon, cacao, cloves and ginger are all neatly packed into baskets large or small, and they make perfect gifts for you or friends. There's even a liqueur made of spices, citrus and rum, called de la Grenade. And like many other Caribbean islands, Grenada has its own rum, Jack Iron. Even ice has a hard time cooling this fiery drink. It sinks!

For pieces of Grenadian history (Carib, British, French, independent), make a stop at the Grenada National Museum (open 9 AM to 3:00 PM, Monday through Friday). Historical bits and pieces tell some of Grenada's checkered history. Petroglyphs carved in stone from the days of the Carib Indians; the Empress Josephine's bathtub; the first telegraph brought to the island—all are housed in this small museum that once was a French army barracks and prison built in 1704.

Other major architectural structures left by the French and the British in their struggles for power in the continual seesaw battles of the Caribbean are the cathedrals, churches and forts that ring the city. The churches mix European architecture with West Indian warm colors, and their walls are lined with plaques and paintings that tell of some of the personal, political and military triumphs of their important parishioners. Military buffs might like to stop by Fort Frederick, which was built by the French and reconstructed by the English to defend themselves against one another, or Fort Matthew. Another major fort, Fort Rupert, built by the French in 1705, is now the Grenada Police Headquarters, and its cannons are still used for the infrequent, official salutes to visiting dignitaries.

Excellent view of town from Fort Frederick

The Esplanade, on the bay side of St. George's, separates the waterfront from Market Square, one of the most fascinating forays a visitor can make. Early Saturday morning is the best time to come, for the fish market, meat market, vegetable and fruit open-air markets are all in full swing. This is the place to buy bananas, papayas, oranges, yams, plantains, mangos, papaya, coconuts and, of course, Grenada spices. The ladies have set up their individual "shops" (spread on clean cloths or used flour bags) and have brought along their own umbrellas to protect them from the Caribbean sun. Of course, they're interested in selling their wares, but this is also the place where they catch up on local gossip. You may have to wait until Maude finishes telling Sadie about recent happenings. Outside busy, bustling Market Square, Grenada's open wooden buses, brightly painted and each individually named, and more modern mini-buses wait for passengers heading to other towns and villages. If you're feeling adventurous, hop aboard; you'll get to meet the country folk. But it's a good idea to be sure there's another bus returning to the area where you want to end your day.

Before heading out of town, you may want to visit the smattering of shops in St. George's (see the Grenada Shopping section), or you might like a crunch or a munch at one of the local restaurants (several on the second story) that provide a voyeur's view of the comings and the goings at the harbor.

A cruise on the glass-bottom barge, Rum Runner, gives a special sea view of picturesque St. George's, as well as a look at the island's underwater life and coral formations. Rum punch flows, and a steel band plays on both daytime and sunset cruises. Call 4233 or 2352 for a schedule.

Outside St. George's

When you leave St. George's, you'll discover the roller-coaster roads of Grenada. Heading east, you'll pass farm country, with ice-cream-colored houses and miles and miles of cocoa, banana, sugar and spice acreage. Westerhall is the residential area of Grenada's affluent, and here you can peek at the best of tropical architecture and manicured gardens. After negotiating many more twists and turns of the road, you'll be in Bacolet Bay, a wide peninsula on the Atlantic side, somewhat windy and wild.

Grenville, called the second city of Grenada, is another spot to relax in. Try the caught-that-morning seafood. A meal of fresh fish with a squeeze of local lime (or the local, very hot, hot sauce), topped off by the local Carib beer, rum, or mauby (it's said that it helps the digestion, but not too many nonlocals agree), sets the relaxed pace for the rest of a discovering-Grenada day. There's a spice factory here that's open and welcoming to visitors and two food markets—one hawking fresh fish and the other, fresh, shiny fruit and vegetables. *[handwritten: Saturday morning is best for the fruit and vegetable market]*

Morne des Sauteurs on the northernmost tip of Grenada is a wave-washed monument to the memory of 40 Carib Indians who leaped to their death from the cliff rather than be captured by the overwhelming French forces. The adjoining expanse of Levera Beach is another swim-stop, where the wilder Atlantic Ocean meets the gentler Caribbean Sea. From here you can usually see Grenada's handful of offshore island dependencies . . . Carriacou; Petit Martinique; Ronde Island; Kick-em-Jenny; Green Bird; Conference Isle. None is exactly a major marketplace, but spending some time on any one of the islands constitutes a fascinating sailing, picnic and beach day.

Betty Mascoll offers lunch consisting of three courses of West Indian cuisine at her plantation greathouse-home nearby in Morne Fendue. The approximately 70-year-old plantation still produces cocoa and bananas. The lunch menu is presided over by Miss Mascoll and her staff. Guests are then invited to look around the sprawling estate.

Twisting back toward the capital, St. George's, you pass through Grand Etang Forest, capped by Grand Etang Lake and a tropical tangle of trees, mountain streams and power-packed waterfalls. It's possible, if strenuous, to hike through the mountain forest, a natural, uncultivated land of orchids, armadillos, monkeys and birds. Nearby are the Annandale Falls, a rushing cascade of fresh, mountain water that falls about 50 feet into a natural pool. Here you can take a sometimes chilly dip or just stroll entranced through what seems like an enchanted forest.

Another adventure takes you along the west coast of Grenada, through small fishing villages. Papaya, cotton, mango, coconut and banana trees line the road . . . workers walk or ride by on donkeys laden with produce . . . until you eventually arrive at the town of Gouyave. At the entrance to the town is Dougaldston Estates, a spice plantation and a factory, where cloves, cinnamon, mace, nutmeg and cocoa are grown and sorted by women who will proudly tell you about their crops . . . how spices are planted and grown, their many uses and the drying and the curing procedure. In town, visit the Nutmeg Processing Station which offers a fascinating half-hour tour.

Most of the individually-stamped and small beach resorts for which Grenada is known are along the southern coast—at Grand Anse and L'ance aux Epines. You may well be staying in this area, and if you are, laid-back beach days will become your normal kind of Grenadian day. If not, be sure to visit the special stretches of beach, particularly Grand Anse. Nearby is the tiny fishing village of Woburn, where you can eat fresh fish cooked in local beach bistros and visit a small sugar factory attached to the Woodlands canefields. Your hotel will pack a picnic lunch, and all you'll need besides a swimsuit will be a broad-brimmed hat to shade you from the Caribbean sun.

Inside Information

Hotels

It's not official, but it's observed in practice: In Grenada there's a rule that says, "No hotel may be higher than a palm tree." And none is. There is no high-rise anything here; even the most modest inns blend into their surroundings. A premium is placed on privacy in the 17 hotels and 16 guesthouses that dot this island off the mainstream. With a room count ranging from four to 30 (except the Holiday Inn's 150 rooms), these small inns are stamped with the personalities of their owner-managers and guests, many of whom are called by their first names. Credit cards are rarely accepted, but we've noted the few exceptions below.

★★★★ SECRET HARBOR HOTEL

Owner-manager is Barbara Stevens, an English expatriate

Each of the 20 suites is furnished in mahogany antiques and carries out the hotel's Spanish-Moorish design—arches, old brick walls, plus interesting accents such as a giant marble chess set and Empire chaise lounges. All suites have their own balconies, two queen-size, four-poster beds, telephone, radio, wall safe, dressing room, living area, and elegant baths with a view of calm Mt. Hartman Bay from the Italian-tiled sunken tub which is as big as a mini-swimming pool. The real pool spreads in free-flow form on several levels and is surrounded by fragrant, brilliantly-hued flora. Dining is Caribbean elegant—formal but in a tropical manner that matches the Continental cuisine. There's one tennis court, a small, private beach on the bay with its own bar. Sailfish and other water sports, excursions to offshore islands for snorkeling, fishing or just a day-away-from-it-all picnic are available. AMEX and VISA cards accepted only. *Cost:* $175 per double MAP, in season.

★★★★ SPICE ISLAND INN
Spread over 8 acres right on Grand Anse beach, Spice Island Inn has ten spacious suites set back from the sea. Each has a king-size bed, enormous bath/dressing room with sunken tub, patio, sun deck, garden and, for starting or ending the day with a skinny dipping splash, your own very private pool. There are also 20 smaller beach suites, all with patio and private garden separating the sleeping area from the bath. These are so closely merged with the beach, these have feet-dipping buckets filled with clear water at the entrance. Something is always doing in the evening—a good combo, steel band, crab races or maybe the weekly movie. Ever-present, ever-charming manager, Desmond Campbell, goes out of his way to assure the total enjoyment of his guests, as does his smiling and efficient staff. *Cost:* $155–$190 per double, MAP in season.

★★★ THE CALABASH
Eight acres of manicured lawn and tropical gardens surround 22 suites in ten two-story cottages on L'ance aux Epines beach. A maid comes each morning to prepare breakfast at the hour you desire in your own small kitchen. There's a charming honeymoon suite with a canopied old mahogany bed, and one enormous suite with its own private pool right in the open living/dining area. Tennis, pool, billiards, snorkeling, and beach bar help guests meet one another while they're engaged in their chosen sport. The stone-walled, vine-covered bar and dining room are beautifully decorated and the kitchen here is one of the island's best. AMEX accepted only. *Cost:* $160 per double, MAP in season; pool suite is $220 per double.

★★★ TWELVE DEGREES NORTH
A unique, idyllic arrangement—eight spacious apartments each with its own terrace looking down over gardens to a private strip of beach in the quiet residential area of L'ance aux Epines. The one or two-bedroom suites are decorated with hot Caribbean colors and original Grenadian art, ranging from watercolors to cloth collages. Each apartment has a fully-equipped kitchen and its own housekeeper who is also an accomplished cook, who works exclusively for you between 8 AM and 3 PM. Spend time doing what you want to do when you want to do it—dive in the pool, volley on the tennis court, swim out and sun on the raft, sail the *Sunfish* or *Mirror* dinghy, waterski or fish. Everything runs like clockwork thanks to owner/manager Joe Gaylord, the American expatriate who built this special spot. *Cost:* $560 per double per week (one bedroom); $805 (two bedrooms), EP in season. Note: No children under 12 permitted.

★★ CINNAMON HILL AND BEACH CLUB
20 hillside villas. Six 2-bedroom and eight 1-bedroom duplexes; 6 one floor hacienda suites. Condominiums run as a resort hotel. Spacious, airy, and also air-conditioned and decorator furnished, each unit has a fully-equipped kitchen (including dishwasher), counter/bar, two baths, queen-size beds, and a living room that could also accommodate two on the commodious sofas. Large terraces, original art on the walls, straw rugs on the red-tile floors and accents of wood all combine to make these apartments some of the island's most attractive. Breakfast is prepared by your own maid and just a bit down the hill is the *Hacienda* bar and restaurant and courtyard swimming pool. The view is magnificent day and night. It's just a short downhill walk to Grand Anse beach and the Sundowner Bar. Still in stage one, this Mediterranean-style resort's plans include the addition of 16 hillside and 22 beachfront suites all with private pools, a second patio restaurant, bar and swimming pool, three tennis, one squash and two badminton courts as well as a putting green. *Cost:* one bedroom villa or Hacienda Suite, $110 EP, $124 CP, $160 MAP, double in season; two bedroom villa, $173 EP, $201 CP, $273 MAP, for four, in season.

★★ HORSESHOE BAY HOTEL
A total of 12 suites in four whitewashed villas furnished with canopied, four-poster beds and authentic antiques with spacious patios overlooking the beach or gardens. The public rooms and dining area are decorated with massive mahogany chairs and tables from Venezuela and Moroccan rugs. A large swimming pool, sunfish sailing and snorkeling off the private beach at L'ance aux Epines provide daytime activities and help build an appetite for the excellent cuisine served nightly. AMEX and DINERS CLUB cards only. *Cost:* $145 per double MAP, in season.

★ BLUE HORIZONS COTTAGE HOTEL
Seventeen units. Six deluxe, six superior, five standard, all nicely furnished one-bedroom suites with full kitchen facilities and verandas all terraced up from the swimming pool. There's a bar and lounge, the 3½ acres of tropical gardens are home to 21 different species of birds (ask for their identification folder), Grand Anse beach is within walking distance, Royston's car rental agency is on the grounds and La Belle Creole restaurant at the crest of the hill is a high spot for à la carte dining. *Cost:* $65–$75, double EP, in season.

★ ROSS POINT INN
A West Indian inn operated in the old manner by Curtis and Audrey Hopkin, situated on a point that affords an expansive view of St. George's and Grand Anse. A reading room, coffee and cocktail lounge, terraced dining room and 12 simple, air-conditioned rooms are nicely laid out on 3½ well-landscaped acres. Food and service are superb and the restaurant is one of the best on the island. The breakfast pavilion, overlooking the sea, serves fresh island fruit . . . the best way possible to greet the morning. Just down the hill is some of Grenada's best snorkeling off the inn's own beach, and there is free transportation to their beach cabana at Grand Anse just ½ mile away. *Cost:* $95 per double MAP, in season.

Sea view rooms are best [handwritten annotation]

Restaurants

Grenada cuisine: Oil Down (breadfruit and salted pork steamed gently in coconut milk and covered with spinachlike callaloo leaves), cold red pepper soup, green turtle soup, rice and pigeon peas, barracuda, flying fish, soursop, nutmeg or mango ice cream. Eating in Grenada is different! For a bit of history to absorb while digesting your Oil Down—breadfruit was orginally brought to Grenada on *The Bounty* from Tahiti. Captain Bligh left one tree in St. Vincent and one in Grenada as an economical means of feeding slaves.

The rum punch here is topped with nutmeg [handwritten annotation]

Reservations are a good idea because chefs usually plan on meals for hotel or inn guests, and many of the inns are small and secluded. Dining in Grenada is informal and is frequently open-air with a view of the sea.

Moderate means $15–$20 per person; expensive would be above $20 per person without drinks.

★★★★ ROSS POINT INN
By far the best of traditional West Indian cuisine. Here Mrs. Audrey Hopkin's special flair with local foods is apparent and her menus offer unending surprises. No outside guests are accepted without reservations and Mr. Curtis Hopkin is likely to answer queries about the evening's bill of fare with a "never mind, you'll like it." And you will. Meals here are unusual, consistently well prepared, and equally well presented. Try for a terrace table, much in demand for the superlative view over St. George's. A few favorite specialties will include classic callaloo or velvety carrot soup; light, airy, and rich breadfruit souffle; conch (lambi in Grenada) and onion pie—a sort of Grenadian quiche; and lambi souse, marinated conch tenderly seasoned to

perfection by Mrs. H's experienced hand. If you're physically able, don't skip dessert—an exotic homemade savory such as soursop (avocado) ice cream, for example. Arrive early to enjoy Ross Point's famous rum punch in the garden bar or gazebo pavilion—or both. Service is careful and diners are treated like guests and never rushed. *Expensive.*

★★★ LA BELLE CREOLE
Audrey Hopkin's two sons, Royston and Arnold, carry on family tradition in their airy hilltop restaurant at the Blue Horizons Hotel in Grand Anse. Their tannia soup is irresistible. (The local tuber vegetable is similar to our potato, but the Hopkin touch in converting the vegetable into something better than vichyssoise is special.) Other creative cooking receiving top billing—sweet and sour pork chops; lobster a la Creole; Imperial Fish (flaked dolphin baked with eggs, vinegar, cream and local spices); and exotic desserts like sweet potato pudding or guava delight. *Moderate.*

Warm water lobster in Grenada is always a sure thing

★★ CALABASH
Food style leans toward genuine West Indian in flavor and is very attractively presented in a flower-filled, outdoor dining pavilion built from local wood and natural gray stone. Buffets at this Lance aux Epines hotel are occasional but memorable happenings. Be sure to inquire about dates when you arrive. Some island specialties not to miss: pungent swordfish Creole pie; green turtle or green pepper soup; fish cakes; coconut brulé and nutmeg ice cream. Everything on the 5-course set menu is freshly prepared and outside dinner guests should make reservations. *Moderate.*

★★ HORSESHOE BAY HOTEL
In L'ance aux Epines overlooking the Caribbean, this is one of Grenada's most romantic settings. Candlelit, widely-spaced mahogany tables provide a warm, intimate atmosphere in the dining area and Mediterranean-style, red-tiled lounge. The menu features West Indian and Continental dishes. Try the pumpkin or chilled cucumber soup for a starter or accras (deep fried codfish fritters); then perhaps Caribbean pepperpot—tender braised chicken or fresh bonita fish with a Creole sauce that shows off the chef's skill. Very popular with the local clientele who know and enjoy good food. *Moderate.*

★ MORNE FONDUE
For a unique Grenadian experience, check to see if Mrs. Betty Mascoll is serving lunch in her 70-year-old plantation home out in picturesque St. Patrick's. Typical noontime fare might include curried titaree (a local fish); barbecued chicken; christophine; boiled plantain; Spanish rice; a hearty pork and oxtail pepperpot; salad; guava stew; and soursop ice cream. All dishes freshly prepared, much of it from produce grown on the 7-acre property. *Inexpensive.*

RUDOLF'S
Another mecca for the boating set. Stop by here if you want to meet local captains, charterers and crew. The comfortable, round window booth gives a good overview of the activity on the carenage. One of the rare late night eating places open until midnight Monday through Saturday. The publike setting on the inner harbor is Austrian owned. In addition to excellent fish (especially the seafood brochette and dolphin), you'll find made-to-order chips, omelettes, cold plates, steak, and lobster any way you want it on the extensive lunch and dinner à la carte menu. The Saturday night buffet is one of Grenada's best bargains—but get there early! *Moderate.*

Like a British pub, but ten times friendlier

THE RED CRAB PUB
A favorite meeting and eating spot among Grenadians and visitors located on Lance aux Epines Road. You can dine in the cozy pub or al fresco under the

trees. Fish and chips, a delightfully-spicy bar-b-qued chicken, chile con carne, fried conch, mixed seafood plate, grilled meats, crab backs, and garlic bread are among Barbara and Reg Blamphin's popular specialties. After luncheon or dinner, stay on to try your hand at a game of darts. *Moderate.*

Nightlife

There are three nightclub/discothèques on Grenada. The atmosphere is free and easy, hours are elastic, the music is eclectic and Grenadians troop there in great numbers on weekends. *Sugar Mill* disco between Grand Anse beach and L'ance aux Epines is a vintage 1750 rum distillery converted into a night spot. Wednesday night features jazz; reggae and disco Friday, Saturday, and Sunday after 9 PM. *Blancos Beach Club,* or the BBC as it is called, is a waterside disco on Quarantine beach. Saturday night is best. When the dancing gets too hot, you can always step outside and take in the view and gaze at the stars as you can at *Loveboat,* next to Grenada Yacht services, but only on Fridays.

The *major hotels* offer more subdued entertainment, with variations on steel or calypso bands. At any of these minitropical resorts, you can dine to the sound of music or stop by later for a drink and dancing in the veranda-like bars overlooking the sea.

For a very special evening, check the Tourist Office for the schedule of the Marryshow Folk Theatre. This new cultural center stages dance exhibitions, musical and theatrical performances and poetry readings. Performers may be local, from other islands or from abroad, but the entertainment is always lively and the setting is unique. The theatre is constructed on the property of a Victorian tropical townhouse built in 1917 by the late T. Albert Marryshow, a prominent, well-loved Grenadian. Be sure to visit the house itself and take an intermission rum punch in the landscaped gardens looking over the lights of St. George's.

Shopping

Shopping in Grenada is limited, and the best bargains are not always found in small shops. Lying on your beach lounge without moving a sun-splashed muscle, you can purchase print cotton sundresses; bits of black coral; spice baskets filled with nutmeg, cloves, cinnamon, mace, saffron or bay leaf; Loofa sponges; woven hats of island straw; or coconut candies from Bernice, Angela, June, or any of the local ladies who gently approach you with their wares. But do be sure to bargain not only because it's expected but because there's quite a difference if you're talking U.S. dollars and they're talking local currency, the EC (Eastern Caribbean) dollar!

When you wander into the capital, St. George's, it's the *Yellow Poui Art Gallery* (on the Esplanade and in Fontenoy, 8 minutes north) for the best selection of art. Jim Rudin, a native New Yorker who was once connected with the New York Museum of Modern Art, has watercolors, oils, seragraphs, engravings and drawings ranging from primitive to highly sophisticated. He also offers antique charts and more recent sculptures and photographs.

For gifts, don't miss Grencraft, the retail outlet of the Grenada National Institute of Handicrafts, also on the Esplanade. Here you'll find straw, wood, bamboo and coconut work; basketry; crocheted items; brown and black coral jewelry; Spice Isle nectars, jams, chutneys, jellies, coffees, sauce and spice baskets; cloth collages; four-poster beds and other furniture all created in Grenada. There are often interesting exhibitions held in the gallery area and it's sometimes possible to visit the workshop classes upstairs. Over on Young Street, is *Tikal,* owned by U.S. expatriate Jeannie Fisher. Her stock is slightly more sophisticated, with many imported items. This is one of the few places that carry Grenada's knock-out liqueur of rum and citrus called *de la*

Try also the yummy guava jelly

Grenade (about $6). The *Blind Handicraft Shop* next to the Turtle Back restaurant and *Noah's Arkade* on Cross Street are two more good stops for local souvenirs and handicrafts.

On the Carenage is *Sea Change,* a tiny shop with an excellent selection of British and U.S. paperbacks (both new and used) as well as West Indian cookbooks, anthologies, children's books, prints, charts, and maps. Pick up a copy of Frances Kay's colorful and amusing profile *This is Grenada* here along with photographic supplies, post cards, shells, spices, even some selected black coral pieces.

The Gift Shop in the Grand Anse shopping center is worth a visit for its crystal and china (Spode, Coalport, Royal Worcester, Waterford, Lalique, Orrefors). Prices are under what you would pay in the United States, from 40% to 60% depending on what you hope to purchase and *if* it's in stock. (The newer patterns are sometimes not available.) It would be a good idea to check hometown prices before your trip.

This modern commercial center also has a beauty salon, record shop, shoe store, supermarket and, just in case you and your luggage didn't arrive together, shop *His 'N Hers.* This is a good address to remember for basic resort wear for the whole family as well as a nice collection of Batik Creole original designs (dress and pareo lengths, scarves, bikinis and other ready to wear). Nearby, the *Spice Island Inn Boutique* stocks a small but tasteful collection of clothing for ladies and some original accessories and gift items. In town, you might turn up a find or two in one of the small dress boutiques; and *Charles of Grenada,* a spacious three-level store on the Esplanade, carries Daks, Liberty, and other British imports for men and women.

Fishermen—deep-sea and underwater, amateur and professional—will find everything they need at *Marine World* on Church Street. This well organized shop prides itself on having the island's most complete selection of rods, reels, lines, spearguns, aqualungs, regulators AND spare parts. Repairs are also made. Hours here are 8 AM to 4 PM Monday through Friday; 8 AM to noon on Saturday.

The newest and prettiest addition to the St. George's Carenage area is *Spice Island Perfumes Ltd.,* a French-Grenadian enterprise that's a store and a factory combined. The perfumes, body oils, natural extracts, potpourris, and teas are made from Grenada's spices and flowers. The salespeople are most willing to explain how the fragrances are captured and invite you to try the unusual tropical scents. Their "Carriacou" line of sun products is excellent, with the after-sun moisturizer one of the best we've tried.

Sports

Choose: There are about 80 miles of coast and more than 65 bays in Grenada. Sixty-five bays with 45 sandy beaches or craggy coastline framed by the gentle blue Caribbean Sea or the more active Atlantic Ocean. The private curves of coast are perfect for an allover tan, beach picnic à deux (packed by your hotel), snorkeling or scuba diving. The more populated beaches offer everything from windsurfing to waterskiing.

Fishing buffs can hug the shore in small powerboats searching for a finned dinner for two or can take up the challenge of serious deep-sea fishing for yellowfin tuna, marlin or dolphin *(not* the mammal; another species of fish), kingfish, wahoo. An International Game Fishing Tournament takes place each January or February.

Underwater explorers (either snorkelers or scuba divers) share this watery home with hundreds of varieties of fish and over 40 species of coral. Many reefs have over 120 feet of visibility, and there are several shipwrecks that attract both resident fish and nonresident divers.

Grand Anse Beach (where several hotels are located) is the center for

[handwritten margin note: Grande Anse is one of the Caribbean's best beaches]

daytime water sports and splashes. This two-mile curve of sand merges into the gentle waters of the Caribbean that are perfect for hesitant novices as well as sprinting swimmers or divers. A cocktail (bring it with you, or go to a hotel patio) sets the mood for a fiery sunset and a last swim of the day.

A full range of *water sports* may be found on the beach between the Holiday Inn and Spice Island Inn—jet skis ($10 for 15 minutes); paddleboats ($10 an hour); catamarans ($12 per hour); speedboat adventures ($100 for four hours, or $200 for eight hours), which can be combined with snorkeling on some of the various offshore islands; windsurfers ($10 an hour); and Sunfish ($8 an hour). Hotels in the L'ance aux Epines section have small Sunfish for their guests' use at no additional cost.

As one of the gateways to the Grenadine chain of islands, Grenada has been a traditional favorite port of call for yachtsmen. Sailors can sample some of the nautical life on ketches, sloops and schooners, all with professional crews for a daylong or full week's charter. Grenada Yacht Services has complete facilities for charter yachts or shorter day trips. The 45-foot *Papagallo* and other boats will take guests for six hours of sailing, snorkeling and sunbathing for $25 a person or deep-sea fishing for $40 an hour, a maximum of four fishermen. (They provide the rum punch; you bring your own lunch packed by your hotel.) Spice Island Charters offers day trips ($150 for six people), with skippers, crew and rum punches or weeklong sailing trips ($1,050 to $3,000, in season); provisioning of the ship is additional, as is the tip for the crew. Day charters ($20 per person); fishing ($30 per person, equipment provided); a cocktail sailing at sunset on Friday (for $12.50 a person); and scuba-diving trips daily 10:00 AM to 4:00 PM ($55 per person with lunch provided) may be arranged through Carin Travel in Grand Anse or Grenada Tours & Travel in town.

For another seagoing adventure, take the drive to Woburn Cove and have a fisherman take you out to Glovers Island or contact Ronald St. Bernard (Tel. 5407) who will take you snorkeling, fishing or shelling around Hog or Calivigny islands ($20–$25 per hour). It's one of Grenada's best snorkeling and private picnic places.

And it's always possible to negotiate *daylong sailing* or *powerboat trips* to Grenada's island offshoots. But here the bargaining is individual, and you're on your own. Better yet, enlist the help of your hotel manager. He knows everyone!

Land challenges come with a good *game of tennis* at a handful of hotels: Secret Harbor; Twelve Degrees North; Calabash; the Holiday Inn. Several private clubs—Richmond Hills and Tanteen Tennis Club—also have courts and will arrange temporary memberships for visitors (at a small fee). It's also a good way to meet Grenadians and perhaps arrange volleys with them.

The Grenada Golf and Country Club between St. George's and Grand Anse (Tel. 4576), has a *nine-hole golf course,* with views of both the Atlantic Ocean and the Caribbean Sea and sandtraps! Many a spliced ball has headed out to sea. An experienced golfer is available for instruction. Greens fee–$5 U.S. per day; club rental–$2; caddy fee $1.

Several of the island's spectator sports are played Saturday mornings near the capital of St. George's from January to May. That's *cricket,* one of the national passions. Another, *soccer,* runs rampant from July through December at the fields of the Botanical Gardens.

Guadeloupe

THE HARD FACTS
Planning Ahead
Costs

With the French franc fluctuating so much right now, it is very difficult to know what the U.S. dollar exchange rate will be next week, much less next month, and this is important in judging prices. At the present rate, Guadeloupe, largely undiscovered by Americans, can be considered one of the Caribbean's best values.

A double room with breakfast in a major resort hotel in season (mid-December–mid-April) will run well below $100 a day. Smaller hotels' prices average around $65 per day, also with breakfast, for two. A package such as "Fête Française"—three- and seven-night programs, including special features such as American-style buffet breakfast, round-trip transfers, a welcome drink, a bottle of rum or wine in your room, one dinner, taxes and service charges—can provide even more savings. Off-season rates go down as much as 45%. Your travel agent or airline will be able to furnish you with the most up-to-date details and prices.

Restaurant prices vary widely—from about $8 per person for an excellent four-course Creole meal at one of the many small restaurants around the island; to $35+ per person at the elegant La Plantation, Guadeloupe's most expensive dining spot.

Note: As long as the dollar is strong do not prepay hotel and meals in dollars before departure from home. A deposit will be necessary, but for substantial savings, leave the balance to be paid in French francs or with a credit card locally.

Climate

Tropical but tempered year round by trade winds, called "les Alizés." Temperatures along the coast average 72°F. to 86°F.; inland from 66°F. to 81°F. The dry season extends from January to April; the rainier (showers may be strong but are of short duration), more humid period from July to December.

Exchange rate at presstime was 8 francs to the U.S. dollar

101

Holidays and Special Events

Public holidays include New Year's Day (Jan. 1); Mid-Lent (March 29, 1984); Easter Monday (April 23, 1984); Labor Day (May 1); Ascension Day (May 31, 1984); Pentecost Monday (June 11, 1984); Bastille Day (July 14); Schoelcher Day (July 21); Assumption Day (August 15); All Saints Day (Nov. 1); Armistice Day (Nov. 11); and Christmas Day (Dec. 25).

Victor Schoelcher abolished slavery here in 1848

Carnival—celebrated from the Sunday after Epiphany through Ash Wednesday. Each Sunday masked dancers frolic in the streets; and various competitions—Miss Carnival, best beguine, beguine vidé, songfests—are organized. Five days of marathon merriment begin the Saturday before Shrove Tuesday, when everyone converges on Pointe-à-Pitre to participate in the traditional parades, parties and balls. The largest parade is presided over by Vaval, King Carnival, and his Queen on Shrove Tuesday; there are elaborate floats, bands, costumes, singing and dancing. The finale comes on Ash Wednesday, when black and white dress is de rigeur for the mourning celebrations when Vaval is burned and buried until next year.

Fête des Cuisinières—the Festival of Cooks is one of Guadeloupe's most animated and colorful events. It takes place annually on the Saturday nearest August 11. On this day, in honor of St. Laurent, the patron saint of cooks, nearly 100 women chefs parade in full Creole costume—madras headdresses, gold jewelry, silk foulards, starched white aprons, and full-skirted, multipetticoated madras dresses. Each carries an elaborately decorated platter of food, flowers and baskets trimmed with miniature kitchen utensils to the Pointe-à-Pitre Cathedral to celebrate High Mass. This is followed by the preparation of a 5-hour feast at the Ecole Amédée Fengarol (rue Henri IV, Pointe-à-Pitre), where the rum flows freely, spirits rise and the beguine plays on. Attendance is limited, and visitors who wish to join the fun should request their free invitations from their hotel activity desks in advance of the festival.

Tour Operators

In the United States—Adventure Tours; Butler Tours; Caribbean Holidays; Cavalcade Tours; Club Med; Flyfaire; Gogo Tours; Hollywood Travel; Jet Vacations; Natrac; Skinny Dip; Tour Trec International; Travel Center; and Travel Light. In Canada—Club Med; Tours Chantecler; Holiday House Multitour and Tours Mt.-Royal.

Sources of Information

In the United States—contact the *French West Indies Tourist Board,* 610 Fifth Avenue, New York, N.Y. 10020 or the *French Government Tourist Office,* 9401 Wilshire Blvd., Beverly Hills, Cal. 90212. They will be glad to furnish information by mail. Telephone or in-person inquiries should be directed to the *French Government Tourist Office, Public Information Service,* 628 Fifth Avenue, New York, N.Y. 10020; tel. (212) 757–1125.

In Canada—contact the *French Government Tourist Office,* 1840 Sherbrooke Ouest, Montreal, Quebec; 109PQ; Tel. (514) 931–3855 or 372 Bay Street, Toronto, Ontario M5H2W9; Tel. (416) 361–1605.

In Pointe-à-Pitre, the *Office du Tourisme* is located on Place de la Victoire; Tel. 82–09–36. Hours are 9:00 A.M.–noon; 2:00 P.M. to 5:00 P.M.; Friday; 9:00 A.M.–noon, Saturday. The cordial, English-speaking staff can furnish an excellent large map of the island, helpful brochures and plenty of good advice. Their informative publication *Bonjour Guadeloupe* in both English and French is designed especially for visitors and contains information about hotels, sightseeing, restaurants, shopping and entertainment as well as history and culture.

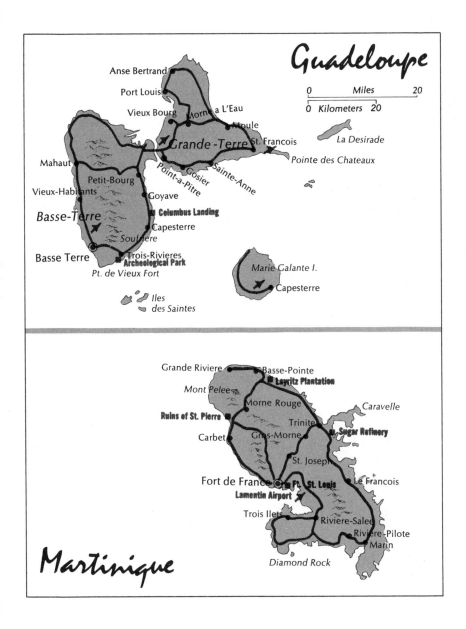

Packing

Lightweight, casual clothing year round, the same as is worn in any summer resort at home. Women will be most comfortable in cotton dresses, skirts and pants; beachwear is not acceptable in urban areas where the Guadeloupean woman is always dressed fashionably and in good taste. Men should include lightweight pants, bermudas and shorts; a jacket and a tie are seldom if ever necessary. Sunglasses, beach cover-ups and a straw hat should not be forgotten; comfortable walking shoes and a sweater or a shawl for the Parc

Naturel and the hilly areas around Basse Terre. Even though prices are by no means inexpensive, visitors will find it hard to resist the chic Parisian and locally-made styles available in the boutiques.

Documentation

U.S. and Canadian citizens need a valid passport. This alone is good for three months; longer stays require a visa.

Getting There

American Airlines offers direct jet service from New York and connecting flights from Dallas and San Francisco (via Miami or San Juan). Eastern Airlines serves Guadeloupe via connecting flights from Miami, and Point-à-Pitre can now be included in Eastern's Unlimited Mileage Fare for a small surcharge. Air France flies from Miami, Port-au-Prince, San Juan and Fort-de-France; Air Canada connects Montreal and Toronto with Guadeloupe. Interisland service is provided by Air Guadeloupe, LIAT and Prinair. During the winter season, cruise ships from the Chandris Line, Costa Line, Cunard, Holland America, Flagship Line, Hapag Lloyd, Norwegian-American, Norwegian-Caribbean and Royal Caribbean Cruise Line call at Pointe-à-Pitre.

Formalities on Arrival

Customs

Items for personal use, in limited quantities, are permitted tax-free entry. Included are one bottle of spirits, three bottles of wine, 400 cigarettes and 125 cigars, two still cameras and 20 rolls of film, one movie camera and 10 rolls of film; one transistor radio, one portable musical instrument; one recording machine with two rolls of tape and one pair of binoculars.

Money

Good news is the exchange rate at presstime — 8 to the dollar.

The French franc is the legal tender; notes and coins are the same as in continental France. U.S. and Canadian dollars are accepted in most establishments, as are major credit cards and travelers' checks. A 20% discount is offered for certain luxury items purchased with travelers' checks. The current exchange rate, which fluctuates daily, is 7.01 FF = $1.00 U.S. The best rates can be obtained from local banks, but these differ from bank to bank, so it's best to investigate several. At our last check BNP and Banque Populaire gave the highest exchange rate; Chase Manhattan the lowest.

Getting into Town

By rental car or taxi only. Rates are posted at the Information Desk just outside the customs area at Le Raizet Airport and in the publication *Bonjour Guadeloupe.* Be sure to check one of these since taxis do not all yet have meters. Settle on your price before leaving the airport. From 9:00 P.M. to 7:00 A.M. there is a 33% night fare surcharge. Sample rates from Le Raizet to popular hotel areas are: Gosier—48 FF; Bas-du-Fort—41.50 FF; Sainte-Anne—89.50 FF; Saint-François—137 FF.

Settling Down

Choosing a Hotel

Guadeloupe now offers about 3,000 rooms—in large resort complexes such as the 273-room Hotel Méridien; small 20-room country inns such as the Relais du Moulin in Chateaubrun or the hotel school Relais de la Grande Soufrière in St. Claude; or simple bungalow accommodations (10) at the Auberge du Grand Large right on one of the island's best beaches at Sainte-Anne. Most hotels are along beaches and larger facilities offer all water sports, entertainment, restaurants and every other amenity visitors could ask for.

Villas, apartments and private rooms are also available through the "Gites de France," which maintains an office at the Tourist Bureau that keeps a list of such properties ranging from simple retreats to comfortable villas.

Gites = resting places

Choosing a Restaurant

It's very difficult to have a bad meal in Guadeloupe. Top restaurants and hotel dining rooms offer Continental, classic French and Creole specialties excellently prepared and presented. But the real fun of eating here is in discovering one of the small, out-of-the-way, Creole places—some are beachside cafes, some in-town bistros, others the front or the back porches of the cooks' homes. Creole food is a blend of French and African, with a bit of East Indian to put spice into dining. The owners of these small culinary corners, usually women, have been aptly named "High Priestesses of Culinary Art"; they are usually ebullient and charming, and if you familiarize yourself with just a few of the local specialties and take along a small phrase book, you'll have a memorable meal. Classic French, nouvelle cuisine, Continental, Italian, Vietnamese, North African, Argentinian, Spanish and Swiss restaurants are among the choices that this island of over 100 restaurants has to offer.

Tipping

A 10%–15% service charge is generally added to all bills; if you are not sure, always ask, "Le service est compris?" Taxi drivers and hotel porters do not generally expect a tip, so base your judgment on the service rendered.

Learning to Cope

Business Hours. Shops generally open at 8:00 or 8:30 A.M. and close for lunch at 12:30 P.M. Most reopen at 2:30 P.M., and closing time ranges from 6:00 in town up to 7:00 in the galleries and shopping centers. Most shops close at 1:00 P.M. on Saturday, with the exception of those in the Centre Commercial in the Bas du Fort Marina. *Banking hours* are 8:00 A.M.–noon and 2:00 P.M.–4:00 P.M., Monday to Friday. In July, August and September, banking hours are continuous from 8:00 A.M. to 3:00 P.M. The day before a legal holiday that falls during the week, banks close at noon.

Electricity. 220 volts, AC; 50 cycles. To use American appliances, a French adapter (round plug) and a current converter are necessary. Hotels have these items in limited supply, so, if possible, bring your own.

Water and Drink. Tap water is potable everywhere. The local bottled mineral waters—Capès-Dolé and Matouba—are delicious, refreshing and very healthful!

Communications. *To telephone* direct from the United States, dial 011–596 plus the local number for station-to-station calls; 01–596 and the local number for person-to-person calls. Direct dialing is not possible from Canada. From Guadeloupe, overseas calls to the United States and Canada go through an English-speaking operator. Local information is 12. *Post office hours* are 8:00 A.M. to 5:30 P.M., Monday to Friday; closed at lunch time and on Saturday afternoons and Sunday.

Airmail postage rates to the United States are 1.40 FF for postcards and 2.50 FF for 15 gramletters; to Canada, 1.20 FF for postcards and 2 FF for 15 gramletters. Stamps can be purchased at post offices, cafés tabacs and hotel desks.

Language. French and Creole are the national languages. There is always someone who speaks English in the larger hotels, shops and restaurants—but non-French-speaking travelers should not leave home or their hotels without a phrase book and a pocket dictionary.

Medical Assistance.   Guadeloupe is well equipped with modern medical facilities. There are five hospitals and 23 clinics. Hotels or the Office du Tourisme can assist in finding an English-speaking doctor if needed.

Getting Around

By Car

Major international car rental agencies—Avis, Budget, Hertz and Europcar (National)—all have desks at Le Raizet Airport just outside the customs area, as do the smaller local companies—D'Arbaud, Guadeloupe Cars, Jumbo, Narcisse, Penchard, Pentier and Sol Tour. Major hotels have car-rental desks as well. Most rentals are by the day or by the week plus kilometer charges, tax (7.5%), insurance and gasoline.

Some unlimited-mileage plans are also available. Cars available include Citroen, Fiat, mini-moke, Peugeot, Renault, and Toyota, usually with stick shifts. Automatic and air-conditioned cars are available but at a much higher rate. A U.S. driver's license is valid for rental. Traffic regulations are basically the same as in the States, with one very important exception—"priorité a droite"—cars coming from the right always have the right of way.

By Moped

Unless you are very familiar with the island, the machine and French driving techniques, this mode of travel is not recommended, especially in town. Competent cyclists may rent motorbikes through Erick, 9 rue de la République in Pointe-à-Pitre (Tel: 82–21–86); in Gosier, Cyclo Tours on Blvd du Général de Gaulle (Tel: 84–11–34 or 84–13–27). In St.-François, Loca Moto, in the Marina.

By Taxi

Taxi rates are posted at the airport, in principal hotels, at the Office du Tourisme and the port. Radio taxis may be contacted by calling—82–42–73; 82–14–21; 82–15–09; 82–54–87; or 82–27–19. Rates increase by one-third from 9:00 P.M. until 7:00 A.M.. Some taxi drivers speak some English, but your phrase book and pocket dictionary will be useful.

By Bus

Buses operate from 6:00 A.M. until 6:00 P.M. and link all the towns of the island. For those who understand some French, this is one of the best and least expensive ways to get around, see the island and meet the people. Bus stops are marked "arrêt-bus," and a wave to the driver stops the bus. Fares are paid when you get off.

GUADELOUPE TODAY

This region of France has been geographically described as a butterfly, for its two halves, Basse-Terre and Grande-Terre. The eastern wing, Grande-Terre, houses the island's hotels, boutiques, discothèques and restaurants; the western wing, Basse-Terre, contains many of the sights and scenes.

You *must* have a working knowledge of French to enjoy the beauties and the special ambience of Guadeloupe. Even in Paris, or on the equally French sister-islands of Martinique and St. Barts, you can get by using English. In Guadeloupe, you really can't rely on English if you want to enjoy this wonderful island.

Almost all Guadeloupeans will tell you that they encourage visitors from everywhere. But most will still tell you in French. North Americans would like everyone to speak English. Guadeloupeans prefer that you speak French. The

The two halves are really two islands, connected by a bridge

solution is a compromise. Go to this special island armed with a French-English dictionary, and plan on using it.

There's also the matter of the Guadeloupean façade. That translates into a proud mien. Guadeloupeans do not always smile or engage in idle chatter in any language. It's merely their way. This is an island-nation where linguistic and other barriers have emerged into an expression that doesn't always look like a smile. But this seeming inscrutability is just part of the privacy and the personality of Guadeloupe.

If you're intrigued and interested, then this may be the experience for you. Pack your French lessons, and head for the airport after you've thrown half a swimsuit (for women) into your suitcase. Like most places that are truly French, no one bothers with the top half of a bikini.

Perhaps a strong sense of identity is the key to Guadeloupe—be yourself. Also, expect that the people of Guadeloupe will be equally *themselves.* A meeting of both nationalities can be fruitful, and it doesn't have to be at the summit of Mt. Soufrière, about 4,812 feet in the clouds. Instead, try a smile and a "Je regrette . . . Je ne parle pas correctement Français." You just might get a smile in return and a "regret" that "the English" is not perfect, either.

The people will welcome you to Guadeloupe, an island that moves more in the mode of a cotillion than a beguine. Its unique charms include a natural park that sprawls across one-fifth of the entire island. You are reminded of Eden as you wander through cool mountain paths tangled with trees of mountain olive, palmetto, white chestnut, red gum-tree, cinnamon, elephant ears and then discover waterfalls, clear lakes, tumbling rivers, even small picnic groves with tables set in private pagodas. Ask for a description of the bois bander tree. It's believed to be an aphrodisiac, and you'll know you've encountered it when you spot many trees with their barks scraped off by Guadeloupeans who boil it into love potions.

Guadeloupe is emerging—from its cocoon stage into its mature butterfly stage.

TOURING

Guadeloupe is a *big* island that offers many touring possibilities; but day trips are long and are thus best done in stages. Guided tours to the various points of interest (by bus) may be arranged through *Petreluzzi Travel* (82–43–41 or 82–13–99), or *Georges Marie Gabrielle* (82–05–38 or 82–91–11), the two operators best equipped to guide English-speaking visitors. Petreluzzi is one of Guadeloupe's largest agencies, whereas Gabrielle's service is a bit more friendly and personalized. Both are very capable having accumulated plenty of experience with foreign visitors, and both have representatives at major hotels and Le Raizet Airport. For those who prefer discovering the island on their own, sightseeing by taxi or by rental car can be easily done by following the self-drive brochure available from the Bureau du Tourisme.

Pointe-à-Pitre, the commercial, industrial and shipping center on Grande-Terre, is a crowded, bustling, prosperous port. In the market a fisherman proffers his day's catch between a madras-dressed spice lady, whose strange and fragrant condiments are spread out in neat bundles before her, and a mound of mangos, avocados, passion fruit, guavas and corossol. The sound of laughter and lilting Creole rises and falls as the haggling goes on from stall to stall. Beautiful rose-colored anthuriums are sold on the street corner; an old woman lugs a large, wrapped bundle of heart of palm, encouraging passersby to make her an offer; elegant Pointoise (as the female residents of Pointe-à-Pitre are called) window-shop in the latest Parisian fashions; and horns honk impatiently in a real Parisian-style traffic jam. Down

Pointe-à-Pitre is not the most beautiful capital in the Caribbean

at the docks, boats of every size, shape and color load and unload exotic cargo and beladen passengers. This is a city where your senses really come alive, provoked by all the fascinating sounds, sights and smells.

The Place de la Victoire is where Victor Hugues defeated the English in 1794, when Pointe-à-Pitre was just a vast marsh surrounded by hills. Unfortunately, half this beautiful park has now been made into a parking lot, but the other half is still a relatively calm oasis with centuries-old royal palm, sandbox, mango and flamboyant trees offering shade from the hot midday sun. Pretty, old, colonial-style wooden houses surround the square and add more color with their brightly-painted balconied facades.

Big modern office, government and apartment complexes present a sharp contrast as you head out of the city toward the beaches and resort areas of the eastern part of Grande-Terre. Drive by the handsome university, newly-built condominiums (some of them are half sold, and the ground has barely been broken for construction), shopping centers and the boat basins of Bas-du-Fort at the base of historic Fort Fleur d'Epée. From these 18th-century ramparts there is an impressive view of Grand-Baie, Gosier Beach and its hotels and the Ilet de Gosier with its red lighthouse just offshore.

Gosier, today Guadeloupe's most popular playground, with seven hotels, fishing, water sports, a host of restaurants, nightclubs and a casino, was an important coffee- and cotton-cultivation center in the 18th-century. Many Pointois businessmen and women come here for lunch and to escape the oppressive midday heat of Pointe-à-Pitre.

Farther east, rolling limestone hills, sugarcane fields and abandoned mills come into view. The shoreline is studded with white sand and reef-protected beaches, where the water is bright turquoise blue. Sainte-Anne has one of the island's best beaches and is one of Guadeloupe's prettiest villages as well. Fifteen kilometers farther is the beautiful Raisins Clairs beach just outside St. François. St. François was a tiny, sleepy fishing village less than ten years ago. Now it's a major resort and residential center, with three hotels, a fine 18-hole golf course, a small airport, restaurants, a casino, a shopping center, a new yacht basin and villas and condominiums in profusion. From here it's a short ride to Pointe des Châteaux (Castle Point), where the Atlantic Ocean and the Caribbean Sea meet and the waves beat against the jagged rocks before being swallowed up by the Trou de Souffleur. On either side of this point are safe, sandy beaches, one reserved for bathing in the buff and enjoying the excellent views of the islands of Desirade and Petite-Terre in the distance.

Return to Pointe-à-Pitre via picturesque cane fields, windmills and the village of Le Moule, once the capital. Before reaching this once-important sugar port—one of the island's oldest settlements—you may want to look at the elegant colonial mansion on the right side of the road at Zévalos. The garden is a well-tended mass of flowers, but the shutters have been closed for years, as it is said that this beautiful, balconied house is haunted.

Le Moule has a pretty town square with an 18th-century church, a nice view from the ruins of the old fort and some excellent Indian restaurants on the beach. You might pass through the Grands Fonds region where chalk hills (mornes) alternate with deep valleys (fonds) full of mango and breadfruit trees. Nearby are the small wooden houses of the last descendants of the "Blancs Matignon," a community of about 400 farmers. These blond-haired, blue-eyed people are said to be of noble blood—Comtes de Matignon, de Montmorency, even Bourbon stock—whose ancestors took refuge in this area during the French Revolution when noble heads were falling right and left. After slavery was abolished in 1848, they were too poor to hire workers to work their land, and so they became farmers themselves. To this day they have never been assimilated into society, marrying exclusively among themselves. The road continues through vegetable farms and sugarcane fields to

[handwritten margin note:] Ste.-Anne boasts a statue of local hero Schoelcher in the Place de la Victoire

[handwritten margin note:] Le Moule was an important town until the hurricane of 1928

the large, residential suburb of Abymes, named after the mangrove marsh that once entirely covered this area. A whole day should be allowed for this excursion in order to enjoy the sights and to have a leisurely lunch at one of the many small restaurants along the road to Pointe des Châteaux.

Another full-day tour will take you to the northernmost tip of Grande-Terre. From Pointe-à-Pitre, follow the road back through Abymes, Morne à l'Eau and Le Moule. From here turn north through sugarcane fields and the pleasant little hamlets of Ste.-Marguerite, Gros Cap and Campèche to the dramatic high cliffs of Porte d'Enfer (the Gates of Hell). There's a charming legend that a certain Mme. Coco was walking across the waves one day, carrying a parasol, when she suddenly disappeared! A few miles farther north is La Pointe de la Grande Vigie (Big Lookout Point), one of the island's most beautiful places. Stark cliffs rise abruptly from the Atlantic and paths lead to the very extremity of the point for a superb view of the sea below—la Pointe de la Petite Tortue (Little Turtle Point)—and back to the Porte d'Enfer.

Now head back down the opposite coast to Anse Bertrand, one of the last refuges of the Carib Indians, who, after fierce fighting, retreated to this spot. There are several good places to stop for lunch in Port Louis and then maybe take a swim and sun yourself on the lovely golden beach—Plage du Souffleur—or farther down the coast at Petit Canal, where there is a pretty 17th-century church and a working sugar factory. Continue on the same road to Morne à l'Eau and back to Pointe-à-Pitre.

For a change of pace and a respite from driving, The Papyrus (Tel: 82–87–26), Guadeloupe's "Bateau Mouche" moored in Bas-du-Fort, does a day excursion that visits the port and crosses the Rivière Salée to Caret Island for swimming, snorkeling and lunch. The evening cruise includes a barbecue under the stars at the Ilet Gosier, free cocktails, dining and dancing until midnight.

Balancing the beach attractions of Grande-Terre are the natural, unspoiled scenic attractions of Basse-Terre, the southwestern, volcanic island. Basse and Grande describe not the terrain but the low and high winds that blow over these two islands. Guadeloupe's capital city, Basse-Terre, is located here.

Leave Pointe-à-Pitre via the new bridge over the Rivière Salée that separates the two wings of the butterfly island of Guadeloupe. Pass through the center of the sugarcane industry at Lamentin, and take the turnoff for Prise d'Eau with its colorful washday scenes. Take a few minutes to visit Vernou, an elegant, residential mountain suburb with weekend villas set amid tropical vegetation and flowers of every variety and color. Then look for the sign for La Traversée, a shortcut to the rugged Caribbean coast that cuts west across the huge 74,100-acre Natural Park, the only preserve of its kind in the Caribbean, via the Deux Mamelles (Pass of the Two Breasts). Marked hiking trails are everywhere, as are rustic picnic areas with tables set in the shade. One must stop is at the Cascade aux Ecrévisses, just a five-minute walk from the parking lot, for a swim in the cool pool at the base of the falls. Get a complete guide with maps, walking trails and points of interest from the Office du Tourisme in Pointe-à-Pitre before leaving. Hikers and casual walkers will enjoy the many paths leading to peaks such as Morne à Louis for a breathtakingly-beautiful view of the mountains and the valleys; through lush foliage; by falls, lakes and rivers—you could spend days here. You probably will also see many exotic birds and forest animals, none poisonous or dangerous, maybe even a raccoon, the park's official mascot. At the Maison de la Forêt, in the heart of the forest, the different kinds of vegetation to be found in the park are identified, and certain, special walks, as well as a slide show on the forest itself, have been devised to enhance your appreciation.

After exploring this part of the Natural Park, continue on to Mahault, and turn south along the leeward coast. The road curves up and down offering

Ecrevisse = crayfish

Leeward means western here

fabulous views extending from Malendure Beach to Ilet Pigeon (excursion boats carry snorkelers and sightseers back and forth all day). Pass Bouillante, a spa with hot springs and geysers; Anse La Barque, with its perfect horseshoe bay; Guadeloupe's oldest church in Vieux-Habitants; and, just before Rocroy Beach, a good view of La Soufrière, if it's not completely covered by clouds. The city of Basse-Terre is not oriented to tourists, but among the sights are Fort St. Charles, built in 1643; a colorful marketplace; the tranquil gardens of the Préfecture; a cathedral and the pilgrimage church of Mont-Carmel; and the Place du Champ-d'Arbaud, surrounded by old colonial houses.

We would suggest continuing 5 km. farther to St. Claude, the cool, elegant, flower-filled suburb in the hills, which is also the location of the Relais de la Grande Soufrière. This hotel school offers comfortable lodging (and do be sure to ask for one of the charming second-floor duplexes) in what was an army rest-and-recreation center over 100 years ago. After a fine dinner and a good night's rest, you'll be ready to tackle the volcano of La Soufrière early the next morning.

In 1976–1977, when La Soufrière started acting up, this entire area was evacuated for several months. Visit the *Maison du Volcan,* just opposite the Relais, where an interesting slide show depicts the events leading to the last eruption; then head up to the volcano. You start to smell the sulfur and see white fumes rising out of roadside cliffs as you follow the twisting road. Unless you go very early in the morning, your chances of seeing the 4,813-foot peak devoid of its usual shroud of mist and clouds are about 50/50. You'll be surprised how cool, almost cold, it is when you reach the lower parking lot. From here you must continue by foot; there is a large map ranking several trails by time and by degree of difficulty, and a guide is recommended for some of the more difficult climbs. But you don't have to climb at all to see the smoking fumeroles; a few of these wisps of hot, sulfurous vapors have penetrated the area right near the parking lot. Once sated with the eerie wonders of La Soufrière, head back down to Matouba for lunch at one of the small restaurants where giant crayfish from nearby mountain streams are considered a highly-prized delicacy. Depending on the time, continue on to Gourbeyre, and do the not-too-difficult excursion to the As de Pique (Ace of Spades) Lake; visit the Archaeological Park with petroglyphs—Carib drawings and inscriptions on the rocks—in the pretty fishing village of Trois Rivières (where boats also depart for Les Saintes); on to St.-Saveur, and its banana plantations and the walk to Carbet Falls (Les Chutes des Carbet), a three-tiered waterfall on the Carbet River that begins with boiling hot water on the east side of La Soufrière and flows cool into the sea at Capesterre. The total drop is about 800 feet. The first level entails an easy, half-an-hour hike; the second, another 20 minutes; but the third and the highest involves a rather difficult trek of over two hours. After this visit, your route continues through Capesterre, with its many flamboyant trees, and the Allée Dumanier, a stretch of the road lined with towering, majestic royal palms. There's a monument commemorating Columbus's landing at Sainte-Marie in 1493; Goyave has a lush tropical forest, and from here and Petit Bourg there are some lovely views extending to Pointe-à-Pitre, Grande-Terre and the offshore islands.

A shorter tour of the northern half of Basse-Terre is also worthwhile and should especially appeal to health and beach buffs. Don't forget swimsuits, for there will be several nice beaches all along this route. Cross the Rivière Salée again, and follow the directions for Lamentin and its rich cane fields. Make the short detour to Ravine Chaude, a thermal station where hot springs flow into outdoor swimming pools surrounded by greenery. These sulfurous waters are said to be excellent for fatigue and beneficial to the skin as well. An hour or so here should give you renewed strength. There's a good restaurant as well, one of whose specialties is crayfish. When you're ready, return to

Lamentin and continue to Ste.-Rose, a pretty, small village with several excellent nearby beaches—Les Amandiers; Plage de Clugny; Plage du Petit Bas-Vent, the latter two offering nice views of the small offshore islands of Kakouanne and the Tête à L'Anglais. Next comes the Plage de Grand'Anse, where Columbus was forced to anchor for six days because his party got lost in the thick forest, now a part of the Park Naturel. There's another small sulfur source at Sofaia. Deshaies, a charming two-street (Ruelle 1 and Ruelle 2) village, has two excellent Creole restaurants and a natural harbor that attracts international yachts. One day the government hopes to develop this area into a resort center with yacht basin, hotels and other attractions to lure visitors into spending more time on this side of the island; but, for the moment, it's an unspoiled oasis of empty beaches, tiny villages and coffee, vanilla and cocoa plantations. The scenic road leads past a dazzling procession of rocky promontories. Then it's back onto the Traversée with plenty of time for a more thorough exploration of some of the trails and sights of the Natural Park.

The larger offshore islands of Marie Galante and Les Saintes are best reached by plane; boat trips are too long and too uncomfortable for most visitors. Air Guadeloupe (82–28–35) and Air Antilles (82–12–25) serve both islands.

Marie Galante lies 27 miles southeast of Pointe-à-Pitre, 15 minutes by air. This is a dry, 59-square-mile island with traditions, untouched charm and a population of 16,000 . . . an island of windmills (at least 100); grazing cows; ox-drawn carts; and beautiful long, white-sand beaches protected by offshore reefs. Rum is still produced, and a visit to one of the five working distilleries can be arranged. Grand-Bourg is the major town. There is no deluxe hotel here, but four small hotels—Soledad (8 rooms); Le Quartier Latin (5 rooms); Le Belvédère (7 rooms) and Le Salut (15 rooms) offer simple, pleasant accommodations. Half a dozen restaurants ("lolos"), naturally, specialize in the freshest of seafood. French is a must here, and if you don't "parlez," you may have some difficulties if you're on your own.

Transport around the island is by taxi, rented car or public bus. Among the most interesting sights are Château Murat, an 18th-century manor house that was undergoing restoration but a lack of funds has postponed the completion of the work, at least for the moment; the grotto Trou à Diable (Devil's Hole) with stalactites and an underground lake; dramatic cliffs in the north; the historic fishing hamlet of Vieux Fort; Grand Bourg, the main town, with an 1845 baroque church; and the seaside towns of Capesterre on the southeast and St. Louis, an attractive market town, on the west.

Désirade lies just five miles off the Pointe des Châteaux, Guadeloupe's easternmost point. Air Guadeloupe flies here several times a day in 20 minutes. Its north coast is a tropical wilderness; the west coast contains the spot where Columbus first saw land during his second voyage to the Americas. This is an island completely outside time. It has only one road, and its 1,800 inhabitants, some the descendants of European exiles, make their living from the sea. There's nothing much here except the little village of Grande Anse, pretty homes, the boat-building village of Le Souffleur, the ruins of an 18th-century leprosarium, a cemetery and a couple of good beaches. Still untouched by tourism, this "longed for land" is much the same as it was 300 years ago.

Les Saintes, a small eight-island archipelago (three are inhabited) 82 miles south of Basse-Terre, is a 15-minute flight from Le Raizet Airport. This is one of the Caribbean's most beautiful, unspoiled corners; islands blanketed by tamarinds, cacti and scrub; rimmed with perfect beaches possessing the kinds of shells collectors are always seeking. There are five hotels on Terre-de-Haute—Le Saintoise (10 rooms); Jeanne d'Arc (10 rooms); La Colline (7

Bois Joli has a nude beach

bungalows); Bois Joli (21 rooms) and Kanaoa (8 rooms). In addition to the hotel dining rooms there are several small seafood places that serve another island specialty—"tourment d'amour" (love's torment), a scrumptious coconut tart.

The descendants of Breton fishermen who settled here over 200 years ago, the men still go out at dawn in fast, brightly-colored longboats—"saintois"—with fanciful names—*Dieu est Bon, Concorde, Belle Doudou*—wearing bright orange and yellow slickers and round, flat "Salakos," (straw hats). Shell horns signal their return to hawk their catches on the beach after having spread out their blue nets to dry.

Columbus and his fleet sighted these islands on their second voyage. He named them Todos los Santos for the religious holiday that had just past. The French later dubbed them Les Saintes.

Ft. Napoleon, restored, is one of the Caribbean's most complete forts

Terre-du-Haut is just three miles long and narrow enough so that nothing is more than a 15-minute walk away. In fact, there are very few island vehicles—a couple of taxi-buses and the doctor's car among them. There is only one street or road that follows the curve of the waterfront and divides this island in half. There's not much to see—Mouillage with some pretty villas; Fort Napoleon and the 1,000-foot mountain, Le Chameau (the camel) offering a spectacular view of the channel and the island itself. Swimming is sublime at the beaches of Pont Pierre and l'Anse du Figuier; they offer soft sand and calm, clear water; Anse Crawen is reserved for "au naturel" bathers and sunseekers; Grand'Anse, with huge waves pounding the ochre sand, is only for expert swimmers. Discover the underwater world as Jacques Cousteau has already done; diving equipment is available for rent at the Hotel La Colline, as are small boats and bikes.

Arrange for a fisherman to take you to Terre-de-Bas, more rural than you probably imagine; citizens will turn in genuine surprise as you pass. There is no bistrôt of any kind; no hotel, no pension; virtually no outsider ever sets foot on these shores, and the Grand'Anse beach on this island is an undiscovered paradise.

Inside Information

Hotels

Guadeloupe has a scattering of hotels spread out on its butterfly wings that spread from Basse-Terre to Grande-Terre. Most, however, are clustered on Grande-Terre, which is where the French-based chains are . . . Frantel, Novotel, PLM, Meridien, Club Med . . . and the sole U.S. representative, the Holiday Inn. There are also two "hotel schools" that are unique in their own right and very special to this island.

Smaller Hotels

★★★★ HAMAK HOTEL (ST. FRANÇOIS)
Flower-filled pathways lead through the gardens to 28 bungalows each with two small, one-bedroom suites. All have a fresh blue and white decor, spacious baths, air conditioning, kitchenettes, rear patios with a second entry door and a high surrounding wall to ensure privacy for you and the outdoor shower, and a front porch with a hammock (but those closest to the beach

have the best view and breezes). The hammock theme is carried out to perfection here—hammocks are everywhere. Water sports and tennis are just out your front door and the golf course is across the road. This is a very special corner of the globe, perhaps the finest of Guadeloupe's hotels. *Cost:* $230 per double with full American breakfast, in season.

★★★ RELAIS DE LA GRANDE SOUFRIERE (ST. CLAUDE)
This is one of Guadeloupe's two very special hotel schools and perhaps the biggest find in the Caribbean. You *must* ask for the duplex rooms that are on the second floor. It's not that all of the 20 rooms aren't spotless and nicely decorated. They are. But the duplexes are special, named for famous hotels such as George V, Crillon, Le Ritz and Grand Hotel. These schools are unique in the Caribbean; they train and then help graduates find jobs in their field—from chef or hotel manager, to waitress or waiter. Staying here couldn't be more delightful since the students try hard to help guests— perhaps one of the nicest ways to meet young Guadeloupeans. *Cost:* 275 FF per double CP, in season.

★★★ RELAIS DU MOULIN (CHATEAUBRUN)
The approach to this hotel is through pastures with grazing cows, purple and red bougainvillea growing free. Although this hotel isn't on a beach, there is a large swimming pool and a very nice feeling of being in the French country-side. The beach is not far, however, and there are horses to ride or take on beach picnics. Each of the 20 bungalows has two rooms, a patio where hammocks can be strung, kitchenettes with refrigerators—so you can sip a cup of coffee in the morning and then dash to the pool. This is where there is also a steep winding staircase up to the top of the sugar-mill bar, which, if you're up to the climb, is a very special place to see the sun go down. Owners and staff are particularly kind and helpful, making this inn one of the nicest possible places to be in Guadeloupe. *Cost:* $56 per double CP, in season.

AUBERGE DU GRAND LARGE (STE. ANNE)
An auberge, or inn, owned and operated by lovely Mme. Georges Damico, the property is chockablock with flowers and is mostly geared to accommo-dating couples or families. The rooms, in ten bungalows, are for two or four; they are simple and small and right next to Ste.-Anne Beach, one of the island's loveliest stretches of sand. Hospitality is the theme here, and you'll thoroughly enjoy meeting Mme.'s daughter, Micheline, an Air France purser, and son-in-law, Luc Michaux-Vignes, American Airline's local representa-tive. Both are fluent in English and will do a great deal to make your stay as relaxed and as enjoyable as possible. *Cost:* 350 FF per double CP, in season.

Mme. features excellent Creole cooking

Larger Hotels
★★★★ AUBERGE DE LA VIEILLE TOUR (GOSIER)
While the rooms tend to be on the simple side, this is a favorite of almost everyone who's been here. Many of the staff have been trained at Guade-loupe's unique hotel schools, and these graduates offer special service. The auberge has been built around an 18th-century sugar mill, which will be your lasting memory of this establishment. There are a total of 84 rooms surround-ing balconies that face the sea or La Soufrière. The inn is now part of the Frantel chain, but it's definitely one of the best places to be, with sports of all sorts, from land to sea. *Cost:* $111 per double with full American breakfast, in season.

★★★★ CLUB MEDITERRANÉE, CARAVELLE (STE. ANNE)
This sister club to the one below is set in a beautifully flowered 45-acre property near one of Guadeloupe's prettiest small towns. 540 beds are available in rooms in two low wings of white stone buildings that, like the

island itself, form a butterfly wing, each facing the beach. For tennis buffs, there's a third wing that faces the courts. Sports are a major factor in any Club Méditerranée vacation, and here the range is from wind surfing, snorkeling, sailing, yoga, calisthenics, volleyball, basketball, tennis, *pétanque,* boat trips, day-long picnics, and archery.

Note: Both of Guadeloupe's Clubs Mediterranees will admit outside visitors for a daily fee. This means you are welcome to explore the club, meet the members and consider becoming a member yourself.

★★★★ CLUB MÉDITERRANÉE, FORT ROYAL (DESHAIES)

Smallest of the Club Med operations in the Caribbean

This is the original club on the island; 17 acres housing 300 people in two-person accommodations that keep the feeling for which Club Med is known—friendliness and family atmosphere. There is a Mini Club here for children from four to twelve exclusively, and this is one of the best places for scuba divers. Pigeon Island, a coral bound haven, is only a short distance away, and daily dives are arranged by the Club. There's even an underwater photography laboratory that has been installed for diving masters.

★★★★ MERIDIEN HOTEL (ST. FRANÇOIS)

While this is part of the French chain, it's very well done with 273 large, nicely decorated rooms and all the conveniences Americans are accustomed to. A welcome drink is offered as you check in; there's a large shopping arcade on the ground level for the purchase of perfume, clothing, art, souvenirs, newspapers and paperbacks; all the tour operators have desks here and nightly entertainment is scheduled. Outdoor activities include a very large pool, long white sand beach, water sports galore and several restaurants and bars where service has continued to improve over the years. *Cost:* $101–139, double EP, in season.

★★★ FRANTEL (BAS-DU-FORT)

A very efficiently-run, 200-room hotel where everything consistently works. Sprawled out over the well-landscaped property are seven 2- or 3-story units and 14 bungalows. All the rooms are attractively decorated and have balconies or patios, radio, telephone, and air conditioning; but the beachside accommodations are stand-outs. These spacious mini-suites offer cathedral ceilings, two twin beds and a comfortable couch, plenty of drawer space and sliding doors that open onto a small, flower-bordered porch just steps from the sea. This is a lively spot with boutiques, tennis, excellent water sports facilities including free scuba lessons in the large pool, three restaurants, a big thatched-roof bar, nightly entertainment, and a popular discothèque. *Cost:* $81 per double EP, in season.

★★ HOLIDAY INN (GOSIER)

This is one of the largest hotels on the island, and the only one with two queen-size beds in each of the 156 rooms, if that's important. Perhaps more important is that there are two beaches, some of the best water sports, a large pool overlooking the sea and several restaurants, both indoor and outdoor. English- and French-speaking guests are about equal, and you can meet and mix accordingly. Other amenities include a swinging disco, sauna, tennis, nightly entertainment and a small meeting room for groups. *Cost:* 500 FF per double CP, in season.

★★ NOVOTEL FLEUR D'EPÉE (BAS-DU-FORT)

The name of the hotel itself came from a French captain, one Captain Fleur d'Epée in the 18th century, when the French and English were vying for Guadeloupe. 190 rooms stretch out in three different wings, each named for island flowers—Anthurium, Hibiscus, Bougainvillea. While the rooms may be small, they're brightly decorated, modern, and comfortable. Water sports here are excellent, the beach is a fine one, and there's also an exchange program for dining with the neighboring Frantel. *Cost:* $99 per double with full American breakfast, in season.

★★ SALAKO (GOSIER)

Under the management of the Novotel chain, this 7-story hotel is spotless, spartan and somewhat stark in decor. It does, however, command the best of the local crowd who come to dance in Le Caraïbe nightclub, one of the hottest of the hot spots in town. The rooms are good size, modern, have telephone, radio, and small balconies. Air conditioning is thorough and the total room count is 120. There are two tennis courts, a large pool and the beach is one of the better ones in this area. *Cost:* $90 per double with full American breakfast, in season.

Restaurants

Guadaloupe's cuisine is as multifaceted as its culture . . . pure, traditional French, French with a tropical touch, Creole dishes, old-fashioned African recipes, subtle spices from India and the Far East. There are over 100 restaurants around the island—some in hotels, others in old, restored colonial houses, some with terraces overhanging the sea, others Chez . . . Doudou, Lydie, Prudence, Nonore, Violetta . . . the porch or the dining room of the cook's home.

You might end your meal with an old dark rum

We've grouped our restaurant selections by location and labeled them inexpensive ($10–$14), moderate ($15–$19) and expensive (above $20).

Pointe-à-Pitre

★★★★ LA CANNE A SUCRE

17 rue Henri IV. Tel. 82–10–19. This 2-year-old restaurant was an instant success and now ranks among the island's five top dining spots. Gérard and Marie-Claude Virginius have restored their charming, old colonial house with taste, care, and eclectic elegance. The two dining rooms are small and crowded and are especially popular at lunch with prominent local businessmen. Reservations are imperative. Gérard's excellent and unusual preparations include *lambi fin gourmet*—conch cooked with eggplant, chives and mushrooms; and turtle steak in a cream port and green peppercorn sauce. Desserts are also delicious with Coupe canne à Sucre—a round of banana, caramel, old rum, sherbet and whipped cream sprinkled with cinnamon, a very special favorite. Virtually no English is spoken. *Expensive.*

Bas-du-Fort

★★★★ L'ALBATROS

Bas-du-Fort next to the Frantel. Tel. 82–39–66. Rosell Aurières loves the sea, and her 2-year-old restaurant is perched right over the Caribbean. This is a lovely spot for a good, leisurely lunch or perhaps Friday dinner when a small band plays romantic music for dancing. The best are on the large terrace, part of which has a glass floor over an aquarium. The decor is very tastefully done in soft tones of rose, brown and orange. Marc, the chef, is from Tarbes, but he's just as adept at Creole recipes as he is with classic French cuisine. Menu highlights, many of which are Rosell's own recipes, include shark in green peppercorn sauce; a superb turtle stew; filet of red snapper with leeks; salade melimelo—a divine creation of potatoes, apples, ham and lumpfish caviar; crab claws in tomato sauce; and coquille de l'Alabatros-lambi, langouste and palourdes gratiné in a light bechamel sauce. Service here is pleasant and very efficient, and the menu contains explanations in English. *Expensive.*

★★★★ LA PLANTATION

Galerie Marina. Tel. 82–39–63 or 83–17–81. We're pleased to report that once again Chef Francois Delage's imaginative cuisine merits raves: the pumpkin soup; lobster bisque; Craig Claiborne's favorite—*salade de gésiers d'oie* (warm goose giblet salad gently flavored with raspberry vinegar, hazelnut oil, croutons, and walnuts); the *civet de ouassous aux morilles* (giant crayfish stew with morel mushrooms); *emince de lambi à la Provencale* (thinly sliced conch in garlic sauce); veal scallops with pistachio nuts. Most of the desserts should be put on your list of "musts." The menu is varied, the presentation elegant. The wine list is outstanding, service smooth; and with the dollar so strong, prices are far less staggering. *Expensive.*

★★★ ESCALE A SAIGON
Route du Fort. Tel. 83–16–22. Antoine and Rosalie N'Guyên's small restaurant is in their home, up on a hill overlooking the sea. If you go early enough, you'll find Maman in the kitchen and the children having dinner in their pajamas. Antoine is a most cordial, English-speaking host who likes Americans and is always delighted to explain in great detail any unfamiliar dish. Service and food are both first rate, and the choice of Vietnamese specialties is endless—ten different hors d'oeuvres (paté Impériale and crab salad, two of the best); 11 soups; 14 shellfish (shrimp Saigonnaise is especially tasty) and 19 desserts—and that's not even counting the beef and pork courses. The house cocktail, a delicate, light mixture of rice wine and lychee juice, is worth a try as well. *Moderate.*

★★★ ROSSINI
Bas-du-Fort across from the Frantel. Tel. 83–07–81. As soon as you walk in the door you're transported to Italy. Just the effect the family Rossini hoped to achieve, since nearly everything in their warm, rustic restaurant is from their home country. The delicious fettuccine, macaroni, lasagne, spaghetti, pasta e fagioli, cakes and tartes are all freshly made in-house by the Venetian chef and Luciano Rossini himself. Signora assures the "style maison" (presentation and decoration) and their two daughters greet, serve and translate for guests. À la carte specialties feature different regions of Italy and change weekly as does the 70 FF 3-course *menu touristique.* Good standard selections include veal marsala flambé; fried squid; osso buco; veal milanese; and ten different pastas. *Moderate* to *expensive.*

★★ LE BOUCANIER
PLM Sun Village, La Marina, Bas-du-Fort. Tel. 83–05–62 or 83–05–76. This is a spacious, hilltop, open-air restaurant and bar with views over the sea, the pool and Port de Plaisance yacht basin. Another favorite lunch place for local businessmen because it's cool and breezy and the food is dependably good. The menu, in both French and English, features mainly French dishes with a few local plates as well. Recommended are stuffed trout with rum sauce; duck à l'orange; snails; veal cordon bleu and a refreshing gazpacho Andalou. There's always a 41 FF menu that changes but could include half a grapefruit, lamb chops, fruit, a split of wine and taxes. *Moderate.*

Gosier
★★★★ LE BAOULE
On the lower road, in town; tel. 84–04–55. Owners Hélène and Jacques Biales warmly welcome guests at their cozy bar lined with huge inviting jars of *punch maison.* This rather sophisticated restaurant—soft lights and soft music, wall-to-wall carpeting, flowers, greenery and a terrace with a picture-postcard view of the Ilet de Gosier—is one of Guadeloupe's most pleasant dining places. Chef Albert's menu is half Creole, half Continental, and includes such delicacies as scallop salad with tarragon; stuffed conch gratiné; chicken fricassé with shrimp; pork chops on a bed of bananas with butter sauce; turtle stew and shark in green peppercorn sauce. *Moderate* to *expensive.*

★★★ AUBERGE DE LA VIEILLE TOUR
Tel. 84−12−04. This hotel restaurant is continuing its long-standing reputation for good service by providing efficient, pretty waitresses in traditional madras. Jean Le Bihan, the young innovative chef, deftly combines exotic local products and fine French cuisine. Among his many new specialties are red snapper with fruit; beef filet with apple wine; doral with mango butter; thyme-grilled lamb chops; fresh, tropical-fruit sherbets and pineapple, coconut or banana crepes flambé in old rum. A well-chosen but costly wine list. *Expensive.*

★★★ CHEZ BACH LIEN
On the lower road, in town; tel. 84−10−91. Open only for dinner, this small second-floor dining spot is always crowded with afficionados of Vietnamese cooking. Reservations are a must. Study the extensive menu while sipping an apértif in the small salon elegantly furnished with antiques. You might choose nems; bobon; one of several delicious soups; noodles on sugarcane; bamboo or ginger chicken; crab claws stuffed with shrimp; caramel pork or order in advance the special lacquered duck or the Vietnamese fondue for two. It's most enjoyable to go here with several companions so that you can taste a good sampling of the many interesting and exotic dishes. *Moderate.*

★★★ LA CHAUBETTE
Route de la Riviera. Tel. 84−14−29. Charming, colorful Gitane Chavalin runs a simple, highly-regarded, neat-as-a-pin place that's popular from lunch till 11:00 P.M. Her Creole recipes include a tasty turtle steak; fine ragout of lambi (conch) or chatrou (small octopus); multiingredient soupe chaubette; and for real Francophiles—a tête de veau salad that is a rare and special treat. *Moderate.*

★★★ L'AUBERGE DU BOUKAROU
Montauban, just outside Gosier. Tel. 84−10−37. New owners, Brigitte and Patrick Salvan create classic cuisine and Creole specialties in their charming country inn. This out-going, young couple speaks good English and they are planning to add such treats as tripe, cassoulet, and lobster stew to the already ambitious menu which includes 19 hot and cold hors d'oeuvres; 11 salads; a dozen different preparations of beef; fish galore including bouillabaisse (order in advance for four persons); and scrumptious desserts. The decor is cool and restful—mainly green and white with accents of wood, wrought iron, and straw; the lighting is subdued and the 12 tables are set far apart in a semi-circle. *Moderate* to *expensive.*

★★★ LE GALION
Ecotel. Tel. 84−15−66. The dining room of Guadeloupe's second hotel school is open for dinner only. It's cool, comfortable and well decorated; if you happen to come to dinner when the students are at the end of their courses, service will be soigné; during their first week, natural confusion, but the very professional maitre d'hotel and the restaurant's manager will be there to ensure that things run as smoothly as possible. This is an interesting menu that changes as often as the cooks. The food is prepared by the students under the tutelage of a trained chef from France. Classic French dishes are the best. Among the recommendations are: machoiran, a fleshy fish that comes only from Guyana, prepared in several different, delicious ways; escargots flavored with Pernod; grilled red snapper and admirable desserts. *Moderate.*

[handwritten margin note: Blaff = fish stew, or bouillabaisse. Boudin = sausage.]

★★ LA CREOLE-CHEZ VIOLETTA
On the edge of town en route to Ste.-Anne. Tel. 84−10−34. One of Guadeloupe's best-known, Creole, grande-dame chefs, Violetta Chaville has

expanded her restaurant and her menu over the years. Every Creole dish imaginable is available. Violetta's experience and expertise really shine in the way she prepares court bouillon, conch, crab, sea urchin, red snapper, blaff and boudin. This is a place very accustomed to U.S. visitors. *Moderate.*

St. Félix (between Gosier and Ste. Anne)
★★ CHEZ JACQUELINE-AUX ARCADES
Tel. 84–17–36. Be prepared for a long but delicious Creole meal in this nicely-decorated, 16-table restaurant. In fact, the surroundings are so pleasant, that you probably won't even mind the wait. Malanga and langouste accras, poisson au gratin, goat stew, cold or grilled lobster are among the two dozen à la carte listings (even steak, pommes frites), and there is a 40 FF menu du jour that always includes a Ti-Punch, hors d'oeuvre, main course, half a bottle of wine and fresh fruit. *Inexpensive.*

★★ CHEZ LYDIE
Tel. 84–13–63. A bit on the hot side at noon, so go after 2:00 PM or in the evening, when there's more of a breeze. A typical, very local, uncommercialized place with 30 tables decorated with colorful, madras tablecloths under plastic and streamers. The no-frills Creole menu changes daily. Lydie's blaff, poulet de pays, stuffed christophine and tiny palourdes in a hot, spicy court bouillon are always good. *Inexpensive.*

★★ LA RESERVE-CHEZ JEANNE
Tel. 84–11–27. The no-nonsense, down-to-earth home cooking of Jeanne Carmelite (the sister of Lydie) has won many awards, and her simple, spotless restaurant is always crowded. Seafood—octopus, mussels, conch, blaff de palourdes, and goat colombo—is Jeanne's special forté, but everything is well prepared. *Inexpensive.*

Petit Havre (between Gosier and Ste. Anne)
★★★★ LE BISTROT
Tel. 84–13–82. This bistro is one of the best—panoramic as well as gastronomic—spots on the island. Jean-Pierre and Martine Dubost's small, open-sided dining room with a thatched roof sits on a hill in quite an elegant residential area. Jean-Pierre's cooking is traditional French with a decidedly tropical flair. There are over a dozen unusual rum punches to try before settling down to some excellent paté du chef; soupe de poissons with aioli; beef rib steak; mixed seafood coquille; the assiette Antillaise—a soupçon of different, local seafood and much more. Service is excellent and personal, and reservations are a must as this bistro is on everybody's list of favorite places to dine. The Dubosts close in the summer when they return to Europe to run their second restaurant on the French Riviera. *Expensive.*

Ste. Anne
★★ L'AMOUR EN FLEURS
Tel. 84–23–72. This roadside restaurant across from the local cemetery doesn't look like much from the outside; in fact, if you're not looking for it, you probably will drive right by. But hidden behind this simple façade is the kitchen of Mme. Trésor Amanthe, whose Creole cuisine has often been honored in island competitions. The lambi (conch) and chatroux (small octopus) were tender beyond belief and were served with a delicious rice and bean mixture. The coconut ice cream was freshly made. We were even able to learn some of Madame's culinary secrets. The presentation is simple, but the preparation of boudin, pork or beef ragout, langouste, poulet pays, blaff, court bouillon is all perfection. *Inexpensive.*

★ AUBERGE DU GRAND LARGE
Tel. 84–20–06. Mme. Georges Damico's small, 12-table restaurant over-looks the lovely tropical garden of her small bungalow hotel two steps from the Ste.-Anne beach. Menus, 45–65 FF, change weekly, with such good specialties as stuffed clams, crabes farcis, matété de crab, meat and fish stew and coconut flan among the choices. Madame does not speak much English, but both she and her staff manage to make you feel very welcome. *Inexpensive.*

Chateaubrun
★★★ LA MARMITE
Relais du Moulin. Tel. 84–23–96. Alphonse, the chef here, is a graduate of the St. Claude Hotel School and the kitchens of the Salako and the Meridien. His ambitious menu includes "Specialités Antillaises," nouvelle cuisine, and classic French dishes that are unusual and unusually good: Paté en pot; eggplant accras; shrimp and banana salad; court bouillon à la Saintoise; turkey scallops à la mode des iles; cheese and leek flan; coquilles St. Jacques à la vapeur; beef filet with girolle mushrooms; and duckling with black currants are just a few of his new recipes that are sure to please. The dining room itself, in an incomparable setting of pastoral fields, magnificent purple bougainvillea and yellow alamanda, is open on two sides and contains windows on the third. Sixteen tables with beige and brown napery comple-ment the natural wood chairs with caned seats; wooden tables and beamed ceiling all contribute to a truly comfortable, Caribbean elegance. *Moderate* to *expensive.*

Anse des Rochers (just outside St.-François)
★★★★ LES OISEAUX
No telephone. An off-the-beaten-track inn set on a plateau amidst flowers and fields. Arthur Rolle and his wife Claudette's "cuisine campagnard" (country cooking) is full of surprises. We highly recommend the tender, spicy clams; seafood casserole; tazard (wahoo) en papillotte or chicken and lobster in cognac sauce. More adventuresome palates will surely enjoy the pork stew Antilles style or pig tails with rice and red peas. If *cigale de mer* (sea cricket) is on the day's menu order it. This odd, ugly member of the shrimp family is extremely difficult to find and catch, but Rollé has his secret source and chances are good you'll be able to try this unforgettable, delicate, sweet crustacean. If you have room, desserts here are also spectacular and the Rollés always offer a *digestif*—old rum, calvados, marc or other unusual liqueur—on the house. This is a very special place that should not be missed. *Moderate* to *expensive.*

St. François
★★ LA LOUISIANE
Grilled meat and fish are always good in this pretty little restaurant in an old colonial house on the road to Ste. Marthe. The menu features Creole special-ties as well as such French classics as filet of turbot with hollandaise sauce; filet mignon with cèpe mushrooms; scallops in vermouth and entrecôte marechal du vin. Quality is consistent, service always with a smile, and the setting is superb. *Moderate.*

★ AU VIEUX PORT
At the old port in the village. No telephone. This is a small, open-air res-taurant facing the sea. It offers 12 tables and a simple wood and straw decor. Daniel and Bernard both speak English, and their service is "sympa," smiling and fast. There's a 75 FF menu that includes grilled fish with sauce Creole, a good rice, pumpkin puree and/or pommes frites; the 85 FF choice is côte

de boeuf, green salad, desert crêpes and a half pitcher of wine. The latest plan is to add really good pizza to the simple, well-prepared menu. *Moderate.*

★ BRASSERIE ST. GEORGES

In the Marina. Tel. 84–48–11. A young, industrious couple, Rene and Nelly Hawai have taken over the management of this very attractive (but never popular) quai-side restaurant. Nelly trained under Roger Vergé, so their new menu, which highlights seafood, is very "nouvelle." Some of the unusual specialties include cuttlefish Chinese style; creamed shark with chives and tomato sauce; crayfish croquettes and tuna cutlets with creamed leeks. The large terrace overlooking the yacht basin is a perfect place for cocktails, and there's usually nice guitar music in the evening. *Moderate* to *expensive.*

★ CHEZ HONORE—AUX FRUITS DE MER

5 Place du Marche. Tel. 84–40–61. Reserve your table, especially in season, because "The Lobster King" has many faithful followers who flock here for his special 6-course dinner. This is a long-standing favorite of Air France crews, locals, and visitors who know and appreciate good value. 70 FF will bring you a crab farci, accras, boudin, salad, grilled lobster, and bananas flambé. A copious meal that's an unbeatable bargain. *Inexpensive.*

★ LA PECHERIE

Rue de la République. Tel. 84–48–41 or 84–48–94. Eight wooden tables and a small bar on the wonderful, upstairs, perched over the sea, porch of an old, old stone-walled warehouse. Owner Camille Rotin is a fisherman at heart, so naturally seafood is the specialty of the house. The menu is decided according to what's best in the market—grilled red snapper; dorade; parrot fish; turtle stew; ceviche; fish soup; court bouillon are among the possibilities. Lobster is available when ordered one day in advance, and there are always one or two meat dishes on the menu as well—steak au poivre or garlic chicken cutlets, for example. You couldn't ask for fresher fish and the informality of this place makes dining a pleasure. *Moderate.*

★ LE ZAGAYA

Rue de la République. Tel. 84–41–99. A small rose-colored house with six tables on the terrace, one on the sand under the palms. Relax and enjoy the classical music and a Creole "starter" or two while your main course— chicken, fish, beef, lamb or lobster grills on the beachside barbecue. Jean Marie's sundaes are rich and tempting. Our favorite is *Coupe mi figue mi raisin* which is a slang expression for bittersweet or so-so (and it is far from being either). Rum raisin and vanilla ice cream and a slice of pineapple topped with figs soaked in old rum is a rich and delicious concoction. *Inexpensive.*

★ MME. JERCO

Rue de l'Egalité, behind the Mairie. Tel. 84–40–19. Hortense Jerco has recovered from her recent illness and is back at the stove of her unpretentious popular restaurant, preparing her hearty, multicourse meals. Just sit back, savor each course as it arrives and accept what's going on around you, you'll really get a feeling for the intricacies and the variety of down-to-earth Creole cooking. *Inexpensive.*

Le Moule

CARAIBE CAT-CHEZ MIMI

81 rue St. Jean. Tel. 84–54–12. Mimi sings and husband Willy tends bar in this small hotel-restaurant where stuffed clams and shark with cream sauce are among the recommendations. *Inexpensive.*

L'ARBRE A PAIN
17 rue Ste.-Anne. Tel. 84–54–29. There are 50 different punches to begin your meal, which might include langouste, grilled fish, crayfish or poulet à la noix coco and its namesake—breadfruit. *Inexpensive.*

LA MANDIANA
Facing the public beach. Colombo and other Creole specialties with an Indian touch are offered in this good-sized restaurant complete with discothèque. *Inexpensive.*

Petit Canal
★★★ **LE BARBAROC**
Tel. 84–72–71. Félicité Doloir prides herself on serving really old-fashioned Creole recipes at her comfortable 12-table bistro. Things you won't find on other menus include porc griots; crab paté, and rissoles; breadfruit purée and soufflé; sweet potato noodles; mouks (mussels) gratiné; paella; soup; congo; bébélé, pork en papilottes and coconut guava or papaya flan. All can be accompanied by "Maby," a healthful drink like a local absinthe or home-made beer, or a very tasty punch made from a secret mixture of fruit. Dinner only during the week; weekends, lunch. *Inexpensive.*

Port Louis
★★ **CHEZ ODETTE**
Rue Gambetta, behind the PTT. Tel. 84–90–16. Rose Mozar is the very pleasant patronne, whose half-open restaurant is surrounded by colorful flowers and birds singing in the trees. A typical meal here might include malanga or pumpkin accras; crabes farcis; goat colombo; Creole chicken with christophine gratiné; cheese; seasonal fruit and homemade coconut ice cream. *Inexpensive.*

★★ **LE POISSON D'OR-CHEZ NONORE**
Rue Sadi Carnot. Tel. 84–90–22. Mme. Eleanore Boulate's very agreeable terrace overlooks the sea, and the view extends to the Basse-Terre Mountains. Excellent, authentic Creole cooking with especially good fish and other seafood. *Inexpensive.*

Anse Bertrand
★★ **FOLIE PLAGE-CHEZ PRUDENCE**
At Anse Laborde, beyond Anse Bertrand. Tel. 84–91–17. Prudence Marcelin is the warm, colorful, temperamental hostess of this large, breezy tin-roof restaurant on the beach. If, for some reason, you don't like her set 8-course menu of that day, she'll want to know precisely why! Seafood is the specialty, but her boudin is one of Guadeloupe's best. Be sure to reserve, especially on Sundays, when people from all over the island come to enjoy the good, consistent food and the beach. There's a shallow pool for occupying the children. A boutique and a weekend disco as well.

Basse-Terre
Baie Mahault, Near Lamentin
★ **RAVINE CHAUDE**
Tel. 85–60–53. Especially popular with those coming to "take the waters." This restaurant, presided over by Mme. Mormont, serves excellent specialties such as crayfish done several ways; goat curry; grilled lobster; lamb brochett-e; boudin omelette; calalou; even a tripe de la Ravine Chaude. The thermal station is the perfect place to relax and get back in form, while Madame's

restaurant offers a handy and a delicious solution to the question of what to do at lunch or dinner. *Inexpensive.*

Sainte-Rose

★ CHEZ CLARA

Across from the beach. Tel. 85–82–99. Good seafood shares the spotlight with Clara herself. This bewitching Guadeloupean beauty with gold-plaited tresses will probably serve you in barefeet. That's just part of the panache of this popular place. The six terrace tables are the best; plan to stay a while because everything is cooked to order. Raie (skate) curry or stew; turtle; poisson coffre (trunk fish); and baby shark are a few of the house specialties. Chicken and beef are added for the weekend crowd. Recipes are family ones and you know the fish is the freshest when you see the fishermen continually stopping by to show Clara their catch. *Moderate.*

Deshales

★★★ LE KARACOLI

North of Deshaies, near Club Med. Tel. 85–81–17. Some tables are practically in the water on this nice beach, shaded with trees. Mme. Lucienne Salcede whips up some of the island's best accras—the spices were mixed to a perfect blend; her coquilles Karakoli, turtle ragout, langouste, palourdes and chicken colombo with rice, or court bouillon de poisson, taste equally good. This is a fairly large place, decorated by combining red and white check, madras material, and flowered plastic tablecloths inside and out, not at all an unpleasing effect. Service is on the slow side, as most dishes are cooked to order, but who cares when there's such a nice beach for a between-course swim! *Inexpensive.*

★★★ LES MOUILLAGES

Ruelle 1. Tel. 85–81–12. In the middle of town, look for the amusing traffic sign that depicts a car falling into the water. Walk down the street next to the general store and enter Mme. Racine's large 10-table dining room via her kitchen. This ingenious lady has been in business for over 15 years and her reputation is a good one. The best tables are out on the porch that looks out over the many international yachts at anchor in the lovely natural harbor. Grilled lobster with a piquant Creole sauce is the house specialty, and for 50 FF you can also have *palourdes* or *crabes farcis,* vegetables or a salad and dessert. There is also a simpler 35 FF "menu touristique" with one entrée, a plat de résistance and dessert; or a more expensive 70 FF offering with accras, langouste, poisson and rice; vegetables or salad and dessert. All are bargains for fine fare such as this. *Inexpensive.*

St. Claude

★★★ RELAIS DE LA GRANDE SOUFRIERE

Tel. 81–41–27. This patrician, blue and white country inn is on a gentle knoll in the elegant residential suburb at the base of La Soufrière. The veranda and dining room are popular luncheon spots for both visitors to the volcano and French government officials who live and work nearby, so reservations are recommended. There's a cozy lounge with padded leather bar and banquettes, and the dining room itself is quite formal: green and white latticed walls; pink napery; fine china, crystal and cutlery; and a beautiful bouquet of flowers on each table. Menus are *prix fixe* (65 FF, all inclusive) or *à la carte,* and both change daily. Beef bourguignon, brochette of veal kidney with sauce Diable, steak tartare, duckling with green peppercorn sauce and smoked salmon with sorrel may be among the always perfectly prepared haute cuisine offerings and fine desserts. *Moderate.*

Staffed by students of government hotel school

Matouba
★ CHEZ PAUL
Tel. 81–41–71. Up in the hills right on the banks of the small Rivière Rouge, this dining room has a circular window overlooking the magnificent view of mountains and valleys. Honest, good Creole and French cooking, with giant crayfish just one of the many specialties. This family-run restaurant is best at lunch, and almost impossible to find after dark by yourself! *Moderate.*

L'Habituee-Capesterre
CHEZ DOLLIN-LE CREPUSCULE
On the road to Carbet Falls. Tel. 86–34–56. This is a simple, but very hospitable place in the middle of a tiny village. But stake out a table on the porch and put your order in for giant crayfish (ouassous) and calalou on your way up to the falls. A hearty lunch will be ready and waiting when you return. *Inexpensive.*

Nightlife

As stated throughout, your best evenings in Guadeloupe will occur if you happen to speak French or a semblance thereof. This is your chance to meet and mix with the citizens who live here, but plan on doing it en Français—or plan on a quiet observation from your table.

One of the most "in" of the in places at the moment is the club Le Caraïbe in the *Hotel Salako,* where owner Gérard Dantevieux draws a nightly crowd ready to flow with the action from about 11:00 P.M. until dawn. The club is chic and crowded, with brown and beige modular cushions and bar stools that you can sink into if you can find one that's vacant. The music is a mix of reggae, disco, beguine and slow to the beat spun by a happy disquaire on a good stereo system. Space is created by the spread-out use of plants and flowers, and lights are dimmed from dusk to dawn.

Martinique claims to have invented the beguine

Over at the *PLM Arawak,* nights begin early with a cocktail in the *Paillotte Bar,* where there's an international mix of visitors and Guadeloupeans. There may be a Brazilian pianist, or Jean Baptiste may have dropped in on his Caribbean circuit that stretches from Montserrat to Antigua, Guadeloupe and Martinique. Later everyone heads downstairs to the *Blue Sky*—for some really late evening action.

You'll hear some English but more French spoken at the *Ti Racoon* in the *Holiday Inn,* the *Frantel's Fou Fou, Le Pharaon* and the *New Land.* In Gosier; *La Chaine* in Stäfélix and *Acapulco* or *Neptune* in St.-François. All are very lively, late-going discos featuring upbeat sounds to recorded music. The dress is Caribbean informal as well as French casual elegance, especially for the ladies.

For a softer, quieter evening of music, stop by the *Auberge de la Vieille Tour,* one of everyone's favorites. Their *Rum Keg Bar* has a good band, albeit a small dance floor, and slow, romantic music prevails. Guadeloupeans often perform at *La Casa Creole.* Check your hotel desk to verify times and dates.

If you're up to risking life and limb for a rare treat, climb the winding, steep, seemingly-endless ship's staircase at the *Relais du Moulin* in Châteaubrun. The steps are inside a restored sugar mill, and once at the top in the tiny bar with taped music for an encore, you'll be in an 18th-century French world. But be forewarned that the difficult climb up can become impossible going down.

Tired of dancing and want to throw the dice? Head for either of the island's two *casinos,* a small one in *St. François,* and the larger and the newer adjoining the PLM Arawak in *Gosier.* Everyone—visitor or French citizen—is required to show identification cards of some form in order to be admitted.

Both the system and the form are European. Each casino is silent and smokey, and serious play is the order of the night; no one-armed bandits here.

In the winter season the *Ballets Caribana* perform different evenings at different hotels. These performances, however, are not wholly folkloric dances. The director has incorporated some Parisian can-can into the repertoire of the troupe. But the ladies of his modest troupe have devised their modest response: They wear concealing pantaloons beneath the can-can come on! All the large hotels schedule different show nights in season, and sometimes they include Ballets Caribana.

Check with your hotel desk, or go directly to the *Centre des Arts et de la Culture* in the capital, Pointe-à-Pitre, to find out what performances are taking place at this architectural and cultural showplace. On different nights in different seasons there are presentations of dance, drama, and theater that change regularly. Although you may not be up to a play by Molière or contemporary drama acted in French, you can enjoy the ballet from Haiti, classical music, jazz or a mime from Paris.

Shopping

Guadeloupe is not quite what you'd call inexpensive, but if you favor fine French products and keep in mind the 20% discount for most luxury items paid for in dollar travelers' checks or credit cards, you'll find some excellent buys here.

Boutiques and more boutiques line the rues Frébault, de Nozières and Schoelcher in the busy commercial center of Pointe-à-Pitre. As the sun gets progressively higher and hotter, your enthusiasm and energy will steadily decrease, so schedule shopping excursions early in the morning (shops open at 8:30) or after 3:30 P.M. when things cool down. Avoid coming into town when cruise ships are in port and on Saturday mornings when everyone does the weekly marketing.

On rue Frébault, *A la Pensée, Rosébleu, Champs Elysées, Vendôme* and *Phoenicia* are practically next door to one another. All are modern, air-conditioned stores whose shelves and showcases are stocked with a well-organized array of luxury labels—silver by Christofle; leather goods from Hermès; Orlane cosmetics; Cartier and Dupont lighters; Nina Ricci sunglasses; Chanel ties; Porcelaine de Paris; Baccarat and Lalique crystal; and hundreds of perfumes from Arpège to Van Cleef and Arpels (a brand carried exclusively by Phoenicia). Prices can represent savings of as much as 30% over those in the States.

Galérie du Port, at the foot of rue Frébault, is a new shopping arcade with plenty of interesting, small specialty stores such as *Ti Moune* for toys; *La Chausserie* for shoes; *La Paillotta aux Trésors* for souvenirs; *Sun Shop* and *Campus Boutique* for clothes; *Coraline* for jewelry; and *La Casserole* for some ovenware and other cookery items that are pretty enough to go from the stove directly to the table.

Rue Frébault is also known for shoe repairs—one-man fixit-stands line the sidewalk. The cobblers work instant miracles for very little effort and expense on your part.

The shops along rue de Nozières concentrate more on clothing. Women of all ages will discover the latest Parisian creations and whatever is the current Riviera rage in sportswear at *Sandra Boutique, La Chamade, Caty, Verouchka, Jennifer, Raquel, Topkapi, Titi Ati* and *ZouZou*—just a few of the dozens of tiny stores in a short four-block area. Very little English will be spoken in shops such as these, but when fashion-conscious women get together, there's no real need for a common language—hand gestures and facial expressions and a few words in French about colors, sizes and so on will be all the propriétaire they will need to understand that your taste is probably the same as hers or you would not have come into the store in the first place. Monsieur will surely be tempted by the lightweight sportswear and men's accessories signed Cacherel, Cardin, Newman or Yves St. Laurent at *Adonis, Borsalino* and *Casanova;* and the children's clothes at *Tom Puce* (Tom Thumb), *Katia, Love, Charly, Kickers* and *Natalys* are beautifully made, as French togs for tots usually are. Galerie Nozières, at the corner of rue Gambetta, is in a big, old brown and cream house with lacy, wrought-iron balconies. The choice here ranges from European health foods at *Santenaire;* herbal beauty products at *Michel Soreg;* bikinis and lingerie at *Tentations;* ladies' clothing at *Mauve Boutique* and *Cannelle;* chocolates at *Sweety* to 18K gold jewelry at *Point d'Or* and fine crystal, pewter, silver and porcelain gifts at *Au Lys d'Or.*

Rue Schoelcher, the third main shopping artery, is the prettiest as well as the most chic. Prices are high, but the quality and the designs are the best France has to offer and the selection is straight out of the pages of the current *Elle* or *French Vogue.* Fabrics are as special as the styles at *Falbala; Jean Laurent; Nicole; Pok; La Pagerie; Elle et Lui; Bleu Marine;* and the two charming, pink-facaded shops of *Paul et Virginie.* A few more places of fashion to note on the side streets include *Dorothée Design, Coloquinte* and *Sophie* on rue Lamartine; *Boutique Carole* and *Anne Onime* on rue Gambetta and *Alamanda, Gipsy Boutique, La Petite Colombia* and *Marie-Claire* on rue Barbès.

Souvenir items—madras dolls, fabric, clothing, aprons and table linens, handcrafted baskets and straw work—may be found at *Au Caraïbe* on rue Frébault and *King Creole Store, Macabou* or *E. Sarkis* on rue de Nozières. Raymond Cellini is the "king of folkloric records," but he also carries a large selection of popular discs at his rue Schoelcher store, *Aux Ondes. Océans,* a unique boutique devoted to shells and some lovely pieces of coral, is located on rue Lamartine. A good address for Creole cookbooks, maps, guides, and other reading matter pertinent to past and present French Antilles lore (mostly in French, but there is a small English selection as well) is *La Librairie Antillaise,* 41 bis rue Schoelcher. You might ask your hotel desk to check with the *Centre des Metiers d'Art* to see if they are holding one of their occasional expositions when the first-class handicrafts—tapestries, ceramics, sculpture, paintings—made there by serious art students are on sale.

Antique buffs will probably turn up a find or two at Simone Schwartz-Bart's *Tim Tim.* This attractive shop in a colonial mansion on rue Henri IV is crammed full of Creole furniture, jewelry, engravings, maps, bibelots, clothes, lingerie, and table linens. *En Temps Longtemps* has a large collection of furniture, pewter, silver and other decorative items that are copies, reproductions, and real antiques. Price tags here are quite realistic considering the fine quality.

Alcohol and wine connoisseurs have one of the best cellars outside France at *Seven Sins,* 6 rue Frébault. This store carries a complete assortment of fine French wines, foreign spirits, cognacs, choice aperitifs and rum galore.

New commercial centers, offering convenient and less hectic shopping, have sprouted up in the Bas-du-Fort area. *Galerie Marina,* just across from Port de Plaisance, features eight restaurants and over 20 shops. Included are *Marina Shop,* a small supermarket; full service beauty salon; *Jumbo Car Rental;* windsurfer and other sports equipment and accessories; *A la Recherche du Passé* for old books, maps and engravings; *Aquarius,* with tropical fish; and *Crazy, Safari, Chabada, Eglantine, Sea and Sun, Ah Nanas* and *Nautilles* for clothing for both men and women. The last has some unusually attractive handpainted silk outfits and T-shirts.

A bit farther on the small road that winds through new apartment complexes overlooking the Marina is *Place Creole.* This small cluster of shops includes *Ti Kai,* with art, handicrafts, furniture and clothing from Haiti and South America; a beauty salon; and *La Véranda,* without a doubt Guadeloupe's prettiest shop. Here interior decorator Bernadette has put together a lovely collection of antique furniture and reproductions. The shop itself is housed in a pink and white building whose wooden doors are painted with flowers and whose windows are trimmed with pink wrought iron. Set off by themselves are *La Maison du Rhum,* where tasting is encouraged before buying, and *La Maison de l'Artisinat,* a cooperative of local craftsmen.

The *Escale Commercial Center,* at the Bas-du-Fort exit on the highway continuing east, has a huge *Mammouth* supermarket. Here will be found not only a lot of cooking gadgets and gourmet foodstuffs but a stylish and a very inexpensive selection of bikinis (40–50 FF); espadrilles; sundresses; shorts (40 FF); T-shirts; and sportswear for the whole family. Also located here is a large and well-stocked *Pharmacie;* a branch of the *Banque Nationale de Paris (BNP); The Magic Store* with all the latest records; *Orchidée* for jewelry and other fine gifts and *La Boite à Malice,* one of our favorites for practical and fun knickknacks with originality and good taste. If you need a grocery store on Sunday, the small "epicerie" on the grounds of the PLM Sun Village Hotel in Bas-du-Fort is the *only* one we were able to find open anywhere. Deli-style salads, charcuterie, quiche, small pizzas, a special "plat du jour," bread, milk, sodas, cheese and other basics can be purchased until 6:00 P.M., during the week until 7:30 P.M..

The booming resort of St. François also has its own shopping center, "La Marina." Next door to the casino, this small, beautifully-landscaped garden grouping of boutiques includes: *Le Bambou* for souvenirs and gifts; *La Goëlane,* for luxury ready-to-wear for the entire family; *Plein Soleil* with decorative objects for the home; *La Boutique du Bee Shirt* for unusual tees; a full service beauty salon; *Alamanda* for costume jewelry and accessories right off the Paris fashion pages; and *Olivier de St. Mande* for books and local handicrafts. Just down the road is another large, well-stocked supermarket, *The Gourmet Shop.*

Finally, one of the nicest remembrances to bring home is a bouquet or two of anthuriums, or bird of paradise. These cut flowers may enter the States (they will be inspected at your U.S. port of entry) and will last for several weeks. *Casafleurs,* at Le Raizet Airport, can pack them securely to travel with your luggage.

Sports

Beaches

The best beaches on Grande-Terre are at Gosier, Sainte-Anne, Saint François up to Pointe des Chateaûx, Port Bertrand, Port Louis and Petit Canal. On Basse-Terre—Viard, Goyave, Sainte-Marie, Deshaies, Grande Anse, Petit-Bas-Vent and Clugny. The major hotels are constructed seaside, and monokini sunning and swimming is the norm. There are a few officially-designated nudist beaches on the island: The most popular are Pointe Tarare near Pointe des Chateaûx; Anse Bourdel on Club Med property (an entrance fee must be paid at the club's gate) in Sainte-Anne.

Camping

Caraibes Loisirs in Petit Bourg (Tel. 85–42–38) rents Datsun camp-car pick-ups with kitchenette, frigidaire, toilet, shower, sheets, blanket and kitchen utensils at 2,495 FF for four people per week; 2,295 FF for two in season, unlimited mileage. Airport transfers, T.V.A. and insurance are also included in these prices. Windsurfers, bikes and diving equipment may also be rented at the same time. There are no organized campsites on the island at

the present time. Camping on private property must be authorized by the landowner. Backpacking is allowed on public beaches and in the Nature Park.

Deep-Sea Fishing

Hotel desks can put you in touch with fishing-boat captains. Three recommendations are Daniel Sanner, Marina Bas-du-Fort (Tel. 82–74–94); the captain of *Thalassa,* a fully-equipped Bertram that can accommodate parties up to ten; and Gilles Gremion, whose 23' Mako, the Flying Lobster, is anchored at the Meridien in St.-François (84–41–00). The barracuda and kingfish season is January–May; December–March for tuna, dolphin and bonito. In Bouillante, near Malendure Beach, the *Fishing Club Antilles* (Tel. 86–73–77) offers overnight excursions including transport to and from Pointe-à-Pitre bungalow sleeping accommodations, all meals and all fishing equipment. Prices range from 1,200–2,300 FF per person, maximum of 3.

Golf

There is an excellent 18-hole, Robert Trent Jones Championship course in St. François with an English-speaking pro, fully-equipped pro shop, electric carts and a clubhouse. There is a daily greens fee of $20.

Hiking

Basse-Terre's Nature Park has well-marked trails that lead through tropical rain forests to mountain waterfalls and natural swimming pools. Hiking is also possible on La Soufrière.

Horseback Riding

Riding can be arranged by contacting *Le Criollo* (Tel. 83–43–63) in St. Félix. Charges 60 FF per hour for a beach and country excursion. The *Relais du Moulin,* in Chateaubrun, also offers lessons, tours and picnics on horseback every day but Monday (Tel. 84–23–96), at 50 FF per hour.

Sailing

Guadeloupe's *Port de Plaisance* has been called the finest facility in the Leeward Islands. Located in Bas-du-Fort, just outside Pointe-à-Pitre, Pleasure Port has 600 anchoring berths that can accommodate yachts up to 92 feet. Other facilities include a wharf with equipment to lift boats; a maintenance department; electrical, diesel, water and ice supplies; a restaurant; and the *Capitainerie* (Welcome Center) with telex (POPPAP919889GL) and telephone (82–54–85). The *Carénage* in Pointe-à-Pitre and the *St. François Yacht Basin* are both being expanded as well. Boats of every size can be rented by the day, week or month, with or without crews, through *Locaraibes* (no tel.) and *Soleil et Voile* (Tel. 82–26–81) in Port de Plaisance; or *Basse-Terre Yachting,* Marina de Rivière-Sens, Gourbeyre (Tel. 81–11–45). Sailfish, Sunfish and Windsurfers (Guadeloupe's most popular and most prevalent sport) can all be rented through water sports centers at the major hotels; lessons are also available.

Scuba and Snorkeling

Diving centers include Pierrick Billard's *Pirate Scuba Club* at the Callinago Beach Hotel; and André Alexander's *GAMA Scuba School,* headquartered at the *Frantel.* The price, which includes an introductory lesson and one dive, ranges from 120 FF–180 FF. Excursions are made by both of these schools to Pigeon Island in Basse-Terre, where there is now an Underwater National Park protected by the government. Jacques Cousteau calls Pigeon Island one of the ten best diving areas in the world, with colorful reefs, shipwrecks, wall diving, caves, slopes and drop-offs.

Scuba-diving charters for certified divers (up to eight people) can be arranged on the *Cadaques* through *Soleil et Voile* (Tel. 82–26–81). This 56-foot ketch is fully equipped with everything from adapters for U.S. and English regulators to a 500 cubic foot, diesel engine compressor. Dany Guignier, the skipper, is a CMA*** international diving instructor with seven years' diving experience in the Caribbean. *For snorkelers,* the *Nautilus,* l'Aquarium and *Les Coraux,* three glass-bottom boats, shuttle back and forth from Malendure Beach to Pigeon Island from 10:00 A.M.–4:00 P.M. There are also excellent, safe reefs to explore off the Meridien and Hamak hotels in St. François and the Ilet de Gosier. Flippers, masks and tubes are usually available free of charge at the major hotels' water sports centers.

Spectator Sports

The *cockfighting* season is November–April. The Bellecourt Race Course at Baie Mahault has several meets and horse races throughout the year.

Tennis

There are 28 courts at hotels around the island, many of them lighted for night play. Included are the Auberge de la Vieille Tour and Hotel Meridien with three courts; Holiday Inn, Fleur d'Epée Novotel, PLM Arawak, Salako and Les Marines de St.-François with two; and Frantel and Hamak with one court each.

Other Water Sports

Pedal boats are usually available to hotel guests at the major resorts for no charge. Waterskiing and lessons can be arranged at all hotel water sports centers.

THE HARD FACTS

Planning Ahead

Chances are that those who come to Haiti with an open mind—a more important commodity here than stacks of spending money—will come away with a rich collection of memories and a fondness for the strength and the spirit of Haiti's people and traditions.

There are problems in Haiti that will take time to solve. But be assured that visitors can walk the streets anytime without fear. There is great poverty here but also incredible resourcefulness . . . just look at the array of home-made products for sale and the recycling of anything into something useful. Nothing is thrown away.

Costs

A trip to Haiti is not inexpensive—a few of the hotels are quite expensive—but most are far more moderately priced than comparable hotels on many other Caribbean islands. (The range is from $35 to $200 per night.) There are many first-rate restaurants, some with dinner checks to match. Most are in the medium price range. (Dinner for two can range from as little as $20 up to $70 without wine.)

And there is excellent shopping. Bargains are everywhere. So is the opportunity to "adopt" a Haitian painting that just might be the kind of find art collectors dream about . . . but don't count on it. Just buy what you like to bring home as a reminder of a very special island in the sun.

Holidays and Special Events

Independence Day and New Year's Day (January 1); Forefathers Day (January 2); Good Friday; Easter; Pan American Day (April 14); Labor Day (May 1); Flag and University Day (May 18); Sovereignty Day (May 22); President-for-Life Day, honoring Jean-Claude Duvalier and his father, François Duvalier (June 22); Assumption Day (August 15); Dessaline's Death Anniversary (the leader who proclaimed Haiti's independence, October 17); U.N. Day (October 24); All Saints' Day (November 1); All Souls Day (November 2); Armed Forces Day (November 18); Discovery Day (the day Columbus sighted Haiti, December 5); Christmas Day; and, most important to visitors, Carnival or Mardi Gras, the three days before Ash Wednesday when parading and dancing transform the streets.

Sources of Information

Questions that need answers before your departure for Haiti? In the *United States,* contact the *Haiti Government Tourist Bureau* in New York, 1270 Ave. of the Americas, New York, NY 10020; or at 150 S.E. 2nd Ave., Miami, FL 33131. *In Canada,* contact the bureau at: 44 Fundy/Etage F, Place Bonaventure, Montreal, H5A 149 or at 920 Yonge Street, Suite 808, Toronto, M4W 3C7. Once you get to Haiti, the *National Office of Tourism* at Avenue Marie Jeanne in Port-au-Prince will be at your service.

Packing

You may well wish to add to your resort wardrobe after strolling through some of Haiti's boutiques offering avant-garde creations, almost all designed and made in Haiti. But since shopping isn't the main reason to come to Haiti (there are so many other things to do), leave room in your suitcases for only a few special purchases.

   You should bring with you informal, conservative, comfortable, light-weight sportswear for sightseeing during the day. (Haitians appreciate a well-groomed approach to dressing.) Some heavier clothing (light sweaters will do), sturdy shoes and pants or jeans are needed for trips to the mountains. On the beaches, or at your hotel swimming pool if you stay in Pétionville, a swimsuit and a cover-up is fine.

   At night some of the hotels and restaurants require gentlemen to wear jackets and ties for dinner; there are no regulations for women, but a simple, long cotton dress or a pants-and-top set is always right.

Getting There

Airline Service: Eastern Airlines and Air Florida offer daily nonstop flights from Miami. Air France has two weekly flights from Miami and five from San Juan; American has daily nonstop jets from New York to Port-au-Prince; Prinair and Air Florida provide daily service between Santo Domingo and Port-au-Prince. Air Canada has service from Montreal.

   A handful of cruise ships (about four or five), departing from New York and Miami, call regularly at Port-au-Prince. A few also stop at Cap Haitien.

Formalities on Arrival

Customs

Entering and leaving Haiti involves formal and thorough procedures. Inspection of bags is courteous but complete, and drug laws are *strictly* enforced. Otherwise, Haiti is like other Caribbean islands. You'll need a passport or a voter's registration card and a return or an ongoing ticket to get in. Before you leave, a $10 departure tax will be levied. Important: If you're coming to Haiti via a private aircraft or a private sailing ship, check with the nearest office of the Haitian Government Tourist Bureau well in advance of departure for information about entry procedures.

Money

The *official currency* is the gourde, divided into 100 units called centimes. It is presently equivalent to 20¢ U.S. However, U.S. dollars are accepted everywhere. Credit cards are accepted at most major hotels, some restaurants and the larger boutiques.

Getting into Town

Rental cars are available at the airport, in Port-au-Prince and in Pétionville. Listings of *taxi fares,* set by the government, are available at the airport, hotels and at the National Office of Tourism. Visitors can also hire *tour cars* available by the hour, half day or whole day; or travel around the capital via one of the *publique* cars identifiable by the red ribbon tied to the rear view mirror. (To use this mode of travel, you should be familiar with your route or speak a little French. Almost all the drivers speak only Creole, but other passengers will try to help you out.) And if you're really feeling brave, jump on one of the wildly-painted *tap-taps* (converted trucks). Along with what seems like most of Haiti, crowd in, and see where you end up!

Settling Down

Choosing a Restaurant

Haitian restaurants are among the finest in the Caribbean. The specialties are French and Creole. It's best to book your hotel European Plan (breakfast only) to give you a lot of evenings to sample the dishes at outside restaurants. (But do dine once at your hotel. Haiti is a personal place, and you'll hurt the owner's feelings if you don't! The cuisine at the hotels is usually quite good.)

Learning to Cope

Business Hours.   Most shops are open from 8:00 A.M. to 5:00 P.M., Monday through Friday, although many close between noon and 2:00 P.M. On Saturday closing time is about 1:00 P.M.

Electricity.   Conventional 110-volt, 60-cycle alternating current permits the use of standard North American appliances.

Communications.   To *telephone Haiti* from the United States, direct dial: 1–509, followed by the number in Haiti. Telephone connections within Haiti are usually quite good.

Language.   Most Haitians who come in daily contact with visitors speak English. Although French is the official language of the country, everyone speaks Creole, a complex mixture of both Norman and classic French, African, Spanish and the native Indian tongue. It's uniquely Haitian.

Medical Assistance.   There are four hospitals in Port-au-Prince, and *every hotel has a doctor on call.* English-speaking physicians, surgeons and dentists in private practice are also available in Port-au-Prince.

HAITI TODAY

Haiti is a passionate state . . . one you love or love to hate. There's seldom an in-between.

The personal I seems out of place with fellow travelers, but with Haiti, there's no other way. It's a personal place. I love Haiti. I love the paintings, including the excellent naive ones sold in art galleries and those peddled on the streets by children who painted them only hours before. I love the restaurants, mostly French, some Creole and almost all good. I love staying at several of the hotels, each individualized with the stamp of the owner-manager. I love the spirit, and most of all, I love the people, among the warmest in the Caribbean or anywhere in the world.

The first black republic in history (1804), Haiti has had as many ups and downs as its undulating hills. The second largest land area in the Caribbean, Haiti rambles for 11,000 square miles over the western part of the island of Hispaniola. (The Dominican Republic occupies the other half.)

In truth, I love being here . . . smelling the coal pots in the streets cooking goat and rice, strolling the streets of Port-au-Prince at any hour, searching for one painting to take home from the hundreds that are offered and stretching my French to converse with a small boy who wants to carry my packages in the hope of a tip.

"Haiti" derives from the Arawak Indian word meaning "High Land."

90% of the population is black

My Haiti begins at the Grand Hotel Oloffson, where the ever-so-attentive major domo puts a rum punch in your hand before you can manage a "bon jour." The Grand Hotel Oloffson is as unique as the country. This is where Graham Greene sat on the veranda typing *The Comedians.* The swimming pool below is the setting for the scene with the floating body. This is where Sir John Gielgud and Anne Bancroft stay. This is where owner Sue Seitz locks up the stationery and leaves the money box open on the desk. Perfectly understandable in Haiti. No one would dream of stealing money, but stationery is hard to come by.

Then it's phoning to see if Issa el Saieh is in residence at his Galerie Issa. If so, would he send a car for me? Minutes later I'm halfway up avenue du Chili at the Galerie looking first for my friend Issa, his lovely lady, Susan, and daughter Babette. Next I look to see what kittens have been added to the ones in permanent residence. Then I look at the paintings that hang, lean, pile or hide in all corners of the Galerie. (Issa handles exclusively about 60 painters and shows about another 60 that other galleries handle as well.)

It's a toss-up between Chez Gerard and La Lanterne for dinner, but Issa has a message for Georges and Edwige Kenn de Balinthazy, the owners of La Lanterne, and that decides it. This elegant restaurant is in a restored colonial house, with an outside court filled with plants and flowers and an inside pool . . . for viewing, not swimming. A highly-valuable art collection hangs on the walls. The extensive menu includes Creole as well as Continental dishes, and we select escargots, followed by stuffed cornish hen and an excellent wine.

This is a Haiti-happening day, shared with special people in a multi-layered, complex island nation. Haiti is the first black republic in history which has survived a past rich in culture, tortured in spirit, bereft of material goods, leaders more than a little mad with power, the spell of voodoo, an incursion of United States forces, and *some* travelers who have understood her complexity.

TOURING

Days and nights are full in Haiti. If you stay in one of the hotels in Pétionville (a "suburb" of Port-au-Prince), it's an easy taxi ride into town. The momentum of the people will stun you unless you're used to New York subways. The sidewalks, streets and curbs are packed with a moving mass of Haitian humanity . . . all polite and good-natured but all on the go. Be prepared to move with them. There's no other way.

There's no better place to get indoctrinated than at the famous Iron Market where hundreds of stands are crowded into a massive, open-air, Byzantine-looking building made of wrought iron. Even before you enter, you'll be hustled by small boys tugging at your sleeve: "I carry your package. I show you best stuff." It's worth the small tip he expects to take one young guide along if only to keep away the others who are tugging at your other sleeve. Once inside, you will see a kaleidescope of goods that is dizzying. Wooden everything . . . vases; masks; bird and animal carvings; plates and bowls; even small tables. Bead everything . . . sandals; purses; necklaces; bracelets; beads in the wooden warri game (a Caribbean specialty brought over from Africa). Paintings everywhere, not "good" ones in the sense of a collection but fun and bright, and if you like one, why not buy it? Mixed in are pots and pans for sale, bicycle tires, recycled rubber dolls. You bargain. There's no other way. The Haitian sellers would be hurt and amazed if you agreed to their first prices. They might not even sell to you. You've spoiled the game!

Your driver should point out the *National Palace,* but even if he doesn't,

Sculpted by albert mangones

you'll recognize it instantly: a smaller-scaled White House that seems most impressive as you drive past (no tours, however) and a sign nearby proclaiming, "Duvalier . . . President A Vie." Stop for a moment at the nearby bronze statue of the *Unknown Slave* blowing a conchshell. It commemorates the call to liberty by the slaves and is truly beautiful, both in concept and conception.

Before heading to any of the well-known art galleries, you may want to visit the *Episcopal Cathedral of St. Trinite,* which will launch your Haitian art education. The first masters—Bigaud, Bottex, Obin, Bazile, Duffaut, Benoit—painted the murals that stun and amaze. They're a permanent reminder of the art world's discovery in 1947 of Haitian art painted by these masters. You may then want to go to the *Museum of Haitian Art* for a look at the past masters as well as the present ones. The museum also offers some paintings for sale in an adjoining annex (but, obviously, not their own collection).

You'll certainly stop by the new Musée du Panthéon National Haitien opened just last spring in downtown Port-au-Prince. This is an underground museum that's a series of connecting chambers dedicated to Haiti past and present, from Toussaint L'Ouverture to present President Jean-Claude Duvalier.

On other days you'll shop in the sophisticated boutiques, discover the excellent galleries of Haitian art, perhaps take the snorkel and glass-bottom boat excursion to the offshore coral reef at Sand Cay, and on Thursday morning, try to schedule the tour of the "gingerbread" houses, sponsored by the Museum, but led by an American, Fran Clarke.

One day (preferably Tuesday or Friday, both market days) should be dedicated to taking a trip to the *Kenscoff Mountains,* south of Port-au-Prince. As your car winds its way up the mountain road, you will see a spectacular view. Most visitors stop off at the *Jane Barbancourt Distillery* for a tour and free samples of their 22 kinds of rum liqueurs. The *Baptist Mission* is another must. Not only is this one of the best (and certainly the most inexpensive) places to shop in Haiti for handicrafts and clothing, but the money you spend is put back into the mission's cooperative for its school and hospital.

The market spreads up a hillside, and this one is strictly functional. It's a food market containing piles of shiny fruit and vegetables. The country folk fill their baskets for the week, and you might well wish to join them in buying some mangos, a coconut (it will be chopped open for you) or in enjoying the new and interesting sights and smells.

Another happening day in Haiti is the two hour drive to Jacmel, one of Haiti's few beach "resort" areas. (Others are Kyona Beach; Kaliko Beach; La Xaragua; the Bay of Gonave; Ibo Beach; Quanga Bay.) These are miniresorts on a low key, genuine scale. You can swim, sun and snorkel (if you've brought your own equipment) and have an excellent lunch, usually of the fish and shellfish from surrounding waters. Some of these beach hotels provide the option of renting horses for a not-too-exerting trot along the beach.

Not all visitors to Haiti take the 40-minute plane ride to Cap Haïten, but we strongly recommend that you do. Here, some 3,000 feet in the clouds, is where Haiti's first (and only) "king," Henri Christophe, built the Citadelle, justly called the eighth wonder of the world. Led by a guide, you journey up the mountain by mule or struggling pony, past wooden shack-homes, trees hanging with fruit, young men who pop out unexpectedly to play you tunes on their flutes. Finally, some 45 minutes later, around another bend in the trail, the Citadelle appears still towering high above you. The effect is staggering. It took about ten years for 200,000 slaves to drag the massive rock up the mountain that you are climbing by pony. Somehow they constructed this massive fortress for their "king," who feared an attack from Napoleon. (It never came.) Finally, inside the fortress, you see the cannon still in place, walk through the chambers built for soldiers and royalty, find your way down

The Citadelle could house 10,000 people

the labyrinth of secret stairways and passages. You leave knowing that you will never forget.

At the base of the mountain is the elaborate Palais de Sans Souci, also ordered built by the king. You should see the remains of this palace that was intended to rival Versailles. But it is the Citadelle you will remember. (The Air Inter Haiti pilots who fly you in and out usually fly over the Citadelle for their passengers. When you see it from the air, you realize the incredibility of the feat.)

Plan to spend at least one night or, preferably, two in Cap Haïtien at any of the handful of hotels. There's an unhurried charm about the town and a smattering of artists to visit. Besides, you'll feel that you're in a world apart from any other.

You'll return to Port-au-Prince knowing you've just scratched the surface of this multilayered island nation but knowing you will return.

Christophe shot himself with a silver bullet in 1820 in the palace

Inside Information

Hotels

Almost all add a 10% service charge and a required 5% tax.

★★★★★ THE GRAND HOTEL OLOFFSON

Picture a Charles Addams cartoon . . . draw in a London duchess, a best-selling novelist, an inveterate globe-trotter; add a dash of some nice people; expect the lights to fail when you're taking a shower, and you have the Grand Hotel Oloffson. You have it, that is, if you can get in. Because the hotel runs at a heavy year-round occupancy rate. Tanned and always trim, owner Sue Seitz is continuing her famed (recently deceased) husband Al's individual "traditions," that care more about attitude than money. In fact, one of their treasures is the painting over the bar (quite good actually) from a guest who couldn't pay his bill. Are you the kind of a person who would complain when the lights, water, whatever, go off? If so, obviously, you don't belong at Oloffson. But if you can convince Oloffson you're the regular sort of interesting person they expect, come on in. There's a swimming pool, and many of the studios and cottages have been named for former residents—John Gielgud, Lillian Hellman, Anne Bancroft, Marlon Brando, James Jones and others. There's also a folkloric show each Monday evening. *Cost:* $65–$125 per double, EP; $50–$60, single, CP.

If you're a little bit crazy, it helps

★★★★★ OLOFFSON MONTROUIS

"Paradise" this is, ensconced in a three-bedroom stone house on the sea, that comes with cook and three (!) staff persons. A 50-minute drive from town. Nights are quiet, with your choice of Sue's extensive collection of tapes and books you've packed or just quiet conversation. *Cost:* $175 per double per day, all meals included; $1,000 per week (six guests maximum), all meals included. Staff tip extra.

★★★★ CLUB MED

The unique and highly-successful French concept that has made Club Med a word known everywhere is in full operation at the village called Magic Isle. There are nonstop activities, most with a sports accent. It's the place to come for continuing activity and the chance to meet some of the 700 people the Club can hold at one time. Only possible drawback: You are about 50 miles north of Port-au-Prince near a small town called Montrouis. *Cost:* Varies according to the time of year and depends on a member's desire to include optional round-trip air transportation. The yearly membership fee is $30; children under 12, $15.

★★★★ RESIDENCE KATHERINE DUNHAM

One of the most special residences in Port-au-Prince. (Don't dare call it a hotel!) Five guest rooms, each individually decorated, are provided in the estate home of Katherine Dunham, the dancer, who is in residence at various times during the year. Long, formal gardens lead to a swimming pool and outdoor patio for informal breakfasts and lunches. Dinners are most formal, and a limited number of outside guests is accepted for dinner if they telephone before 10:00 A.M. on the day of dining. In Miss Dunham's absence, Egyptian-born, Israeli-raised Rosie Rubenstein is the manager, sharing honors with "Nudnick," a parrot who's partial to vodka and tonic. *Cost:* $120 per double with breakfast; $90 single with breakfast; year round.

★★★ CORMIER PLACE

Each of the 35 rooms are on a superb beach with hammocks privately placed in palm trees and luxuriant foliage among fifteen acres. All rooms have separate balconies and are decorated in Caribbean-collage spreads, offset by Haitian paintings. There are tennis courts, boardsailing, fishing, and spontaneous beach picnics where char-broiled lobster and chilled white wine are standards. *Cost:* $70–$75 per double MAP (breakfast and dinner), in season.

★★★ EL RANCHO

The archways, white walls, red-tile roof and dramatic, geometrically-patterned entrance, 10 minutes and 1,200 feet above the capital (in Petion-ville), are reminiscent of the earlier Spanish presence. Once the private home of proprietor and vintage auto collector Albert Silvera, it has sprouted wings, expanding to 115 rooms ranging from simply furnished to sumptuously appointed. On the grounds are two connecting pools, hot whirlpool baths, two bars—one beneath a waterfall—tennis and badminton courts, a gym and saunas. There's an indoor-outdoor restaurant and dancing at night in the Flamboyant nightclub, open to the wee hours. Need we add there's a spruced-up sparkling casino featuring blackjack, crap tables and keno. *Cost:* $80–$130 per double CP; $72–$110 per single CP.

★★★ HABITATION LECLERC RESORT AND CASINO

A few steps away is your semiprivate pool. A stroll away, over grounds, past statues gathered from around the world, is Habitation Leclerc's main pool, with a slide and a sunken bar, a native band playing nearby and a poolside buffet lunch—or on Sundays, brunches of Haitian fruits, chicken and champagne.

Possibly the retreat of Pauline Bonaparte Leclerc, Napoleon's sister, this 30-acre estate is an exotic mix of hedonistic pleasures, from the 44 luxuriously-appointed villa suites with bright Haitian accents, fresh-cut flowers, two king-size beds and sunken circular bath tubs offering eye level voyeur views of you and the Haitian foliage, to dinners served in the elegant main restaurant, to the international sophistication of the casino—a striking contrast of pale ivorylike carved wood walls and gaming tables for blackjack, roulette, craps and slot machines. Some of the decor was imported from New York's *El Morocco,* and there are on-the-house nightly cocktail parties. For those with sporting inclinations, there are tennis courts and a riding stable, and arrangements can be made for golf or water sports on secluded Cocoyer Beach (45

Pauline and her husband, a general, were sent here by Napoleon to get her out of his sight minutes away). *Cost:* $170, villa/suite EP; $130 per single EP; summer plans from $65 to $105 EP.

★★★ HOTEL LA JACMELIENNE SUR PLAGE
An unexpected resort in an unexpected town. Erick and Marlene Danies have created a first-rate hotel nestled in a perfect spot right on the fringe of Jacmel Bay's expansive sweep of unspoiled beach. The hotel's main bar area, filled with plants and ferns in bright copper pots, set against intricate iron grillwork, is also open-air. Another bar is perched beside a huge swimming pool. Waitresses, clad in lacy, white-skirted Haitian dress and white headdress, serve superb variations of traditional Creole dishes created by ex-New Yorker Marlene Danies. *Cost:* $45 per person, with two meals, in season.

★★★ HOTEL SPLENDID
The oldest hotel in Port-au-Prince (the main house dates from 1905). Most of the 50 rooms are modern, air conditioned, and grouped around a swimming pool. All is crisp and clean, under the eagle-eye of German owner, Wolfgang Wagner. *Cost:* $50–$55 per double EP, in season. Suite prices not yet set.

★★★ VILLA CREOLE
Like so many of Haiti's hotels, Villa Creole used to be a private mansion. It has since gradually and continuously expanded. There are now 80 comfortable, air-conditioned rooms, private gardens, a large, gently-angular swimming pool and veranda dining featuring many excellent French-Creole dishes. Every night there's dancing under the stars; three nights a week there's a Haitian show. *Cost:* $70 per double CP. $45–$65, single CP.

★★ IBO LELE
At Ibo Lele, enthroned in regal isolation high up in the mountains, every day is a clear day, and you *can* see for miles and miles—at least 100 miles. The spectacular view is a favorite feature of the terraced pool, whirlpool, dining area, and many of the 70 air-conditioned rooms and suites. As a bonus, guests have exchange privileges with the Ibo Beach resort located on Cacique Island, a 20-mile and a five-minute boat ride away. Here guests can scuba dive or snorkel, play tennis, windsurf, sail, swim or just wander. *Cost:* $65 per double CP.

Ibo Lele is a Voodoo god

★★ HOTEL BECK
The 15 oversize rooms on 36 acres with over 50 variations of shrub and tree, each have fresh-plucked flowers renewed at bedside daily, and any car left in the parking lot is washed by unknown hands! The hotel also has the largest swimming pool in Cap Haitien, filled with mountain spring water, and there's a show each Thursday afternoon of folkloric arts. *Cost:* $55–$75 per double MAP (breakfast and dinner), year round.

★★ KALIKO BEACH CLUB
Forty "choucounes" or Creole-style beach houses. Fifteen acres of gardens, surround, and there's a wide range of sports. Kaliko is a diver's by-word for sensational scuba diving and full water sports. *Cost:* $70–$75 per double MAP (breakfast and dinner), in season.

★★ MONT JOLI
There's indoor and outdoor dining, a large pool surrounded by a fragrant hedge and, 20 minutes away (by foot), a beach for sailing, swimming and snorkeling. (Cannons from sunken French galleons are visible a mere five feet below the surface.) The hotel has 45 air-conditioned rooms, many with a panoramic view almost equaling that from the bar. Arrangements can be made for Sans Souci and Citadelle tours. *Cost:* $70–$75 per double, breakfast and dinner.

A hotel since 1956, this is now the most "active" hotel in Cap Haitien

★★ ROI CHRISTOPHE
Though recently renovated, this pleasant, bougainvillea-covered, 19-room hotel built in 1724 with its quiet little courtyards and lantern-lit passageways, has kept the style of a more graceful era. Roi Christophe was orginally the mansion of the island's French governor. One of his most famous guests, Pauline Bonaparte Leclerc, stayed here in the early 1800s while her own estate was being built; today's guests can stay in the same suite (ask for room number 3). There are personalized "touches" everywhere . . . in the antiques that are . . . rich selection of Haitian paintings . . . private terraces to every large room. The food, served in a pretty, beamed dining room, is good. Outside are a fresh-water swimming pool and a bar, both surrounded by a lovely garden. The manager is Henri-Paul Mourral. *Cost:* $60–$75 per double MAP.

★★ XARAGUA
This is a comfortable beach resort in the town of Délugé on the north shore, about an hour and one-half from Port-au-Prince. The 48 rooms are spread out in a three-story modern villa that is most unusual for Haiti. Other beach hotels are hut style. The beach is just outside the front door, and the accent here is on water sports at ocean or poolside. There are tennis courts, and if you get restless, Club Med is ten minutes away. *If* they have space, they will allow paying visitors on a day basis (not overnight). But phone in advance. *Cost:* $100–$145 per double MAP.

★★ TAINO BEACH
One of the nicest of Haiti's handful of beach resorts, Taino Beach is on the southern shore in the town of Grand Goave. One-, two-, or three-bedroom accommodations are available in A-frame huts, all well decorated in the Haitian style. Besides the swimming pool, all water sports and tennis courts are available, and the owning Herau family is present. *Cost:* $85–$110 per double MAP.

★ PENSION CRAFT
Pension Craft, offering 12 small, scrupulously-clean rooms (10 with private baths), was once a home of Bernard Craft, the grandfather of owner Adeline Danies. Adeline converted it to a guest house 40 years ago with the help of Lucy Craft, her mother, who still oversees the kitchen. *Cost:* $35 per double with two meals.

★ ROYAL HAITIAN HOTEL AND CASINO
Set on the bay and surrounded by acres of lush, lovely gardens, the Royal Haitian, recently adopted by Quality Inns, with 80 modern, air-conditioned rooms, is a convenient base for shopping sprees and the place to stay for those who enjoy the tempo and the glitter of an elegant gambling casino. Afterwards dancing and other live entertainment are provided. The grounds contain a large pool with poolside bar and tennis courts. *Cost:* $70–$90 BP per double.

IBO BEACH CLUB
One of Haiti's oldest beach resorts, and the closest to Port-au-Prince (about a 25-minute drive), Ibo Beach is on its own island, Cacique, and that's reached via water taxi from the mainland. While there are accommodations for some 200 guests in A-frame bungalows, rooms are pretty basic, and more for day usage. *Cost:* $65–$75 per double, breakfast only, in season; $60–$70 per double, breakfast only, off season.

RELAIS DE L'EMPEREUR
This is the "house" that Parisian entrepreneur Olivier Coquelin rebuilt, a good hour's drive from the capital to Petit Goave. The ten, special great rooms date

from 1849. The town of Petit Goave itself surrounds, and the fantasy is a sharp contradiction to much of Haitian village reality. Guests are whisked by water taxi to Cocoyer Beach where beach dress is undress, and there's a truly magnificent three mile stretch of beach and a 150-foot swimming pool. *Cost:* $250 per double, in season; breakfast, lunch and dinner; drinks are free at Cocoyer Beach and sea-taxi to and from the Relais.

Restaurants
Port Au Prince - Petionville

★★★★ CHEZ GERARD
(Tel. 7–1949). Named for and created by Gerard Lancelot, this is a truly elegant restaurant. Tables are set with pure white linen, candles, fresh-cut flowers, silver and sparkling crystal glasses. Though the menu sounds a bit ambitious, the dishes—from rabbit to duck to frogs legs to red snapper to tournedos bearnaise—are excellent. (The check will run around $25 per person not including wine.)

Dining indoors and out

★★★★ LA LANTERNE
(Tel. 7–0479). Owned by Georges and Edwige Kenn de Balinthazy, this is a restaurant you won't want to miss, and you'd be remiss if you didn't strike up a conversation with Georges. He's a total charmer with an irreverent wit and a lover of all things aquatic, as evidenced by the elaborate aquarium in the restaurant and his long list of scuba-diving stories. Originally from Hungary, he served as a purser on one of the first cruise ships to call on Haiti; here he met Edwige and "jumped ship." The restaurant is in a lovely restored home; dining is by candlelight at poolside from an extensive menu, including some flambé Creole dishes. Georges recommends the black bean soup, langouste (lobster), steak au poivre and chicken djon-djon, but it's difficult to go wrong with your selection. (Dinner averages around $22 per person without wine.)

★★★ CÔTÉ JARDIN
(Tel. 7–1247). It's like dining in a Haitian country home, and you have a choice of the main house or the flower-filled courtyard. There's a selection of homemade pasta, and fish or meat as the main dishes: filet of captain fish with sorrel; grilled filet of sarde with mustard sauce; breast of duck with port wine sauce. Two house specialties are fisherman's marmite (for two) or the Bombay chicken with rice, raisins, bananas, pineapple, coconut, and fresh mint. Open for lunch or dinner, averages about $18 to $20 without wine. Reservations required.

★★★ LA BELLE EPOQUE
(Tel. 7–0984). The setting: One of Haiti's restored gingerbread houses, with Tiffany chandeliers and a dark intimate bar. The dining room is crisp and formal. The food: lambi (conch) done Creole style; grilled langouste; curried chicken; grilled red snapper, all first rate. (Dinner is about $15 per person.)

★★★ LA CASCADE
(Tel. 7–6704). The menu is Paris-inspired with a sprinkling of Port-au-Prince: mussels with basil sauce; mushrooms from Kenscoff in a salad; terrine of provençal pâte; lamb with noilly and safran; a glazed shrimp with cognac. Dinner is about $20 without wine; reservations are a must.

★★★ LE CHALET
(Tel. 7–1504). Informally Haitian, this restaurant specializes in Creole cooking, some of it hot; all of it good and interesting. There are some strictly French dishes, but the Creole specialties bring customers back. (Prices average around $12 a person.)

★★ KINAM
(Tel. 7–0462). A Haitian gingerbread house turned restaurant, with French-born Colette Gillet, the multi-lingual hostess. It's as heavy with ambience as with spicy possibilities. Fountains splash . . . ceiling fans whir . . . flowers blossom. Dishes are a mixture of French, Creole and Middle Eastern. Crepe aux fruits de mer is one specialty; another is a pepper steak with a sauce for visitors and a sauce for locals. Guess which is hotter! Dinner runs about $14 without wine.

★★ LE BELVEDERE
(Tel. 7–1115). Poised on a cliff overlooking Port-au-Prince, this restaurant gets the prize for a most spectacular setting. The place to sit is at one of the five tables on the terrace, farthest on the brink. However, unless your dining companion is among the local "in" set, don't be too disappointed if you can't get this prime spot. Actually, any window table has a view nearly as breathtaking. Two features of the menu are la bisque de langouste au Barbancourt and sole de Douvres. (Dinner is about $20–$25 without wine.)

★★ LE PICARDIE
(Tel. 7–1822). A small, informal restaurant with bright red and white checkered tablecloths. The waiters and other patrons talk freely in French, Creole and English. The menu is simple but delicious: snails from Kenscoff; langouste grilled; barbecued shrimp; and homemade ice cream for dessert. (Dinners average around $12 per person.)

★★ PHOENICIA
(Tel. 7–4171). Assorted Middle Eastern dishes. The decor is Mediterranean, with pebble white stucco walls, Aladdin brass lamps, and softly lit Doric columns. If you didn't know you were in Petionville, you could be on Mediterranean heights. Dinner is about $18 without wine.

★ LE ROND-POINT
(Tel. 2–0621). This is the best of the downtown lunching spots, where many of Haiti's working folk gather. An unpretentious but bustling restaurant, it serves freshly-caught local fish done in intriguing Creole styles . . . many flambé. (Lunch averages around $10 per person.)

Jacmel
★★★ LA JACMELIENNE
(Tel. 8–3331 or 8–3451). The newest and the largest hotel-restaurant in Jacmel, La Jacmelienne is right on the ocean. You can swim there or in the large swimming pool as you wait for lunch or dinner to be prepared. In fact, the swimming pool almost merges with the bar, and you can call in your drink order and do a few more laps. The menu is both Creole and Continental. (Cost: about $12 per person.)

★★ PENSION CRAFT
This is the colonial home of the Danies family. Now it's a pension and a small, perfect restaurant, where owner Adeline Danies reigns. And reign she does, turning out perfections such as pisquet, a caviar-like delicacy marinated with spices found only in Jacmel. Course after course follows, all for about $10 a person.

★ MANOIR ALEXANDRA
(Tel. 8–2111). Set in a colonial mansion, this is both a pension and a restaurant. Mme. Alex Vital is the owner. Her Creole menu features unusual tastes such as cooked cornmeal mixed with meat and rice, topped by red or black beans.

Nightlife

Ibo Lele's *Shango Club* provides more of a Haitian rhythm. On another level of the hotel there's dancing to a modern beat.

There's a "folklorique" show every night at one of Haiti's major hotels—*Oloffson; Ibo Lele; Villa Creole; Mont Joli*—and the show, performed by different show troupes, changes nightly. You can visit a hotel a night although you're apt to be following the same show. Each hotel follows a schedule.

Nightly voodoo shows, complete with lights and costumes, are staged at *Le Peristyle* in downtown Port-au-Prince. Without lights and with participants wearing their regular clothing, similar but more authentic performances are held at *Ticousin.* And on special, prearranged occasions, Katherine Dunham, the famous dancer, choreographs an evening ceremony at her *Residence Katherine Dunham.* Miss Dunham, now in her seventies, is an adamant follower of the voodoo religion, and if you can arrange to be part of this experience, it will be as close as you can get to the real thing without going into the hills. Even if there's not a special performance, it's more than worth the day-ahead request to come for a superb dinner with international, intelligent, conversation.

Voodoo is not a joke - it is a religion

When the urge to roll some dice strikes, gambling can be found in many Haitian haunts . . . the *Royal Haitian Hotel* and the *International Casino,* both in Port-au-Prince Dunes, El Rancho; Habitation le Clerc; L'Insolite, all in Petionville; and *International Hotel and Casino* on the road to Kenscoff. In addition to craps, blackjack, roulette and slot machines are available.

If you'd like to go where upper-class Haitians on the go, go, drop out of the hotel scene, and head to Petionville. It's the center of all PM activity. The *Shango Club* on a Friday night has a live show that draws a mixture of residents and visitors, and *Bubbles,* an outdoor cafe is very European in mood with its taped music, but Haitian in fact with Creole food and conversation in the French-based patois. After 10 PM, you might give *Luigi's Club Privé* a try where owner Luigi Roy draws the local elite for dinner and disco dancing. An after-dinner drink is still popular at *Le Bock,* but among the "in" places on weekends is *Mister P's;* you'll be warmly welcomed by regulars surprised at a face from out of Petionville-town. All are best on weekends.

Shopping

A tip: At the Iron Market, young Haitian boys will offer to help you. Take *one* of them up on the offer. He'll guide you through the crowds, ward off pushy vendors and carry your purchases for you. (For this he expects and deserves a $1 tip.)

(Two notes of caution: Wooden objects should go directly into your freezer when you get home and stay there for 24 hours to kill any insects that may still be lingering within. Also, do *not* buy goat rugs, tortoise shell combs or tortoise shell anything; all such items will be confiscated before you enter the United States.)

The goat rugs might harbor anthrax; the tortoise is an endangered species

Now that you've gotten a taste for things Haitian, on to the shops. Bargaining is not the order of the day here! Most of the shops are located on the long rue Panaméricaine. But one of our favorites, *Ambiance,* is slightly off the beaten track (15 avenue M) in a classic gingerbread house. It's owned by Mike Wallace's wife, and stocks a lovely collection of lace and cotton camisoles, handpainted cottons for sunwear by two young, chic French girls who design some 45 styles under the Lechuza label; exquisite silk sarongs, Haitian ceramic dinnerware and tapestries. There's lots of Haitian-made decorator items—lampshades; embroidered and woven pillows; printed Haitian cotton by the yard.

A telephone call to Sharona Albalak's Atelier (Tel. 55691) arranges a viewing of her handmade sweaters and sweater-dresses or Haitian cotton bikinis, all in the $20 to $30-line. It's also a chance to meet this charming Israeli, as well as see her work.

Two offbeat shops are *Jane Barbancourt's Castle,* with a sugarcane press and a replica of a distillery outside. Inside is the opportunity to sip and buy 22 kinds of rum liqueurs (from mango to hibiscus), made by the Barbancourt family since 1765. The Barbancourt rum outlet in the heart (and heat) of Port-au-Prince is where you buy the serious rich rums from one star to a five star that can be used as a cognac or you can buy the few remaining numbered bottles over 15 years old. You must bring your passport in order to make a purchase. Sue Seitz's *Perfume Factory,* on the main road to Petionville, specializes in aloe-based moisturizers, shampoos, perfumes and suntan products. (The aloe plant is an excellent burn remedy; for a product made from aloe, the price is based on the percent of aloe content.)

Galleries

In 1944 DeWitt Peters, an American artist, came to Haiti, recognized the artistic potential here, opened the Centre d'Art, and Haitian artists began to express themselves on canvas. Thus began Haiti's artistic explosion. The first of the famous Haitian painters were Hector Hypolite, a houngan priest, Philome Obin and Rigaud Benoit. Then followed Wilson Bigaud, Prefete Duffaut, Castera Bazile, Gerand Valcin and Andre Pierre. Theirs was a rich, diversified and spontaneous talent; their style was called naif by Madison Avenue's galleries, and their works were sought by art collectors around the world.

The Centre d'Art still blossoms, two floors in a white and grey ginger-bread house in Port-au-Prince, where the lower floor usually is devoted to the work of one artist at a time. The off-shoot rooms on the lower floor staircase leading to upstairs cul-de-sacs are filled and flowing with work of painters past and present.

We suggest therefore that if you're not an expert on Haitian painting but are seriously interested in buying a piece of art, you spend an hour or so in the Museum of Haitian Art at the College of St. Pierre in Port-au-Prince to acquaint yourself with the Haitian styles and get a "feeling" for the qualities that distinguish this work from the work sold on street corners. (We are *not* suggesting that you try to buy a Haitian painting as an investment, however. Select a painting that you love because you love it—not because you think it will dramatically increase in value.) The galleries handle fine artists—and there's no bargaining over prices.

Galerie Issa, located up the hill from the Hotel Oloffson, is one of the best. Issa, an engaging and helpful "patron" of the arts, handles 60 painters exclusively and another 60 on a nonexclusive basis. His selections, piled against one another and leaning against all available walls, number into the hundreds. His prices are fair—ranging from $25 to $900; occasional pieces go for more.

A recent addition is the Galerie Issa en Ville, downtown in the heart of Port-au-Prince. The new gallery is air conditioned, with paintings properly framed, hung and labeled, each with its own "space."

Another good gallery is the *Galerie Monnin,* owned by Swiss-born Michael Monnin and his father, Roger. They handle about 20 artists exclusively and show some 45 more. Many works are in their downtown Port-au-Prince location, but a better selection is housed in a second Monnin gallery on the road to Kenscoff. Prices range from $25 to around $2,000. Among the artists handled by Monnin are St. Louis Blaise; Éric JN-Louis; Simil; Fabolon Blaise; Pierre Joseph Valcin; Agénor.

The *Museum of Haitian Art* in downtown Port-au-Prince sells as well as shows Haitian painters. Of course, they do not sell past masters or museum pieces (such as Philome Obin, Hector Hyppolite, Philippe Auguste). But they do sell present masters in a rotating exhibit. Recently they showed Hilda Williams, whose style is more modern and whose works sell for $600 to $750. Or they might have an Andre Pierre in the same price category. More affordable are the handicrafts in the small shop attached to the museum . . . the carnival masks made from papier-mache; the vive (voodoo) dolls; masks wrought from tin drums.

Nader's Gallery has an established reputation largely because of Georges Nader, the man who supports it. He too handles painters, such as Lyonal Laurenceau, who's internationally known in the art world, on an exclusive basis.

The Galerie Marassa in Petionville has high prices. The art works they display is a true gallery advantage with proper space, lighting, etc. (This is a rarity in Haiti.)

In Cap Haitien, Luticia Schutt teaches and paints in her Atelier Arc en Ciel where a roomful of artists are usually at work, and other work is for sale. (Actually, so are the canvases in progress, if you'll wait for them to dry!) The average cost of a painting here is under $50.

At the Galerie des Trois Visages in Cap Haitien, serious artists are displayed at serious prices. It's sometimes possible to visit Philomé Obin, now 91, by special arrangement at his Cap Haitien home. And it's always possible to visit the new forerunner of Cap Haitien artists, Max Gerbier, who has a gallery at Bennett Plaza and where his wife Margot is usually "minding the store."

Sports

Spectator sports in Haiti are the Haitian sports . . . the ones the people love. There's usually a soccer game, the national passion, going on somewhere. Or if you really want to see a cock fight, your hotel waiter will know where next Saturday's fight is going to be held.

Active sports center at your hotel? It's the swimming pool; tennis courts; dance floor or the water activities at the beach resorts not located in Port-au-Prince. Until recently, scuba diving and snorkeling was strictly only if you'd brought your own equipment. Now there are three excellent centers for scuba diving and all water sports that are drawing aquatic raves from everyone. Georges Kenn, the owner of the well-known restaurant, *La Lanterne,* has turned his life-long love of all things below the sea into special water-borne weekends. Guests arrive in Port-au-Prince in time for Thursday night dinner at *La Lanterne,* then are driven to Cap d'Estree on the southern coast of Haiti where they spend four days diving through tunnels, down walls, into caves, and over wrecks. You will be staying at M. Kenn's private villa on two and a-half acres of beachfront. Only four to six privileged, if paying, guests are invited at a time, and communication is best directly via M. Kenn at his restaurant: La Lanterne, 41 Rive Borno, Petionville, Haiti.

Another excellent dive operation where you stay on the premises for as short or as long as you like, is Cormier Divers at Cormier Plage, P.O. Box 70, Cap-Haitien, Haiti. Here, on lovely resort grounds (complete with resident peacocks), with full sports facilities, the dive program is under the direction of co-divers Jane and Jerry Barnes, originally from New York. A resort scuba diving course for beginners of four hours and $50, equipment provided. There are limitless choices for those certified.

At the Kaliko Beach Club (about an hour or so from Port-au-Prince), all water sports—particularly diving—is personally handled by Alan Baskin and Eva Cope, owners of Baskin-in-the-Sun and themselves professional divers.

Another day or weekend water activity—precious in Haiti, since the captial, Port-au-Prince, has swimming pools only—is the chance to book the 51-foot sloop *Guachinango* skippered by Jean-Louie Richard and his mate Cornelia Schutt (who has recorded local songs), for a day on the ocean. The *Guachinango* has won several international races and its home port is at Ibo Beach (about two hours drive from Port-au-Prince). She leaves the dock each day at 9:30 AM for a day sail that includes reef explorations by zodiac or snorkeling gear, a Creole lunch, and sometimes songs by Cornelia (known locally as TiCorn) if she's in the mood. Cost is $50 per person for the day sail that returns by 4:30 PM. An overnight sail to the offshore island of Gonave is possible to arrange for two to six passengers. Call 2–0381 in Cap Haitien or 7–2889 in Port-au-Prince.

One of the newest and nicest possible sports activities in Haiti is an outside membership ($5) in the Athletic Club of Port-au-Prince. Not only do you get full use of the club's modern equipment, but there are classes in dancercize, self defense (karate), along with racquet ball, a huge swimming pool where diving is taught, and lots of torturous-looking body-building equipment. Your first clue that this is where upper-class, active Haitians spend free time is the international tapes that are always going, as are the "bon jour's" and "bon soir's" of the three international owners: Manou el Saieh; Raymond Smith, and Patrick Chemaly. Port-au-Prince telephone: 6–4381.

Within Port-au-Prince, snorkeling is only possible at Sand Cay Reef and there are daily boat excursions to the reef and guides to help you once you get there. Riding is usually the best along the beaches (an hour and one-half from Port-au-Prince), but ponies or mules are used on the long trip up to the Citadelle at Cap Haïtien, where it's not really riding as much as a laborious climb. Hunting for duck, guinea hen, water turkey and alligators can also be arranged. Deep-sea fishing is a possibility, but it's not easy to arrange.

If you're a serious sports fan, bring your own equipment. Otherwise, count on renting or borrowing a racquet or a snorkel mask.

Jamaica

THE HARD FACTS

Planning Ahead

Costs

It's the third largest Caribbean island

Jamaica, one of the largest and certainly one of the most developed of the Caribbean islands, does not fall into the inexpensive category . . . nor does the entire Caribbean these days. There are hideaways that are affordable, but in Jamaica . . . $60 a day per person would be considered moderate . . . and that doesn't count food. In the off season, April 16–December 15, rates fall as much as 50%. Most hotels and restaurants add a 10% to 15% service charge to bills. There is also a room tax which varies according to season and category of hotel ($2–$6US, per day).

Climate

Average temperature hovers around 80°F., with November to April the coolest months. Constant sea winds, called the "Doctor Breeze" keep coastal temperatures comfortable during the day. At night the wind comes from the land so temperatures fall to pleasantly cool levels. As you get up into the hills it gets cooler—generally in the 70s during the day; in the 60s or even 50s at night in the Blue Mountains. Average rainfall is 80", with heavy but brief showers in May, June, October, and November.

Holidays and Special Events

There are nine public holidays in Jamaica: New Year's Day (January 1); Ash Wednesday; Good Friday; Easter Monday; National Labour Day (always in May); Independence Day (August); National Heroes Day (October); Christmas Day and Boxing Day (the day after Christmas).

The annual 4-day Reggae Sunsplash International Music Festival, usually held in July, draws fans of this very popular, unique to Jamaica music, from all over the world. The best, brightest and newest stars—Peter Tosh, Jimmy Cliff, Bunny Wailer, Rita Marley, Yellowman Chalice and countless others—perform almost nonstop, open-air concerts in Montego Bay's new Freeport Bob Marley Memorial Performing Center.

144

Tour Operators

In the United States: Caribbean Holidays, Cavalcade Tours, Inc., Club Universe, Flyfaire, Inc., Jamaica Travel Center, Adventure Tours, Lib-Go Travel, Inc.; Lotus Hedonism Holidays; Thompson Travel, Sun-Time Trips; Brendan Tours; and Caribbean Tourist Consultants. In Canada: Fairway Tours (Canada Ltd.).

Sources of Information

In the United States; call or write the *Jamaica Tourist Board,* 866 Second Avenue, New York, NY 10017, Tel. (212) 688–7650; 36 S. Wabash Avenue, Chicago, IL 60603, Tel. (312) 346–1546; 3440 Wilshire Blvd., Los Angeles, CA 90010, Tel. (213) 384–1123 or 1320 S. Dixie Highway, Coral Gables, FL 33146, Tel. (305) 665–0557. In Canada: 2221 Yonge Street, Toronto, Ontario M4S 2B4, Tel. (416) 482–7850. In Jamaica, the local Tourist Board headquarters are in Kingston in the New Kingston Hotel, 77–83 Knutsford Blvd., Tel. 929–8070 with branches at the Cornwall Beach Complex, Montego Bay, Tel. 952–4425 or 952–2462; Ocean Village Shopping Center in Ocho Rios, Tel. 974–2570, 974–2582, and Port Antonio at the City Center Plaza, Tel. 993–3051. There is a Negril Visitors Service Bureau, Tel. 957–4243 as well.

Packing

Jamaica offers both boutique and beach-bought goods. However, it's not the best shopping in the Caribbean, and you should plan on putting almost everything you need into your suitcases. Laundering of cottons is quick, easy and inexpensive. We still suggest that you don't send things to the cleaners . . . unless you're staying for a month or longer. And when it comes to primping time, you have your choice of jumping in the shower for shampooing or going to any of the many expert hairdressers in Jamaica. Film here is *very* expensive—as much as $12U.S. for 36 exposures—so be sure to bring plenty along with you.

Documentation

The usual for Caribbean destinations . . . proof of citizenship (passport, birth certificate, voter's registration card) and an ongoing airline or cruise-ship ticket. This qualifies U.S. citizens to stay up to six months. Citizens of other countries should check with their nearest Jamaica Tourist Office. You are presented with an immigration form on the plane . . . and you're required to turn that in with about $6 U.S. when leaving (government tax).

U.S. and Canadian citizens don't need passports - all others do

Getting There

Getting to and from Jamaica is easy. From the United States to Kingston: Air Florida flies from Burlington, Vt., Boston and Miami; Air Jamaica from Baltimore, Chicago, New York, Miami, Philadelphia, San Juan and Washington, D.C. American Airlines has flights from New York; BWIA from San Juan; and Eastern Airlines from Miami. To Montego Bay: Air Florida comes in from the above cities; Air Jamaica from Baltimore, Chicago, New York, Miami, Philadelphia, and San Juan; American from New York; Arrow from Los Angeles and San Francisco; Eastern from Atlanta and Miami; Guy Airlines and Pan American from New York. From Canada: Kingston is served by Air Canada and Air Jamaica from Toronto; Montego Bay by Air Canada from Toronto, Halifax, Calgary, Winnepeg and Montreal and by Air Jamaica from Toronto. Within the Caribbean: Air Jamaica flies to Barbados, Grand Cayman, Haiti, Nassau and Trinidad; ALM from Curaçao and Haiti; British Airways from Nassau and Bermuda; BWIA from Antigua, Barbados and

Trinidad; Cubana from Cuba, Barbados, Georgetown, and Trinidad and VIASA serves Jamaica from Aruba.

Kingston, Port Antonio, Montego Bay and Ocho Rios are regular stops for most cruise ship lines.

Formalities on Arrival

Customs

Efficient but friendly officials now make spot checks only. Flowers, plants, fruit, meat, and vegetables are not allowed entry unless in cans.

Money

The Jamaican dollar is attached to the U.S. dollar, but like other currencies in the international monetary systems, it fluctuates. However, Jamaica does require that none of its currency be brought in or out of the country. IMPORTANT: It's also required that all hotel bills, in-bond purchases and car rentals be paid in foreign currency, travelers' checks or by credit card. American and Canadian dollars can now be exchanged at *open market rates* (which fluctuate daily) at commercial banks or airport exchange counters. This rate— $2.55 to $2.80JM for $1US—is much better than the Central Bank Exchange Rate ($1.78JM for $1US) that hotels are allowed to give. Keep bank receipts for reconversion—a maximum of $200JM—at the airport before departure. It is definitely an advantage to change your currency for shopping, taxis (though many drivers quote fares in $US), sightseeing, restaurants, etc., and places quoting in Jamaican dollars are often cheaper.

Getting into Town

Some hotels offer complimentary transfers and there are city buses that serve both Norman Manley Airport in Kingston and Donald Sangster Airport in Montego Bay, the two international airports. Taxi stands are just out the door of baggage claim areas. JUTA (Jamaica Union of Travellers Association) taxis are the most reliable and have set point-to-point fares. The usual price for the 11- to 13-mile trip to Kingston hotels is about $15US; $5–$9US from Sangster to most Montego Bay hotels. Major car rental agencies maintain desks at both international airports.

Settling Down

Tipping

If a service charge has not been automatically added to bills, tip the same as you would at home: from 10 to 15% depending on just how good the service was. 50¢JM a bag for bellmen; $2 to $5JM for raft trips; $1JM for great house guides are gratuity guidelines suggested by the Tourist Board, but these are, again, entirely up to each individual.

Learning to Cope

Business Hours.   Banks are open 9 AM to 2 PM Monday through Thursday; 9 AM to noon then 2:30 PM to 5 PM on Fridays. Shops are generally open from 8:30 AM to 4 PM in Kingston; 'til 4:30 PM in Montego Bay; til 5 PM in Ocho Rios Monday through Saturday. In Montego Bay on Thursday, shops close at noon; on Saturday in Ocho Rios they close at 2 PM; and on Wednesday in downtown Kingston and Thursday in New Kingston noon closings are the rule.

Electricity.   The standard voltage within Jamaica is 110 volts, although some hotels use the European 220 volts. Check with the reception desk, and if the hotel's voltage doesn't match yours, ask for a converter.

Water and Drink.   Tap water is chlorinated and filtered and safe to drink all over the island. Jamaica's Blue Mountain coffee is world famous and do be sure to try some of the unusual liqueurs—Tia Maria (coffee flavored), Rumona (rum flavored), Wild Orange, Pimento, Spirit of Forget-Me-Not or Ortanique (a mixture of orange and tangerine). Appleton is the best known and the best rum, coconut water is a cool, refreshing beverage; Red Stripe is the excellent local beer.

Communications.   Cables can be sent from almost all hotels and post offices throughout Jamaica, as can telegrams within the country. The telephone system is good and operates 24 hours a day, seven days a week, inside and outside the country. Main post offices are open 7 AM to 5 PM Monday through Saturday. Postcards cost 35¢JM; 1/2-oz. letters 75¢JM to the U.S. and Canada.

Jamaica is an Arawak Indian word meaning "Land of Water and Wood"

Language.   Everyone speaks English and the Jamaican patois of Welsh, English, and African.

Medical Assistance.   Major specialized hospitals are located in Kingston (University of the West Indies Hospital, Kingston Public Hospital) and Montego Bay (Cornwall Regional Hospital). Elsewhere, should you need to contact a physician, get your hotel desk or manager to recommend a good local practitioner.

Getting Around

By Plane

Trans-Jamaican Airlines has internal light plane service between Kingston, Ocho Rios, Port Antonio, Montego Bay, Negril, and Mandeville. Express Air Ltd. has several daily scheduled flights between Kingston and Montego Bay. Wings Jamaica Ltd. provides charter service, sightseeing rides, flying instruction, and sky diving flights.

By Train

There is daily train service between Kingston and Montego Bay. This is a picturesque four to six hour trip that goes through the mountains and along the coast. It's not posh comfort but you can't beat the price ($13.60J first class; $6.80 second) or the scenery.

By Bus

Both Montego Bay and Kingston have municipal bus services that go just about anywhere you might need or want to go. For very adventurous travelers, country mini-buses serve the entire island. Be prepared for chickens and ducks as fellow passengers, frequent stops, back roads, loud music, and drivers who seem to be practicing for Le Mans. Some excellent and quite unusual bus excursions are organized by Blue Danube Tours in Montego Bay and Martin's J.U.T.A. Tours with offices in Kingston, Ocho Rios, and Montego Bay.

By Car

Reserve rental cars well in advance in season. Most of the major U.S. companies such as Avis, Budget, Dollar, Hertz, National, and some reliable local agencies (Martins, Sunshine, Vacation Car Rentals) have desks at Montego Bay and Kingston airports and in major hotels. U.S. and Canadian driving licenses are valid up to one year. A credit card must be used as deposit or you will be required to put down $400 U.S. which will be refunded upon

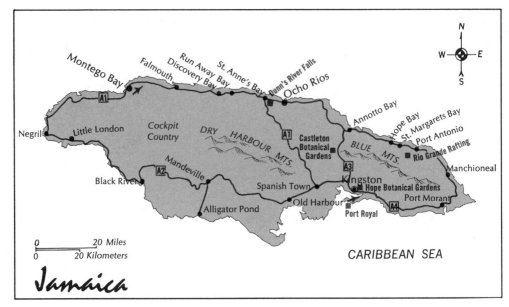

Jamaica

safe return of the car. Each company has a different insurance coverage so be sure to ask full details. Minimum age for renting a car is 25. Driving is on the left.

By Taxi

Most taxis (except in Kingston) do not have meters. J.U.T.A. taxis work as "contract carriages" with set point-to-point or hourly rates for touring. Get a taxi tariff sheet from the Tourist Board or check the fare with your hotel desk or doorman; then settle on the price with your driver *before* departing. All taxis that are licensed have red PPV (Public Passenger Vehicle) plates in addition to regular license plates.

TOURING

Jamaica is a large island . . . in fact, the third largest in the Caribbean and the largest of all the former British West Indies. It's 146 miles long and 51 miles at its widest point, totaling about 4,411 square miles. That will mean a lot of driving time if you want to see much of this country.

The capital, Kingston, has traditionally been a nontourist town. But for the traveler with a thirst to discover the pulse of Jamaica (and, indeed, of the entire business-oriented Caribbean), this is a "must" stop. Anyone who gets seriously bitten by the Caribbean-learning bug stops off here for a day or a year. This is where the art galleries are located . . . the centers where excellent Jamaican painters display their talents. Kingston is *not* a pretty town; it's a functional town. Don't underrate it.

Devon House was built in 1881 by a black mining millionaire

Although most visitors don't drop by the Parliament building or the foreign embassies, they're worth seeing. Far more likely on a visitor's agenda is a visit to Devon House, a beautifully restored, classical 18th-century mansion with courtyard restaurant and interesting shops; Ward Theatre—a pretty blue and white structure that is the Western Hemisphere's oldest theater; Hope Botanical Gardens—200 acres of tropical flora and a children's zoo; Kings House, the residence of the Governor-General; the crafts market and the new National Art Gallery, now located in downtown Kingston Mall in the Riy West Building that houses a wide range of Jamaican art from the 1700s to the present. There are serious art displays around the city . . . sometimes in front of painters' homes . . . the Bolivar, John Peartree, Little Gallery, Gallery Barrington and Olympia International Art Centre are just a few. Jamaican art deserves more than a passing glance. It's one of the few islands, including Haiti and the Dominican Republic, that have serious, internationally-recognized art, and although you may or may not plan to purchase, you will probably want to see and appreciate it. Much recognition came as the result of the work of Mrs. Edna Manley, the widow of Norman Manley (a national hero). She is considered to be one of the unquestioned leaders in sculpting. Much of her work is in the National Gallery or in private homes in Jamaica, but some of it is for sale. (Don't expect low prices; expect excellent artistic work.)

The Institute of Jamaica on East Street contains a lending and a reference library on art, history and philosophy that are well worth as much time as a serious student of the Caribbean can spare.

About a 20-minute drive or ferry ride from Kingston is Port Royal. In the 1700s it was considered to be the most wicked and the richest city in the world. Charles II was on the throne of England, and Captain Henry Morgan was on board his privateers outside Port Royal, fending off and attacking ships flying other flags in the area. (He even ranged as far as Panama.) Today about 90% of Fort Charles, where a lad named Horatio Nelson once served as a member of the British naval services, still stands. He served in Jamaica before he became admiral and lord and head of the entire British war effort based in Antigua. Some Jamaicans still say his spirit is here, but you'll get an argument on that from Antiguans! Much of Port Royal was destroyed by the 1692 earthquake, but the Jamaican Archaeological Museum, housed in the town's original hospital, displays many "finds," some dating back to the Arawaks.

To stay in or to visit Montego Bay is definitely on many travelers' itineraries. Dashed across the north coast, it's home to the best of resort hotels (along with those at Ocho Rios) and offers one of the best natural beaches in Jamaica. Doctor's Cave Beach was willed to the people of Montego Bay by Doctor McCatty, the former owner. It's a splendid stretch of natural sand; the waters form a mix of salty ocean and infeeding mineral springs. In daylight it's yours to enjoy (along with other Jamaicans). On Friday evenings there's the beach party at adjoining Cornwall Beach. (See the Nightlife section.)

There may be a band on board

Don't miss the Governor's Coach . . . a good, old-fashioned train of about three or four cars that does what trains are supposed to do . . . transport people in style. Once the private domain of the governor of Jamaica, this train has been turned into an all-day special coach that's very popular with visitors. It chugs its way about 40 miles into the interior, stopping at the Appleton Rum Distillery; the Ipswich Caves; and two stops—one on the way up, the other on the way down—to order custom-made shirts or dresses stitched up within the few hours that the ride consumes.

There's a clustering of great houses (former plantation estates) on the north shore. Many of these have been kept in original, mint condition and are open for visitors who want to glimpse estate life as it once was in Jamaica . . . on a grand scale. Rose Hall, just outside MoBay, is certainly one of the most infamous plantations, and several books have been written about Annie Palmer, its owner, who supposedly killed here several husbands and slaves whom she had made her lovers. Her ghost is said to still walk here. John Rollins, a former lieutenant-governor of Delaware, has purchased and restored the estate. In the same area, Greenwood House belonged to the family of Elizabeth Barrett Browning. The Barrett's original property once extended from Rose Hall almost all the way up the coast to Falmouth, 22 miles away.

Her husbands totaled seven, of whom six were murdered

Furnished with fine antiques, this great house has a collection of rare books and musical instruments, Barrett memorabilia, and supposedly two ghosts in residence. Good Hope, near Falmouth, was owned in the 18th century by one of Jamaica's richest planters, John Thorpe. Visitors can wander through this mansion of countless rooms and antiques and also arrange to traverse, on thoroughbred horses, some of the estate's 6,000 acres bordering the banks of the Martha Brae River.

Next, you'll pass through Runaway Bay. But this is not a place to pass through. Stop off at the Runaway Caves where escaped slaves once hid. It's now possible to take a boat ride through the underground Green Grotto Lake and feel the haunting presence of men desperate to obtain their freedom.

If you've kept driving, you're now in or near Ocho Rios, another resort center for visitors. Adjacent to the town itself are Dunn's River Falls, a day or an evening excursion. We suggest evening. That's when torches are lit and planted in the 600' tumbling falls, the sand and next to the picnic tables. For about $28 U.S. you'll be treated to a barbecue under the stars, a rushing waterfall and a very good show from a beachside stage. Dancing is barefoot. There's no other way to dance in the sand, and if you haven't learned Jamaica's slithery movements, you will now.

Also on the list of "Ochee's" attractions are Shaw Park Botanical Gardens, 34 acres set high on a hill with cascading falls, limpid pools, nature trails and a spectacular view of the town and coastline. There are long beaches, lush vegetation, excellent shopping, and dining and sports facilities. Do drive through Fern Gully, a 3-mile winding stretch of road that was once a river bed and is shaded by a living canopy of rain forest foliage and giant ferns up to 30 feet tall. Two more great houses are also nearby, both still working plantations. Prospect Estate's grounds can be viewed from wagons or on horseback on three specially designed trails that pass by herds of grazing Red Poll cattle, and through groves of lime, papaya, pimento, coffee and banana cultivations. At Brimmer Hall, closer to Port Maria, guests can lunch, swim in the pool, browse the shops, and visit the great house and its sprawling property.

The lush, tranquil area around Oracabessa was once the favorite retreat of the rich and the famous. This is the location of "Golden Eye," the long-time winter residence of Ian Fleming. It was here that he brought to life secret agent 007, admittedly borrowing his name, James Bond, from the author of one of his ever-ready references, *Birds of the West Indies*. Nearby, Noel Coward's "Firefly" is open to visitors as part of the National Trust of Jamaica. Miguel, Coward's former butler, will guide you around this small, unpretentious cottage filled with nostalgia. His simple grave—just a stone marker protected by a white wrought iron fence, is at the edge of the promontory with a spectacular vista up and down the coast.

Outside Port Antonio (about 67 miles east of Ocho Rios) is the Rio Grande River, the most famous of the rafting rivers. Harry Belafonte's (whose mother was Jamaican, his father from Martinique) lyrics, "work all day . . . drink of rum . . . Come Mista Tallyman, tally me banana . . ." depicts the hard life of a banana loader during the days when Port Antonio was a top banana port and the Rio Grande was used to transport the "green gold."

Port Antonio is known to Jamaicans for its civic attitude. Its houses are primed and painted; its gardens are kept neat and bloom with flowers. Visitors are apt to know Port Antonio for its Blue Lagoon. (Some say it's bottomless; others estimate its depth at around 160 feet.) Here it's possible to swim, snorkel or even water-ski surrounded by unrelieved stretches of beach and cliffs that tower behind. Excursions can (and should) also be made to Somerset and Reach Falls; Nonsuch Caves; Athenry Gardens and Boston Beach for a taste of the island's *best* jerk pork.

Ian Fleming, creator of James Bond, lived near Ocho Rios

Inside Information

Hotels

Smaller Hotels

★★★★★ ROUND HILL (MONTEGO BAY)

Eight miles west of town on a hilly peninsula, this resort is open only from mid-December through Easter, but when it's open, it's "the" place to be in Jamaica. Twenty-seven villas are scattered over the 98 acres that once contained a working sugar plantation. Each villa assigns a personal maid who cooks breakfast and even dinners if guests request this additional service. Thirteen villas have private swimming pools, one of the most spectacular being the former home of the William Paleys whose pool extends partly into the house! There are also 36 hotel rooms—all redecorated this year—in a two-story building overlooking the sea and a brand new main swimming pool. Guests enjoy breakfast brought to them each morning on their own private terraces. A team of European chefs is responsible for the superb cuisine served in the covered, candlelit Georgian dining room or on the open terrace. At the next table may be Lord and Lady Harberton, Joanne Woodward and Paul Newman, the Marchioness of Dufferin or Mr. and Mrs. Paul McCartney. Both the personal service given to all and the entire resort are impeccable. There's music every evening, Monday beach parties, Wednesday barbeques, and Saturday night's Gala dinner dances (where tie and jacket for men is obligatory, black tie requested . . . other nights dress is informal). A broad beach, water sports, three tennis courts, shops, beauty salon, massage, and car hire complete the rosy picture. *Cost:* $250 to $260 hotel rooms; $280 to $360 villa suites, double with three meals in season.

Jamaica's leading hotel since 1954, a warm and wonderful place

★★★★★ TRYALL GOLF AND BEACH CLUB (MONTEGO BAY)

Twelve miles west of MoBay, this 3,000 acre estate is known for having one of the Caribbean's most challenging and beautiful golf courses. A stately great house with 44 newly decorated guest rooms (the 20 ocean view and patio suites are the most spacious) is the core of activity, just as it was the hub of a sugar plantation when it was built in 1834. Scattered around the golf course, down on the beach and in the hills are 40 elegant, secluded two-, three-, and four-bedroom villas which can be rented by the week. Each is staffed by a cook, maid, laundress, and gardener and almost all have a swimming pool. Service, facilities and food here are superb and there's a heavy repeat business from pleased guests. Breakfast on the terrace features such tropical delicacies as coconut pancakes, eggs Caribe (Eggs Benedict with lobster instead of ham), fresh fish and homemade muffins. Lunch is enjoyed poolside or across the road at the beach bar. High tea is served each afternoon on the comfortable veranda and the evening meal taken in the multi-level, formal dining room or out under the stars. Guests can ride through the hills and by the sea on one of the resort's twenty polo ponies; play tennis on six courts (two lit for night play) or have Vincent, the ever-helpful concierge, arrange for scuba diving, sailing, water skiing, or deep-sea fishing. Some evenings a small band is invited for dancing but guests generally retire quite early after an active day on the green or courts or make their own fun at their villas. *Cost:* Great house rooms are from $140 to $230 double MAP in season. Villas (two bedrooms) from $1500 per week; three bedrooms from $2400 per week; four bedrooms from $2800 per week, EP in season.

a Mo' Bay favorite

★★★★ JAMAICA INN (OCHO RIOS)

A 50-room inn that serves high tea every afternoon on the open porch while guests play croquet on the lawn. This is the well-mannered (coat and tie are

On the beach

requested after 7 PM) ambience of this very popular resort where 75% of the guests return time and time again and the average stay is three weeks. The rooms are spacious and decorated with antique touches. Each has its own patio with well-cushioned furniture, fresh flowers and a spectacular view of the ocean, small pool or private cove beach. In addition to socializing, the inn offers such sports as waterskiing, snorkeling and fishing. It also makes arrangements for guests to play golf and tennis at the nearby Upton Country Club or ride at Prospect Plantation. *Costs:* $195–$240, double occupancy, full American plan. Children under 14 are not permited

★★★★ TRIDENT VILLAS AND HOTEL (PORT ANTONIO)
A very special place where genteel, gracious living is the golden rule. Peacocks stroll the lawns or may roost on your roof. High tea is a late afternoon ritual. Manager Josef Forstmayr, a wonderfully efficient young Austrian, has just the right amount of Old World charm and savoir-faire. Newly rebuilt, there are now 14 spacious studio apartments grouped around a lovely courtyard and 14 one-bedroom villa suites set down by the sea. No two are alike and all are exquisitely decorated. There's a large pool, a small sheltered cove for sunning, swimming, snorkeling or sailing and two tennis courts across the road. Days begin on the terrace with breakfast of freshly squeezed orange juice, myriad local fruit—otaheite apples, papaya, mango, bananas, sweet grapefruit, plus homemade banana bread and eggs (any style you like them). *Cost:* Studios $250; villas $290 double MAP in season. Imperial suite $470; Prime Minister's suite $400 EP.

(handwritten margin note: Between Port antonio and Frenchman's Cove)

★★★ JAMAICA HILL (PORT ANTONIO)
There's a philosophy at this hotel that can be summarized by the statement, "Our patrons are called guests, and when they leave, they're called friends." Such a philosophy guarantees a nice welcome to the 28 one- or two-bedroom villa apartments high on a hill overlooking the sea. Meals are served on the pretty blue and white terrace of the main house and table decor features some of the 18 varieties of bougainvillea and 37 varieties of hibiscus grown on the estate. Visit the Almond Tree Lookout for a fabulous view; sip a rum punch in the Tree Bar built around a 100-year-old fig tree; play tennis day or night on the two courts; ride—horse or bike—around the 700-acre property; jog down the 126 steps to crescent shaped San San Beach for snorkeling or sailing. Then if you still have some energy, arrangements will be made for you to visit the villages, falls, and farms of the countryside by foot, coach, raft, horse, bicycle or even a taxi. Included in the weekly rates are round-trip charter flights from MoBay or Kingston; hotel transfers; meals and drinks; tennis instruction and all other sports; room service, tax and gratuities. *Cost:* One bedroom villas $1,000 per person double; two bedrooms $1,350 per person double; $900 per person for four, full American Plan per week in season.

★★★ PLANTATION INN (OCHO RIOS)
120 guests are well accommodated in a rather formal, but friendly country club atmosphere. The decor of the spacious main building is fresh and bright. Lots of green, rose, and white. Flowers abound and the walls are hung with interesting original art work. They offer 65 compact but comfortable rooms that continue the color theme; all have terraces, ceiling fans, air conditioning, and the plushiest dusty-rose, oversize Martex bath and beach towels you've ever seen. Three large corner suites are also available. There's plenty to keep you busy . . . two white sand beaches; free snorkeling equipment, rubber dinghies, sunfish and windsurfers; a large fresh water pool and two tennis courts. Riding and golf are nearby. A resident band provides nightly dance music and there are frequent floor or cabaret shows, beach parties, and

(handwritten margin note: On one of Ocho Rios' beaches)

a not-to-be-missed "Plantation Evening," that celebrates Jamaica's cultural and culinary heritage. A beauty salon and boutique are also on the premises and the Coconut Grove Shopping Center is just across the road. Dress is casually elegant but during the winter season, jackets are required for men after 7 PM Monday through Thursday; ties on Friday and Saturday. *Cost:* $220 to $275 double, MAP in season; suite $350. Children under 12 on request only.

★★★ SANS SOUCI (OCHO RIOS)
A luxurious hideaway with a very Mediterranean feeling. Take an elevator or the stone steps lead down through the multi-level tropical gardens to two pools—one fresh water, the second fed by mineral springs—and a very private strip of white sand. Five pink and white buildings housing 45 suites (ranging from garden view to duplex penthouses) are hidden among the foliage. All are attractive and roomy and have living and dining areas, full kitchens and large terraces. Meals may be taken in Casanova, a romantic gourmet Italian restaurant (jackets required after 7 PM in winter) or on "Temptation Terrace" where there are evening buffet dinner dances. There are two tennis courts and guests here have complimentary membership for golf at the Upton Country Club. *Cost:* One bedroom suites $150 to $190; two bedrooms $240–$280; penthouses $260 to $360, EP in season.

★★ COCONUT COVE (NEGRIL)
Seven miles of beautiful beach stretch along the coast at Negril, and the Coconut Cove is one of a handful of resorts here. It has 44 luxury apartments with one or two bedrooms, living room, balcony or patio. Besides the beauties of this beach, there's a freshwater swimming pool, tennis, horseback riding, sailing, scuba diving, deep-sea fishing and windsurfing. Breakfast is served on the beach, dinner in the very attractive open air restaurant where some evenings there's a calypso band. *Cost:* One bedroom $180 double, two bedrooms $270 triple, $320 quad MAP, in season.

★ CHARELA INN (NEGRIL)
Sylvie (she's French) and Daniel (he's Jamaican) Grizzle have turned this Spanish-style hacienda on a quieter section of beach into one of Negril's nicest places to stay. There are ten simple but comfortably furnished rooms. Two of the rooms are considered deluxe and are upstairs with sea views (the honeymoon suite is, of course, most in demand). The Grizzle's sophisticated sense of style, warm hospitality and fine cuisine are drawing lots of repeat customers to their relaxed little inn, tiny provincial dining room, very Parisian bar, and delightful dinner terrace. *Cost:* Standard $120; deluxe and honeymoon $130, double MAP in season.

★ TERRA NOVA (19 WATERLOO ROAD, KINGSTON)
On the grounds of a lovely city mansion (which houses one of Kingston's most fashionable restaurants), the 35 balconied, comfortable rooms (all air conditioned and each room has a telephone) are built around the nicely landscaped gardens and small pool. This well-run hotel has a firm repeat trade of mainly business travelers who enjoy its good service and proximity to New Kingston. *Cost:* $70 double, EP

★ THE COURTLEIGH (31 TRAFALGAR RD., KINGSTON)
Recently renovated inside and out, this small hotel in a pretty residential area has lots of character. It's conveniently located for shopping, theater, gallery visiting as well as business; 35 rooms with terraces, telephones and radio, plus three elegant suites look out over the glorious gardens, the large pool or the Blue Mountains. *Cost:* $55 to $66 double; $86–$88 suites, EP.

HIBISCUS LODGE HOTEL (OCHO RIOS)
Ceiling fans and terrace breezes cool these 19 simple, modern rooms (4 are right on the sea) set in a garden on the same property as the popular Almond Tree restaurant. There's no beach but swimming and snorkeling are excellent right off the "sand deck" built into the rocks and there's a raft for sunning just a few yards offshore. This is one of Jamaica's best bargains for its location alone, secluded yet within walking distance of Ocho Rios' activities. *Cost:* $48 double, EP in season.

Larger Hotels

★★★ JAMAICA HILTON (OCHO RIOS)
A resort with all the Hilton amenities plus the stamp of its own personality. There are 265 rooms spread over 22 acres. Most of the rooms have ocean views. All have private patios or balconies. There's a lot of action here. The best aquatic center, "See and Dive Jamaica, Ltd.," offers everything from basic snorkeling to a full certification course in scuba diving. There are also tennis clinics, sailing, fishing and boating. *Cost:* ($166–$199 double; $260–$445 suites, MAP, in season.

On the beach

★★★ JAMAICA PEGASUS (KNUTSFORD RD., NEW KINGSTON)
This seventeen-story tower is the city's largest hotel with 350 deluxe, wall-to-wall carpeted rooms, 3 luxury suites and 112 studio suites. The accent is definitely on conventions. There are meeting rooms for up to 1,000 people. Trusthouse Forte runs everything smoothly, efficiently and very personal for such a large, busy place. Vacationers have not been forgotten—there's an Olympic-size swimming pool and a smaller one for children; shops, beauty salon; jogging track; putting green and arrangements can be made for golf and tennis nearby. There's lot's of activity here with nightly entertainment and several bars and restaurants. The rooftop "Talk of the Town" with its panorama view is Kingston's best. *Cost:* $100–$125 double; $150–$250 suites, EP.

★★★ HALF MOON CLUB (MONTEGO BAY)
An 18-hole championship golf course as well as 13 tennis courts draw visitors to this 191-room resort near Montego Bay. Recently 62 self-catering apartments have been added for those who want to be on their own (although management will stock them for you at your request and the services of a cook/maid are included in the rent). Everyone shares in the joys of 2 freshwater pools, 4 squash courts, sauna and massage, beach-bonfire picnics and nightly activities. It's a country club atmosphere, where most guests have preferred the richly-decorated villa suites, some with their own pools; but over the summer all the deluxe and superior rooms have been completely refurbished—including new baths. The grounds are sprawling, there's a mile-long white-sand beach and a good sports center for water activities. *Cost:* $229–$248 double rooms; $298–$378 suites MAP; $74.50–$139 apartments, EP, in season.

★★ ROSE HALL BEACH HOTEL AND COUNTRY CLUB (MONTEGO BAY)
This large (508 rooms and 36 suites) seven-story resort complex has just received a 4½ million dollar face-lift. A lot of action takes place on the 18-hole golf course and six tennis courts. There are water-sports activities and a choice of swimming pools. There's also a choice of dining rooms, one on the veranda of the great house, followed by late-night discoing in the bistro. Most guests go home well satisfied. *Cost:* $90–$200, double, EP

a Montego Bay stalwart

★★ ROYAL CARIBBEAN (MONTEGO BAY)
Sunfish dot the shore . . . a diving boat waits . . . and a fully equipped Sport Fisherman takes guests out to do battle with blue marlin, yellowfin tuna, wahoo. The 168-room resort contains a tennis complex with a resident pro, and a golf course is minutes away. The architecture is Jamaican colonial, with flowers and tropical greenery both inside and out. A lot of evening activities are overseen by the friendly staff eager to assist. *Cost:* $109–$280, double, EP, in season.

near Mo'Bay's airport

★★ SHAW PARK BEACH HOTEL (OCHO RIOS)
120 rooms fan out down the 1500-foot, palm-shaded beach. All face the sea and have wall-to-wall carpeting, air conditioning, balconies or patios. The 60 deluxe accommodations in the Mermaid and Neptune wings are, by far, the most attractive. There are also 12 extra nice, newly-spruced, two-bedroom apartments with two baths and kitchenettes. Activities are endless—two tennis courts, a new free-form swimming pool in the gardens, a children's pool, and a branch of the excellent See and Dive Jamaica Ltd. water sports school, all on the premises, and golf at the Upton Country Club, just 10 minutes away or horseback riding to can easily be arranged. Three bars, and a restaurant with a good reputation and "Silks," Ocho Rios' most "in" discothèque keep guests occupied until the wee hours. *Cost:* $128 to $141 per double; $336 suites quad, with full breakfast in season.

★ SANDALS (MONTEGO BAY)
Also for couples only but somewhat more upscale, less frenetic. Clothing is casual but guests seem to dress up more. There's a choice of accommodations ranging from superior or deluxe rooms to villas with their own swimming pools. All are air conditioned, spacious and have telephones. In addition to the usual long list of water sports and tennis, there's a complete health club with sauna, gym, exercise classes, jacuzzi, racquet ball and squash courts. Food is above average with a breakfast buffet; lunch served by the pool or on the beach; sit down dinners with full waiter service and there's also a beach barbecue. Champagne is offered on arrival, there's a champagne brunch on Sunday, a 24-hour juice bar, and late night snacks. The staff (called "Playmakers") is 100% Jamaican and couldn't be more helpful. *Cost:* $1,550 to $2,000 for two all-inclusive, depending on accommodations chosen in season.

COUPLES (TOWER ISLE, ST. MARY)
The first resort of its kind, 6 years old and still going strong with the island's highest occupancy record. These 141 rooms are reserved for twosomes only, singles and children need not apply. Breakfast and lunch are buffet, dinner more formal in the dining room with tables for four or six. Activities can get rather frantic but the staff (called "coordinators") is genuinely friendly and energetically conducts the ongoing lessons in every conceivable sport, both indoor and out. If you get tired of all the activity, take the boat over to the private offshore island for sunbathing in the buff; visit the well-stocked shopping center that carries everything from aspirin to expensive jewelry designed by an *ex*-Miss World or just stake out one of the double hammocks on the beach. If action for two is your aim, this is the place. *Cost:* $1,780 to $1,860, all-inclusive for two. Rates depend on particular week and room choice of ocean or mountain view.

HEDONISM II (NEGRIL)
For those who enjoy a nonstop party atmosphere; bodies in barely-basic bikinis; contests and games galore . . . wet T-shirt, find your husband blindfolded, pass the banana, and so on. Casual living and total freedom are the bywords of this 280-room resort that attracts mostly singles but welcomes

couples too. Dive into the pool at midnight and show off your form to dancers in the disco watching through the underwater window; then play tennis if you feel the urge. Dress or undress . . . there's an official nude beach. Join in the planned mixers to meet a maximum of fellow guests or walk for hours on the beach (7 miles long). Learn or perfect almost any sport or just roll a chaise into a secluded spot on the 22 acres and daydream. Meals are all buffet style, rooms are large and have recently been completely redone. *Cost:* $650 to $790 per person all-inclusive, depending on the week chosen.

HOTEL OCEANA
On the waterfront, Kingston. In the heart of town, this hotel has 330 large rooms and suites and all the amenities of a former Inter-Continental. Although it caters to the needs of businessmen, there's a swimming pool, tennis courts, boutiques and several restaurants and bars to enliven your nights. *Cost:* $73–$83 double; $80–$160 suites, EP.

NEW KINGSTON HOTEL
Knutsford Rd., New Kingston. Even though the name has been changed, most local folk still call this the Sheraton. This spruced-up 17-story hotel with 196 rooms, 6 jr. suites and 2 penthouse suites is a long-established residence for people on business. Since Kingston is the crossroads of business in the Caribbean, this hotel is ready with a convention hall and meeting rooms. But it also provides amenities for tourists: 2 tennis courts, a swimming pool with poolside bar, several restaurants and a lively nightclub. *Cost:* From $70–$90; jr. suites $149; penthouses $200, double EP.

Restaurants

Montego Bay, Port Antonio, and Ocho Rios
Do ask your hotel desk to find out if the restaurant of your choice arranges round-trip transportation. Most do at no charge or at considerably lower tariffs than taxis.

★★★★ TRIDENT VILLAS AND HOTEL (PORT ANTONIO)
Just east of town (Tel. 993–2602). Part of the prestigious Relais de Campagne-Châteaux Hotel group (one of four in the Caribbean) whose rules for membership require the highest standards of quality and cuisine that is *haute*. The six-course gourmet dinners are always superlative but change nightly depending on what is in season and freshest on the market. Tiny sweet spring lobster, caviar blinis and tournedos Rossini are always a treat, but rest assured whatever is on the menu will be good. The atmosphere is very formal, yet somehow relaxed and relaxing—something like that of a very pleasant but very elegant country inn in France or England. Reservations are absolutely essential as the timbered dining room is always popular with the hotel's guests. *Expensive.*

★★★★ TRYALL GOLF AND BEACH CLUB (OCHO RIOS)
Hanover (Tel. 952–5110). Specialties include veal sauteed in rosé wine with papaya and coconut; crispy tamarind duckling; tender lobster with scallions in a mornay sauce; boned breast of chicken on a bed of *callaloo;* double sirloin with a green pepper sauce. There are 17 different menus in all. Dress is always elegant in the multi-level dining room and terrace of the Great House. If you have your own transportation the 12-mile trip out here for dinner is well worthwhile; taxi fare will run a steep $25U.S. one way. Reserve your table well in advance. *Expensive.*

★★★ ALMOND TREE (OCHO RIOS)
Hibiscus Lodge on Main Street (Tel. 974–2676/2813). Lunch is served under the almond tree surrounded by bougainvillea and hibiscus; at dinner the upper, open terrace overlooking the sea is available for dining. This is;

outdoor, informal dining at its best. Hors d'oeuvres include escargots smoked marlin; island-style fish cakes and two kinds of crepes. Main course specialties are medallion of beef Anne Palmer (three small filet steaks with a very spicy pepper sauce); chicken Hibiscus—pieces of chicken wrapped with bacon, topped with a special herb sauce then gratineed. Reservations are imperative. *Moderate.*

★★★ CALABASH (MONTEGO BAY)

Queens Drive (Tel. 952–3891 or 952–5986). Mrs. Berryl Hall's cuisine is more creative than the usual island fare . . . cream of celery and conch soup; spicy pork flavored with allspice and ginger; boneless curried goat; roast lamb in a creme de menthe sauce with cherry tomatoes and scallions and the house specialty, a tasty mixture of shrimp, lobster, crab and other seafood baked in brandy, then gratineed. Effervescent owner, Roma Chin-Sue's careful attention to detail, style and cuisine make this spot one of MoBay's best. *Moderate.*

★★★ CHEZ ROBERT (OCHO RIOS)

Main Street, Turtle Beach (Tel. 974–5007/8). The large air-conditioned dining room is under a spectacular conical wooden roof, hung with a dramatically tiered chandelier. There is also a long, open terrace overlooking the water. The strictly Continental food is deftly prepared and artfully seasoned; tasty sauces are the chef's forté. Most will be accompanied by the classic Swiss dish of crusty pan fried potato and onion slivers. Service is *soigné* and the elegant surroundings very relaxing. Reserve in season, well in advance for terrace tables. *Moderate.*

★★★ HALF MOON HOTEL CLUB HOUSE GRILL (OCHO RIOS)

Rose Hall area (Tel. 953–2228/2314). One of two excellent restaurants in this hotel which has Jamaica's most complete wine cellar. The grill is set on a very large outside patio overlooking the golf course. The specialty is prime rib carved from a silver trolley; flambéed shrimp and steak—Diane or au poivre; and broiled lobster. *Expensive.*

★★★ MOXON'S (OCHO RIOS)

Boscobel, St. Mary (Tel. 974–3234). This candlelit patio with soft music is one of the most romantic dinner spots in Ocho Rios. You can hear the waves below, but unfortunately you cannot see them in the inky blackness that could benefit from some illumination. We can heartily recommend the homemade liver paté Normande (an unusual taste treat made from calves liver); lobster thermidor in a creamy sherry and lime sauce; the Jamaican beef curry and the Hungry Monk (a filet steak with cheese and raw onion cooked in Red Stripe beer). Reserve your table. *Expensive.*

★★ CASANOVA (OCHO RIOS)

Located in the Sans Souci Hotel. The chef concentrates on pasta and other Italian dishes. It's the place to come when you're tired of local dishes and standard international cuisine no matter how well done. Jacket and tie are requested at dinner. *Expensive.*

★★ RICHMOND HILL INN (MONTEGO BAY)

Top of Union Street (Tel. 962–3859 or 952–5432). In a colonial house once owned by the Dewars family of Scotch whiskey fame. This hotel-restaurant's somewhat limited menu offers well-prepared dolphin, lobster, steak, veal, and lamb. Both lunch and dinner are served on a poolside terrace above the bay and below the Jamaican hills. *Expensive.*

★★ TOWN HOUSE (MONTEGO BAY)

16 Church Street (Tel. 952–2660). An "in" spot with Montego Bay executives and knowledgeable visitors. Julia and Jim Snead now run this English

not far from The Parade

pub which is situated in the cellars of an 18th-century, all-brick townhouse. Red snapper, "papillotte," is the house specialty and it's cooked in a brown paper bag in a light lobster and shrimp sauce with just a touch of cheese. *Moderate.*

★ FRONT PORCH RESTAURANT (MONTEGO BAY)
Gloucester Avenue (Tel. 952–2854/3679). Located in the Wexford Court Hotel, this restaurant is simple but authentic in its preparation and presentation of Jamaican specialties. The owner, Godfrey Dyer, features the national dish, ackee and saltfish, also curried goat or mutton and, of course, "jerk" pork or beef. But it's the delicious local fruit that most visitors truly enjoy . . . paw-paw, pineapple, bananas, guava, mangos. *Inexpensive.*

★ GEORGIAN HOUSE (MONTEGO BAY)
19 Union Street (Tel. 952–4914). A personal place in a 300-year-old stone townhouse. Indoors, 6 tables seat just 30 guests in a cozy room with flagstone floor and stucco walls which frame the colonial furniture. You can also ask to have a place set in the garden. The menu is small and simple, but the competent lady chef has a way with chicken, lobster (sauteed with green pepper and onion or spiced-up and stuffed in classic patties), crab (baked or in a delicious omelette with cheese), and there's always a good daily special. *Inexpensive* to *moderate.*

★ KING ARTHUR'S RESTAURANT (MONTEGO BAY)
Ironshore (Tel. 953–2250). Ray and Roy Watkin's large new restaurant has 32 tables inside, 42 on a terrace hung out over the waves. Food features grilled meat, seafood, and Jamaican specialties at both lunch and dinner. *Moderate.*

★ MARGUERITE'S (MONTEGO BAY)
Gloucester Avenue (Tel. 952–4777). The stunning batiks of Muriel Chandler decorate the walls of this good size (120 seats), very popular seaside spot. The menu is small . . . quiche du jour, lobster bisque and a daily special soup, broiled fish, lobster sauteed or baked, chicken two ways, steak, and pork. The fare is generally good and the service and ambience most agreeable. Dinner only. *Expensive.*

★ THE DIPLOMAT (MONTEGO BAY)
9 Queens Drive (Tel. 952–3353/4). The setting, in a colonial mansion, couldn't be more elegant . . . a drawing card for upper class Jamaicans as well as visitors. The emphasis is on Continental, steak, seafood and some Jamaican specialties. Service is impeccable, and the atmosphere more than makes up for the rather undistinguished cuisine. Dinner only. *Expensive.*

VERANDAH (MONTEGO BAY)
Gloucester Avenue (Tel. 952–4130). Columns, delicate latticework, and wicker chairs in white are set off by flaming red nappery on large, well-spaced tables decorated with sprays of fresh flowers. This pleasant, second-floor porch of the Coral Cliff Hotel is primarily for guests, but outsiders may dine here with reservations. Stop by for sunset cocktails and check the menu (it changes daily). If lobster is featured keep in mind that this is one of the few places we were able to enjoy lobster tender . . . not overcooked and tough as we too often found, even in far more pretentious places. Service is careful and cheerful, the airy atmosphere very relaxed. Open breakfast, lunch and dinner. *Inexpensive* to *moderate.*

THE RUINS (OCHO RIOS)
Tel. 974–2442/2789. Chinese and Continental cuisine in a very special setting of cascading waterfalls, lush tropical gardens, natural streams and pools. They serve a buffet lunch daily for $9.50 U.S.; dinner is à la carte with

[handwritten note in margin: Finish up with Blue mountain coffee]

such specialties as chicken with pineapple; lotus lily lobster; seafood quiche; grilled meat and fresh fish. Take a tour of the grounds before you try the special house drink—rum, vodka, Tia Maria, cherry brandy, pineapple juice, and sugar syrup—quite a knockout combination. *Expensive.*

Negril

★★★★ TALK OF THE TOWN

Jamaica Pegasus Hotel (Tel. 926–3691 ext. 531–4). The view is breathtaking with the sparkling lights of Kingston spread out for miles below. The fare is international with just a touch of Jamaican flavor. The wine list is excellent and costly but you might try one of the quite pleasing, locally blended Montpeliers (red) or Monterey (white). Very attentive service from the maitre d' down to the busboys and top-notch food make this 17th-floor aerie as popular with Jamaicans as it is with visiting businessmen and tourists. *Expensive.*

★★★ CHARELA INN

Negril Beach (Tel. 957–4277). Lunch is served in a pretty provincial style dining room and features local specialties—curried goat or chicken; ackee and saltfish as well as those fabulous French pizzas and crepes. Dinner is set by candlelight on the hotel's patio just a few steps from the sea. This is healthy French Jamaican cooking, no artificial coloring or preservatives. The chef-owner does all her own baking, makes the fresh cream and utilizes many products from her own farm. In season reservations are recommended at both places. *Moderate.*

★★ CAFE AU LAIT

Lighthouse Road, no telephone. The menu is decorated with hand-drawn flowers and features quiche of the day; crepes—cheese and calaloo, chicken and mushroom or lobster; vegetarian, fish, bacon or lobster pizza with homemade crust and tomato sauce; several salads and about a dozen main courses to choose from. This is a very casual, homey little place where Preacher, the Jamaican manager, maitre d', bartender, etc., will look after you well. *Inexpensive* to *moderate.*

★★ COCONUT COVE

This hotel-restaurant nests on Negril's nearly perfect seven-mile stretch of sand. Breakfast is served on the beach, while the hotel "dining room" contains tables formally set on a terrace at the edge of the beach. By day it offers an oceanic panorama; by night, sparkling moonlit waters. Continental food (steaks, chops, chicken and so on) is served, as are some Jamaican dishes. *Moderate.*

★★ SUNDOWNER

This is a special guest house on Negril Beach—in fact, the oldest "hotel" here—that accepts a limited number of outside reservations for dinner. Wednesday night is the buffet special, with honest Jamaican cooking all hot and fresh from the oven. The atmosphere is low-key, beachside—you dine inside or out, depending on the weather. Some of the unlimited amounts of cuisine can be partly walked off in a stroll after dinner, to the other end of the beach. *Moderate.*

★★ TERRA NOVA

17 Waterloo Road (Tel. 926–2211/9334). A good day for lunch is Friday when there's an especially good seafood buffet which might be preferable eaten on the terrace with a view of the lovely gardens. Food is international with several interesting specialties—hard-to-find baked crab; a rich fish chowder; entrecôte Cafe de Paris; steak au poivre; roast prime ribs with horseradish cream and lobster thermidor. *Expensive.*

★ **PIRATE'S COVE**
On the waterfront. This pretty, very popular new seafood restaurant is right on the water in downtown Kingston. The best tables are under the awning on the side terrace upstairs. Lunch is light—seafood chowder, salads, fish and chips, etc., with a buffet twice a week. At night the atmosphere becomes romantic and the menu more varied. The Sunday brunch from 10 AM to 2 PM is Jamaican style. *Inexpensive.*

★ **ST ANDREW GUEST HOUSE**
13 West Kings House Road. You won't see many tourists here in this tucked-away, old house. What you will see are lots of Jamaicans who love good, home-style cooking. All the local specialties you've heard about, and some you haven't, may be tasted—gungoo pea soup; ackee and saltfish; mackerel run-down; tripe and beans; smoked pork chops; pickled ox tongue. Everyone we talked to considers this cuisine some of the best and most authentic in town, maybe on the island. There's a small bar that stays open fairly late and the ambience is homey and friendly. *Inexpensive* to *moderate.*

Kingston

BLUE MOUNTAIN INN
20 minutes from New Kingston (Tel. 927–7400). The setting is sublime. An elegant dining room in an 18th-century, antique-filled great house 1,000 feet up in the lush foothills above Kingston. Cocktails are taken on the terrace overlooking the Mammee River and the gardens, which are both nicely illuminated. The menu is extensive and *seems* quite intriguing, unfortunately, far more intriguing than the food itself. Bland is the kindest description; tasteless could even be used in some cases. *Expensive.*

   Note: $8 round-trip limousine service can be arranged when making reservations.

Nightlife

When the sun goes down, Jamaicans and guests come out. There aren't any casinos in Jamaica, but there's a lot of live entertainment at the big hotels, clubs and dicothèques all over the island. You could spend a month discovering Jamaican nightlife and not once repeat an evening out!

   Jamaica also offers several beach parties that are unique to this country . . . one where you canoe down a river to the beach . . . another involving falls that cascade down to a beach lit by flaming torches.

   Montego Bay is one of the main centers for visitors to Jamaica, and clubs and discos vie for their attention. The *Disco Inferno,* with plush red carpets and doormen in tuxedos, is the largest in Jamaica. The club is across from the Holiday Inn and draws Jamaicans as well as guests. It's a true disco, with flashing lights, that starts swinging around 10:00 and goes till dawn.

   Footprints, in the Coconut Grove (shopping) Plaza, Ocho Rios, is distinctive and popular with young local folk. Phosphorescent footprints lead visitors to and through the door, where there are more day-glow footprints. The music is taped, and there's a cover charge (small), but paying it guarantees an evening well danced.

   Two other special evenings are popular in Ocho Rios . . . the beach parties given at Dunn's River Falls and the White River Feast. At *Dunn's River Falls,* a natural cascade of water tumbles onto the sandy beach where picnic tables have been set for munching visitors. Each Thursday torches are lit both in the sand next to the tables and, somehow, in the falls themselves! There's an open, nonstop bar featuring the local (and excellent) Jamaican rum that complements the buffet supper. Pumpkin soup is one specialty (spicy and

a good drink anytime can be made from appleton's white rum

Wear your swimsuits

delicious), and then the "jerk" pork or beef or perhaps the more sedate roasted chicken. Curries abound . . . goat, beef, mutton . . . as do local fruits and vegetables. Dinner is followed by a folkloric show of costumed dancers, singers and musicians. Then guests follow the professional show with their own show . . . dancing on the beach to the live music that keeps pace with the guests' mood. (The cost is about $28U.S. per person, and that includes everything.) Sunday, when the *White River Feast* is held, is a special evening. Guests board canoes to be poled for the 15-minute ride up the White River to picnic at beachside spreads. There's another opulent buffet set on groaning boards; limitless rum drinks; a beach show with professional entertainers and dancing barefoot (or with sand in your shoes) under a star-splashed sky. (The all-inclusive cost here is about the same: $28U.S. per person.) *Most important:* Check your hotel desk for these once-a-week evenings of beaching, dancing and dining. They have been known to change unexpectedly.

For those who stop off in *Kingston,* Jamaica's capital, this is where there are *several theater and dance companies.* Tickets aren't easy to come by, but if you're lucky (talk to the hotel desk), you'll know you've been in the cultural heart of Jamaica, in fact, of the entire Caribbean. Night owls won't be at a loss either. Epiphany, Exodus, Toppsi and Turntable are popular discos that spin the latest local and U.S. records from Wednesday to Sunday. The real action begins at happy hour after work on Friday and continues on full blast through the weekend.

Shopping

Shopping in Jamaica seems to fall into two categories: the serious (for valued and valuable art or the island's famed Blue Mountain gemstones) and the not-so-serious buys of handicrafts or island designs. On beaches and in some of the simpler centers for crafts where sellers rent stalls, you bargain or, as it's called locally, higgle (meaning haggle).

Kingston is the center of the *Jamaican art world.* So if you're art oriented, this is the place to spend at least a day. The painters who began much of this art movement in the late 1930s and 1940s are John Dunkley, Henry Daley, and, more recently, Edna Manley, the widow of a national hero and former prime minister, who is also a highly regarded sculptress.

Perhaps the best place for visitors to start is at the *National Art Gallery* now housed in spacious new quarters in downtown's Kingston Mall. Although they're not about to sell you the works that are in trust for the Jamaican people, you can begin to appreciate the fine art that has emerged from this island. Then if you feel their artistic approach is in tune with yours, continue on to the *School of Art at the Cultural Training Center,* the *Institute of Jamaica,* or the better known art galleries such as The Olympia International Art Center (across from Hope Gardens); Gallery Barrington Union Square; John Peartree (3 Haughton Ave.); Bolivar (1D Grove Rd.) or the Little Gallery (3 Norbrook Drive). There's also the respected sculptor and naïf painter *Kapo,* on Gandhi Road in Kingston, but he can be hard to locate.

Once you move out of Kingston you will discover that most of the art treasures are scattered; you'll have to ask for exact locations. *Gloria Escoffery* displays her work in her Wayfarer's Gallery in Rio Bueno (on the north coast). This is also where *Joe James* and seaside restaurant has a gallery. In Port Antonio, *Herb Rose* presides over the Rosart Gallery. In Montego Bay, the *Montego Bay Gallery of West Indian Art* (1 Orange Lane) has Haitian primitives as well as Jamaican works. The *Lisa Gallery* does fired clay vases with delicate flowers, all handmade, all one of a kind, signed with a blackbrush scrawl (from $5 to $8 dollars U.S.). *Gallery Makonde* at the Half Moon Hotel carries Jamaican, African, and international art—paintings, drawings, prints, and carvings. Kingston's prestigious *Bolivar Gallery* has opened a branch in the Westgate Shopping Center and Rio Bueno's *Gallery Joe James* now has a second outlet at Holiday Village Shopping Center.

In Ocho Rios, *Harmony Hall,* a restored great house just outside of town, has a fine gallery with paintings by Jonathan Routh (of Queen Victoria's Visit fame) and several interesting local artists.

At *Round Hill* (a very exclusive resort) outside Montego Bay, the small but very special boutique has paintings by *Lionel Walker, L. Chuck* and *Clarence Roussell.*

The other really serious offerings in Jamaica are the *Blue Mountain Gems* (with prices that range from $18 to $2,000). The semiprecious stones . . . agate, jasper, quartz, local black coral . . . were discovered by Alan O'Hara in the hills of Jamaica (hence the name). But some of the finer work mixes those stones with some that are imported. There's blue lapis from the Soviet Union; opals from Australia; amber from the Dominican Republic; and an occasional emerald from Colombia.

Perhaps the best of the best jewelry is designed by O'Hara's son, Mike, with the help of his wife, Denise. Many of their designs are one of a kind and may be seen in Blue Mountain Gem's shop in the Holiday Village Shopping Center in MoBay.

One of the finest ways to spend a day in Jamaica is to visit the Falmouth workshop of Muriel Chandler, an American expatriate, who introduced some of the finest *batik work* (mostly on silk) to Jamaica in 1970. Since then, her cotton and silk *Caribatik* designs have been used by almost every top fashion designer—American and European—and she produces the largest quantity of batiks in the western hemisphere. Drawing on patterns from nature, Mrs. Chandler has tranlated the flowers, birds, seascapes, flora and fauna into true works of art . . . wall hangings or framed treasures that hang in many Jamaican hotels and private residences around the world. She's been exhibited at one-woman shows in the United States and is now also designing a small collection of clothing for both men and women. Don't miss Caribatik's adjoining boutique.

As a country formerly associated with Britain, Jamaica claims the standard 25% to 35% discount on *crystal and china* made in the British Isles. There's also a large selection of antique silver, prints, stoles, and sweaters. BUT we strongly suggest that you check hometown prices. Not only have costs gone up tremendously in all the islands, but there's the problem of carrying or shipping them back home. This is not meant to be negative: It's only meant to warn you that whatever you buy that's breakable may well be what you'll have to carry!

No matter what you've read, *cameras, stereo, tapes and electronic equipment* in general aren't inexpensive. But for smokers, the *Macanudo cigars* grown in the hills of Jamaica are (unless your next stop is Cuba); *coffee* under any name (Blue Mountain is the best if you can find it . . . most is exported; if you can't, ask for High Mountain Coffee grown farther down the hillside) is a good buy you can take home for yourself or for friends. Rum and the Sangsters Old Jamaica liqueurs also make nice gifts as do the local fragrances—Khus Khus for the ladies; Royall Lyme, Spyce or Bay Rhum for men. All of these products are available in the airport shops so you can leave these purchases until the last minute.

There are in-bond shops throughout the island. They claim good values in all the major towns that attract visitors. Again, we suggest that you compare prices with hometown prices of . . . cameras, china, crystal, watches, whatever. Jamaica's prices may or may not be bargains. Comparison shopping is not just something you should follow in Jamaica—it's a good procedure anywhere in the Caribbean. What your decision should be based on is:

Do you love your find enough to carry it, wear it or decorate your home with it? If you do, grab it . . . and treasure it as a happy memento of your Jamaican stay.

Sports

Jamaica has more *golf courses* than any other island in the Caribbean . . . nine in all. Montego Bay has four championship courses. The Tryall in Hanover, one of Jamaica's most demanding and spectacular; Half Moon, with a course designed by Robert Trent Jones; Rose Hall, which has modeled each of its 18 holes after the most famous in the world; and the leisurely Ironshore Golf Club. Still on the north coast, Runaway Bay's Golf and Country Club also has an 18-hole course. In Ocho Rios, the Upton Country Club seems well named, for it's golf course contains a bewildering series of ups and downs. (Upton also offers riding.)

Kingston has two challenging golf layouts. Constant Spring, with 18 holes, is in the foothills of the Blue Mountains. Slightly west of Kingston, the 18-hole Caymanas course is surrounded by sugarcane fields, a golf club-house, a swimming pool, a bar and a restaurant. The smaller (but cooler) nine-hole Manchester Club in Mandeville, high in the hills above the south-west coast, is in the traditional British manner. It's a little-known hideaway for resident golfers.

Tennis buffs will find over 120 courts in Jamaica. Most of the larger MoBay and Ocho Rios hotels have their own courts. In Kingston, guests of the Pegasus and The Courtleigh have privileges at Liguaneas' six hard courts; the New Kingston has two courts of their own. All four Port Antonio hotels have courts; in Negril, Hedonism II has six courts, Coconut Cove two.

Something new and quite unusual is the exploration of Negril's Great Morass, one of the western hemisphere's largest wild life preserves. The Swamp Dragon, a huge airboat that can transport 15 people, leaves from under the big bridge over the N. Negril River about two miles from the airport from 9 AM to 5 PM, 7 days a week. Three tours ($25–$50JM) head up river, pass through handcut tunnels in a giant mangrove forest and penetrate as far as two miles into the swamp to an abandoned airstrip with three crashed ganja planes.

Jamaica offers both *freshwater and saltwater angling,* and no license is required. In freshwater, you can match your skill with mullet, tarpon and snook. Serious fishermen who decide to charter a boat can do so at Port Antonio, Kingston, Ocho Rios and Montego Bay. It could easily run between $100 to $250 a day, but the catch possible is marlin, blackfin and yellowfin tuna, albacore, bonito, jackfish, kingfish, barracuda and wahoo. The biggest event is the annual International Marlin Tournament held in Port Antonio, usually in October.

Glass-bottom boat trips and the rental of Sunfish or Sailfish can be arranged at most hotels on the north coast (where most visitors stay). For larger, crewed *charter yachts,* contact the Royal Jamaica Yacht Club, in Kingston, the Montego Bay Yacht Club, and the Ocho Rios Sailing Club.

Diving, either snorkel or scuba, offers special rewards in Jamaica. In Ocho Rios, if you head to *Sea and Dive Jamaica* at either the Hilton or the Shaw Park Beach Hotel, directed by Mike Drakulich, you'll be taught by the best in the business. An ex-aide to New York City's ex-mayor Lindsay, Mike and his staff have a way of qualifying you for certification *(if* you work with them daily) and of giving you great confidence. Free Spirit, based at the Ocho Rios Sheraton, is also well recommended. In Montego Bay, a Dutch couple, Theo and Hannie Smits, run Poseidon Nemrod Club at the Chalet Caribe where diver certification can be obtained in four languages. You could also try Scuba Jamaica at the Half Moon Hotel and the Holiday Inn or Seaworld at the Cariblue Beach Hotel. In Negril, Peter Metrick's Negril Scuba Center has facilities at Rick's Cafe and the Negril Beach Club Hotel. Three of Jamaica's all-inclusive resorts—Hedonism II in Negril, the Trelawney Beach Hotel and Club Caribbean at Runaway Bay also have good programs for their guests.

Both *windsurfing* and *para sailing* are available on the north shore of Jamaica (where most hotels are located) and in Negril. Just ask at your hotel desk for advice and assistance, in case these water sports are not available there.

It's possible—and delightful—*to ride* in Jamaica's hills. Jaunts can be arranged through the Blue Mountains . . . past wild orchids, waterfalls, rocky streams and thick forests, where Jamaica's famous coffee is grown. There are stables in Falmouth, Port Antonio, Mandeville, Ocho Rios, Montego Bay and at Negril's long stretch of beach.

Squash, a British institution, is becoming increasingly popular with visitors. There are two courts at Sandals and four at the Half Moon Bay Hotel in Montego Bay and 11 in Kingston.

Would you believe there are even *jogging trails* in Kingston, Montego Bay, Ocho Rios, and along Negril Beach? It's, of course, possible to jog along your hotel's beach, no matter where you stay. But for serious runners, there's an annual jogging tournament called the Red Stripe Light 10-K Fun Run, which is held each November at a trail near the Rose Hall Inter-Continental. (Warning: You'll be in competition with Jamaicans as well as other visitors, and the Jamaicans are very good!)

Spectator Sports

Cricket is viewed from January to August. Most of the best matches take place in Kingston on Saturdays. Tickets are *not* easy to come by, for this sport is one of the national passions, and Jamaicans arrange for tickets months in advance. After cricket, *soccer* is the most popular spectator sport. September through April is the time of play everywhere in Jamaica, but most leading matches are held in October and November at the National Stadium in Kingston.

The speed, the rush, the hurl and the clash of *polo* are marked by the thunder of hooves that pound the four polo fields on the island. Near Montego Bay is the Hanover Polo Club at Blue Hole (on the north coast). On the west coast there are fields at the St. Elizabeth Polo Club, Gilnock. In Ocho Rios, head to the St. Ann Polo Club at Drax Hall. In Kingston the Polo Club plays on field grounds at the Caymanas Race Track. All these clubs play year round and all welcome visitors.

Horse racing takes place every Wednesday, Saturday, and on public holidays at Kingston's Caymanas Race Track.

Martinique

THE HARD FACTS
Planning Ahead
Costs

The *French franc* is Martinique's *legal tender.* Because the franc-dollar exchange rate fluctuates (as much as 10%), the number of francs you'll get for your dollar will vary. Simultaneously, the actual dollar amounts that hotels charge for meals and services go up and down. As long as the dollar is strong, prepay only the minimum deposit before leaving home. Pay the balance and all meals locally in francs or with a credit card and your savings could be substantial. To avoid surprises and the necessity of adjusting your bill should the dollar dramatically dip, then get hotel rates and package-tour prices guaranteed in U.S. dollars by your travel agent before you depart. The average *in-season* price for a *double room* in one of the major *deluxe resorts* is about $90 per day, CP (with breakfast). And there's a fine choice of accommodations in the $35–$40-for-two category that also includes a generous breakfast. Off-season (April 16–December 15) rates are reduced 30%–50%. Packages, such as the Annual "Fete Française" tours, which combine air fare with hotels, meals and other special features, represent good savings. Your travel agent or airline or hotel representative will be able to furnish the most up-to-date information on prices and packages.

    If you're traveling during "The Caribbean Season of Sweet Savings" (mid-April–mid-December), ask your travel agent for a "Sweetener Voucher." Present this at the tourist office when you arrive and you'll be given a little madras bag with generous perfume and rum samples and a local souvenir.

With the franc so deflated, Martinique has become a real bargain

Climate

Tropical, tempered by trade winds called Les Alizés. Along the coast temperatures average 72° to 86°F.; cooler in the highlands. December to April is the driest, coolest season; May to August is slightly warmer; September to November is the wet season; but rains, though heavy, are of short duration, and there should be sunshine every day.

Holidays and Special Events

Official holidays include New Year's Day; Easter Monday (April 23, 1984); Labor Day (May 1); Ascension Thursday (May 31); Pentecost Monday (June 11); Bastille Day (July 14); Assumption Day (August 15); All Saint's Day (November 1); Armistice Day (November 11) and Christmas Day. *Mardi gras* or *carnival* in the French West Indies is one of the Caribbean's longest and most colorful. Townspeople start preparing their costumes and floats in January, and dances and parades are held each weekend: celebrations reach a fever pitch just before Lent. The weekend before Ash Wednesday (March 7) business comes to a halt, and carnival becomes everyone's occupation. Musical contests, the election of the Queen of the Carnival, parades, street dancing, special children's competitions and gala balls fill the day and the night. Shrove Tuesday is a day for red devils, floats, marching bands and parades; on Ash Wednesday, the first day of Lent, white and black costumes prevail for Vaval's (King Carnival's) funeral procession during which rum flows freely, the streets are packed with costumed revelers and anything goes. After dusk, the coffin is taken off for burial until the following year. *Epiphany* (January 8, 1984), "Le Fête des Rois" (the kings' festival), is celebrated by observing the old French custom of serving a cake called a gallette des rois in most homes and many hotels. Whoever finds the replica of the king in the cake is crowned king for a night and gets to choose his reigning partner for feasting and dancing. On *Mi Carême* (Mid-Lent, March 29), all Lenten fasting is suspended for the day, and galas are held in towns and villages all over the island. July 21 is *Schoelcher Day,* a celebration that honors Victor Schoelcher, the leading spokesman for the abolition of slavery, which was achieved in 1848. In September is the *Fête Nautique de Robert* (Festival of the Sea), a nighttime celebration in the Atlantic coast town of Robert—boat races, lighted flotillas and folk dances done on rafts.

[handwritten margin note: The birthday of Napoleon's Josephine, born here, is not a holiday]

Tour Operators

Major tour operators are: Adventure Tours; Butler Travel; Caribbean Holidays; Cavalcade Tours; Club Med; Flyfaire; Gogo Tours; Hollywood Travel; ITW; Jet Vacations; Natrac; Skinny Dip; Travel Contes and Travel Light.

Sources of Information

In the United States, contact the *French West Indies Tourist Board,* 610 Fifth Avenue, New York, NY 10020, or the French Government Tourist Office at 9401 Wilshire Blvd., Beverly Hills, CA 90212. Send for their recently published *Helpful Hints for Visitors to Guadeloupe and Martinique.* Once *in Martinique, the Office du Tourisme* (Tel. 71–79–60) is located on the harbor in Fort-de-France and has a desk in the main arrival terminal of Lamentin Airport. Pick up free copies of *Ici Martinique,* a publication put out by the Tourist Office; and *Choubouloute*—a weekly listing of events and useful addresses. *Les Bonnes Adresses de Martinique,* an excellent little guide with a good map, may be purchased in either French or English at bookstores and most hotel shops.

Packing

Again, leave room in your suitcase for the designer and Paris-to-French-Riviera-style sportswear sold in Fort-de-France's boutiques. Pack the same sportswear, streetwear and evening clothes you'd wear in any summer resort. Women usually dress up in the evening—long pants or skirts; men dress down—slacks and sports shirts. Ties are not really necessary; jackets are suggested but not obligatory in top restaurants and the casinos. Straw hats are helpful for shielding yourself from the sun, and a shawl or a sweater for the mountains and air-conditioned places is always a good idea.

Documentation

U.S. and Canadian citizens need a valid passport and return or on-going ticket. This is good for three months; longer stays require a visa. No vaccination certificate is needed for U.S. and Canadian citizens arriving from North America. Smallpox certificates will be needed by travelers arriving from Haiti, St. Andres Island, Montserrat, and Venezuela.

Getting There

Air Florida serves the island with flights from Miami. American Airlines offers nonstop flights between New York and Fort-de-France. Eastern has direct flights from Miami and St. Lucia; connecting services via Miami from other major U.S. cities. Air France links Miami to Martinique via Guadeloupe, San Juan and Port-au-Prince. Air Canada flies from both Montreal and Toronto; LIAT services most neighboring islands; Air Martinique connects Fort-de-France with Union Island, St. Vincent, St. Lucia and Barbados and International Caribbean Airways flies to and from Barbados.

Martinique is one of the most popular ports of call for cruise ships out of Miami, Port Everglades, New York, and San Juan as well as Windjammer "Barefoot" cruises on the 197-foot sailing ship *Yankee Clipper.*

Formalities on Arrival

Customs

Show your passport, return or onward ticket and the tourist form filled out on the plane. The immigration officer will ask you how long you are staying and where. The baggage claim area is clearly marked, and carts are available. Customs officers are courteous, and usually only spot checks are made. Showing your U.S. passport will usually elicit a "Bienvenu" and a wave of the hand to direct you to pass on through. Items for personal use in limited quantities are allowed tax-free entry. Included are 1 bottle of liquor; 3 bottles of wine; 400 cigarettes or 125 cigars; 2 still cameras and 20 rolls of film; 1 movie camera and 10 rolls; a transistor radio; a portable musical instrument; a recording machine with 2 rolls of tape and 1 pair of binoculars.

Money

Martinique's official currency is the French franc (about 7 FF to the U.S. dollar). U.S. and Canadian dollars are accepted by many establishments, as are travelers' checks and credit cards. Dollars are best exchanged for francs in local banks, where the rate is more advantageous than at hotels and restaurants. Many specialized shops selling luxury items give a 20% discount for goods paid for in travelers' checks or credit cards.

Rate of exchange at presstime = 8 francs to the U.S. dollar

Getting into Town

There is no hotel shuttle or limousine service from the airport. Taxi rates, to specific touristic destinations, in French francs *only,* are posted at the tourist office desk and in the baggage claim area. Most taxis now have meters, but some may prefer to offer a set price—this may or may not be to your advantage. Sample daytime fares are: airport to Pointe du Bout hotels—about 104 FF; to Fort-de-France—about 40 FF. Fares go up 40% between 10:00 PM and 6:00 AM Rental cars are also available at Lamentin Airport.

Settling Down

Choosing a Hotel

Martinique's choice of hotels ranges from large (the Méridien Martinique has 303 rooms) to tiny (the 12-room Caraïbe Auberge). They include deluxe resorts; country manor houses; small, comfortable, family-run inns; and furnished villas to rent by the week or month. As always, choosing a hotel is a very personal thing. Looking for a luxury, self-contained resort with every possible water sport? Try the Méridien or the Bakoua Beach. You're a tennis buff? The PLM Batelière has the island's best courts. You want to get away from it all? Leyritz Plantation at the northern tip of the island may well be the place for you. The local Office du Tourisme is a good, reliable source for villa and bungalow listings. Most of the houses offered are the simple summer homes of affluent local families and are generally near a beach or at least have a sea view—Le Diamant, Ste. Luce, Anse à l'Ane or Les Anses d'Arlets. Dishes, utensils and linens are furnished, and a maid can also be engaged.

Choosing a Restaurant

Martinique's gastronomic reputation is upheld by even the plainest, smallest bistro. Although some meals will, of course, be more memorable than others, it's pretty difficult to have a really bad experience in any of the 60 restaurants scattered around the island. It's just a matter of deciding on French, Creole, Spanish, Argentine, Vietnamese, Chinese or Continental and the price you want to pay. There's something to please every palate and pocketbook. Fresh seafood, in an astounding variety, is a good choice on any menu; typical selections are red snapper, cod and a wide array of shellfish. Lunch hours are 12:30 to 2:00 or 3:00. A two-hour lunch is the norm here. Dinner is served from 7:00 to 8:00 until 10:00 or 11:00. Reservations should be made almost everywhere but especially in the small, popular Creole places for both lunch and dinner.

Tipping

A 10%–15% service charge is usually added to the bill or included in the listed price. If not, a 10% tip is a good rule of thumb; more, of course, if service has been very special. Most taxis are privately owned, and drivers do not expect a tip. Neither do hotel porters, but tipping depends on service rendered.

Learning to Cope

Business Hours.   Shop hours vary slightly but are roughly 9:00 A.M. to 12:30 P.M. and 3:00 to 6:00 Monday through Friday. Saturday closing time is 12:30–1:00 PM. Shops are closed on Sunday. But when cruise ships are in port, some of the larger shops open on weekends. Banking hours are 8:00 A.M.–noon and 2:30 –4:00 P.M. Monday through Friday. Banks are closed the afternoons preceding public holidays.

Electricity.   American-made appliances will require French plug converters and transformers because the voltage is 220 AC, 50 cycles. Bring your own as those devices are generally hard to come by, even in major hotels.

Water and Drink.   Water from taps is drinkable throughout the island; Didier, a locally-produced mineral water, is available everywhere.

Communications.   *To call* Martinique from the United States, dial directly 011 (or 01 for person-to-person calls), then 596 and the six-digit number. *Post offices* are open weekdays from 8:00 A.M.–5:30 P.M.; closed at lunchtime and on Saturday afternoons and Sunday. Airport post offices are open on weekends. To the U.S. and Canada, the rate for postcards is 2F05; letters are 3F30 to the U.S.; 2F60 to Canada.

Language.   Although French is the national language, many people speak the colorful Creole dialect or patois. English is understood at the large hotels and shops as well as by some taxi drivers and restaurateurs. An English-French dictionary will be very useful to you.

Medical Assistance.   Martinique has 18 hospitals and clinics and doctors who specialize in every branch of medicine. Many speak only French but hotel desks and the Tourist Office can be of assistance if an English-speaking doctor is needed. Medical services may not be paid by credit card.

Getting Around

By Car

There are about a dozen car-rental agencies in Fort-de-France center. Avis, Budget, Europcar-National, and Hertz have branches at the airport and in Pointe du Bout. Budget is represented at the PLM-La Batelière. Cars are Renault, Citroen, Peugeot, Fiat, Toyota or VW. Some automatics and air-conditioned models are available. Your valid U.S. driver's license will enable you to rent a car for up to 20 days; after that an International Driver's Permit will be required. Driving is on the right, and it's important to learn the French "Priorité à droite," priority always goes to the vehicle on the right at intersections unless signs to the contrary are posted. Parisian style means moving fast!

By Taxi

Rates are published for standard taxi excursions to different parts of the island. Both *Choubouloute* and the Office du Tourisme have these listings. Sample prices are: Fort-de-France, Trois Ilets, Le Diamant–Fort-de-France (53 miles, 4 hours) 225 F 60 FF; Fort-de-France–Ste. Anne, Salines, Fort-de-France (79.3 miles, 5 hours) 386 F 85 FF; or Fort-de-France, St. Pierre via the Caribbean coast, Morne Rouge, La Trace, Fort-de-France (43.7 miles, 3 hours) 225 F 60 FF.

Martinique is about 50 miles long, 15 wide

By Bus

Most public transportation is operated by collective taxis, eight-seat vehicles displaying signs marked TC. They run from early morning until about 8:00 P.M. and serve all the principal towns of the island. The main terminal is at Pointe Simon on the Fort-de-France waterfront.

By Ferry

Fort-de-France is linked with Pointe du Bout, Anse Mitan and Anse à l'Ane by scheduled ferryboats. The fare to any of these destinations is 5 FF one way, 12 FF round trip. The first 20-minute trip to Pointe du Bout is at 6:30 A.M., and the last is 12:45 A.M. (1:45 A.M. on Fridays and Saturdays). From Pointe du Bout to Fort-de-France, the first boat leaves at 6:10 A.M., the last at 12:20 A.M. (1:20 A.M. on Fridays and Saturdays).

It is not known how many points the future mme. de Maintenon, Louis XIV's mistress, had on her foulard

MARTINIQUE TODAY

In the days when the capital of Martinique was the Paris of the West Indies, women followed a sensible and romantic practice. Each wore a foulard, an intricately-tied madras headscarf. Each scarf was tied with one, two, three or four points. One point meant my heart is free. Two points meant my heart is promised . . . but only promised. Three points meant my heart is legally taken. . . . Attention! Four points? I'm married, but who worries about that!

    Unfortunately, in sophisticated Martinique today, madras foulards are worn by only the Grand Ballet de la Martinique of folkloric dancing, by the ladies selling dolls in madras costumes on street corners in Fort-de-France and by ladies attending local festivals in the country. But the mystique remains, and the ladies of Martinique turn many an eye their way. There is a pride in the bearing of the Martiniquais, descendants of French plantation owners and African slaves. The Creole mix seems to have combined the best of two opposite worlds. Theirs is a lithe and a lively charm.

The island was made a full department of France in 1946, a status that is still proudly held. It is governed by a Prefect appointed by the French minister of the Interior. The electorate sends three deputies and two senators to the French Parliament. The benefits of this political status have been clear to all, except small groups that organize occasional demonstrations in support of "independence." Most Martiniquais are proud of their French citizenship and want no part of any independence movement. Why give up all those francs from Paris that pay for free schools, hospitals, 200 miles of good roads—some of the best social services and security in the Caribbean?

This undercurrent of opposition will not affect visitors at all. They usually set up housekeeping in one of three areas—the busy capital of Fort-de-France, which is accessible to everything but contains no beaches; the large hotel-resort complexes across the bay from the capital at Pointe du Bout and L'Anse Mitan; along the more remote southern and northern coasts.

The opening of the modern hotels in Pointe du Bout has brought about changes in the older, adjoining section of L'Anse Mitan, which, nevertheless, remains the setting for a perfect Martinique day. If you're not staying here (and we suggest that you consider this stretch of beach frequented by local residents), it's a 20-minute ferry ride from Fort-de-France. Wear your swimsuit, and discard both your cover-up and your shoes when the ferry docks. Wander this stretch of not uncrowded but interesting beach barefoot. You'll pass seaside, open bistros, exuding spicy, inviting smells. Stop at almost any one and order crabes farcis, a salad of fresh greens, a large langouste and a bottle of wine. The bread and cheese will come after you've finished your meal. As you stand in the water waiting for your order to be prepared, Madame or Monsieur le Proprietaire hand down to you a "petit punch." This is a knock-out mixture of jeune acajou (poetically, young mahogany), white rum gently laced with sugar syrup and fresh lime. Martinique makes some of the best rum in the Caribbean; it's almost cognaclike in its smoothness and in its capacity to induce you to overindulge. Until well into the 19th century, Martinique prospered because of its sugarcane and rum production, and several of the plantation estates built at that time are now special vacation hideaways in the countryside.

You'll be called from the surf when lunch is ready, and as you sit at a simple table with a red-and-white-checkered tablecloth, poised to attack your order, several cats will inevitably position themselves as close to you as they dare . . . hoping. In the distance, the usually cloud-capped top of 4,656-foot Mt. Pelée dominates your vista, dwarfing the now small village of St. Pierre at its feet. As you sip your wine, you think about May 8, 1902, the day when the mountain literally blew its top and killed all but one of the 30,000 people living in the "Paris of the West Indies."

L'Anse Mitan is a beach where you'll hear the local patois, a mélange of French and African languages spoken in a singsong tone. But everyone speaks Parisian French as well, so use yours or a French-English dictionary. Not everyone speaks English. Why should they? You're in France, mon ami!

Bienvenue à la Martinique—still a French coquette who dances the beguine—where it all began. It's still going on.

[handwritten margin note: Guadeloupe also claims the beguine, but who cares?]

TOURING

Verdant hills and volcanic peaks provide a dramatic backdrop for the yacht-filled harbor of Fort-de-France situated on one of the finest bays in the Caribbean. A bustling, sophisticated commercial center, the capital is best visited on foot. Traffic gets easily and frequently clogged, and parking is next to impossible.

Start at *La Savane,* an open park facing the sea and lined with three small hotels, boutiques and sidewalk cafes. A bronze statue of Belain d'Esnambuc, the Norman nobleman who claimed possession of the island in the name of the king of France in 1635, greets visitors at the entrance to this recently relandscaped gathering place. A white Carrara marble statue of the Empress Josephine, sculpted by Vital Dubray, stands at the edge of the park looking out to Trois-Ilets, her birthplace. La Savane, at the city's center, is animated day and night. This is the best place to see the spectacular show of the sun sinking into the sea each evening around 6:00; football matches often take place here, and at carnival it's the focal place for the wildest celebrations.

The rococo building, set amid royal palms and tamarind trees at the park's far corner, is the *Schoelcher Library.* Built for the 1889 Paris Exposition, it was transported here in pieces and reconstructed on the spot. Nearby is the *Musée Départemental de la Martinique* in a lovely, restored colonial house on rue de la Liberté. Its collection includes Arawak and Carib artifacts, local documents, old maps, period clothing and furniture. An interesting color slide show as well as a commentary is presented once a day, unfortunately, usually only in French.

Explore *Fort Saint Louis,* the historic fortress built by Vauban on the other side of the square. Visit the *St. Louis Cathedral,* constructed in 1895 in the Romanesque-Byzantine style in vogue at that time. Shop for handmade souvenirs and Paris fashions along the balconied streets named for some of France's foremost literary figures—Victor Hugo, Ernest Renan, Lamartine. Stop by the rue Isambert market where avocados, bananas, breadfruit, corossol, guavas, mangos, pineapple and other luscious tropical delights crowd the stalls and the aroma of cloves, sandalwood, vanilla and cinnamon makes the air heady.

When you're ready to discover the countryside, visit the tourist office on Harborfront Blvd. It has designed some full and half-day tours that are meant to be taken at one's leisure in a rental car or in a taxi. However, if you have any hesitation about driving and *parlez*-ing on your own, the office can develop something for you with an English-speaking guide or driver.

Twenty minutes across the bay from Fort-de-France is Trois-Ilets containing pretty, little, flowered houses and the *Musée de la Pagerie,* evoking memories of Josephine Tascher de la Pagerie, the Creole beauty who became the wife of Napoleon Bonaparte and the empress of France. Take the ferry from Fort-de-France, and pick up your car in Pointe du Bout, the island's resort center where most of the major hotels, sports and other tourist facilities are centered. Then it's just 3½ km to the small stone house that was once the kitchen of the estate of La Pagerie. The collection of Josephine's memorabilia includes the bed she used as a child; portraits of the imperial couple; ball invitations; bills clearly itemizing the extravaganzas that the empress created; period furniture; even a passionate letter from a lovelorn Napoleon. The museum is open all day, every day but Monday; and admission is $1.50 for adults and 50¢ for children.

A well-paved road leads to dry, sun-bleached southern landscapes. All along the road are magnificent views of Fort-de-France Bay to the Pitons du Carbet, even Mt. Pelée on a cloudless day; then it's beach country. At Anse à l'Ane, take time to visit the tiny (15 by 30 feet) *Musée d'Art en Coquillage,* which is entirely devoted to seashell art. Intricate tableaux, completely fashioned from local shells, depict Napoleon's crowning, a folk festival and a typical pastoral scene. Continue to Anse d'Arlets, a picturesque village containing three small beaches, each with colorful fishermen's "gommiers" (slim-shaped fishing boats) pulled up on the sand and nets spread out to dry. Have lunch at Diamant, take a swim, and enjoy the two-mile beach but not before you salute the *H.M.S. Diamond Rock,* as all passing British ships must do. This 600-foot pinnacle was officially commissioned as a sloop of war by England in 1804. A force of 110 British soldiers held the rock for 18 months against the French, who held the entire island. The story goes that the British finally succumbed after the French floated out barrels of rum from Diamant, waited until the fiery spirits produced the desired effect, and then unleashed their regiments.

Stop off at Sainte Luce, another important, pretty, little fishing village and the site of the Montravail Forest that contains good hiking trails, and then bear left to Rivière Pilote, a lush agricultural center in the mountains. Return to Fort-de-France via Petit Bourg and Ducos.

Another full day of touring could include the Atlantic Coast and the fine Caribbean beaches near Sainte-Anne. Drive back through Ducos and Rivière Pilote; then take the road that starts the steep climb affording good glimpses over the bay of Le Marin, an historic village with an interesting 18th-century church and a nice, well-protected, white-sand beach. Continue south through Sainte-Anne, a quiet, little town with a charming square, good restaurants, a splendid view of the Sainte Lucia Canal and the Club Mediterranée's Buccaneer Creek and Le Manoir de Beauregard. The road gets very rocky, rutted and rough, but don't let these conditions dissuade you. Once you arrive at Les Salines, Martinique's most beautiful beach, you'll realize what you might have missed. Nearby is also the Petrified Savannah Forest, a desertlike stretch of land with almost no vegetation, whose jagged cliffs descend like a jackknife into the sea; salt marshes; Ilet Cabris and the Table du Diable, a flat rock surrounded by water. Return to Ste. Anne for a seafood lunch at Poi et Virginie or Les Filets Bleus and another swim while your fish is grilling.

After lunch, head north again to the historic village of Vauclin where excursions can be made to Mt. Vauclin, the highest point in the south, for spectacular views. Continue on to St. François, another picturesque port with old colonial homes, a rum distillery and a coral reef perfect for snorkeling. Perhaps on another day you'll decide to return to St. François to take a fishing boat to the small, offshore islets and La Baignoire de Josephine (Josephine's Bath), shallow, sand-bottomed waters near the reef. There are also two excellent beachside bistros, Club Nautique and Les Brisants, for lunch, an afternoon petit punch or even an early dinner.

Then return to Fort-de-France via Lamentin, a vast sugarcane-covered plain.

A visit to *St. Pierre,* just 42 miles from Fort-de-France, usually ranks high on everyone's list of things to see and do. Head north out of the city, through the hilly, residential areas of Bellevue, Desrochers and Didier. The road is bordered by flamboyants and big, old, colonial-style houses graced by columns and verandas. Most are surrounded by extensive gardens bright with hibiscus, bougainvillea, alamanda, canna, frangipani and other exotic trees and plants.

The coast is rugged; the road winds up and up and the views are breathtaking. Creeks flow between rocky cliffs. These inlets shelter picturesque fishing villages such as Fond Lahaye, Case Pilote, Bellefontaine, Fond Capot and Le Carbet. It was at Carbet that Columbus landed in 1502. After a three-day stay, he wrote, "It is the best, the richest, the sweetest, the evenest, the most charming country in the world. It is the finest thing that I have ever seen, and therefore I cannot tire myself of looking at such greenness." *Mt. Pelée,* as it did in 1502, towers over the northern end of the island, its volcanic soil the cradle for banana, pineapple and coconut plantations. The sweet smoke of burning sugarcane hangs in the crisp, volcanic air, and children smile and wave at you on backcountry roads. It's not exactly the world that Columbus saw, but the beauty and charm are still here.

Just outside Carbet is Martinique's newest museum, *Centre d'Art Musée Paul Gauguin.* This memorial to the work that the noted French painter completed during a four-month stay in Martinique in 1887 exhibits quality reproductions of a dozen paintings, books and biographical information as well as some of his letters.

Saint Pierre, the first French city in Martinique, was once the cultural and the economic center of the island. The "Paris of the West Indies" was completely destroyed in just three minutes by the eruption of Mt. Pelée on May 8, 1902. The town was rebuilt among the ruins and now has a population of just over 6,000.

Of 40,000 souls in the town, only 1 survived

The *Musée Volcanologique,* founded by an American volcanologist, Dr. Franck Perret, houses photos, engravings and documents recalling life in St. Pierre before the eruption as well as fascinating artifacts recovered from the debris. These include petrified spaghetti, singed newspapers, furniture fragments and clocks and watches stopped precisely at 8:00 A.M., the hour of destruction. Nearby is the hillside jail of the only survivor, a prisoner named Auguste Siparis, who escaped death in his dungeon and went on to become a circus curiosity.

It's a short drive north to Prêcheur, one of the oldest villages on the island. Mme. de Maintenon, the second wife of Louis XIV, grew up here. Visit the 18th-century chapel and monument honoring Jacques Du Parquet, one of the most important colonizers, and then return to St. Pierre. Head inland to either Fond St. Denis, where you can see the scenic *Morne des Cadets Volcanic Observatory,* or to Morne Rouge, where you can climb to the crater of the sleeping but well-monitored Mt. Pelée and behold a panoramic view of Martinique and all the neighboring islands.

Return to Fort-de-France via La Trace Road. This mountain route cuts through a rain forest thick with plants—a real botanical garden. Mahogany, bamboo, red-flowered canna, palms of every variety, ferns, lianas, colorful orchids and immense ancient trees dwarf your car, and tropical vines, interwoven with flowers, hang overhead creating an eerie silence.

The last stops will be just beyond Camp de Balata for an overview of the center of the island and the tiny islets around Robert and a quick look at Balata Church, a replica of Sacre Coeur in Paris. Then you'll descend into Fort-de-France in time for a late lunch.

Take another full day for the Grand Rivière tour to the northernmost point of the island, about 100 miles from Fort-de-France. Leaving the capital via the expressway, you should pause at Robert, a natural, well-protected harbor and a busy fishing village with old-time character. Aimée Dubuc de Rivery, who was captured by Barbary pirates, taken to the Grand Turk of Istambul and eventually became the mother of Emperor Mahmoud II, was born here. If you're in the mood for a boat ride, you can easily arrange an excursion to one of the small offshore islets in a fishing boat. Turn inland, and wind through banana and pineapple groves, bordered by hibiscus and bougainvillea, to Vert Près and Gros Morne, where you can see a panorama of the Caravelle Peninsula below. Trinité, with its broad, seafront promenade abutting interesting, old buildings, is the gateway to the Presqu'ile de la Caravelle, worth half a day by itself. This sharply-indented peninsula juts into the Atlantic and ends in rocky cliffs topped by a lighthouse offering spectacular views on all

At Robert, they dance on rafts in the sea at a September festival

sides. The southern part of La Caravelle has beautiful calm bays: the Baie du Galion, the Baie Grandjean and the Baie du Trésor. On the north is La Tartane, where you can enjoy good swimming on a beach shaded by coconut palms, seafood restaurants and the ruins of Chateau Dubuc. Return to Trinité, and then continue on to Sainte Marie, with its Jesuit-style church, and Fond Saint-Jacques. Here in 1664, Dominican friars set up one of the first sugar mills on the island—a model of its kind. The buildings—a chapel, a monastery, an aqueduct, a mill, a drying house and an oven—appear to be intact and form an interesting ensemble amid luxuriant vegetation.

Continue on to Marigot and Le Lorrain, Martinique's most fertile areas where rich alluvial plains nurture plantations of pineapple, coffee, banana, sugar, cocoa, cotton and tobacco. Just after Basse Pointe, there's a small road that leads up to Leyritz Plantation. This magnificent, 200-year-old estate overlooking Mt. Pelée and the sea has been painstakingly restored by Charles and Yveline de Lucy de Fossarieu. Wander through their complex of great house, sugar mill, granary, rum refinery, slave quarters turned into guest rooms, guardhouse and chapel. Then enjoy a leisurely drink at the poolside bar. This is a Martinique sheltered from the cosmopolitan milieu of Fort-de-France, a gentle, peaceful place.

Now head down to Macouba, a village with a small 17th-century church perched atop the cliffs. Walk down the small road at the edge of town to visit the caves. The route then twists and turns through another lush rain forest, crosses the Rivière Pitiche and weaves down to Grand Rivière, the northernmost fishing village on a spectacular wave-lashed site . . . it's almost like the end of the earth.

Return through Ajoupa Bouillon on Mt. Pelée's slopes, Morne Rouge and La Trace rain forest. Then end your afternoon by stopping at the anthurium nurseries at Dans les Nuages before returning to Fort-de-France.

Inside Information

Hotels

Martinique's 30 hotels range from internationally known seaside establishments to restored manor houses furnished with cherished antiques to small, homey guesthouses where the ability to speak French is indispensable. We've chosen what we consider the best this island has to offer . . . expensive and modest; large (303 rooms) and small (12 rooms); complete resorts offering every amenity and family-run country inns where the proprietor will personally greet you.

Smaller Hotels

★★★★ LEYRITZ PLANTATION (BASSE POINTE)

This is a carefully and authentically-restored country inn, perched above a working banana and pineapple plantation at the northern tip of the island. It's 35 miles from the airport; let the proprietors know your flight number well in advance, and transportation will be waiting. Charles and Yveline de Lucy de Fossarieu have decorated their 25 rooms with taste and flair. Those in the 200-year-old manor house contain the original tile or marble floors and elegant antique furnishings, whereas the old slave-quarter chambers are

Presidents Ford and Giscard d'Estaing met here for a mini-summit

more rustic. Food here is traditional French and Creole. Visiting lunch tours often crowd the poolside restaurant, but there's always a peaceful spot in the main house or in the formal gardens. Tennis, hiking to the base of Mt. Pelée, through some of the island's most verdant vegetation and swimming in the spring-fed pool are among the activities offered, and free daily transport is provided to Atlantic and Caribbean beaches about ½ hour away. *Cost:* $80–$125 per double, with breakfast, in season.

★★ HOTEL ST. AUBIN (TRINITÉ)
This is a wonderful, old, three-story, gray gingerbread house encircled by wide, white-columned verandas. It's situated on a hill looking down on the midisland village of Trinité, the Atlantic, and sugar plantations. Fifteen air-conditioned rooms feature modern furnishings, wall-to-wall carpeting and one-way windows to protect your privacy from veranda strollers. There's very good French and Creole cooking prepared by Guy Foret for guests only. A new pool has been added and cars may be rented for a drive to the nearby white-sand beach at Presqu'ile de la Caravelle. *Cost:* $48, double, with breakfast, in season.

★★ MANOIR DE BEAUREGARD (CHEMIN DES SALINES, SAINTE ANNE)
Near the main road of the southern village of Sainte-Anne and 31 miles from the hustle and the bustle of Fort-de-France. The 18th-century manor-house hotel is now managed by Plantation Leyritz. There are 35 air-conditioned rooms in the main house that face the pool or gardens. An additional 15 rooms with patios are set back away from the house. By this summer, 70 new studios with kitchenettes should be completed. The decor reflects the past and the present: four posters, turn-of-the-century lamps and every modern comfort. Home-style Creole and French food is served on the terrace; breakfast is poolside. Sainte-Anne Beach is within walking distance, and it's just a short drive to Les Salines, Martinique's most beautiful beach. *Cost:* $83 per double, with full American breakfast, in season.

★ AUBERGE DE L'ANSE MITAN (ANSE MITAN)
This is an offbeat, little three-story inn with a lot of charm. Twenty air-conditioned rooms provide seaviews and balconies. There's also a one-bedroom beachside bungalow. Although it's a quiet spot at the far end of the bay, it's just a few hundred yards from the ferry to Fort-de-France and the many sports facilities at Anse Mitan beach. You'll be happy here if you speak some French. *Cost:* $36 per double, with breakfast, in season.

VICTORIA (DIDIER)
A tastefully restored Creole home on a hilltop in the quiet, residential suburb of Didier, where's there's always a cool breeze. The 29 rooms are very pleasantly situated in five units adjacent to the main house. Terraces, gardens, solariums, and a nice pool complete the country picture, and it's just a mile and a half from the center of Fort-de-France. *Cost:* $35–$45 per double, with breakfast, in season.

Larger Hotels

★★★★ BAKOUA BEACH (POINTE DU BOUT)
Luxurious and elegant, this well-run locally-owned resort hotel is one of the most delightful. Ninety-three of the 98 rooms have sea views, and all have balconies or patios. Some are perched hillside (older, larger rooms); others (new and small) are right on the recently-widened, white-sand beach. There are also three one-bedroom suites with refrigerators. A 60-foot oval pool, two tennis courts, volleyball, snorkeling equipment, Sunfish, windsurfers and pedal boats are free to guests. A social director organizes cocktail parties,

bar-b-ques, beach parties, nightly dinner-dances under the stars and, on Friday nights, a buffet highlighted by Grand Ballet performances. *Cost:* $140–$167 per double, with full American breakfast, in season.

★★★★ BUCCANEER'S CREEK CLUB MEDITERRANEE (SAINTE ANNE)
One of the most attractive clubs . . . pastel-colored bungalows with blue shutters and wooden balconies, flowered cobblestone walkways, fountains and small plazas, all custom-built. This 48-acre resort, on a prize expanse of white-sand beach studded with palms, features a marina, open-air disco-thèque, boutique, coiffeur, six tennis courts, open-air bridge salon, an English–French language lab, complete fitness program, sailing, snorkeling, yoga, waterskiing, volleyball, pétanque, calisthenics, sailing picnics and cruises. The only problem here is that you hardly know you've left the States . . . although Canadians and Europeans are represented in the guest list, for the most part, the group is the same you'd see in a singles bar on New York City's upper east side. *Cost:* $530–$830 per person, per week, with three meals a day, depending on time of year.

★★★★ MÉRIDIEN MARTINIQUE (POINTE DU BOUT)
This deluxe resort is Martinique's largest hotel . . . 303 handsomely-furnished but rather small rooms with balconies that offer sea or marina views. Included are five junior and five one-bedroom suites; those on the corners are the nicest. Every convenience to please a cosmopolitan clientele has been incorporated here . . . two restaurants, bars, a large casino, lively discothèque, convention facilities, shops, a freshwater pool, beach, two tennis courts, Sunfish, pedal boat, sailing excursions, snorkeling, waterskiing, a scuba-diving center, Ping Pong, volleyball, even a health club. Golf and horseback riding are nearby. *Cost:* $102–$140 per double, EP, in season.

★★★★ PLM LA BATELIÈRE (BATELIÈRE)
A mile north of Fort-de-France, this deluxe, multilevel resort was formerly the Martinique Hilton. The 218 balconied rooms are the most spacious—and we think, the nicest—on the island! They include seven fabulous duplex suites with nautical names and decor. Facilities here are excellent—direct telephone lines, radio, 24-hour room service, beauty salon, sauna, shops, quick laundry and dry cleaning—and businessmen as well as vacations keep the occupancy rate high year round. The tropical garden is filled with flamboyant and other flora, there's a white-sand cove beach and six tennis courts. All water sports are offered—Sunfish, pedal boats, snorkeling, waterskiing, windsurfing and cruises on the 58-foot ketch, *Bois Normand II*. An open-air terrace restaurant now overlooks the huge, oval pool, the casino has been refurbished, and the Club 21 disco, built into the rocks above the sea, is romantic and lively . . . a very popular nighttime spot for both visitors and residents. *Cost:* $100–$123, double, with full American breakfast, in season.

★★★ HOTEL DU DIAMANT-NOVOTEL (DIAMANT)
Just 20 minutes from the airport via the new superhighway to the southwest coast, this is the former Hotel Diamond Roc, now under Novotel management. Expanded to 180 rooms, all have been redecorated and many have terraces overlooking the Rock that rocked history. This is a self-contained 5-acre resort with its own night club, shops, video room, 2 bars, 3 good restaurants, 3 pools, 4 sheltered cove beaches, water sports and two tennis courts. The small fishing village of Diamant is just minutes away where you can watch the fishermen bring in their catch. *Cost:* $98 per double, with breakfast, in season.

★★ FRANTEL (POINTE DU BOUT)

Built on a peninsula jutting into the bay, this facility offers unobstructed views extending to Fort-de-France and the marina. These accommodations are not luxurious, but the 213 balconied, comfortable rooms are pleasantly and colorfully decorated with bamboo furniture, bright bedspreads and curtains. There's a large convention hall, a restaurant with an outdoor terrace, a poolside snack bar, discothèque, a small, white-sand beach with pedal and sailboats, a freshwater pool with a sundeck, two tennis courts, a scuba center and other water sports. A daily newsletter listing events and an attractive, helpful staff round out the attractions of this resort complex. *Cost:* $85 per double, EP, in season.

★★ PLM MARINA-PAGERIE (POINTE DU BOUT MARINA)

A new wing, containing 100 comfortable, well-furnished accommodations, overlooks the garden of this apartment hotel built around the marina. The 140 older studio, one-, two- or three-bedroom apartments, are simply furnished, but all are air-conditioned and contain kitchenettes and balconies that overlook the marina or the pool. This Mediterranean-style complex offers fine values for families and a location right in the center of the action. *Cost:* $69–$80, studio; $87–$102, two- or three-room apartment, EP, in season.

LATITUDE HOTEL (CARBET)

This hotel is 16 miles north of Fort-de-France, on a gray-sand beach at the edge of the village of Carbet. It's arranged around an old Creole plantation house now used as an activity center. The 90, odd-looking, octagonal bungalows are surrounded by coconut and mango trees. All have patios, simple furnishings, paper-thin walls and almost no cross ventilation, so get accustomed to the cacophony of air-conditioning sounds . . . yours and your neighbors. Most of the guests are scuba enthusiasts here to use the excellent facilities offered by the diving school and to explore a dozen or more sunken ships that went down in nearby St. Pierre's harbor when Mt. Pelée destroyed the old capital in 1902. The atmosphere is group, and 90% European, and so it's best to come with a friend or a group of friends. *Cost:* double $110, with three meals, in season.

[handwritten margin note: Gauguin lived in Le Carbet in 1887, before his Tahiti period]

Restaurants

One fact cannot be challenged: Wherever the French have settled, food is treated as a form of art and a very special part of life. Martinique is well known for the variety and the excellence of its restaurants, both large and small, plain and fancy. At last count, there were about 60 scattered around the island. We've listed those we feel are the best, the most unusual and the most interesting in every price category.

As a guide, an *inexpensive* dinner (depending on your selection, this can vastly change) ranges from $8 to $13; *moderate* from $13 to $20; and *expensive* would be anything over $20.

Fort-de-France

★★★★ LA GRAND'VOILE

Pointe Simon (Tel. 70–29–29). The Big Sail has a lovely view of the harbor from its terrace above the Yacht Club. Owner-chef Raymond Benoit is from Lyon. He is known for his classic preparation of seafood and shellfish and steak tartar as well as quenelles de brochet (pike dumplings) and terrines. A special five-course menu and a gastronomic menu are featured as well. The decor is nautical, and there is an excellent wine list. *Expensive.*

★★ EL RACO

23 rue Lazare Carnot (Tel. 73–29–16). This restaurant reflects a typically

Castillian setting with wrought-iron doors, arched, white-stucco ceiling and grillwork on the windows. This small, intimate spot offers music and a choice of Spanish dishes from Andalusia, Catalonia and Valencia. *Moderate.*

★★ L'ESCALIER
19 rue de la Republique (Tel. 70–25–22). Look carefully for the sign pointing to the entrance of this small, downtown building. The restaurant is on the second floor of a walk-up. It has a lot of atmosphere, wood paneling and a charming, flowered balcony. The authentic Creole cookery includes excellent crabes farcis, crayfish, colombo and fresh fish. *Moderate.*

★★ TYPIC BELLEVUE
Bd. de la Marne (Tel. 71–68–87). Taken over last year by Bruno Raphael-Amanrich, whose savoir-faire with food has brought this formerly so-so place up to something quite special. The view from the terrace over the Baie des Flamands is spectacular, especially at lunch or cocktail hour. Interesting specialties here include sea urchin pie and soup; baby shark in a spicy tomato sauce; fish in a fennel sauce flambé with Pernod, conch kebab, cochon de lait Boucanier (roast suckling pig) and breadfruit croquettes. *Moderate.*

★ LE D'ESNAMBUC
1 rue de la Liberte (Tel. 71–46–51). This small, stylish, rather formal restaurant serves traditional French food and some Creole specialties. A green-carpeted stairway leads to a green and white room filled with flowers. This is the old Le Foyal with a new name, a new chef, a new management and a new look. Very little English spoken here. *Expensive.*

★ THE CREW
42 rue Ernest Deproge (Tel. 73–04–14). Nice cool, little bar and three rustic dining rooms conveniently located just behind the tourist office. Your hosts are Jean and Françoise; their Creole and classic French cooking are both excellent AND the price is right. Among the specialties are paté de campagne, escargots, frogs legs, grilled meats, steak tartare, turbot and trout. A 3-course tourist menu (45F), and 3-course conventional menu with a carafe of wine (50F) are always available in addition to the large à la carte selection. Open lunch and dinner. *Inexpensive.*

In the Suburbs

★★★★★ LE TIFFANY
Croix de Bellevue, 1.5 miles north of Fort-de-France. (Tel. 71–33–82). This hard-to-find Victorian gingerbread mansion is high on a hill in a quiet residential area. It's the island's best and most charming dining place, decorated with antiques, Haitian art, and cooled by old ceiling fans. Claude and Odile Pradines serve artfully-prepared and artistically-presented fine French fare with a tropical touch. Smoked salmon with blinis; goat cheese in a warm, creamy sauce; fresh foie gras with sauterne; sole with leeks; duckling in cider; coconut, lemon, almond and prune tartes and homemade chocolate truffles are only a few of their delicious and unusual creations. *Expensive.*

★★★ LE FOULARD
Schoelcher (Tel. 71–05–72). An air-conditioned dining room in a private home on the sea where the dependably delicious French and Creole specialties of Guy Karchesz have been drawing crowds for nearly 12 years. The lobster bisque maison; snapper dumplings; tournedos Rossini; veal chops Zinguara; confit of goose or duck and the wild mushrooms (girolles and crepes) are especially recommended. *Expensive.*

★★★ LE JARDIN DE JADE
Schoelcher (Tel. 70–05–50). Refined Chinese cuisine is served as you enjoy a panoramic view from the large, cool dining room of the former Lido Hotel. Service is efficient, the choices are extensive and at lunch you'll be in the company of many prominent Fort-de-France businessmen who rate this the top Oriental restaurant in town. *Moderate.*

★★ LA BAIE D'ALONG
Schoelcher (Tel. 72–31–40). Popular for Vietnamese specialties at lunch and dinner. It's open every day except Monday and Sunday evening. *Inexpensive.*

★ LE BITACO
Ravine Vilaine residential area (Tel. 71–35–16). In the hills amid dense tropical vegetation, this small, rustic restaurant has gracious service, a pretty setting in the flower garden of a plantation house and authentic Creole dishes. For a good sampling, order the Bouquet Bitaco—boudin, accras and stuffed crabs—and then follow with paté en pot (a thick Creole mutton soup) and grilled red fish. Top it off with Creole rum cake or a lemon ice. *Expensive.*

Pointe du Bout
★★★★ CHATEAUBRIAND
Hotel Bakoua (Tel. 73–62–02). The dining room opens on a lovely garden with a bay view. The menu is a gastronomic list of over 135 items to choose from: quail, veal, and filet mignon from the classic French; soudons (tiny clams on the half shell); blaff d'oursins (sea-urchin stew) from the Creole. Monday nights there's a special seafood feast. The wine list is extensive. After Friday night's buffet, there's a performance of the excellent Grand Ballet de Martinique's folkloric show. *Expensive.*

★★ CHEZ SIDONIE
Hotel Madinina on the Marina (Tel. 76–30–54). It's one of the island's best known restaurants for fine Creole cooking, very popular and thus very busy. There's a feeling of being in the south of France, but the cooking is pure Creole, with a few French dishes for the unadventurous. Specialties include paté en pot (a thick soup of finely-chopped mutton and vegetables); gambas (large, grilled shrimp, with a spicy, piquant sauce); conch salad (salade de lambi); grilled turtle steak marinated in white wine, hot pepper and garlic; raw clams (soudons). Dessert may be fresh guava, passion fruit or other sherbets or stunning sundaes (coupes) with ice cream, fruit, rum and liqueurs. *Expensive.*

Good view of marina from upstairs dining room

★★ LES CANTONNAIS
Inside the shopping center of the Marina (Tel. 73–63–53). This restaurant is operated most elegantly by a Chinese family. Its eye-catching, laquered red and black decor is relieved by the presence of Chinese antiques in the formal dining room. The Cantonese dishes include birds-nest soup with minced chicken, a soup that combines prawns and assorted meats, main courses featuring steamed chicken with vegetables, sliced duck with black bean sauce and sliced peppers and prawns with fresh mushrooms. *Moderate* to *expensive.*

L'Anse Mitan
★★★ LA VILLA CREOLE
(Tel. 76–35–53). The accent is on cuisine and atmosphere on the back porch of this Creole wooden house, owned by Guy and Ghislaine-Dawson, who jointly run the restaurant. Guy, a guitarist, entertains, while his wife supervises the dining. The food is French and Creole and a combination of both. It

includes salade de morue Creole (codfish, avocado, cucumber, tomato and onion salad); conch tarte, terrine of local salmon; Colombo aux 3 viandes (a curry of chicken, pork and lamb); coquelet du chef (young chicken wrapped in bacon then flambé in cognac); coconut chicken; chocolate mousse; creme coco caramel and "Dessert Villa Creole," a crepelike concoction that is really an omelette of fruit that has been macerated, caramelized and flambéed in old rum. Open for lunch and dinner in the low season; dinner only high season. *Moderate.*

★★★ LE MATADOR
Just across from the beach (Tel. 76–35–36). Raymonde and François Crico were formerly affiliated with the Bakoua. This charming couple recently moved their popular restaurant to the other side of the road from their original location. Do reserve in the evening as their reputation is good, their seafood something special. Creole and cuisine française are both featured on the menu. *Moderate.*

Diamant
HOTEL DIAMANT LES BAINS
(Tel. 76–40–14). A pleasant, very local bar and terrace restaurant that overlooks the seaside gardens of this little south coast hotel. M. and Mme. Andrieux love to practice their English, and are most friendly and accommodating inn keepers. Try their fresh vegetable soup, shrimp or sea urchin omelette or burgot (sea snail) salad, then one of the stuffed avocado dishes. Stop to visit this charming fishing village and take time out to savor the marvelous view of Diamond Rock. *Inexpensive.*

Sainte-Anne
★★★ LES FILETS BLEUS
(Tel. 76–73–42). An open-air restaurant surrounded by palms. The glass-topped floor enables patrons to view the langouste on the rocks below and to dance after dinner without shoes of course. Seafood is the specialty, and it's the best on the island. Reservations are a must here, especially at dinner. Turtle soup; fried sea urchins; langouste; fricassée of conch with red beans and rice and turtle steak would be good choices. But in fact, everything here is of the freshest, finest quality. Continental and French-style food is also served. *Moderate* to *expensive.*

LE TOULOULOU
(Tel. 76–73–27). A large airy, "feet in the water" place right on Pt. Marin Beach. Beachwear is the quite acceptable attire for a good Creole lunch between dips in the sea. Portions are more than generous here, so it's advisable to slow down and let everything digest well before undertaking any ambitious water sports. The usual Creole specialties are available and well prepared. We especially favor the fish soup with the flavor of capers, served with garlic croutons. The 35F, 3-course menu attracts a big crowd, especially on Mondays, when all the other beachside restaurants are closed. *Inexpensive.*

POI ET VIRGINIE
(Tel. 76–73–12). A small, thatched-roof hut on a little square, serving grilled fish and lobster. One of the owners is a former G.O. at Club Med; the recipes reflect that experience. *Moderate.*

Basse Pointe (the northernmost point on the island)
★★★ CHEZ MALLY EDJAM
(Tel. 75–51–18). Reserve in advance because this is one of the most highly praised little places on the island. Go for a leisurely lunch where you'll dine

[handwritten margin note: G.O. = the term for an employee at Club Med (gentil organisateur)]

on the side porch of Mally's home under an orange and white awning, among the hummingbirds and hibiscus. If you can't understand French, your phrase book better be the best. This is family-style cooking and among Mally's delicacies are lobster vinaigrette, conch tarte, crayfish, broiled red snapper with lime, capers and onion, papaya souffle and fresh light coconut cake served with homemade tropical fruit, jams and preserves. *Inexpensive.*

Morne-Des-Esses (a mountain village in the north, near the Atlantic Coast)

★★★★ LE COLIBRI
(Tel. 75–32–19). There's only one main street here, so it's not too hard to find. Go with someone who speaks French if at all possible. Madame Palladino or one of her twin daughters explains their menu in great detail but only in French. However, if he's here, her son does speak English. This is a friendly place. Half a dozen tables on the porch of la patronne's modest maison look out over banana trees, the mountains and the sea. Reserve your place because local gourmets give Le Colibri rave reviews. You'll get an idea of why this restaurant is rated so highly from this list of her delectable dishes: callaloo des crabes (a stew made with crab, callaloo greens, garlic and hot pepper); buisson d'écrevisses (a half dozen giant crayfish served in a grand goblet with chive sauce for dipping); stuffed pigeon on a nest of shoestring potatoes; purée or soufflé of christophine (the local squash) and chicken in wine with coconut. *Moderate.*

Le Francois

(On the Atlantic Coast, about mid-island.) At the following two restaurants lunch is usually preceded by a short trip to the nearby coral reef for some snorkeling off a boat owned by a fisherman who may be just the one who's caught your lunch.

CLUB NAUTIQUE
(Tel. 74–31–00). This snack bar on the waterfront offers only lunch. The choice of fresh fish depends on what is caught that day. Try a "décollage" (take-off) as an apéritif—rum aged with herbs and a chaser of fruit juice. Two or three of these will propel you right under the table. *Inexpensive.*

St. Pierre

LA FACTORERIE
Quartier Fort (Tel. 77–12–53). The best spot to stop for lunch when touring historic St. Pierre. This large, open-air restaurant is part of a rural agricultural school so all the food—eggs, chicken, rabbit, pork, vegetables and fruit—is grown on the property by the students themselves. There's always a choice of two 65F 3-course menus and an extensive à la carte listing that features fish, fowl and meat Creole style. *Inexpensive.*

LES BRISANTS
(Tel. 74–32–57). The name translates to ocean breakers, a perfect description for this exceptional site on the Atlantic. Creole seafood is the specialty— fresh sweet clams served with peppers and limes; squid; urchin roe and charcoal-broiled fish and lobster. *Inexpensive.*

Nightlife

Noctambules (night owls) will find plenty of diversion in Martinique . . . dinner-dances under the stars; nightclubs featuring steel bands, limbo and folkloric shows; discothèques and casinos.

The most popular *discos* in *Point du Bout* are lively, roomy *Le Vesou* at the Frantel and the Méridien's dark, intimate *Vonvon. Club 21* at the PLM La Batelière is very fashionable as well as romantic; it's perched on the rocks above the sea. Music may be live or recorded; a mixture of beguine, slow and rock. There's usually an admission charge of about $5 (which includes one drink) or an equivalent minimum; hotel guests are generally admitted free or are given a 50% discount. Scotch, Bourbon and American-style drinks are expensive, so it's best to stick to tropical concoctions made from local rum or French wines.

In *Fort-de-France* "in spots" change from time to time, so it's always a good idea to check with the tourist office or your hotel to find out the number 1 boîte.

Club 78 swings Tuesday through Sunday from 10:00 until dawn; so does its neighbor on Boulevard Allegre, *The Hippo Club,* making Friday or Saturday night a special night out on the town. *Le Manoir* (1.5 km out of town on the Route des Religieuses) is THE place for authentic Martiniquais music, wild entertainment (limbo, fire-eaters, exotic dancers), plenty of local color and a restaurant for late night snacks.

Gambling buffs will find two European-style casinos (no slot machines) on the island at the PLM La Batelière and at the Méridien. Minimum bets are $2.50 for baccarat, craps, blackjack and roulette. Hours are 9:00 P.M.– 3:00 A.M.; you must be 21; show identification with a photo. Most people dress up.

Shopping

If you like shopping, you'll thoroughly enjoy a full day of wandering in and out of the many boutiques that line the four main commercial streets of Fort-de-France. To ensure maximum enjoyment, however, pick a day when there's no cruise ship in port.

All along rue Victor Hugo, rue Antoine Siger, rue Lamartine and rue Schoelcher pastel buildings house tiny stores whose ground-floor windows display merchandise almost as bright and as beautiful as the gorgeous greenery and fabulous flowers hung on the balconies above.

The best buys here are French luxury labels—crystal, porcelain, haute couture from Paris and chic resortwear from the Côte d'Azur, cooking gadgets, wines and liqueurs and, of course, *perfume.* In fact, savvy shoppers generally head straight for *Roger Albert,* a slick showcase on rue Victor Hugo that's stocked to the rafters with every size and shape of the world's most famous fragrances plus many you've never heard of . . . the Caribbean's most complete selection of scents. You'll also find fine lingerie, leather goods, designer ties and scarves, Lacoste shirts, Cartier and Dupont lighters, cosmetics, atomizers, watches, Limoges and Lalique at Roger Albert's and across the street at *Beaufrand,* a quality gift shop on a smaller scale. The prices of these items usually beat or at least match prices in France, but these two merchants (and some others) offer an additional, hard-to-resist, buying incentive–a 20% discount on goods paid for by travelers' checks or major credit cards.

For jewelry ranging from ornamental, heavy (and therefore quite expensive) gold beads known as *collier chou* (darling's necklace)—an integral part of every Creole costume—to imported, modern designs in silver or gold, try the always reliable *Cadet Daniel* (established in 1840) and *Thomas De Rogatis* on rue Antoine Siger; *R. Montaclair, Venutolo,* and *L'Or et L'Argent* on rue Victor Hugo.

Fashion boutiques abound; every season there's a new list of names to note; *Biba, Al Nanas, Le Carcibi, Chantilly, La Chamade Folie-Foloi* and *Olympe* are only a few of the current favorites for Madame. Monsieur will find his designs at *Jean Laurent, Brumel* or *Lui;* and both can browse at *Mod* and *Aventure.* The owners and sales personnel are charming and helpful, but a French phrase book and an understanding of European size equivalents will probably be of more assistance to you.

Your best identification is with-photo is your passport

Creole *antiques* are hard to locate; but *La Malle des Indes,* on Rte. Didier carries old maps and prints. A visit to *Les Puces* or one of the stores at the suburban *Cluny Shopping Center* may turn up a find or two.

Traditional *madras* . . . yards and yards of it, all colorful and all inexpensive . . . is everywhere. The difficulty involves choosing a pattern to give to a local tailor so that he or she can get to work on a bikini, blouse, long skirt or man's shirt and finish it before you go home. *Hit Parade,* on rue Lamartine, has the island's best choice of *records;* and *straw* items can be found at *Gommier* and the *market* that is set up daily in *La Savanne.*

Some of the best *rum* in the Caribbean comes from Martinique. Hemingway's favorite is reputed to have been St. James. There are over a dozen distilleries on the island. From January to June, visitors are invited by Le Syndicat des Rhums de la Martinique for tasting tours. In town, do your tasting at La Case à Rhum on avenue de la Liberté, *Boulevard du Rhum* or *La Boutique du Rhum* on rue Victor Hugo.

La Boutique has a nice garden and teahouse, too

Sports

Beaches

Martinique is partly of coral and partly of volcanic origin; consequently, beaches are white in the south and dark gray in the north. The scalloped Caribbean southern coast offers dazzling, long, white expanses of sand as well as secluded "petites plages" that begin at Anses d'Arlets and continue through Diamant, Sainte Luce and Sainte-Anne—a fishing village with several good beachside bistros. Just beyond Sainte-Anne is the Plage des Salines, miles of palm-shaded, nearly deserted beach during the week. Because this is considered to be the island's most beautiful beach, it is well-populated on weekends but less crowded during the week.

Swimmers should approach the rougher Atlantic coast with caution except at Vauclin in the south and the Presqu'ile de la Caravelle at mid-island. The latter, a peninsula jutting into the ocean from Trinité, contains several good-size bays and tiny, calm coves.

There is no official nudist beach on the island, but topless sunning and bathing are acceptable and popular practices at the resort hotels, much less so at beaches out on the island.

Showers and facilities for changing are available at a nominal charge at hotel beaches.

Golf

The Empress Josephine, an 18-hole, Robert Trent Jones-designed course, is located at Trois Ilets. This 140-acre course has a par of 71. Rental carts, clubs, caddies, changing rooms and showers are available, and there is an English-speaking pro. Special greens fees are accorded to guests of the major Pointe du Bout hotels.

Fishing

Kingfish, tuna, barracuda, dolphin (NOT the mammal . . . a different species), bonito are some of the deep-sea fish that are popular catches. Arrangements for charters should be made through your hotel desk a few days in advance. Surf casting for jackfish, parrotfish, yellowtail snapper is best at Cap Ferré, Cap Macré and Cap Chevalier in the southeast.

This dolphin is similar to the Hawaiian mahi mahi fish

Hiking

Tourists are welcome to participate in the inexpensive, guided excursions organized by the Parc Regional (Tel. 72–17–25). Possibilities include a Mt. Pelée climb; exploration of the Gorges de la Falaise and the rain forest between Grand Rivière and Le Prêcheur (a six-hour walk). The nature preserve at Presqu'ile de la Caravelle has well-marked trails leading to the ruins of Château Dubuc and through the tropical wetlands.

Horseback Riding

The Ranch Jack Galochat in Anse d'Arlets (Tel. 76–43–97) arranges half hour, one hour or half day excursions. Small, sure-footed Creole horses—a South American-Spanish breed—are used, and prices are about $5 per hour.

Sailing

Excursions can be arranged through major resort hotels' activities desks. Most hotels on the beach provide Sunfish and sail boards for guests who windsurf. Latitude Hotel has a windsurfing school with a practice simulator.

Cardholding members of yacht clubs may use the facilities at the Club de la Voile de Fort-de-France at Pointe Simon (Tel. 70–26–63) or the Yacht Club de la Martinique (Tel. 71–23–60).

Yacht charters and boat rental by the day, week or month can be arranged through Dufour Antilles (Tel. 76–35–35); Tabarly Yachting (76–34–09); Captains Shop (76–35–64); Cariberick (76–30–76) or Voile Voyages (76–34–09) in Pointe du Bout. In Fort-de-France, try the Ship Shop (Tel. 71–43–40). In Schoelcher, Carib Charter (71–58–96).

Scuba Diving and Snorkeling

Scuba centers, all with licensed instructors, are: at the Méridien, PLM La Botelière, and Diamant Novotel, the Hotel Latitude; and the Club Méditerranée (for their guests only).

Snorkelers will find plenty of fish, coral and sea ferns right off Pointe du Bout and Anse Mitan beaches, in the small bays near Anse d'Arlets, and off the southern beaches near Ste. Anne. Snorkeling is usually a feature of sailing excursions, and most hotels provide equipment to their guests free of charge.

Spectator Sports

Sailboat races are popular, and local "bloodsports," such as cockfights and mongoose versus snake contests, draw big local crowds. But the classic sports event of the year takes place on Easter Monday when Martinique and Guadeloupe meet for their annual soccer clash.

Tennis

The PLM La Batelière has six courts (four floodlit); the Bakoua, Méridien and Frantel each offers two (also lighted for night play). One court is available at Leyritz Plantation and Hotel Latitude. In addition, temporary memberships are available to visitors at the Tennis Club de Fort-de-France (Tel. 71–64–15) or at the Tennis Club du Vieux Moulin (Tel. 71–33–82). Fees run about $7 per hour.

Other Water Sports

The PLM La Batelière, Frantel, Bakoua, Méridien and Latitude offer pedal boats and waterskiing and provide about every conceivable piece of equipment for water sports.

Your taxi driver is likely to know of any mongoose- snake fight, but we don't want to know about it

Nevis

THE HARD FACTS
Planning Ahead
Costs

Nevis is one of the few Caribbean islands that do not charge astronomical rates for accommodations. In the winter season, a stay at one of the plantation inns runs about $150, double occupancy MAP. In summer, rates range from $80 to $100, double occupancy MAP.

It's pronounced knee-vis, not neh-vis

Since shopping and nightlife are limited, don't plan on allocating large sums for these activities. (A little will go a long way.) There is no casino or disco, although some of the inns feature string bands once a week. You'll spend a lot of time strolling miles of beaches, black-volcanic as well as standard Caribbean sugar-white beaches, many fringed with coconut palms. You'll stay at one of a handful of great-house plantation estates that have been turned into villa-like inns—each possessing a distinct personality and some boasting of ghosts "in residence." Travelers visit Nevis for its quiet and peacefulness.

Climate

The cooling northeast trade winds keep the average temperature at 78°F. year round.

Holidays and Special Events

The following public holidays are celebrated each year in Nevis: New Year's day (January 1); Statehood Day (February 27); Good Friday; Easter Monday; Labour Day (the first Monday in May); Whit Monday (40 days after Lent); the Queen's official birthday (about June 10); August Monday (the first Monday in August); Prince Charles's birthday (November 14); Christmas Day; Boxing Day (the day after Christmas, December 26).

A special event is Culturama (really Nevis's special style of carnival), which is celebrated the last week in July and part of the first week in August. There's jamming in the streets to steel bands; drama shows enacted on wooden platforms; calypso singing; string-band performances; a lot of local dishes sold from streetside booths set up for the occasion; and great quantities of rum consumed. There's also a local cure for carnival that Nevisians swear by: "One cup of Goat Water (a stew with a lot of spices) takes care of a lot of liquor!"

185

Tour Operators

Major U.S. operators: Caribbean Holidays, Lib/Go Travel, Inc., and Travel Impressions Ltd.; Tour-Trec International; Thompson Vacations.

Sources of Information

Call or write the *Eastern Caribbean Tourist Association Office* at 220 East 42nd Street, New York, NY 10017, (212) 986–9370. Or contact the *Caribbean Tourist Association,* 20 East 46th Street, New York, NY 10017, (212) 682–0435.

Packing

Take along casual, comfortable, lightweight summer clothing. Men are not required to wear ties and jackets. Women may want to tuck in one casual, long dress or skirt, also lightweight shawls for evenings. Take along any prescription medication that you might need, although prescriptions can be filled in the drugstores of Charlestown. The small inns of Nevis do not employ hairdressers, so bring your blow dryer, along with your favorite shampoo. If you plan to tour the island—and you should—pack a pair of sturdy shoes that will protect your feet from the underbrush, which is thick and prickly. There's plenty of it around the old plantation houses and in nonbeach areas. Do your vacation-wardrobe shopping before you leave the United States: The local selection of resortwear is scarce and sizes are limited. Photo fiends should pack more film than they think they'll need. Film costs almost double U.S. prices.

Documentation

To enter Nevis travelers from the United States need only show proof of citizenship. A birth certificate, a passport (current or expired), a valid driver's license or naturalization papers all serve the purpose, although presenting a current passport enables you to whisk through U.S. Customs. Also, you must show an ongoing or a return airline or ship ticket.

This applies also to Canadian visitors

Getting There

British West Indian Airways (BWIA) have weekly, nonstop flights from the United States to St. Kitts, the neighboring sister isle of Nevis. Regular ferry service is provided between Nevis and St. Kitts. The trip takes 40 minutes and costs $7.00 each way. LIAT provides air service from Antigua, and Eastern Caribbean Air Service flies from St. Croix. Small planes offer charter service from St. Kitts, Antigua and other nearby islands. ALM serves neighboring St. Martin via Miami, where WINAIR connects to Nevis. (WINAIR also connects from St. Barts.) But all hoteliers stress they will get you there if you contact them or their representative directly.

Formalities on Arrival

Personal belongings are admitted free of duty. Each person may also bring along one carton of cigarettes, one bottle of wine and one bottle of liquor.

Money

The Eastern Caribbean dollar ("Bee Wee") is used in Nevis. Hotels and taxis accept U.S. dollars. You can convert U.S. dollars at commercial banks or your hotel. The latter will give a rate almost equivalent to that offered by the banks. Some establishments accept major credit cards. If you anticipate that you'll have to cash a personal check, be sure to register your request for such privileges with your hotel management in advance of the transaction. There is a $8.00 EC departure tax, which can be paid in U.S. dollars.

Learning to Cope

Business Hours.   From 8:00 A.M. to noon daily except Saturday and Sunday. On Friday the St. Kitts–Nevis National Bank Ltd. in Charlestown stays open from 3:30 P.M. to 4:30 P.M. Saturday hours are 8:30 A.M. to 11:00 A.M.

Electricity.   Nevis has the European, or 220-voltage, current. You will need a converter for any appliance you bring along. Bring your own, or ask to borrow one from the owner/manager of your inn.

Language.   English is the offical language . . . sometimes referred to as the Queen's English . . . with a distinct island lilt.

NEVIS TODAY

He used to come down from the hills very slowly, this old man and his old donkey. They waited patiently and watched from their home on the hill until there were visitors gathered on the golden sand of Pinney's Beach. And when there appeared to be even a small handful, the pair wended their way down to the beach. This gentle pair went over to the sunseekers, asking for nothing. This proud old man and his aged companion—the flower-bedecked donkey—just wanted to welcome the visitors to Nevis. This greeting became a tradition in Nevis. The old man loved his island, and he wanted all newcomers to love it too. Before he came down from his hillside home, he lovingly decorated his donkey with garlands of island flowers: hibiscus, bougainvillea and frangipani, perhaps to symbolize the tranquility of Nevis. The highlight of his greeting was the serenade that he played on his fife. This gentle, old man, John Woodburn, is gone now, but the Nevisian tradition he started lives on. Small boys borrow their fathers' donkeys and "dress" them with flowers. Then they watch, poised to greet new arrivals.

The people of Nevis give to this special, tucked-away island—a member of the State of St. Kitts and Nevis—its special character. You may not meet Marcia and Wendy, ages four and five, who wave and plead for visitors to stop their cars so that they can shake your finger. Momentarily overcome by shyness when visitors ask their names, they finally manage to answer and ask the same question, but you'll meet your own Marcia and Wendy on the road somewhere in Nevis.

You may want to journey to Clay Ghaut Estate to meet Eva Wilkin, a respected artist now in her 70s. She lives in a plantation great house and paints in a restored sugar mill, where she shows or sells some of her works to visitors. Although she was born in Montserrat and was schooled in London, Miss Wilkin has spent over 50 years of her life in Nevis. For her, it is home. She plans to concentrate her talent on painting portraits of the people of Nevis, mostly the children. If you're lucky, you may be able to buy a few of her prints. She'll gladly tell you the history of each, such as the time many years ago when she sat sketching "The Mill" the day before the actual mill was torn down. She cried as she worked.

Unquestionably, you'll meet the owner of the inn where you've elected to stay. So, too, will you meet the proprietors who will serve you lunch and dinner. At the *Golden Rock* owners Pam and Frank Barry will guide you around their 200-acre estate, showing you the great house (built in 1815) and the counting house (built in 1801). The former plantation was built and owned by Pam's great, great, great, great grandfather, Edward Huggins, whose descendants sold it to nonfamily members. Pam is glad to have it back in the family. If you've arranged to stay at *Zetland Plantation,* you will discover that host Richard Lupinacci, his wife Maureen and their four children are eager to become your friends.

[handwritten marginal note:] "Nevis" comes from Las Nieves, Columbus' name for the place, "The Snows"

At the *Montepelier Estate,* owner James Milnes Gaskell will welcome you to his rock-hewn great house and will proudly escort you around his three-acre vegetable and fruit garden. He'll gladly give you information about his garden—all fruits and vegatables are organically grown—but will probably forget to tell you that he's a second cousin of Queen Elizabeth II and that his cousin, Prince Charles, intended to stop here on his royal honeymoon to visit his royal relative. If you decide to lunch at the *Rest Haven Hotel and Restaurant,* built around an Olympic swimming pool, you may hear its elegant owner, Almon Nisett, saying to a guest, "I hope that whatever your dreams may be, they become a reality."

The people of Nevis live for today and remember yesterday. They revere their traditions and their past. It is a past that embodied gracious living built on the foundations of prosperous sugar plantations. It is a past that revolved around the gentry who came from Europe to "take the waters" at the sulfur springs of the Bath House Spa. Nevis's sugar, sun and sulfur springs earned the tiny island the name Queen of the Caribbee in those seemingly-simpler days. Alexander Hamilton was born in Nevis; Lord Horatio Nelson was married in Nevis to Frances Nisbet, the daughter of a wealthy plantation owner.

[handwritten margin note: Nelson and Hamilton were contemporaries]

Despite its aura of tranquility, Nevis was born in a series of volcanic eruptions, the evidence of which is still apparent in the black-sand beaches developed from volcanic-tinted strains of sand. The island's past speaks of pirates and slaves; duels for honor and for love; Indian massacres; haunted great houses on sugar estates.

For an island so diminutive (36 square miles), Nevis has had more than its share of ups and downs. The island is now politically stable, for it is a state in association with St. Kitts (the association maintains ties to Great Britain). Unlike St. Kitts, smaller Nevis is not now courting hotel development on a large scale.

TOURING

Discovering Nevis entails a bit of driving either on your own in a rented car or by booking a taxi and a driver. Whatever your choice, you'll encounter unexpected coves, countless 17th- and 18th-century ruins, deep coconut groves and tiny, undisturbed villages. Even though the island is small, there's no reason to rush the journey. Allow time for a swim, a leisurely lunch at one of the restored plantation great houses, or for something that suggests it will be more than a passing interest.

If you decide to hire a taxi, you'll find the drivers to be knowledgeable about the island. Spencer Howell is always in demand; he's a fund of local lore and a very pleasant companion. Your inn will arrange to book either a taxi and a driver or a car that you can drive. If you choose the latter, you must get a temporary driving permit at the police station in Charlestown. Simply present a valid U.S. driver's license and pay $4.00 (U.S.). The charge for a taxi with a driver varies according to the length of your island trip and your destination. It's possible to rent a standard car or a mini-moke for about $30 a day. Mopeds rent for about $20 a day. All costs are based on unlimited mileage, but gas is not included. The rules of the road in Nevis are: Keep to the left, and drive with an eye for stray goats or donkeys that sometimes, appear around a bend in the road and claim the right to exercise their territorial imperative. Your plantation inn will gladly pack a picnic basket, or you can make reservations at one of the other excellent plantations for lunch. Before you set out, you may want to read one of the best possible guides: Janet Cotner's *A Motoring Guide to Nevis.* Try to get the edition that's been revised by Sunny Northrup. It should be available in the shops of Charlestown or at the Tourist Office there.

Charlestown may well be the place to begin your Nevisian adventure. It's a typical West Indian, ex-British, port town. Nothing much happens here in too much of a hurry (except for the arrivals and the departures of the ferry from neighboring St. Kitts). In the center of town, see the *Customs House* and the stone *Court House,* where pirates confronted justice. The building contains the *Library,* which has a small, select exhibit of Carib stone carvings. One of the most interesting stops in town is the large *marketplace* where ladies display local fruit and vegetables, some of which will turn up on your dining table. You may want to buy some mangos, papayas, avocados, oranges or grapefruit for your journey. If you come early in the morning when market life is at its best (particularly on Saturday), you may be in time to see the impromptu *fish selling* that takes place directly across the street on the beach. Before heading out of town, stop by the Nevis Bakery and try their freshly-made coconut tarts, bread or cookies.

As you head south out of town, you'll come to the restored *Jews Cemetary.* To enter it, you will need to get the key from Mr. Hunkins' office, next door. Twenty-five percent of Nevis's population used to be Sephardic Jews (many from Brazil) who worked as shopkeepers or helped introduce sugarcane to Nevis. The tombstones date to 1684, and the inscriptions are in Hebrew, English and Portuguese. Near the cemetery grounds are the remains of a synagogue and a school. It's believed that Alexander Hamilton started school here.

If you continue on the road south of Charlestown, you'll come to *Fort Charles.* Once, by firing its 23 cannons (a few remain), the British did their best to hold this fortress when the Spanish fleet attacked Nevis. Later, an English nobleman, Sir Timothy Thornhill, made Nevis his headquarters for launching attacks against the French in St. Barts, St. Martin and St. Kitts. Today most of the fort is in ruin, but it's still possible to see the rusted seal of the English Crown affixed to some of the cannon and a bit of the original parade ground, cistern and the powder magazine.

The remains of other edifices are also historically important. Among the most significant are those of *the Bath Hotel,* built in 1778 by John Huggins (the same man who built the Golden Rock Estate). When it was opened, the hotel could accommodate 50 guests, many of whom came from Europe to take the thermal baths (temperatures rose as high as 108°F.). Many Canadians came via what was called the Lady boats, for *Lady Drake, Lady Hawkins* and *Lady Nelson* started their runs in Canada. The elite of Nevis also came to the hotel to drink and gamble . . . and they gambled for the possible reward of land, not money. During those days of high living, the hotel was characterized as "the most ambitious structure ever erected in the West Indies." Its mineral waters were appreciated by Captain John Smith, the leader of the Jamestown colony in Virginia, who came to recover from manchineel burns (the tree that bears the name still bears the poisonous fruit). In a letter home, he noted: "Here we found a great poole, wherein bathing found much ease. . . . We were well cured in two or three days."

The abolishment of slavery, which coincided with the start of a world war, brought to a close the heyday of the Bath Hotel. And earthquakes in 1950 destroyed what remained of the cane houses, great house and bath house that then contained six separate cubicles. Although there have been several prospective buyers, the government hopes to preserve the remains as an historical monument.

Your next stop in discovering Nevis should be *Government House,* built in 1909. It's now used for occasional offical cocktail parties. A well-built house of thick, local stone, it contains an expansive porch graced by well-tended plants. Visitors are welcome to enter and open the guest book, see who's come before them, and leave their signatures for other guests to note.

The next stop of note is at *Fig Tree Church,* still quiet, perhaps reflecting the atmosphere that prevailed when Frances Nisbet married Captain Horatio Nelson in 1787. The church register shows the official recording: "1787. March 11th. Horatio Nelson, Esquire, Captain of His Majesty's Ship *The Boreas,* to Frances Herbert Nisbet, Widow." Unfortunately for her, he left her and sailed back to Lady Hamilton in England.

One of the most fascinating stops along the meandering road is a visit to *Morning Star Plantation,* the private home of Robert Abrahams. Inspired by love for their chosen island retreat, Mr. Abrahams (a Philadelphia lawyer, the author of several books and a knowledgeable historian) and his late wife, Florence, created the Lord Nelson Museum. (They were also responsible for the restoration of the Jews Cemetery.) Time stopped, literally, when Elizabeth II and Prince Phillip visited the museum on February 22, 1966: The hands of the great clock were stopped at the time of their visit, 3:15 P.M., not to be started until their return. There's a print reputed to depict Horatio Nelson and Frances Nisbet. If it's genuine (no one is certain), it would be the only visual recording of the couple. There are faded letters written by Nelson with his left hand after the right had been shot off, and other Nelson memorabilia.

The next historic stop should be *Cottle Church,* the first church in the West Indies in which slaves were allowed to worship with their masters. To commemorate its opening on May 5, 1824, Mr. Cottle proclaimed the day an official holiday for his slaves. In fact, he built the church so that it would be used by both the owned and the owners.

It's possible to stay, lunch or dine at *Montpelier Estate.* Even if you choose none of these options, you should certainly stop at this restored inn, built on the ruins of the sugar works of the original Montpelier Estate. Because the restoration is authentic in every way, it's impossible to perceive the scope of the restoration project. It was here, under an ancient silk-cotton tree, that Lord Nelson and the widow Frances Nisbet exchanged their wedding vows. There's a tablet on one of the original stone pillars that records the event. Before her marriage, Frances Nisbet lived at Montpelier with her uncle, Mr. Herbert, who was the president of Nevis.

You may decide to lunch at Montpelier or move on to neighboring *Zetland Plantation,* another of the island's great houses built on a sprawling estate that extends more than 1,000 feet up towering Mount Nevis. The plantation is one of the several places where you can begin the 3,500-foot climb to the top of Mount Nevis if you're so inclined.

When she's in residence (and that's most of the year), Eva Wilkin, Nevis's most famous artist who is respected throughout the island as well as the world, will greet you. Her plantation home is at *Clay Ghaut Estate,* where she welcomes guests before noon or after three in the afternoon. She has been decorated for her work by Elizabeth II and more recently hosted a visit by Prince Charles. Most of her original works depict the children of Nevis and its abundant island flowers. Her pastel portraits, pen and ink drawings and watercolors are for sale. Meeting and talking with Miss Wilkin will be the capstone of your visit to her sugar-mill studio on the estate.

Old Manor Estate in the village of Gingerland is certainly worth a stop. We recommend that you stay for drinks and dinner. Officially called Croney's Old Manor Estate, the plantation inn takes its name from the Croney family, its first residents. Built as a sugar plantation, local lore recounts that the property was used as a stud farm for the breeding of slaves until 1834, when they were freed. In the 1970s, the estate was painstakingly restored by King A. Koch from Texas and is presently owned by Mrs. Vicki Knorr and her son from Ohio.

The windmill is now a honeymoon duplex

You may well want to make dinner reservations at the *Golden Rock Estate* and stay long enough to look at this magnificent plantation inn. It's now owned by Frank and Pam Barry (she's a direct descendant of the builder Edward Huggins whose initials [E. H.] can be seen on the main door along with a date, 1815). It's said that the ghost of a slave walks on some nights. According to the story, after the master, Edward Huggins, locked the slave in a small dungeon, Huggins set sail for England.

Your belief in the existence of a ghost at Golden Rock may depend on whether your ear is attuned to moans and the sound of chains clanking on cement. But you may accept the story of the ghost of the *Eden Brown Estate* because it is "historic." Cries of shock and disbelief echo (for believers) through the ruins of the estate. It seems that in the 18th century there was a prenuptial party held on the eve of the wedding for the bridegroom, a member of the leading Maynard family. For reasons not clearly discernible but that seem to center on the amount of liquor consumed, Mr. Maynard and his best-man-to-be challenged each other to a duel at dawn. As the sun rose over the Atlantic, both men lay dying. The almost-bride was so distraught that she could not be restrained from roaming and raving in her room. She never recovered her sanity. Her father closed the house, fully-furnished, and took her back to England. Although she never returned in body, her spirit, or so it's said, continues to roam here.

It's worthwhile to make a brief stop at *Saint James Church,* one of five Anglican churches on the island, for a look at one of three black figures of Christ known to exist in the Caribbean. You may want to make another brief stop at *St. Thomas Church,* the oldest church in Nevis. The adjoining graveyard had some interesting epitaphs on its weathered gravestones.

You'll next come to another of Nevis's plantation inns, the *Nisbet Plantation,* where Frances Nisbet lived with her uncle. Today you can stop for a proper English tea in the afternoon or book a table for lunch or dinner and sense the unhappy past and feel the happier present.

Unless you're accompanied by a guide-driver, you'll pass by *Nelson Spring* and not even know you've missed it. It's where Nelson is said to have taken on board fresh water for his ship and where, it's also believed, he first met Frances Nisbet. Today ladies may walk by balancing sacks of coconut shells on their heads, which they'll use at home for fuel, or a donkey, laden with goods, may stagger along.

Along the winding roads, you may pass one of the island's most fascinating trees, the tremendous *baobab tree,* imported from Africa. The story goes that God was annoyed at this tree, tore it from its roots, and replanted it upside down. Starting from seeds, these incredible trees take over 250 years to mature. A few are thought to be over 2,000 years old. Troops of the island's famous "monkey population" have been seen eating the fruit of the trees, now called monkey bread.

Circling back toward Charlestown, you'll come on the remains of the *Alexander Hamilton House.* Alexander Hamilton was born in Nevis on January 11, 1757, and spent his first 11 years here. The ruins of his birthplace are crumbling, but the local residents honor his memory. Each year, on the anniversary of his birthday, William and Marion Trott, now in their 80s celebrate by holding a garden party. They ask guests to make small donations which they send to a secondary school on the island. Hamilton, as you may remember, was the illegitimate son of Scotsman James Hamilton and Rachel Fawcett, a Creole beauty. His mother died when he was 11, and Alexander was sent to the island of St. Croix to be raised by an aunt. He developed his genius for business matters, and at the age of 15, he set sail for North America. He graduated from what is now called Columbia University in New York City. A patroit during the American Revolution, he became Secretary of the

Columbia was then King's College

Treasury and then died from wounds sustained in a duel with the then Vice-President of the United States, Aaron Burr, in 1804.

Inside Information

Hotels

There are no "hotels" in Nevis. There are a handful of restored villa-style inns built around the remains of great houses or restored sugar plantations. Each inn has a distinct personality based on its link to the past. If your inn is not located on its own sands (and many aren't), the management will gladly arrange a lift to get you to the beach. Almost all the inns have their own swimming pools, and a few have tennis courts.

The estates add a 10% service charge and a 5% government tax to your bill. If you prefer to rent a villa or a cottage with cook and maid service, contact the Nevis Tourist Committee, Charlestown, West Indies. You must reserve any accommodation far in advance. (The largest of the inns has only 36 rooms.) Inns are at full capacity in season (December 15 to April 15); and with the recent influx of European visitors, most are booked in summer as well (April 16 to December 14).

The atmosphere of all the inns is relaxed, friendly and quiet, and at a few, refined British manner is evident. Flow with the current.

★★★ GOLDEN ROCK ESTATE

This former sugar plantation elicits the personal attention of Pam and Frank Barry, which reflects the concerns of generations past. Pam's great, great, great, great, grandfather, Edward Huggins, built Golden Rock (his initials can still be seen in some of the stone facing), as well as the stately remains of the Bath House. Twelve rooms accommodate 24 guests in period settings that range from the Sugar Mill, with antique four-posters bearing carved head-boards, to sprawling large rooms in other buildings, all with a lot of bamboo, bright fabrics and English antiques. The estate roams over 200 acres of flower-filled, undulating hills, including a special 25-acre garden manicured to English-tropical perfection. There is a swimming pool, but there's also transportation to two private beaches; one on the windward side of the island, the other on the leeward (or calmer side). There's also tennis on an all-weather court, and deep-sea fishing as well as waterskiing, snorkeling and scuba diving can be arranged. *Cost:* $175 per double MAP, in season. Golden Rock is closed from August 1 to October 31. Bringing children under 12 is not recommended. Off-season rates are $125, double MAP.

★★★ MONTPELIER

Although owner James Milnes Gaskell is a relative of Queen Elizabeth, he writes in his invitation to visit Montpelier: "You don't need to be rich or successful; just intelligent, interesting and fun." And that's the way life is on this 100-acre estate rebuilt by Mr. Gaskell and Nevis's builder, Sam Hunkins, in 1965 on the ruins of the former estate. The eight cottages house a total of 16 rooms, each redecorated last year by Jacqueline Chenoweth (formerly of Baltimore and now of Nevis) in sophisticated prints with Caribbean touches (wicker headboards; flowers on the table). The beach bar, by the Olympic swimming pool, also shows Jackie's touches: wicker basket swinging chairs;

matching tables; a deep, ocean-blue print fabric flecked with flowers adorning the sink-in chairs. This is where lunch or afternoon tea is served or where you can sip a before-dinner drink. There's a pool, off-shore fishing, riding and tennis for the energetic and fruit and flower picking, shell hunting, and visits to historic sights for the not-so-energetic. *Cost:* $135 per double MAP, in season (December 15 to April 15); $95 per double MAP, off season (April 16 to December 14).

★★★★ NISBET PLANTATION INN
A long avenue of palm trees on a perfect English lawn leads guests down to the half-mile stretch of gentle beach; hammocks for two swing from the trees; beachside gazebos provide drinks or snacks and there's usually a barbecue fire going. The great house was rebuilt on 18th-century foundations. The main rooms offer English country-style decor with formal evening dining. Managing directors Michael and Marianne Brewer run the great house and the 30 rooms provided in adjacent buildings. Each is individually named— Gingerland; Paradise; Hard Times; Crook's Ground—and individually decorated with varying touches of the English "motherland." Tennis, croquet and archery are available on the estate; fishing, sailing, waterskiing, climbing Mt. Nevis, and horseback riding can be arranged. This is where Frances Nisbet played as a child. You can play as an adult. *Cost:* $175–$225, per double MAP (including wine), in season (December 15 to April 14); $100 per double MAP (including wine), off season (April 15 to December 14).

Good beach here

★★★★ THE HERMITAGE
This is the oldest known house in Nevis and was probably built around 1690. It is owned by Maureen and Richard Lupinacci who intended it to be their private get-away from managing Zetlands Plantation. But due to constant requests, they've now added four period apartments to satisfy repeat visitors, each with kitchenette and maid service. But it's the two-story house that's in constant demand, with cross beams made of lignum vitae (no longer even grown on the island). There's a view of the ocean through century-old trees . . . truly a place where time has stood still. *Cost:* $200 a week.

★★★ CRONEY'S OLD MANOR ESTATE
Set in the village of Gingerland, 800 feet above the ocean, this 19th-century great house and estate accommodates 20 guests in ten rooms along with a resident ghost who roams at will! Plans call for the addition of three rooms this year in keeping with the old-world ambience. Walls, almost three feet thick, are built of Nevis's face stone work; the rooms are actually suites in duplex settings reminiscent of a private wing in an English castle, where the king-size beds are draped in filmy mosquito netting. The Knorr family will arrange complimentary transportation to a beach, or a gallop through the surrounding hillsides. *Cost:* $140 per double MAP, in season. Even the bar is run on the honor system. Off-season rates are $96 per double MAP.

★★★ ZETLAND PLANTATION
This plantation-inn nestles high on the slope of Mt. Nevis, offering spectacular views of the Caribbean Sea and the Atlantic Ocean. Separate cottages with kitchenettes give guests the choice of preparing their own meals or dining at the excellent restaurant in the main house. Managers Richard and Maureen Lupinacci have found that most of their guests make occasional cups of coffee in their cottages but lunch poolside or dine inside where they find friendly companionship. Because the Lupinaccis have four children, they welcome families here. Their teenaged daughters even offer to baby-sit. There are 15 rooms, and four are under construction. Two rooms have sunken roman baths outside sliding glass doors. Sports include tennis, horseback riding, sailing, fishing, a trek up Mt. Nevis, a jaunt around the island by Moped

Trade wind breezes keep Zetland cool

bikes. *Cost:* $135 per double MAP, in season (December 15 to April 13); off-season rates (April 14 to December 14) dip considerably to $95 per double MAP.

★★ CLIFF DWELLERS

Ten cottages containing a total of 14 rooms perch hillside on Tamarind Bay, about 150 feet above the sea and below towering Mt. Nevis. Managed by English-born Harriet Turner, each room has a sitting area and a dressing room as well as the standard bed area and adjoining bath. All rooms have semi-canopied beds draped in dramatic print fabrics. Straw rugs from Dominica grace the floor. Each room has a terrace offering a view of the white-crested ocean or the white, cloud-covered mountain. There's a tramway for transport to and from the different levels of cottages and the main house on the top of the hill where guests dine, chat, or listen to the Thursday evening string band. Besides pool swimming (they have the largest pool on the island), the hotel provides ocean swims or snorkels, free use of a tennis court, day sails for lunch and drinks to Cockleshell Beach Resort on the neighboring island of St. Kitts, a climb up to Mt. Nevis and the chance to trot along the sands or into the hills on horseback. *Cost:* $165 per double MAP, in season; $110 per double MAP, off season. Closed in September and October. Bringing small children is not encouraged.

Restaurants

The standard price seems to be about $18 for dinner, and at most inns that does not include wine. At some, it does. Lunch costs range from a low of $3.50 in a local Charlestown snack and drink meeting place to about $15 at one of the plantation inns for lobster with all the fixings. Remember to make reservations at all plantation inns. They're a *must.*

★★★★ CRONEY'S OLD MANOR ESTATE

This 18th-century estate is presided over by Mrs. Vicki Knorr with such dedication that she even shipped her china from her home in Ohio. An evening begins with the drink of your choice ordered from the bar. As you sit down to dine, you face lighted candles and dinner napkins folded into perfect Easter lilies or roses. The menu might feature chicken creole in a tomato, onion, pepper and olive sauce; a side dish of cabbage casserole with tomatoes and sweet peppers; crisp tania fritters; baked plantains or conch fritters. Then if you can manage it, dessert might be coconut cream pie topped off with baked coconut. *Moderate.*

★★★★ HUSAVIK

Husavik, as every Icelandic native knows, means "house by the sea." And that's exactly where you are, in the seaside house of Lloyd and Laurie Gillies (although it took their daughter to name their idea for a restaurant). Quite understandably, lunch or dinner is by reservation only (which has to be made via your inn manager or jungle drums, since there is no telephone at present) and includes dips in the ocean by their bar-patio. Each night has a different theme. Lunches are mostly pub-style, with shepherds pie; steak and kidney pie; or fish and chips served English-style in newspapers (unless someone has "borrowed" the newspaper, a highly-valued item on any Caribbean island!). *Moderate.*

★★★★ NISBET PLANTATION

As you might expect in an 18th-century plantation that has been turned into an inn, restored and decorated with English elegance, dinners are formal in the great house dining room. Antiques enhance the ambience, and serve for dining as well. Marianne Brewer, wife of the managing director Michael Brewer, has taken special pains with the kitchen, which turns out both Creole and Continental cuisine. Dinner might start with a fish, pepper-pot or pump-kin soup, followed by West Indian main dishes: salt fish with avocado or eggplant; lamb kebab; a curried chicken with all the accoutrements; island langouste simply prepared in a butter sauce or spiced-up Creole style. Side dishes might be stuffed crab-back, goija (coconut-cornmeal bread), any of Nevis's endless variety of fruits and vegetables. And since Mr. Brewer is English (Mrs. Brewer is originally from Holland), there are a few basic steaks and chops and an occasional Dutch dish. Wine is complimentary at dinner. Lunch is usually served on the half-mile stretch of beach framed by palm trees in a new beach gazebo that turns out charcoal-broiled lobster and grilled fish—red snapper, Spanish mackerel, small tuna, wahoo, dolphin, *not* the mammal—or whatever local fishermen were able to catch that morning. Simple salads and sandwiches are also available. Sunday is usually the day for a super beach barbecue. *Moderate.*

★★★★ MONTPELIER
The pride of this 100-acre estate is actually centered on the three-acre organic fruit and vegetable garden. The owner uses no pesticides or defoliants. James Milnes Gaskell can often be seen tending to his personal passion, which results in avocados, grapefruits, tangerines, sweet potatoes, tomatoes, car-rots, beans and aubergines being placed on your lunch or dinner table. Even the sprinklings of parsley and basil come from the garden. The constantly-changing menu surprises even repeat guests. A few dishes that are favorites are lobster creole, fish crepes, turtle steaks, fish pie, peppers stuffed with lamb or beef, conch balls in a tomato sauce, stuffed eggplant, pumpkin fritters and stuffed green paw-paw. Lunch is served informally, but dinner is usually served in the formal English-style dining room in the great house. Occasional-ly a barbecue or a wine-tasting dinner is served in an informal setting. *Moderate.*

★★★★ ZETLAND PLANTATION
The cuisine at Zetland is legendary. So accustomed to the cuisine are mana-gers Maureen and Richard Lupinacci that when they visited their summer home in Pennsylvania last year, they took two of their cooks with them. The menu seems to change nightly. Maureen works closely with her cooks in order "to take local foods and together make them more exciting." Some dishes are local: goat water (a blend of stewed goat meat, breadfruit, carrots and spices); a salt fish stew with coconut dumplings; curried conch or conch fritters. Other nights the Zetland special—minted lamb; a red snapper stuffed with lobster; or lobster simply prepared in butter and spice sauce—might be served. Island vegetables and fruit always accompany the main dish; papaya, breadfruit, soursop, coconut, bananas, plantains, mangos, strawberries, lemons and limes, all served hundreds of ways. Lunches, served poolside or on the veranda, are simpler. Dinner is always served in the main house, except on Wednesday nights when it's served around the swimming pool to the accompaniment of a string or a steel band. *Moderate.*

★★★ CLIFF DWELLERS
The cuisine for both lunch and dinner accentuates Caribbean dishes. Like the owners of all the inns, the proprietor insists that locally-grown produce be used. Lunch is usually on the cliff-hanging patio (unless it's Sunday, when a king-size lunch is served by the king-size swimming pool, while a band serenades). More formal dinners are served in the hilltop main house, which is reached by a single-gauge tram that travels part way up the hill. Some of the featured dishes include snapper sauteed with plantains and peanuts; Creole crayfish in a sauce of tomatoes, peppers, onions and spices; glazed pork sweetened with pineapple; a baked grouper, with an eggplant mélange

stuffing. Soups are some of the best (although, in fairness, they're excellent at other inns too). A few of Cliff Dwellers' specialties are conch chowder; peanut soup; pumpkin soup with bacon bits; an unusual breadfruit soup. *Moderate.*

★★★ GOLDEN ROCK

Imagine dining in a 175-year-old great house, where owner Pam Barry is a direct descendant of the original builder. She presides over the candle-lit dining room with husband Frank, just as she earlier presided over the menu. Dinner might begin with a fish or a lobster chowder or possibly a callaloo soup; then it might move on to a baked snapper in a white-wine sauce with tania fritters; a tureen of turtle in an olive and tomato Creole sauce; simply spiced broiled lobster; Spanish mackerel, wahoo or grouper stuffed with a "secret" recipe. The select Saturday night buffet always features West Indian dishes. If possible one of the Golden Rock's special curries, such as their lamb curry with grated coconut, chopped egg, and homemade mango chutney, is served. Lunches, served in a flower-filled courtyard, are informal. The menu ranges from simple salads and sandwiches to grilled fish or chops and local lobster with all the fixings. The reasonable dinner bill includes the house wine. *Moderate.*

★★★ MRS. WELTON HOWE, AT HOME

Actually, this "restaurant" has no name, since it's truly the home of Mrs. Howe, and features West Indian cuisine for those guests who have managed to let her know they plan on dropping in. The menu might include pumpkin soup; a spicy lambi curry or conch—fried, frittered or stewed. Dessert could be a local fruit in any form, from nature's freshest in a thick sauce or frozen into ice cream. *Moderate.*

★★ THE LONGSTONE

This is the in-town gathering place for locals and visitors to lunch and gossip over a game of backgammon in the restored townhouse of George Edward Huggins, dating between 1817 to 1837. Now it's owned by Dick and Liz Pingel who have transformed it into an interesting bar, hung with nautical flags. There is an expansive dining room presided over by a wall mural of six ceiling-to-floor parrots, with a haughty watch kept by the granddaddy mural parrot of all. Drinks feature (naturally) a parrot special of rum, Grand Marnier, pineapple juice, and bananas; dishes are a Longstone lobster with chunks fried in a spicy sauce; chicken Kona (a Hawaiian recipe); imported steaks; or basic sandwiches and salads. *Moderate.*

★ REST HAVEN AND ★★ PINNEY'S BEACH HOTEL

These establishments are located on opposite ends of the three-and-a-half mile stretch of Pinney's Beach, one of Nevis's finest. After a morning swim, you might well want to lunch at either . . . your choice should be based on which one is closer to your staked-out spot of sand. Their menus are similar, emphasizing seafood (including grilled lobster), Creole and some Continental dishes. Following your afternoon swim, why not plan to stop off at the one where you didn't lunch for a late afternoon cocktail. Watch the sun slowly slip below the horizon. You might even see the famous Caribbean "green flash," that split second as the sun gives way to night and there's a shock of green at the edge of the horizon. *Inexpensive* to *moderate* at both.

THE (ROOKERY) NOOK

Tucked away in the heart of the capital, Charlestown, this is where Nevisians meet for lunch. One American who has a winter house here informs his island friends of his whereabouts by two signs: "Joe Bailey Gone Away to Come Back," or "Joe Bailey in Residence." Simple, like the local decor (or lack of it)

One of the few non-hotel restaurants on Nevis

but effective, like the food that's sufficient for your needs. A backyard stretches to the sea, and there are small tables and chairs for the lunching crowd. It's also an after-work drinking spot, until 6:00 PM., when everyone goes home. *Inexpensive.*

Nightlife

Your evenings will be mostly quiet and relaxing, and you'll probably find yourself settling in early with a good book or a quiet conversation. But during the week, some of the inns set aside one special evening as jump-up night. In Nevis this translates into a string band at Zetlands Plantation (on Wednesday); the Cliff Dwellers (Thursday); Croney's Old Manor Estate (Friday); and the Golden Rock (Saturday). The "do" at Zetlands is one of the best because its barman "King Meko," is a former Calypso King (a high honor in these islands of many-talented performers) and he turns to his true trade, magic and music, each Thursday night.

The string band, incidentally, is a cultural band featuring only Nevisian music. The lead instrument is the flute, made from locally-grown bamboo. The bass is a long, tubular instrument produced from trumpet-tree wood with a hollowed-out center. There are guitars, quatros, banjos, a small number of steel drums, and a scratch-can called gero. The performance is certainly worth catching at least once.

On weekends, if you feel like casual, barefoot dancing and a sip of the local rum, head out to Dick's Bar at Bricklyn Village, where a band imported from the sister isle of St. Kitts keeps everyone jumping. Decor is simple . . . the bar is open-air and freeflowing. It's a real chance to meet the people you've been reading about . . . the people who really live here. Or you might head out to the Conch Shell on the outskirts of Charlestown, where the "Mighty Sparrow" performs some evenings. Its leader is simply "the" Calypso King of the World, and as you sit around the open courtyard surrounding the raised stage, you'll come to understand why. There are several bars . . . no food (unless you count peanuts) . . . and while it's definitely local, it's uptown local.

"Uptown" as in Upper East Side, or upscale

Shopping

Shopping in Nevis is limited but interesting and sometimes results in the "find" that your neighbors back home definitely won't have. Nevisian-only specials are always worth checking out. They range from woven straw work (often done by the blind); painstakingly-embroidered cottons; bits of jewelry made with local materials (seeds, shells, fish fins, and the U.S. customs-forbidden turtleshell); a local hot sauce that's unique in taste but equally hot on each Caribbean island, to jars of jams and marmalades from locally-grown fruits. Although Nevis is far from a shopper's mecca, you'll find browsing a combination of discovering things to buy and stimulating conversation with knowledgeable shopkeepers. With the exception of the pottery sold in the village of Newcastle, all the shopping is confined to the capital of Charlestown.

Caribbee Clothes Ltd. is one of the best of the clothing shops for men, women and children, but prices are definitely expensive. The boutique carries a full range of cotton designs, all with bits of bouquets of embroidery. Designs are unique, displaying strong styles and colors. Its trademark is an embroidered yellow, smiling sunburst that may be familiar to habitués of some U.S. and Canadian boutiques. Women's long or short designs can run well over $100; embroidered short robes are $60; men's shirts are about $50; sheer, voile classic shirts for women are surprisingly low at $20. Each garment is an original, sewn by a single seamstress and embroidered with her initials. The tag accompanying the garment gives you both the seamstress' and the embroiderer's full name. The shop was opened about 12 years ago by an American, Bette Roby, with one sewing machine and a lot of design talent. Long ago, when Mrs. Roby moved the store to another building, her seamstresses failed to show up for work. It seemed that a rumor had spread in town that the building was inhabited by "jumbies" (the local term for evil spirits). Matters were eventually resolved by a bit of exorcism. Both the shop and the workroom are now run by Cathy and Rip Todd who carry on the Roby tradition and have expanded the stock. Although the designs are expensive, they are unique. If you happen to be there in mid-May, you might well find a sale in progress.

Betty Roby's latest enterprise is *Tradewinds Ltd.,* where there's a cottage-size industry in full force. Local ladies faithfully reproduce her designs on canvases for needlepoint or embroidery; the completion is up to you. These highly-stylized canvases depict island life, and scenes from ocean to dominating mountain offer striking contrasts; flowers and fauna; and fanciful interpretations of practically everything. You're bound to find something appealing here for yourself or a friend. But, unfortunately, canvases are all *exported,* and if you manage to edge your way into the bustling workroom and find something you can't live without, you'll have to look plaintive and hope for permission to buy.

A delicious buy comes when you stop by Caribbean Confections in the heart of Charlestown, for a scoop of cherry, banana, coconut, guava, or other island fruit ice creams, and a talk with the manager, Mrs. Helen Hood, who came out of retirement to manage this caloric establishment.

At Zetlands Plantation, their in-house boutique has some of the liveliest styles on the island, and is presided over by "one of the Lupinacci clan," daughter Jenny. Indian cotton dresses (long and short), sexy swim-wear, handpainted T-shirts of pastels by John Woodland (now of Antigua), and the Zetlands' own light wool sweaters with their crest for the cool night air are just a few of the many finds.

A very special look at life in Nevis comes with a stroll through the *Nevis Handicraft Cooperative Society,* where any purchase ensures that about three-fourths of the money is given to the artist and the remaining one-fourth is reinvested in the cooperative. Presided over by knowledgeable Nevisian women, the shop constitutes a fund of local lore, legend and merchandise. Although the inventory changes according to availability of raw materials and the whims of the artists, there are usually straw baskets crafted by the Nevis Workshop for the Blind and coconut shell birds carved by a deaf and mute young man, Kennedy Tyrell. There are also Caribbean-standard shirts for men and skirts for women of flour-bag materials, each stenciled flour-bag sack once actually held flour! One of the most special buys is the variety of preserves made from local fruits . . . Mamma Apple jam; guava jelly; Sour-gage brown-sugar, health marmalade . . . the superhot, local hot sauce made of red, green, yellow or purple peppers (the yellow is the hottest). Here you can also pick up inside booklets (not available outside Nevis and St. Kitts)—*A Motoring Guide to Nevis* (being updated); *Some Nevis Families; A Recipe Book of Local Foods*—all for under $4 U.S. and all invaluable buys.

At the *Nevis Philatelic Office* you can send home postcards or letters displaying some of the Caribbean—standard but very special—postage stamps, or better yet, buy a collection or one of the first-day issues when the cruise ship *Queen Elizabeth II* came to call and the windjammer "Barefoot" Cruise *Polynesia II* dropped anchor for the first of twice-monthly visits.

Although *Caribelle Batik* is headquartered in St. Kitts, it also has a gallery in Nevis, and here you'll find some special designs made into halters, dresses, draped skirts for women; shirts and foulards for men. Many designs are made from the supersoft Sea-Island cotton, but that's becoming harder and harder to secure, so some fabrics are a mixture. Even though they're not the best of all possible worldwide batiks (Jamaica and Kuala Lumpur in Malaysia offer batiks overshaded with hand paintings that are true works of art, which should never be cut or made into clothing . . . hung on walls, yes, but not worn), the batiks fashioned in Caribelle's workroom are quite good.

One of the most special of all possible shopping days in Nevis comes when you drive to the village of Newcastle and stop at the *Newcastle Pottery Outlet.* Here American-born Jackie Chenoweth (originally from Maryland) joined forces, when she arrived in Nevis, with Mrs. Helena Jones, a famous local potter. Mrs. Jones specializes in small, primitive pottery heads of Nevisians. On the route out of town toward Newcastle village, you'll pass Craftshouse. But don't! Stop instead, for a look at the coconut "everything": string bags, a coconut husk plant hanger that's a true size mourning dove, hair ornaments made from polished coconut shells, placemats from the plant fiber, and hanging mobiles of coconut molded fish. You can also watch the ladies who make these items in the adjoining room. The outlet in Newcastle features the work of all Nevisian potters. Jackie Chenoweth, Helena Jones and her niece, Almena Cornelius, all train young hopeful artisans, and it's still strictly a cottage industry. Some of the designs date to 800 A.D., the time of the Arawak Indians, and the first rudimentary pottery. It's very much a Nevis specialty. Prices range from $3 U.S. to $85 U.S., and each piece is inscribed with the initials of the potter.

There's a potpourri of items at the *Yellow Shutters,* another boutique tucked away in the capital, Charlestown, where almost all shopping is centered along the main street. Here you'll find unexpected items such as long wool capes made in Nevis for $60; French berets for $9; T-shirts that proclaim "Nevis" in varying designs at $5; mahogany bowls and bird carvings made and signed by Kennedy Tyrell. Personal cards and signatures on work seem to be a Nevisian tradition, and when you buy a carved calabash (later to be used as a planter) for $6, the card that accompanies it says, "Michael Brookes is the young Nevis artist who hand carved these calabashes. The calabash tree was brought from Africa during the slavery years and the gourds were used as eating vessels." You take home not only a Nevis treasure but a bit of its history with it.

Sports

There are no organized sports activities on Nevis. But the island's *beaches* are excellent. You'll find Pinney's Beach spectacular but may also discover your own private cove. Several inns have their own freshwater swimming pools. Hotels stock limited gear for scuba diving and snorkeling. We advise bringing your own along so that you won't have to wait for equipment that may well be in use.

Nisbet Plantation Beach is also great

You can opt for day or week membership at the new *Oualie Beach Club* on Mosquito Bay. By paying the nominal amount of $1 U.S. a day or $2 U.S. a week, you can have the fun and the run of this small beachside club. Alastair Yearwood is the young, active manager. The operation is owned by him and his Nevisian family. It offers *Sunfish sailing; Hobie Cat racing; windsurfing,* and a Zodiac *for snorkeling* (with equipment available). Snacks and drinks are sold and then munched at long, wooden picnic tables or small, round tables for two. On Fridays they have a string band that plays until everyone goes home (often in the wee, small hours). The name "Oualie" (which you'll spot throughout Nevis) is the original name that the Carib Indians gave the island.

Deep-sea fishing can be arranged via the Golden Rock Hotel, which has its own boats. Arrangement can also be made directly with local Charlestown skippers. With luck, you'll run into snapper, kingfish, grouper and bonita. Take along your own gear, or take a chance on what's available.

Six of the plantation inns offer *tennis* (although it's usually a one- or two-court limit): Croney's Old Manor; Nisbet Plantation; the Golden Rock; Montpelier; Zetland Plantation; Cliff Dwellers.

Surprisingly, *horseback riding* is available in Nevis. It's a sport that's extremely limited on most Caribbean islands. Nisbet Plantation rents horses right on the estate, and arrangements can also be made to ride at Garner's Estate or at the Big H Riding Stables at Cane Gardens. Your inn manager will discuss your needs and degree of expertise with you and will then contact the stable that seems appropriate. Almost all riders follow trails that go partly up towering Mt. Nevis through the foothills or trot along coastal paths. Both good English and Western tack are available, and all establishments strongly suggest that an experienced guide accompany riding parties.

Another Nevis adventure is *hiking* or *climbing* part way up or all the way to the crest of 3,500-foot Mt. Nevis. It's not for everyone, but it's possible to reach the top. Wear the sturdiest of your most comfortable shoes, and have your inn manager pack something cold and a snack for the journey. Be sure to watch for the shy, wild monkey population along the way. It's now estimated that Nevis has 9,000 people and over 15,000 monkeys! Fascinating speculation has led some people to conclude that a "monkey tunnel" runs under the sea between Nevis and St. Kitts, but so far, no one has been able to prove the suspicion. Guides can be hired for the trek up Mt. Nevis for about $18 per day, and they're well worth it, both for their expert guidance and knowledge of local lore.

Relaxing poolside, beachside or in the hills is what Nevis is all about. Take a selection of paperbooks, needlepoint, or the materials necessary for your personal passion.

Depending on the time of year, there are occasional *soccer matches,* and Nevisians hope to resume *horseracing* soon. (It did exist but suffered an eclipse.)

THE HARD FACTS
Planning Ahead
Climate

The *temperature range is more extreme* than in some Caribbean islands thanks to the towering range of Mt. Scenery. Days are usually warm (range: 78°F. to 82°F.), and the trade winds make the climate very pleasant; evenings are cooler—the temperature can dip to the mid-60s in Windwardside, where two of the best guests houses are located. The average rainfall is 42 inches.

Holidays and Special Events

Scout Thirkield's birthday (Dec. 15). This is also Kingdom Day, and that might well be the real "official holiday." Try to convince Scout! Because this is a Dutch island, the Queen's birthday is a major event (April 30); Good Friday; Easter; Easter Monday; Labor Day (May 1); Ascension Day; Whit-monday; Christmas; Boxing Day (Dec. 26). The first weekend in December, there are a few days of sports events, called *Saba Days* that feature contests of all kinds; donkey races; local bands, booths selling island snacks and general merriment. Carnival is held in July with costume dancing in the streets and visiting bands from neighboring Anguilla and St. Maarten.

Sources of Information

Questions that need answers before you leave on your Saba holiday? In the United States, contact the St. Maarten–Saba–St. Eustatius Tourist Information Office at 25 West 39th St. New York, NY, 10018. In Canada, contact the office at 243 Ellerslie Avenue, Willowdale, Toronto, M2N 1Y5. Once in Saba, meet Glenn Holm, the director of the Saba Tourist Board. He loves to meet visitors to "his" island.

Packing

When you're packing for Saba, you should emphasize informality. Jackets, ties and long dresses, are useless (unless you'll be spending a few days on St. Martin or another larger island). You should take everything you need, however, because shopping is limited. You'll also want some sturdy shoes for climbing and a hat with some sort of a brim for protecting your head from the sun. Since evenings can get cool, a shawl or a wrap of some sort will come in handy. What you can plan on buying is a collection of Saba T-shirts that we can almost guarantee the neighbors back home don't have! Remember to pack *film* and *prescriptions*. They're not always available. The same goes for *toiletry items* and *cosmetics*.

Documentation

Non-U.S. or non-Canadian visitors need a passport

Saba, like most islands of the Caribbean, requires only a passport, a birth certificate or a voter's registration card plus a return or onward-bound airline or cruise ship ticket.

Getting There

Considering its tiny size, *airline service to Saba is good.* Windward Island Airways makes three daily trips on STOL (Short-Take-Off-and-Landing) aircraft from St. Martin. Round-trip airfare is $40.

There were no cruise ship calls last year (so who knows if one will call in 1984), and the only regularly scheduled daylong stop is aboard a Windjammer "Barefoot" Cruises sailing ship.

Learning to Cope

Money. The Netherlands Antilles florin is the *official currency,* but U.S. dollars are accepted everywhere. *Credit cards,* even those rated the best, are not.

Communications. The *telephone system* is surprisingly good, and you can usually telephone from the reception area of your guest house. Or, for privacy, go to the Cable and Wireless Building in Windwardside.

Medical Assistance. There is a *small hospital* in Saba, but patients considered emergency cases are flown to St. Martin, a 15-minute flight away.

Getting into Town. A *taxi from the airport to your guest house* will be about $6. A tour of the island (about two hours) is $25 a carful . . . and we've packed as many as nine into a sagging station wagon!

Electricity. The *electrical current* in Saba is the same as that in the United States—110 volts; 60 cycles—bring whatever appliances you want.

SABA TODAY

The Road is only 34 years old

Saba is a five-mile, round island off St. Maarten that flies the flag of the Netherlands Antilles. Time either stopped here or never started. It's an island shrouded in mist and mystery: 3,000-foot Mt. Scenery dominates lesser peaks; four make-believe villages—Hell's Gate, Windwardside, St. John's, the Bottom—are scattered throughout the hills. The Road (the only one), which experts from Holland said couldn't be built, corkscrews its way for six and one-half miles connecting the villages. It was built over a 20-year period by Sabans, led by Josephus Lambert Hassel. He took a correspondence course in engineering after the road was finished!

Perhaps the captain of a British West Indian Airways jet, Captain Eric Mowser, said it best as he dipped his wings over Saba, en route to St. Kitts . . . "In 1945, Saba got their first transport, a jeep. In 1946, they got their second transport, another jeep. Then in 1947, they joined the rest of civilization and had their first collision!"

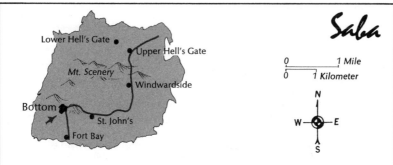

Saba

Lower Hell's Gate
Upper Hell's Gate
Mt. Scenery
Windwardside
Bottom
St. John's
Fort Bay

0 — 1 Mile
0 — 1 Kilometer

N
W — E
S

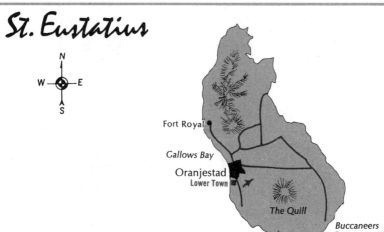

St. Eustatius

N
W — E
S

Fort Royal
Gallows Bay
Oranjestad
Lower Town
The Quill
Buccaneers Bay

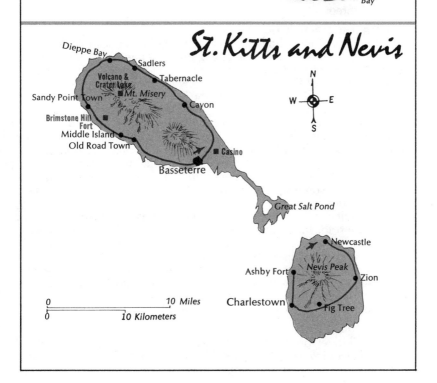

St. Kitts and Nevis

Dieppe Bay
Sadlers
Volcano & Crater Lake
Tabernacle
Sandy Point Town
■ *Mt. Misery*
Cayon
Brimstone Hill Fort
Middle Island
Old Road Town
■ Casino
Basseterre

N
W — E
S

Great Salt Pond

Newcastle
Ashby Fort
Nevis Peak
Zion
Charlestown
Fig Tree

0 — 10 Miles
0 — 10 Kilometers

Orchids, poinsettas and moonflowers grow everywhere sometimes aided by the human hand, sometimes not. Fruit trees are heavy with coconut, guava, avocado, soursop, orange, breadfruit, sugar apple, lemon and mango that hang from roadside branches.

Saba's people project an unreal quality appropriate to their island. They not only like each other (all 958 of them), they like the occasional "strangers" who drop from the sky on STOL aircraft from St. Maarten, 28 miles away. Everyone speaks to and smiles at everyone, and you never have to ask for a ride; each driver of the island's 900 cars offers everyone else rides . . . even "strangers."

It's possible to meet the entire island on Saturday night, when everyone, from the youngest to the oldest Saban, makes his or her way to the Lido Club, turning it into Brigadoon. An accordion, a guitar, drums . . . hammer the night and punctuate the eerie silence outside, where the mist from Mt. Scenery envelops the entire island and ghostly figures appear, headed for the community of the Lido.

Inside Information

Hotels

There are four "hotels"—translation: guest houses—in Saba, but we recommend three:

★★★ THE CAPTAIN'S QUARTERS

Ten rooms in the village of Windwardside are chockablock with antiques, including four-posters. Officially opened for guests in 1966 by H.R.H. Princess Beatrix of the Netherlands on her honeymoon visit, the main building was built about 1900. It was originally the home of the daughter of a Saban sea captain but now does duty as the hotel's office, library, sitting room, and parlor for late afternoon tea.

Adjacent to this Victorian building is the sea captain's home, built in 1832. It is now used to provide accommodations for guests. The remaining rooms are in a third building that was added onto the hotel. All the guest rooms feature antiques, white wicker, and hot Caribbean colors in spreads, drapes and pillows. The big news though is that ten more rooms are being added, and some will open by 1984. There's also a spiffy boutique under construction.

What was the village dispensary-clinic has become the hotel bar. There's a pavilion for lunch and snacks, and you just slide the ten paces into the swimming pool. . . . Or order a drink as you float in one of the inflatable chairs in the water. It will be handed to you in the middle of the pool. As you gently sway, the Caribbean Sea splashes on giant rocks some 1,500 feet below . . . the scent of hibiscus, poinsetta, orchids, roses and bougainvillea is in the air . . . hammocks for two hang in the trees . . . and you're in Saba. *Cost:* $55 per double EP; $45 per single EP; MAP is $22 per person.

★★ SCOUT'S PLACE

Scout Thirkiel, once of Ohio, came to Saba to manage the Captain's Quarters, but after doing that, he opened his own place in Windwardside. And his former guests and most of Saba followed. Now it's Scout's Place housing four

The decor is Early Eclectic

and one-half rooms which Scout visits daily letting Mrs. Diana Madero do the managing, while he plays "guest." One smaller than small room is the Fox Hole, and tucks "sideways" one of either gender inside the miniroom. This place is known as Bed'n'Board, Cheap'n'Cheerful. The rooms are medium sized, but you'll spend all your time on the bar-terrace anyhow, talking, listening, and being glad you're there. *Cost:* Approx. $50 per double MAP; $42 per single.

★ CRANSTON'S ANTIQUE INN
This was once a government guest house, and none other than Queen Juliana occupied Room #1 during an official visit to Saba. Now it's privately owned. The six rooms all have mahogany four-posters, colonial sideboards and rocking chairs. (Only three have private bathrooms, however.) Saba Artisans Foundation's colorful fabric was used to make the bedspreads and curtains. Possible handicap: It's in the Bottom and if you want to socialize at Scout's, you'll have to hitchhike—not difficult. *Cost:* $50 per double MAP; $42 per single.

Restaurants

Believe it or not, they exist . . . sort of. You can always call ahead for a proper table at *Scout's Place* or at *The Captain's Quarters,* but one of those guest houses is apt to be home, where you'll take many of your meals.

Your only other choice is the Blue Wave, across the street from Cranston's Antique Inn. The decor is early motel, but food is lip-smacking local, and your chef is none other than Chuck Maxwell who cooked for Queen Beatrix when he was at the Captain's Quarters in 1981. Now he turns out local dishes here—goat water (a hearty and delicious stew); callaloo soup; stuffed christophene; blaff (a local fish, poached, then marinated in lime and herbs); curried goat or lamb; possibly steak Creole style (a tomato base with lots of spices).

There's also a Chinese Restaurant (named just that) with one of the most ambitious menus south of Chinatown . . . any Chinatown. Some 18 dishes cover the gamut from Moo Goo Gai Pan; pineapple with chicken; abalone with oyster sauce; to local fish of all kinds in all kinds of sauces.

Costs everywhere in Saba are *inexpensive* to *moderate. The Lido* in Windwardside will always make you a simple sandwich or a salad and will be more than happy to let you sample *Saba Spice,* a lethal brew of 150-proof rum, with brown sugar, cinnamon, cloves, nutmeg and fennel seed, that's home-brewed in Saba. It tastes rather like a sweet liqueur. One taste is usually enough. (It makes a great item to take home with you.)

But the most open invitation of all, will be the one you receive from individual Sabans you've met along the way. A dinner at home in Saba is the nicest "evening out" of all.

Nightlife

Nightlife . . . in Saba? Well, there is the *Saturday dance at the Lido,* and that's where everyone will be. Late evenings, and the Blue Wave turns into a lively, loud, local disco.

Other than that, it's patio conversations at *Scout's Place* or *The Captain's Quarters.* Sounds dull? Then you've never heard the conversations. Saba is an individual island that draws individualists. They're well worth talking to.

Shopping

The true *treasures of Saba* are the *ladies* who make the drawn threadwork that so closely resembles lace. They will invite you into their parlors to see the work of which they are so justifiably proud. And if you're staying a few days, they will custom-make a shirt, linen and lace purse, almost anything in your choice of color and thread pattern.

Most of the shops are in Windwardside, and hours are loosely: 8:00 A.M. to noon; 2:00 to 6:00 P.M. The *drawn thread work* is also carried at *the Saba Shop, the Yellow House,* and *the Handcrafts Shop.*

That bottle of Saba Spice can be bought at *the Green Shutters,* an annex of the Lido, at about $6.

There's a small boutique adjacent to The Captain's Quarters offering local handicrafts and casual clothes at reasonable prices. T-shirts have recently arrived in Saba, and some great ones can be found at a tiny shop, the *Treasure Chest.* (They also have clothes imported from the United States, but that's probably not what you came to Saba to buy!)

In the 1970s the United Nations sent craftsmen to Saba to teach artisans more modern crafts that could be set up as cottage industries. The result is the *Saba Artisans Foundation* in the Bottom and in a one-room showcase next to The Captain's Quarters featuring batiks and silk-screened fabrics made into dresses. Fabric for shirts, scarves, and T-shirts is sold by the yard. There are also hand-embroidered shirts made from denim that are excellent and useful (big pockets).

Sports

Sports in Saba are limited. The Captain's Quarters has one of two *swimming pools* on the island (the other is a community swimming pool just opened in Windwardside). They also offer the island's *badminton table.* There's one *tennis court* at Cranston's Antique Inn at the Bottom, and another in the "discussion" stage. But in Saba, that could take awhile! *Climbs to the top of Mt. Scenery* are popular with guests staying more than a few days. Robert Hassell of Saba and Edward Arnold of Rhode Island have recently combined forces to form *Saba Deep.* They specialize in *scuba diving* (providing all the equipment) and a resort course if needed. The most popular "sport" remains cocktail conversation at *Scout's.*

There are no beaches in Saba

St. Barts

THE HARD FACTS
Planning Ahead
Costs

From mid-December to mid-April 1984, most of the best hotels in St. Barts were charging over $100 a day, some well over; but a few were slightly below that figure. That's for a double room, and it might or might not include breakfast. In other months, hotel rates decrease about one-third. Over the entire expanse of the Caribbean, this could be considered moderate to expensive. But you do have your choice of about 200 hotel rooms (most in small villa-like hotels; two in slightly larger ones); and the possibility of renting a private villa with a maid and a cook.

All restaurants in St. Barts take their cuisine seriously, including the special beachside bistros and the more formal haute-cuisine restaurants for evening dining. Prices in all (without wine) seem to range from $12–$40 per person.

Surprisingly, taxis (in this world of high gasoline prices) aren't that high. It will cost you about $4–$6 to go almost any place you want, mainly because destinations are very close on this island of eight square miles.

Holidays and Special Events

Legal holidays are Christmas and New Year's Day; Mardi Gras and Ash Wednesday; Mi-Careme (mid-Lent); Easter Monday; Ascension Day; Pentecost Monday; Bastille Day (July 14); All Saints' Day (November 1); Armistice Day (November 11).

One of the nicest annual happenings is the Festival of St. Barthélemy celebrated for three days the last week in August. It honors the patron saint of the island. Small booths selling food and wine line the streets of the capital, Gustavia, and people dance in the streets. It goes on nonstop from day to night. It's your only chance to photograph the five gendarmes on the island. It's the one time of year when they get together. There's practically no crime here!

There's usually, but not always a St. Barts Sailing Regatta, held in late February and early March, featuring team races, single-handed races, and a flotilla of schooners. Over 100 yachts participate.

Pronounced san bartel mee, accenting mee

Sources of Information

In New York, contact the French West Indies Tourist Board at: 610 Fifth Avenue New York, NY 10020; or call them at: (212) 757–1125. On the West Coast, contact the French Government Tourist Office at: 9401 Wilshire Blvd., Beverly Hills CA. In Canada, contact: The French Government Tourist Office, 1840 Ouest rue Sherbrooke, Montreal, Quebec, Canada. H3 H1 E4; in Toronto, 342 Bay Street, 610, Toronto, Ontario, Canada. In St. Barts stop by the Office du Tourisme Saint Barthelemy in Gustavia.

Packing

Depending on your desire to spend francs—or not to spend them—St. Barts has limited but excellent clothes from France. Officially a "duty-free" port, it also has French perfumes, crystal, watches, jewelry, liquor, tobacco and linens. Also featured are the specialties of St. Barts: the hand-screened designs of a master craftsman, Jean-Yves Froment, are exported to the other islands and to the United States. There's also woven reed work that's unique in St. Barts. Prices are not inexpensive so you may want to pack all you'll need. Otherwise plan to stock up on some very exclusive warm weather wear during your stay.

Documentation

Both U.S. and Canadian citizens need a valid passport. This alone is good for three weeks; longer stays require a visa.

Getting There
Airline Service

You have to make a connecting flight (although a short one) to get to St. Barts. You can fly via St. Martin, St. Thomas or Guadeloupe, but the shortest connection is from St. Martin—a ten minute hop by Windward Islands Airways, a 19-seat STOL aircraft. However, do appreciate the landing at St. Barts. It's on a short take-off-and-landing strip that starts in the hills and ends in the sea! (But they haven't lost a passenger or a pilot yet.) Also Air Safari's twin-engine five passenger Piper Aztecs, based in St. Barts will meet clients at any airport in the Caribbean and fly them, with baggage, to St. Barts or other West Indies destinations.

Cruise Ships

Occasionally a few drop anchor here, but crewed yachts (both chartered and private) make this a very special port of call. Bareboaters from St. Martin also drop in from time to time. You can meet and mix if you're in the mood.

Formalities on Arrival
Customs

The customs officer is offical and courteous. You just present your documents, and you're on your way. There is no tax on entering or departure. Although personal firearms are not permitted, yachts may and do carry them for valid reasons. If you're arriving in your own yacht, it's fine. Otherwise, leave it to the captain or the crew.

Getting Into Town

You have your choice of taxi, car rental, motorbike, or your own feet. Taxis are inexpensive and drivers know their way around. Car rental is usually a VW beetle or an open minimoke, which seems best on St. Bart's hilly terrain.

A valid driver's license is required. Cars can be picked up either at the airport or in town (Gustavia). Motorbikes are also available (best arranged by your hotel), but walking is the least expensive of all!

Settling Down
Choosing a Hotel

There's a total of 200 hotel rooms in St. Barts. Should this sound overwhelming for an island of this size, you should be told that most are in small and special auberges containing fewer than 20 rooms. Two others are somewhat larger with 36 and 50 rooms respectively. Most are scattered beachside or are within a few minutes' walk of the beach.

Small and special? Head for the Eden Rock. Larger with a selection of water-sports facilities? The St. Barth Beach Hotel. Interested in doing some of your own cooking? Then consider the Village St. Jean. In a mood for a little more tropical elegance (and don't mind the lack of a beach)? The answer might be Les Castelets. Or if you want one of the newest and nicest on the island, book into the Hibiscus in Gustavia or the Filao on the St. Jean Beach.

There's also the chance to rent a villa or a beach house (see hotel section). All come with full maid or cook services.

Think about what you want from a hotel. Read hotel brochures carefully. Discuss accommodations with your travel agent (and make sure he or she has been there recently). And your selection should turn out to be perfection.

Money

Officially the tender is the French franc, which, like all currencies these days, fluctuates. It has been over 7 francs to the U.S. dollar. At one time, it was necessary to race to a local bank to change money. But these days, dollars are accepted almost everywhere. Some prices are even quoted in both currencies. However, you may get slightly more for your dollar if you change it into francs. The slight difference may not be worth the bother.

Rate of exchange at presstime was 8 francs to the U.S. dollar

Choosing a Restaurant

We beg off: they're all good. You have a choice of over 20 restaurants ranging from beach bistro to French formal. Cuisine consists of local Creole or the haute cuisine of Dijon, Lyon and other cities in France that evolved into Paris dining and then enriched the world.

Tipping

This is based on the European system of automatically adding a 10% service charge to your bill. This does not mean, however, that if a waiter has been especially kind or courteous, a small additional tip would be out of order. In fact, it would be very much appreciated.

Learning to Cope

Business Hours.   In offices, banks and boutiques in the capital, Gustavia, they're from 8:00 A.M. to noon (when everyone takes a lunch break) and then from 2:00 to 4:00 P.M. weekdays. Only boutiques are open a half day (mornings) on Saturday.

Electricity.   Voltage is European, 220 AC, 50 cycles. This means that American appliances require special plugs, converters and transformers. Some "travel" items these days are made for both stateside use and the European systems. If you bring such items, you'll need only a small plug with three prongs. Your hotel may or may not have all these devices. If you're going to need them, bring the additives with you. Our suggestion is to let your hair blow free in the wind and take an old-fashioned razor.

Water.   Safe (as it is throughout the Caribbean) unless you have medical problems of a delicate sort, a highly overrated subject these days.

Communications.   To telephone directly from the United States, dial 011–596 plus the St. Barts number for station-to-station calls. For a person-to-person call, dial 01–596 from the States. Telephoning within St. Barts is good, although you may have to place calls from your hotel desk since not many rooms have private telephones. Letters and postcards can take a couple weeks to be delivered to the States.

Medical Assistance.   In the capital, Gustavia, there is one clinic. There are also several doctors and one dentist on the island. For anything really serious, you would probably be flown to neighboring St. Martin or Guadeloupe.

ST. BARTS TODAY

We don't like writing about St. Barts (officially St. Barthélemy) for a very simple reason. It was our secret until a short while ago, our hiding place, where we went when we were bone weary and in need of escape. But since the word is out, we might as well tell you: St. Barts is perfection. It's not big (8 square miles to be exact), and it's not easy to get to (you connect on a small airline via St. Martin for a ten-minute flight). Arrival at the airport is dramatic and sometimes traumatic . . . the STOL aircraft . . . slides in through tree crusted hills and then stalls as it drops onto a field where crosscurrents may be blowing. It's not for the fainthearted.

   A few years ago, it was said in St. Barts that what Mr. Rothschild didn't own, Mr. Rockefeller did. That's changed. They maintain their property holdings, and family members or friends drop in from time to time. But now other visitors come to St. Barts (mainly French since this is a French island), and some quick-on-the-draw Americans and Canadians have snapped up a little property. But it's not easy to do any longer. In fact, it's almost impossible.

   What makes St. Barts so special?

   A combination of many things. Small, secluded, perfect curves of beach; a few beach bistros scattered where you lunch (or dine) on langouste, boudin creole (blood sausage), grilled fish from the sea with a squeeze of lime off the trees; of course, a wine that has perfectly traveled from mainland France; children who run along the beach and into the waves naked and natural . . . women who beach or lunch topless since here it's natural and normal. For evening dining there are more formal restaurants—the sophistication of Les Castelets or perhaps ducking into Le Pelican. After dinner drinks can be enjoyed pool-side at the Hibiscus with the lights of Gustavia competing with starlight. Shopping for some of the best of imports from the French mainland (not inexpensive, just excellent) . . . sexy, Caribbean-suited cottons and a visit to a very special local designer, Jean-Yves Froment, the creator of the finest batiks anywhere. Jean-Yves designs have been selected and imported by New York City's Saks Fifth Avenue, Henri Bendel's, and other fine department stores. Then there's the chance to rent your own villa for however long you're able to stay (and you won't want to leave) and set up private housekeeping; then shop in La Rotisserie in Gustavia for casseroles . . . langouste creole; thon en chartreuse . . . almost anything you care to order. This is the way Craig Claiborne (*The New York's Times's* cuisine expert) does it along with preparing his own dishes from the freshest foods imaginable. Does this sound like a rave notice? It is. As long as you realize that not everyone speaks English. If you can manage a bit of French, this is the Caribbean's secret (well, once it was) hideaway for Caribbean buffs. Welcome aboard!

The island belonged to Sweden from 1784 to 1877

A St. Barts day is languid and leisurely . . . a stroll down the streets of Gustavia (named for a king of Sweden) . . . a chat with the shopkeepers, possibly purchasing something from them, possibly not . . . then a short nap, and on to an evening of delicate cuisine, perhaps followed by a stop at the harbor to see the offshore yachts with their lights twinkling invitations for you to call next time. (There's always a next time in St. Barts.) Or if you've met some local citizens, you've had the special experience of being in their homes or in their favorite restaurant.

TOURING

St. Barts has been called the smuggler's isle, and insiders know it's true. But the smuggling is hardly serious. A little booze, perfume and cigarettes are removed in the night by boat to other islands since St. Barts' prices are among the lowest in the Caribbean. True pirates did hide out here in the 18th century, but there are no tributes to their memory.

You might, however, find one or two discreet indications of their existence in the tiny museum set up in a centuries-old stone house across the harbor from the main port of Gustavia along with a few remnants from the period when Sweden exercised sovereignty over the island (from 1784 to 1877).

When you meander back into Gustavia, you'll notice that the tiny town is a mixture of Swedish colonial architecture (at City Hall where there are original records in Swedish of laws and town plans) and in the Clock Tower's design. The French influence from the past to the present is best seen in the boutiques, bistros and businesses. It's rumored that there's treasure buried in or near Gustavia that can be traced to the late 1700s, the days of French and occasional Dutch pirates, but so far, no one's found a trace. Unless you feel like trying your hand at excavating, lunching or shopping, that's about it in the capital of Gustavia.

In case you sailed rather than flew in, a look at the airport is a must. Named the Aérodrome la Tourmente, the airport reflects the great sense of irony that the namer must have had. Only 19-seat STOL planes can fly in from neighboring islands since this almost nonexistent airport starts in the hills and ends in the sea. A few aircraft that didn't quite make it decorate the airfield, perhaps as a reminder. (But these were all Air Safari private pilots, not Windward Air or Air Guadeloupe pilots who fly professionally and haven't lost a passenger or one of their own yet.)

You'll now be heading along the north shore, past some of the best beaches in the Caribbean—one in particular, the Baie de St. Jean, where there's a clustering of beachside bistros—and you must stop off at least one day on your exploration of this island. This experience is worth a full day's stay and many more.

When you drive on to the area of Grand Fond, the gentle mood changes. Here the shore is pounded by the Atlantic surf, and it's not the place to stop for a swim. Minutes later you reach Vitet, displaying a mixture of stones in the fields and untropical short grass mixed with dry branches on the hillsides. The houses of the farmers are topped with roofs of red or green, and their lands are divided by stone fences against mountains that form a backdrop. You could easily be in Normandy, with cacti, blossoming in yellow, white and red, blending in with the mood of the unusual landscape.

It's possible to continue on to the village of Corossol, where the men dress in long-sleeved white shirts tucked into dark pants and the women wear long-sleeved dresses adapted from their French ancestor's provincial mode along with the unique shoulder-length crisp sunbonnets (called quichenottes). The only reason that we suggest you make this another day's excursion is that you'll become fascinated with the people—the ladies' straw work made at home and for sale—and you'll want to stay a while. Although it's tempting, most people would be very offended if you tried to photograph them. The same situation applies in the nearby village of Colombier. Just store away in your mind the experience of a special time at a special place. There are several "chez's" in both areas (the word originally meant dining in someone's home), but these are more suitable for an apéritif than a complete lunch.

A smattering of minibuses (about ten) in St. Barts will put eight passengers together for a tour but it's really much more fun to do it on your own by rental car or minimoke. And the roads, although winding and hilly, aren't that hard to follow.

In St. Barts there's not that much to "tour." There's just a very small, special slice of the world to see.

The population of St. Barts is mostly European in background

Inside Information

Hotels

Almost all St. Barts' hotels are small and secluded, as is the island itself. Although there is one large hotel—for St. Barts—that has 50 rooms, most of the others have capacities of under 20 rooms. There's also a limited selection of private villas available for rent. But all residences have their year-after-year devotées, and it's not easy to get in anywhere in St. Barts. Make your reservation early, no matter what time of year you plan on visiting.

★★★★ EDEN ROCK

For us this is the place to be in St. Barts. Formerly owned by Mayor Remy de Haenen (who also flies the mail plane when he's not too busy and still comes to call), and now managed by Martine and Gilbert Molina, it's a small cluster of seven rooms against an ocean, with antiques in the main house from France. Each of the rooms has ceiling fans in lieu of air conditioners and the shower water is "island temperature." Mornings, and you race down to the beach that waits a few paces below your room. Evenings, and you may decide to have an apéritif in an unexpected, intimate bar, hung with soft-lighted ships' lanterns, that's connected to the hotel by a twisting path. Dinner is served in the formal French style but also in the casual style of the Caribbean under a star-splashed sky on an outside terrace. *Cost:* $65 + 10% tax per double CP (with breakfast), in season.

This was the mayor's home, in fact

★★★★ FILAO

The Filao, named for a local tree, is a new and very special hotel. Its location is one of St. Barts' best: right on St. Jean Beach. And its 15 white stucco villas—each with private terraces, each named for a château in France, offer both elegance and such extra niceties as huge bathrooms with built-in, recessed hair-dryers and wall safes for valuables. Guests are served breakfast on their terraces. For dinner many opt for the excellent Le Pelican (same ownership and just up the road). In between, water play can be enjoyed in the hotel's swimming pool—or in the sea. A word of advice. Plan to book a room here at least a year in advance. It's that popular. *Cost:* $160 per double EP.

★★★★ HIBISCUS
A hotel of nine individual bedrooms and one large duplex that the local citizens call the prettiest on the island! It's also one of the newest. Set on a hill overlooking Gustavia, all rooms have balconies, and there's a small swimming pool below. The rooms have been done in soft, soothing colors that contrast with the overhead wooden ceiling fans. Jean-Yves Froment, the local master fabric designer, designed the curtains. The linens are by Descamps of international repute. There's a special restaurant a few feet up the hill—du Vieux Clocher, named for a bell tower. It's popular with yachtsmen and you're quite likely to meet many of them here. *Cost:* Duplex: $160 (sleeps from two to six guests); rooms: $85, single or double, in season.

★★★★ LES CASTELETS
One of the most "in" places in St. Barts that is truly sophisticated if you desire formality. Its elegance is orchestrated by Mme. Genevieve Jounay, part of the management since its opening 10 years ago. There are 10 guest rooms in chalets, each decorated with antiques in areas separate from the expansive bedrooms, and all have patio decks. The castle is not beachside, but there is a small swimming pool and its hilltop site offers wonderful sunrise and sunset views. If you arrange for a minimoke, you're a short driving time away from one of the best beaches on an island filled with perfect beaches. *Cost:* $100 to $240 double CP (with breakfast), in season.

★★★★ VILLA RENTALS
If you want to rent a villa, American-born Brook Lacour and her French husband Roger (from Guadeloupe) can arrange it through their company, Sibarth Real Estate. They handle over 50 villas and bungalows, some booked all year. Almost all the villas are beachside, but a few are scattered among the foliage-decked hills. Cost varies and the only way to match your taste with what's available is to call the Lacours directly at 87–62–38, or if time permits, write them at: BP 30, St. Barthélemy, French West Indies.

★★ AUTOUR DU ROCHER
This hotel with eight rooms has had a checkered reputation, but it's now very much on the rise. Once it was par excellence, then it took a downturn. Now it's in the hands of new owners' singer Jimmy Buffet and some dozen partners. The setting is one of St. Barts' best: hilltop, with a wide range of beach at the base. Antique four-posters have been added to several of the rooms, which are strung out among the hillside cottages. Dinner (or lunch) is in the main house where both Continental and French cuisine is served. Tortoises meander their way through an inner courtyard, and dancing barefoot and casual to taped music takes place on a terrace set into a cliff. *Cost:* $74–$95 per double CP (with breakfast), in season.

★★ HOTEL TROPICAL
There are 20 twin-bedded rooms in this newly-opened auberge on a flower-filled hill above the St. Jean Bay. Owners Monsieur and Madame Paul Vial, originally from France, have created this special place with the help of François Pécard, a highly-respected architect. The rooms are decorated in muted cream and salmon, arranged in a U-shape around a cloistered garden. True to the best of French traditions, there are a music and a reading room: small but a very nice touch. *Cost:* $110 + 10% tax per double EP, in season.

★★ PLM JEAN-BART
The island's largest hotel with 50 rooms (although that's not really large). Suites come with kitchenettes if you're in the mood to do some of your own

cooking. There's a choice of swimming pool or a languid, lovely beach a five minute walk away. True to the PLM's high standards (this is just one of a French chain of hotels), there are sports activities on the nearby beach: snorkeling, scuba diving, windsurfing, small boat sailing, and occasional day sails to offshore islands. Sports activists might consider important the fact that this is one of two hotels in St. Barts that offers these activities. *Cost:* $108 per double (American breakfast), in season.

★★ SERENO BEACH HOTEL

20 rooms decorated with taste and distinction. You enter the A-frame bunga-lows through a flower-filled garden and later decide to swim at the beach that's literally at the front door or in the swimming pool, called the Garden Pool, with plants sprouting from an inner, free-form flower box. The rooms range around an inner court where the large swimming pool, beach bar and dining room share daylight or nightlight space. *Cost:* $113–$160 per double EP, in season.

★★ ST. BARTH BEACH HOTEL

This is the second largest hotel in St. Barts. All 36 rooms have balconies and ocean views. The decor, however, is more modern than the Caribbean touches that you'll find in the smaller hotels. And the location in Grand Cul de Sac is a bit removed from the capital, Gustavia (mostly visited for shopping), and some beach bistros. Families seem to enjoy this hotel best since it's a "self-contained center." There are water sports and Sunfish sailing, pedal boats, snorkeling, windsurfing, all available along a long section of beach. A nice plus is that owner Guy Turbé also owns the Baie des Flamands Hotel and will arrange dinner for you there whenever you desire a change in menu. *Cost:* $114, double CP (with breakfast), in season.

★★ VILLAGE ST. JEAN

Twenty rooms, all with kitchenettes, that have been a favorite of Craig Claiborne of *The New York Times.* Although you won't be directly on the beach, you'll only be a few minutes' walk away. There are beach bistros scattered along the shores for a leisurely lunch. Or you can take a swim or windsurf (one of the newer, hotter French passions) in waters that really are "crystal clear." When dinner time comes, you might stock up in the food commissary right on the property or drop into one of our favorites, La Rotisserie, where casseroles are already prepared . . . hot and ready to go. *Cost:* $64–$152 per double EP, in season.

a do-it-yourself kind of place

Restaurants

★★★★ CASTELETS

(Tel. 87–61–73). Unquestionably, this is one of the island's most chic, tucked-away hotels with a restaurant. And here the restaurant is most formal and elegant from the china to the silver to the crystal. The chef is Michel Viali, a native of Marseilles, and he turns out the most classic of French haute cuisine. It may be the only kitchen on the island to have its own pasta maker and fish smoker! The owner, Mme. Geneviève Jouany, presides over her dining room, which features French provincial antiques, discretely and pre-cisely. It's the place to come on the island for the most perfect service and, need we add, reservations for lunch or dinner are an absolute must. *Expen-sive.*

also, a good wine cellar

★★★★ L'ANANAS

(Tel. 87–63–77). Dining here is in an elegant colonial St. Bartian house, with ships' lights sparkling below in Gustavia. The owner Mme. France Cornu-Leducq created the entire ambience from rattan furniture, Italian beige fabrics and Korean light fans. It's possible to dine inside and outside on an open terrace,where pavé sauce roquefort or ouassous (a freshwater crayfish from Guadeloupe) highlights the menu. It's also an in spot for gathering before or after dinner. *Expensive.*

★★★ AU PORT
(Tel. 87–62–63). New owner Gerard Balageas greets guests in a second-story dining room overlooking the port in Gustavia. A few tables are also on the balcony, open to the sea and the sky. Here it's strictly dinner, not open for lunch. Specialties of the house are cassolette de langouste, foie gras maison, and filet d'agneau a la creme d'ail. Service is excellent—and friendly; the clientele is international (many live here or visit regularly). *Moderate.*

★★★ AUTOUR DU ROCHER
(Tel. 87–60–73). This hotel with dining room is high on a hill overlooking L'Orient Bay, where the only "night lights" are those from stars that resemble bits of shattered crystal. Owned by singer Jimmy Buffet (and partners), this place against the sky serves Continental and Creole cuisine . . . steaks, roast beef, langouste and salads mixed with island vegetables. The decor is rustic . . . the almost-English-style food is unusual for St. Barts . . . and on a few special nights, if he's there, Jimmy Buffet may play for himself and guests. *Moderate.*

★★★ BOULANGERIE ROTISSERIE—HEDIARD
(Tel. 87–63–13). We refuse to be drawn into the debate over which of St. Barts' two rotisseries is the best. They're both good. This one, located in Pont Milou (St. Jean shopping center), has a resplendent selection of mouth-watering, take-out fare displayed in a sleek-chic new shop. You be the judge! Both rotisseries are well worth a visit, if only to "window shop." *Moderate to expensive.*

★★★ LE PELICAN
(Tel. 87–64–64). Mostly because of the chef from Brittany, visitors and St. Bartians have been vying for reservations at this beach terrace or at the inside, formal dining room. Lunchtime is casual; at dinner the accent is definitely on formality; service is provided for about 40. They do prepare some "nouvelle cuisine" that is true to the original intent. There are also omelettes soufflées flamed in rum, a caramel île flottante along with other highly creative dishes. *Expensive.*

★★★ OLD YACHT CLUB—LA BRIGANTINE
La Brigantine, meaning either a ship (in English) or spanker sail (in French) is the former Dinzey home and St. Barts' oldest yacht club. But since a new yacht club opened before the old yacht club reopened, the old yacht club had to choose another name to avoid confusion. Confused? Anyway, under the direction of Dantès Magras and Maria Beronius the old yacht club/La Brigantine's 200 year old walls have been retucked and pointed and the bar, made from the planking of a wrecked sailing ship, has been restored. Soft indirect lighting has been added and there's foliage everywhere. The result is one of the most beautiful restaurants on the island—some say in the Caribbean. Dining is either inside or on an outdoor patio overlooking Gustavia Harbor. Menu choices range from langouste to boeuf . . . and we haven't been disappointed with any selection. *Expensive.*

★★★ ROTISSERIE-BERTRAND
For great take-out picnics or "chez moi" evenings, head to this Craig Claiborne favorite . . . it'll provide everything except your chez moi companion. The menu changes frequently, but crabs, lobster, barbecued chicken and salads are apt to be among the offerings. (Rotisserie offers only take outs; there's no in-house seating.) *Moderate* to *expensive.*

★★★ SERENO BEACH
(Tel. 87–64–80). Set within a relatively new hotel in St. Barts, this bistro serves classic French Creole dishes. *Expensive.*

★★ BRASSERIE ASSERIE
An honest, metropolitan French-style brasserie with no pretentions of being anything else. This is the place to come for a thick cup of French coffee and a hot buttery croissant. There's a scattering of small marble tables inside (beneath twirling wooden fans) and an outside patio ideally situated for people-watching. Or patrons can seat themselves on small wooden stools lined up at a solid wood bar with metallic silver finish. Attached to the brasserie is a small boutique. *Inexpensive.*

★★ EDEN ROCK
(Tel. 87–60–01). This is one of the island's first and oldest pensions with a restaurant on a veranda where you hear the sounds of the sea splashing below. It was begun by Remy de Haenen, a former mayor of St. Barts, but now he's handed it over to a young couple Martine and Gilbert Molina, from mainland France. The cooking is Provençal, with the accent on fish and shellfish from the seas that surround, all spiced and sauced by a superb French chef. Before or after dinner, there's a small bar separated from the main house by a few wobbly steps along a stone path that's rocky but worth the effort. Once in the dimly-lit bar, the decor is nautical, the drinks are fine, and the gossip (mostly in French) is some of the best on the island. *Expensive.*

★★ CHEZ FRANCINE
(Tel. 87–60–49). A total change in mood. This is a place to come for lunch and a swim on the perfect curve of beach at St. Jean Bay. While you wait for your langouste, shish kebab, boudin creole (blood sausage), all served with pommes frites and salad, to be prepared, you dash in and out of the sea. At lunch ladies may or may not be topless (as on the beach), and children run naked. It's totally French, totally busy, and totally part of that perfect St. Barts day: lunching and beaching combined. *Moderate.*

★★ FLAMBOYANT
Only slightly more expensive than the decidedly inexpensive Normandie. *Flamboyant* has some 8 to 10 tables clustered in the cozy living room of this once private house and on the airy front porch with a view. Its basically French fare, including wonderful lamb dishes and an always good "catch of the day," is often accompanied by hair-curling hot Creole sauce. (Beware!) Sometimes—depending on the chef's mood and the availability of fresh ingredients—such dishes as eggplant parmesan find their way onto the menu. Dinner runs around $16. *Inexpensive.*

★★ TAIWANA CLUB
(Tel. 87–63–82). This is St. Barts' only sports club. Owned by Mme. Valentine Montero, it offers one tennis court, a swimming pool, a shallow, separate pool for children, and that's about it. But it does have excellent soups, salads and meat en brochette. It's another lovely way to spend a St. Barts day. The setting is on the crescent-shaped Baie des Flamands, and you can combine the limited sports with a leisurely, consistently good lunch. *Moderate.*

★ CHEZ JACKI
Owned by Jacki Brin, and located right on the beach, this informal new St. Barts' bistro offers grilled French and Creole dishes, including brochettes, langouste, poulet grillé, poisson grillé. *Moderate.*

★ LA CREMAILLERE

(Tel. 87–63–89). Located in the heart of Gustavia, next to fabric designer Jean-Yves Froment's boutique, this is a small casual lunch or dinner spot with a simple, basic French menu. Dining is in a bougainvillea bedecked garden illuminated at night by the soft glow of candles. *Moderate.*

★ NORMANDIE HOTEL

(Tel. 87–61–66). Yes, it is possible to find a good, inexpensive dinner in St. Barts. Benjamin LaPlace's recently enlarged and redecorated Normandie Hotel offers very good French food for around $12 per person. *Inexpensive.*

Nightlife

Nightlife is limited to say the least, unless your idea matches ours of cocktails, conversation and a gourmet dinner to the sound of splashing waves at a choice of almost 40 restaurants.

For an after dinner cognac, you might head for Gustavia's chic L'Ananas, with a terraced patio that overlooks the boat-filled harbor or to Hibiscus' poolside terrace which overlooks Gustavia.

If you're in the mood for the really local scene, drop in to Le Select, a basic bar, where dominoes and backgammon go with the beer and wine. It's also a place where visiting yachtsmen gather and the place to meet Caribbean people. It helps if you speak some French.

No casinos, no real island jump-ups, mostly quiet nights under quiet stars.

Shopping

Shopping in St. Barts is limited, but good, if not always inexpensive when you buy an import from Paris. Once not so long ago, liquor prices here were even lower than in the Virgin Islands. Now we're not sure, but they are well under stateside prices, and if you feel up to carrying home the one duty-free bottle allowed per person, it's a value. (Liqueurs are always the best buy.)

Everything for sale in St. Barts is tax free

There's jewelry and crystal from Europe and hand-embroidered linens from China that are limited but definite good buys. And perfume from Paris. (You may not be able to find Yves St. Laurent perfumes, like *Opium*, however. When last we visited, perfume prices had been dropped below French standards, so in retaliation Paris stopped sending the goods!) This is also the home-studio of Jean-Yves Froment, whose hand-blocked fabrics are distributed in St. Barts and throughout the entire Caribbean, the United States and Europe. They're among the best; the only rivals we've seen are in Jamaica.

Almost all the boutiques are in Gustavia, although there's a new shopping area on St. Jean Bay. In Gustavia, the *boutique next to* La Trinquette (on the harbor), has some expensive but select buys in Paris-imported cotton day or night dresses; bikinis for the slim; and T-shirts for everyone (all hand-painted). Across the street, the *Boutique sur le Quai* has a collection of Parisian cosmetics and leathers that are exclusive and expensive. The leathers range from wallets to purses to very fine luggage, all designed and produced by internationally-known names. At *Bijouterie*, on the quay, just off the docks, is very Parisian jewelry, Rolex, Hermes, et al. There are two sides to *Alma's;* one offering crystal, watches, perfumes and liquors; the other neighboring shop carrying nautical supplies for yachts and, for visitors, lamps with anchors for a base, green-glass ball lights strung in hemp ropes that make dim but soft light for outside patios. Their marine shop is also the place to buy French scuba or snorkeling equipment, probably the best manufactured anywhere.

A la Calèche, recently redecorated and enlarged, displays Bette Robey's designs from her Caribee shop in Nevis, American Indian jewelry, a few watercolors depicting the ambience of St. Barts and a scattering of paperback books. The *Doll's House,* near the Eden Rock, has handicrafts made in St. Barts: watercolors, macrame, basketware, clothes, candles. Tina Wright, the young, international and interesting owner, creates many of the candles herself.

A very recent addition is the shopping area in the Baie de St. Jean, where there are *several boutiques* with off-the-rack designs from Parisian couturiers. They're the kinds of beachwear and sportswear designs that you can take home and live in for years to come. Possibly of interest if you're staying at a hotel with kitchenette facilities is the small *grocery store.* Of note too, is *La Cave,* near Marigot Bay, a wine shop with some 60,000 bottles of 80 varieties of French wines. The owners Mr. & Mrs. Julien Courtois, also cultivate a hydroponic garden near their shop, so sometimes offer fruits and vegetables straight from the garden. Probably not of interest is a *hairdresser.* In the Caribbean?

But the most special of all has to be the boutique of *Jean-Yves Froment* in Gustavia, where he has hand-screened both silks and cottons into pareos, dresses (long and short), T-shirts, and cut-at-will fabrics. Each bears his initials (JYF), and each is a very special work of art to wear and to remember him and his chosen home.

Sports

In St. Barts sports revolve around the water. There's no golf and tennis is limited, but the special coves of beaches make possible anything water oriented.

Yachts can be rented for half-day, full-day, or even longer sails. For *deep-sea fishing,* there are local fishermen who will make individual arrangements. *Snorkeling* and *scuba diving* are perfection, and if you didn't bring your own equipment, you can rent it or purchase it (the French manufacture some of the best scuba and snorkeling equipment). *Windsurfing* can be done almost anywhere since it's now a new international passion. *Sunfish* and *Sailfish* rentals and *pedal boat* rentals are more limited but can be arranged at the St. Jean Beach or at Grand Cul de Sac. *Waterskiing* can be arranged in Gustavia's harbor, but since it's usually filled with yachts, be very good or you'll receive a warning. *Tennis* can be played at the Taiwana Club and at the St. Barth Beach Hotel, but the courts are not for semipros. If you feel like batting a ball around, they're fine.

Several sports concerns on the island can arrange everything: There's the *St. Barth Water Sports Center* on St. Jean Bay, with an even larger headquarters in Gustavia; Filao has three catamarans and snorkling gear for rent; the *West Indies New District for Surfing* (WINDS) is based at the Eden Rock, but it also offers windsurfing equipment (their specialty) at the Sereno Beach Hotel, the Grand Cul de Sac and St. Barths Beach.

St. Eustatius

THE HARD FACTS
Planning Ahead
Costs

'Statia, one of the smaller and the least commercial of the Caribbean islands, has not yet geared up to accommodate high-volume tourism. Group tours and "tourists" have not invaded its shores. Visitors with discriminating taste come to 'Statia. But their numbers are small. There is no large, deluxe hotel or high-rise complex. There are, however, two small, distinctive inns on 'Statia that we recommend highly. Considering prices at other islands throughout the Caribbean, a stay in 'Statia is considered monetarily moderate. Rates average $160 a day, double occupancy MAP, in the winter season. Tariffs depend on the room's location and usually include complimentary wine with dinner. A 10% service charge is added to the cost of your accommodations.

Holidays and Special Events

New Year's Day; Good Friday; Easter; Easter Monday; Labor Day (May 1); Ascension Day; Whitmonday; Christmas Day and Boxing Day (December 26). The island's really big holiday is Statia-America Day (Nov. 16), the really big holiday that commemorates 'Statia's salute to the new U.S. flag in 1776. Each Nov. 16, there's a local "jump up" with costumed residents and visitors dancing in the streets, a reenacting of Rodney's firing on a U.S. ship, and local goodies sold, including the spicy meat and fish-filled "pastechis." Kingdom Day (December 15) is also alive with festivities including parades, governmental events and general celebrating that continues well into the night.

Tour Operators

There are no wholesalers serving St. Eustatius.

Sources of Information

Write directly to the St. Eustatius Tourist Office, St. Eustatius, Netherlands Antilles. Or contact Sontheimer & Co., 25 West 39th St., New York, NY 10018, for additional background information.

219

Packing

There are a handful of tiny shops where you may pick up an extra item of clothing or find a gift to take home. But remember that in small 'Statia, even boutiques come in miniature, so pack what you'll need for your visit. You will not need an elaborate wardrobe. Casual summer clothes will suffice. You might take along an extra swimsuit and beach cover-up. If you're planning to make the fairly rigorous hike up the Quill, the island's extinct volcano, be sure to toss in a pair of sturdy shoes and socks and a pair of lightweight pants. You'll also need a wide-brimmed hat for protection from the Caribbean sun. Fill-in drugstore items can be picked up in Oranjestad. Be sure to pack more film than you think you'll need. Film is almost double the U.S. price if purchased locally, and it's not always available. Wines and liquors are very reasonably priced in 'Statia, so don't worry about packing a bottle of your favorite beverage.

Documentation

This applies also to Canadian citizens

U.S. citizens need carry only proof of citizenship to enter 'Statia. A passport (which is best), a voter's registration card, a birth certificate, or naturalization papers will do plus proof of return or ongoing transportation.

Getting There

Airline Service

Windward Island Airways serves 'Statia, St. Kitts and Saba. Daily scheduled flights leave from St. Maarten. Either the Old Gin House or Mooshay Bay Publick House will arrange charters from nearby islands.

Cruise Ships

Statia is not a stop for cruise ships, although Windjammer 'Barefoot' Cruises' 4-masted, 248-foot barquentine, "Polynesia" stops twice monthly, and the newly renovated square-rigger, "Sea Cloud" makes occasional winter visits.

Formalities on Arrival

Money

Official currency in 'Statia is the Netherlands Antilles guilder. U.S. dollars are accepted everywhere on the island. All restaurants but one quote prices in U.S. dollars.

Getting into Town

Taxis meet all incoming flights, and many drivers will offer to take you on a tour of the island once you've settled in your hotel. Considering the price of gasoline, the trip into town is reasonable—about $3.00. Car rentals can also be arranged.

Settling Down

Choosing a Hotel

When you're thinking about a place to stay in 'Statia, you'll realize that the choice is definitely limited since there are only five possibilities—and the largest inn has only 40 rooms. Winter rates average $160, double occupancy MAP. Several of the guest houses are less expensive but we think most travelers want to experience a special service and charm—especially when the cost is moderate. And considering the cost of hotels throughout the Caribbean, these inns fall into the moderate class in season. Rates drop 30% in summer.

Tipping
Most inns and restaurants add a 10% service charge to your bill; a 5% government tax, and there's a 5% electrical charge. Additional tipping is at your own discretion.

Learning to Cope
Business Hours.   Generally, stores are open from 8:00 A.M. to noon and from 1:30 to 5:30 P.M., Monday through Friday. Saturday hours are from 10:00 A.M. to noon and from 2:30 to 5:30 P.M. But since many shop owners are Seventh Day Adventists, it's lock up at sundown on Friday and all day Saturday.

Electricity.   'Statia has the same current as the United States—110 volts AC, 60 cycles.

Water and Drink.   Drinking water is considered safe. But if you have a delicate stomach, rely on drinks special to the island, club soda or any of the choices of inexpensive liquor. Complimentary wine is often served with dinner.

Communications.   'Statia has 24-hour-a-day telephone service. But if you're planning to make an international call, plan ahead with your operator or your inn's proprietor. Your inn can also arrange to send a cable for you. Again, arrange in advance. Remember that 'Statia uses Eastern Daylight Time all year.

Medical Assistance.   A Dutch licensed physician is available at Princess Beatrix Hospital in Oranjestad.

ST. EUSTATIUS TODAY
Once upon a time, an elderly resident of eight-square-mile St. Eustatius was asked by a visitor, "Do you have many tourists here?" The reply with pride and a bit of hurt was, "My dear, we don't have tourists in 'Statia. We have guests."

The mood of 'Statia is as quiet and as gentle as the people. In the capital, Oranjestad, there's a donkey cart that occasionally carries official visitors about. Apparently there used to be a bit of trouble with the donkey. He didn't want to move. "But we'll work that out," the man in charge confided. And, apparently, he did. During the Christmas holiday season, elderly Henry Newton practices jibs and quadrilles on his fiddle. Cyril Hill stitches ribbons and silver foil onto his costume for a forthcoming party, and teenager Evie Blyden practices carols in her parents' home. At any time of year there's the chance to meet Marty Scofield and John May, both from the United States, who have made 'Statia home and who have also made genuine contributions to the island by building the Old Gin House and the neighboring Mooshay Bay Publick House, two of the best of the limited places to stay.

If you're a true Caribbean buff, you'll be impressed by the following: Tiny 'Statia has one of the best steel bands in the entire Caribbean. Led by Buck Duinkere, the 'Statia Steel Band has made tours of Europe and recordings. They not only take their drums, carved out of used oil drums and beaten into precision instruments, and make the usual kind of Caribbean music, "Bang-Bang Lu-Lu," they play Bach as well, and the "Hallelujah Chorus." It's hard to believe, but it's true.

you'll love or hate the steel bands

TOURING

A walk or a drive through 'Statia is a rendezvous with history, so much so that the under-200-member Historical Foundation, composed of 'Statian, Dutch and American members, has written and designed both an eight-page *Walking Tour Guide* and a map that are available free of charge once you're on the island.

It's really best to walk rather than drive into this land of history for several reasons. Distances are short, and although hills are steep from Lower Town to Upper Town, it's easier to rest your feet than park a car on narrow, cobblestone streets. (On another day, if you visit "the Quill," an extinct volcano, you will require a car or a taxi.)

Following the route of the Historical Foundation's walking tour, you begin among the ruins of "Lower Town," part of the capital of Oranjestad. This was the busiest port in the Caribbean in the 1700s and although little evidence of this prosperous commercial life remains today, the visitor can sit on benches provided by the society under flowering shrubs and almond trees and contemplate what once was. Offshore, the crumbling remains of the "city beneath the sea" can sometimes be seen, and it's tempting to plan a snorkeling or a diving excursion. The "Happy Hooker" Water Sport Center is here. It provides dive, snorkel, or fishing excursions and equipment at an extra charge.

Take a ten-minute stroll along the beach to the ruins of Crooks Castle, the 18th-century home of a wealthy Dutch merchant. It's not the ruins themselves that are worth the walk; it's the chance to scratch around the grounds and possibly turn up some of the blue beads, called slave beads, that are found nowhere else in the Caribbean. There are several theories about these beads; among them they were brought over by the slaves from Africa or, that they were used for trading purposes in lieu of currency.

The route from Lower Town to Upper Town is a long, hot, but worthwhile climb over the blue-gray cobblestones that once served as ship's ballast in the Atlantic crossings from Europe. (They were left behind on the island since the ships left laden with goods.)

Once there, puffing and panting, you'll understand why the Fort Road was so named. Fort Oranje sits in majestic and magnificent silence, one of the most—if not the most—complete forts in the Caribbean. It was restored in honor of the U.S. Bicentennial in 1976. You wander in through an arch . . . past flowered grounds . . . to thick stone fortifications. Cannon are in place, aimed at the sea, waiting for the man-o'-wars that used to come frequently.

A short walk away from the fort is the Historical Foundation Museum, housed in a 19th-century, gingerbread-trimmed wooden building kept Dutch-clean. Inside the small museum, an 18th-century engraving of 'Statia's harbor greets newcomers. There are prints and photographs of the island's past as well as drawings by children of 'Statia present. Display cases contain broken bits of 18th-century delftware and porcelain, buttons, musket balls and glass bottles discovered when Fort Oranje was restored. A 19th-century parlor has been created in a separate room, with period chaise lounges and needlepoint-covered chairs. Both the needlepoint and the crocheted curtains were handstitched by several island women. In another room, the island's first telephone switchboard resides in a place of respect. And if you try to make a phone call, even today, to or from 'Statia, you'll know why! Although there is no admittance charge to the museum, a donation is very much appreciated.

Also on the walking tour is a visit to the Gertrude Judson Library, which everyone in 'Statia calls Three Widows' Corner, for three widowed sisters

Cannon from the fort were the first foreign guns to salute the new U.S.A. flag on an arriving ship in 1776

who lived at the crossroads in the late 19th century. Today two of their houses constitute the local library that is used by the people who live here. Any interested visitor who cares to drop in is invited to do so. Inside the 18th-century town house, a staircase built of yellow brick leads to an upper floor. The neighboring 19th-century building is a fine example of gingerbread architecture.

The misnamed Huis de Graaff is being restored. It was named for Johannes de Graaff, the governor, who never actually lived here; he lived in a neighboring house. The restoration of Huis de Graaff, which dates from the 18th century, will result in a new, very luxurious restaurant, expected to open by 1984, once the restoration, true to the original architecture, is complete.

The facade of the Dutch Reformed Church is in the process of being spruced up with the help of the central Dutch government. Consecrated on November 2, 1775, the church was severely damaged in the hurricane of 1792 (which destroyed many other buildings as well). The shell of the church still stands . . . the outside walls and square tower. Originally there was a rectangular nave and a transept on the north side; a straight wall in back of the choir; and a square tower against the northwest wall of the nave. What remains gives the visitor a feeling of 'Statia when horse-drawn carriages drew up at the wooden doors of the church and citizens, dressed in their Sunday best, went in to prayer.

The Honen Dalim Synagogue was rebuilt after being damaged by the *This was one* same hurricane that destroyed much of the Dutch Reformed Church. The *of the first* restoration was financed by donations from New York's Jewish community. *synagogues* In the 18th century the synagogue had the traditional two floors; the ladies' *in the New* gallery and even a ritual bath were on the first floor. However, when 'Statia's *World* economic fortunes changed, so did the well-being of the synagogue: It was abandoned about 1880. But a walk through the ruins, recalling the many Jews who left Europe for islands throughout the Caribbean, established homes and synagogues and made their contributions to each island, is a worthwhile experience.

Perhaps on another day, you might want to take a car or a cab to the foot of the Quill (the extinct mountain volcano) and make the climb upward. There's a shaded rain forest spilling flowers, ferns and trees that makes a perfect resting place for a picnic (packed by your hotel). Cactus and cassia also grow here on the shaded slopes. If you continue to circle the island, you'll come on fields of flowering sisal, white cedar, tamarind, yellow elder, and, of course, many colors of hibiscus and bougainvillea.

Now may be the time for that snorkel or scuba dive off the shores of Lower Town to see the city that crumbled into the sea and to meet some of the fish in residence. Or you may prefer to soak up some sun and reflect on the days when there were hundreds of ships in the harbor, loading goods needed in America and in Europe. Today a sloop or a ketch, carrying private sailing parties, may sail past. Wave, smile, and go back to remembering things past.

Inside Information

Hotels

There's a choice of five inns in St. Eustatius (the largest has 14 rooms), but we recommend that you choose among three. The others are basic guest houses and probably not the place you want to hang your hat the first time in 'Statia. There's a 10% service charge added for all accommodations. And all are quiet places where you can rest.

★★★★ MOOSHAY BAY PUBLICK HOUSE

This is 'Statia's "largest" hotel (14 rooms), owned by John May and his partner, Marty Scofield, who abandoned their native U.S.A. for 'Statia's charms. They also own the Old Gin House directly across the street. (Guests flow back and forth from one place to the other.) Built of stone from the 18th century and stonework added from bricks once used as ship's ballast in the crossing from Europe, the rooms, which contain genuine antiques, reflect the charm of the Caribbean. Almost all guests choose to spend a few quiet moments in the second floor loft, with library, oversized chandelier, and taped classical music. All the rooms have balconies and overlook the swimming pool, which is in a cistern rebuilt from colonial days. Guests are more than welcome to walk a few paces across the road to the Old Gin House, which is on the ocean, and use its beach facilities. *Cost:* $100, double EP, in season; $160, double MAP, in season.

★★★★ THE OLD GIN HOUSE

Owned by the same team that owns the neighboring Mooshay Bay Publick House (partners Scofield and May), this was their first, highly-successful effort to establish an inn after starting a small, special restaurant after they arrived in 'Statia. (Although the real "owner" may well be Magee, an island dog with the good life, who escorts guests as they go.) Each of the six rooms faces the sea above an onyx-black beach of volcanic sand. All rooms are decorated with antiques from the owners' travels to Europe, Africa and other Caribbean isles. Mosquito netting facilitates nighttime sleeping when the no-see-'ums (miniature mosquitos) come out. All have overhead, revolving wood fans. Meals are served by a courteous, friendly staff in an open patio that overlooks the ocean. The grounds are covered by the Caribbean's sunset-shaded flowers. There's also a boutique in miniature, called the Goobie Boutique, which, in the local patois, means the calabash, a local squashlike vegetable. *Cost:* $100, double EP, in season; $160, double MAP, in season.

★★ GOLDEN ROCK RESORT

It's impossible to be very far from anything on an island of this small size, but the Golden Rock is on its own point of the two-mile stretch of beach at Zeelandia, directly opposite the capital of Oranjestad. There's a total of ten rooms in several bungalows along the hillside on the eastern coast of the dangerously rough Atlantic side of the island. (The Caribbean Sea on the opposite side is gentler.) The rooms are spacious and brightly decorated by owner Don Lewis from New York. If the wind whips up and you don't feel like conquering the black-sand volcanic beach and churning waves, you can use the swimming pool and adjoining beach bar. *Cost:* $130, double MAP, in season; $104, EP.

Stay here if you want to join the guest roster with Queen Beatrix and Prince Claus, as well as "known" theatre luminaries

Restaurants

In the 18th century, when the English and the French were colonizing islands to plant sugar, tobacco and cotton crops, the Dutch were far more interested in seeking salt for their North Sea fisheries. Mostly because the community in the Dutch associated islands was clannish, two unique customs developed based on food: one, the birthday reception, which is an open house held from dawn to dusk and attended by anyone who cares to come; two, tea time, now fading from the scene, was similar to the English custom of high tea, but unlike high tea, the main purpose was to participate in the gossip hour, known in Papiamento as *awa di redu,* or gossip water. Even though both these customs are no longer strictly observed, what remains of the Dutch traditions can be found in local spots, and happily for all, prices are *moderate* (approx. $25 per person, without drinks) to *inexpensive.*

★★★★ THE OLD GIN HOUSE
A few tables are set on the patio that offers an ocean view, and waiters offer you your choice of drink, followed by cuisine thought out by Martin Scofield, one of the owners. At lunch, it might be salads (chicken, warm-water lobster, fresh fruits from the trees). There's also the standard sandwich you'll remember from home, but here it comes decorated with local fruits and flowers. Special soups, from callaloo to pumpkin, are always featured. Dinners become more elaborate; Mr. Scofield presides over his sous-chef from Haiti. The menu might offer an unusual peanut soup; a chilled curry of green coconut soup; a half pound of langouste in butter sauce; a spiced red snapper or perhaps "lobster Antillean," the Caribbean spiny lobster, decked with tomatoes, celery, onions, dill, wine and Pernod. *Moderate.*

★★★★ MOOSHAY BAY
Dinner here is special, served on Dutch Delft and pewter dinnerware, shadowed by candlelight and formally presented. Some of the best dishes mix French influence with local availability . . . grapefruit or pepper-pot soup; red snapper served with a pink horseradish sauce and broccoli; quiche Niçoise (a combination of anchovies, sausages, capers and tomatoes). Lunches, which are served in the jointly-owned Old Gin House across the road, aren't quite that elaborate. The accent is placed on salads and simpler fare for midday; perhaps a seafood plate or homemade pasta. But there are always flowers on the table and smiles on the faces of the people serving you their proud culinary creations. *Moderate.*

★ L'ÉTOILE
A second-floor local restaurant with a few simple tables, and a basic menu, but what's done is done well. Eric and Caren Henriquez have owned this place for some time. One of the specialties of the house is pastechis (turnovers deep-fried and stuffed with meat). *Inexpensive* to *moderate.*

a favorite with 'Statians

★ TALK OF THE TOWN
The name is appropriate for despite the fact that it's not formal, this restaurant has the most ambitious menu on the island. The cook, Melvina Niss, learned her craft in Aruba, and when given some notice, she can prepare dishes that range from Dutch to Chinese to Italian to Caribbean Creole. Soups include sharks fin; a local bouillabaisse; Dutch-accented green pea and island callaloo. Many of the main dishes are West Indian curries (hot and spicy), but also available are crisp duck flavored with Curaçao sauce; Caribbean red snapper flavored with a tomato-and-spice, Spanish-type sauce; the Indonesian dish nasi-goreng (a meat, vegetable and noodle combination); pepper steak in oyster sauce. There's usually Mrs. Niss's own "Happy Family" dinner, a combination of several Chinese dishes ranging from the mild Cantonese to the spicier Szechuan and Hunan dishes. *Inexpensive* to *moderate.*

Nightlife

To put it mildly, nightlife in 'Statia is just about that . . . the night, the splashing sea and the stars above. Really big excitment is generated when an occasional falling star shoots from the heavens into time itself.

However, there are nightly cocktails and dancing to a live band at the small Twilight Inn.

There may—or may not—be informal dances on Saturday night at *Charlie's,* a local favorite for drinks and island gossip. It's a spot you might call unpretentious. But there's usually an island dance somewhere . . . ask around.

Infrequently, 'Statia's famous steel band, simply known as the *Statia Steel Band,* which has given concerts abroad, may perform on shore. If so, go . . . no matter what plans you have to cancel. They really are among the best. The only way to know when they are going to perform is to talk with your hotel manager. He has the answer to everything.

If you stay at least a week, you'll undoubtedly meet some of 'Statia's citizens and may be invited to dinner or to private parties in their homes. Socializing is the lifeblood of 'Statia and why visitors return time and time again.

Shopping

You didn't come to 'Statia to shop, but you may find a handful of treasures to take home. Don't neglect the opportunity that a beach walk may afford to gather shells. Once home, you can shellac them and put them into clear-based glass lamps, under glass on small tables, into framed shell montages or even into string jewelry.

It's worth stopping at the *Sign of Goobie,* attached to the Old Gin House, where there are clothes for men and women imported from Italy, Haiti, and Saba and 'Statia, of course. Most are classic in design (although the Italian imports are somewhat more sophisticated), and some are hand-embroidered. If you forgot to pack a shirt or a skirt, you can find something here. Tags on some of the 'Statia designs state, "This printed fabric is based upon shards of 18th-century porcelain found along the shores of St. Eustatius." There are also some craft items: wooden wine goblets; shell and scrimshaw jewelry; a smattering of 'Statia sketches and watercolors. One of their newest additions (and well worth the $7.50 price) are unusual soup recipes from the Old Gin House, soon to be followed by their appetizer, entrée, and dessert recipes. Learn to cook at home as you eat away.

There's also the *Mazinga Gift Shop,* the name taken from the highest point on the "Quill." It's a true general store: Delft china mixed with hardware; French bikinis nestled next to tennis sneakers; T-shirts that proclaim Statia's charms in several ways; postcards; even snacks and cokes for sale.

A very special find comes *occasionally* at the Information Center at the end of the pier (hours: 9:30 A.M. to 4 P.M., Monday to Friday). A handful of "slave beads" for sale, dug up by enterprising young men. We've seen a single dark blue bead (most are five-sided, and both condition and size set the price) for sale on neighboring island jewelry shops on simple chains just under $100. Here, the asking price is $10.

Sports

'Statia lacks a golf course, but does have a new tennis court at the community center with night lights. There are lovely beaches—some volcanic, some not. Choose the more rugged Atlantic side with extreme caution or swim in the gentler Caribbean. One of the best volcanic beaches—with black sand—is on the southwest shore of 'Statia. Any cab driver will know the spot. *Hiking.*

There's volcano climbing for the stout of heart. Pack a picnic, and take your time exploring the Quill. The extinct volcano, Mt. Mazinga, has one of the most perfectly formed cones in the Caribbean, and contains a rain forest where birdwatchers may sight a rare species of hummingbird. It is not seen anywhere else in the world. If you don't want to walk up to the volcano crest, there are donkeys to rent. (The donkey population in 'Statia consists of one for every three humans.) The Old Gin House can arrange for deep-sea fishing trips, snorkeling, scuba diving and a guided trip to a reef. It's thought there are over 150 submerged wrecks in 'Statia's reefs, as well as some of the original town sacked by Admiral Rodney. It's seldom you get the chance to swim through history! It might not be a bad idea to take along your own equipment, but rentals are usually available. Be sure to check with your airline regarding regulations on transporting oxygen tanks. Some plane cabins are not pressurized. *Spearfishing* is legal in 'Statia. Go *surfing* (at your own risk) on the very challenging Atlantic side of 'Statia. And if you don't like surfing, at least walk along the beach a bit and even jog if you want to.

St. Kitts

THE HARD FACTS
Planning Ahead
Costs

In general, St. Kitts is still considered a "good buy" if such a thing any longer exists in the Caribbean. A double room, in season, can run about $100 per day at one of the best inns. This includes breakfast and dinner. Other double rooms may be obtained for $85, double, in season (December 15 to April 15). Housekeeping cottages, where you do your own cooking, are available for less. It is customary for hotels to add to your bill a 10% service charge and a 5% room tax.

Holidays and Special Events

Public holidays in St. Kitts each year are: New Year's Day (January 1); Statehood Day (February 27); Good Friday; Easter Monday; Labour Day (first Monday in May); Whit Monday (40 days after Lent); Queen's Birthday (June); August Monday (first Monday in August); Prince of Wales' Birthday (November 14); Christmas Day; Boxing Day (the day after Christmas, December 26). Other local events are: the Queen's Birthday Parade (June 2); Carnival (December 26 to January 2).

　　Businesses and banks all close down on the above dates, so don't make shopping plans around any of them.

Tour Operators

Caribbean Holidays, Lib/Go Travel, Inc., and Travel Impressions Ltd.

Sources of Information

Call or write, the *Eastern Caribbean Tourist Association,* 220 East 42nd Street, New York, NY 10017 (212) 986–9370. Or write the St. Kitts Tourist Bureau, Treasury Pier, Basseterre, St. Kitts, W.I. You may also find the Caribbean Tourist Association helpful. They're at: 20 East 46th Street, New York, NY 10017 (212) 682–0435.

Packing

Life in St. Kitts is laid back—casual and low key. Pack your wardrobe accordingly. Temperatures average 78°F., and thanks to the northeast trade winds, there's a cooling breeze year-round. In addition to packing sandals,

No special day for Christopher Columbus, who gave the island his name — St. Christopher

take along a pair of sturdy hiking shoes if you're up to making the trek up Brimstone Hill or Mount Misery. You'll need no prescription for standard medications. Remember to pack shampoo and hair blower although what may be the best hairdresser in the Caribbean, Rene, is at the Royal St. Kitts. There are some Sea-Island cotton skirts and dresses for sale; they are of a limited supply and are quite costly, so don't plan on "winging it" and completing your wardrobe after arrival at St. Kitts. You may be disappointed. A long or a short summer evening dress is in keeping with the surroundings of the gracious great house inn dining rooms. Men are not requested to wear jackets and ties. Camera buffs will want to take along more film than they think they'll need. Prices are often double those in the United States.

Documentation

As is usual for most Caribbean islands, U.S. travelers need only carry proof of citizenship to enter St. Kitts and to stay up to six months. A passport, a birth certificate, a valid driver's license or naturalization papers will suffice. Also, an ongoing or a return airline or ship ticket is required. Personal belongings are admitted duty-free. You are also allowed to bring along one carton of cigarettes, one bottle of liquor and one bottle of wine.

These comments apply also to Canadian citizens

Getting There

From New York and Miami, British West Indian Airways (BWIA) has weekly nonstop flights to St. Kitts, and the list is growing. Visitors can also use ALM, American or Eastern to other points in the Caribbean and then transfer via Prinair, LIAT, WINAIR or Air BVI (from Tortola, B.V.I), Carib Aviation or Coral Air. Cruise ships also visit St. Kitts, including the Cunard's "Princess." Occasional visits of the QE II are also slated in winter and the Sun Lines, and the Windjammer "Barefoot" Cruises' 248-foot sailing ship *Polynesia* make stops at St. Kitts and Nevis regularly. A modern, comfortable ferry, *The Carib Queen,* makes daily trips to and from Nevis. The trip takes 40 minutes and costs $3.00 (U.S.) each way.

Money

Currency used in St. Kitts is the Eastern Caribbean ("Bee Wee") dollar. U.S. currency is accepted by hotels, taxis and restaurants. You can convert foreign currency at commercial banks at the prevailing rate of exchange, which follows U.S. dollar fluctuations closely. Hotels will also change your money for you at just about as good a rate as the local bank. Most hotels and stores accept major credit cards, but if you're planning to cash a personal check, be sure to register a request for check-cashing privileges with your hotel management in advance of the transaction. Also, when engaging a taxi, always check with the driver to see if the fare is being quoted U.S. or EC dollars. Set aside $8.00 EC for the airport departure tax (although U.S. dollars are accepted everywhere).

Learning to Cope

Business Hours. From 8:00 A.M. to noon, daily except Saturday and Sundays, then 1 P.M. to 4 P.M.. Thursday is a halfday, most stores closing at noon. On Friday most banks remain open between 3:30 P.M. and 5:30 P.M. The St. Kitts-Nevis National Bank Ltd., in Basseterre, opens from 8:30 A.M. to 11:00 A.M. on Saturday.

Electricity. The standard voltage within St. Kitts is the European 230 volts. Request a converter at your hotel's reception desk or, better yet, take along appliances with built-in adapters.

Communications.   All major hotels and inns can send cables for guests. The local telephone system is adequate and operates 24 hours a day, 7 days a week, inside and outside the island. No additional tax is levied on international calls.

ST. KITTS TODAY

The sleepy, slumbering island of St. Kitts (officially St. Christopher) isn't sleepy or slumbering any more. It is, it seems, going to be among the newest of the "in" islands among the American, Canadian and European well-traveled set.

The rediscovery of St. Kitts (Columbus dropped by in 1493) began through a combination of circumstances. First BWIA airlines (with a bit of push from the government) inaugurated nonstop service from the United States that proved so successful that there are hot rumors that American, Air Canada and British Airways intend to follow in BWIA's jet stream. Then there are the major condominium developments. At Frigate Bay, a long stretch of land on the southern side of the island, with shores washed by Caribbean and Atlantic waves, 12 developments are projected over a period of from 10 to 15 years. When these are complete (and a few will be partially open this winter), visitors will be able to book into individually-decorated villa-style condominiums or, if they're in a buying mood, to purchase them. The largest development now underway projects 450 rooms, with tennis courts, swimming pools (most are also projected to have private beaches), restaurant complexes and golf on an 18-hole course (one course is already in full swing). Several of the 12 resorts plan to add to the island's only casino (also on Frigate Bay).

The aim, best characterized by Michael Oliver Powell, minister of tourism, is: "to keep the other small, select inns as they are on the rest of the island, but to permit these large resorts to congregate on this neck of the island, where visitors who want this range of condominium activity will have a very full choice."

Until 1981, when ground was broken for some of the condominium projects, sugar was the main industry, accounting for about 90% of St. Kitts's income. But now the accent seems to have shifted toward tourism.

It's hoped that this booming land development will not disturb the comparatively tranquil life on the rest of this 68-square-mile island, whose population totals about 40,000. The people of St. Kitts, like the people of Nevis (the sister island of St. Kitts), will make your visit to their island special and unique.

Depending on what you choose to do, day might bring a meeting with Arthur Leaman at his elegant, 12-room Golden Lemon Inn. (Arthur occupies one room.) The antique-filled Golden Lemon is a true find in St. Kitts or anywhere else in the Caribbean. If you can't manage to make a room reservation, do make one for lunch or dinner. Mr. Leaman may tell you the story behind the naming of the Golden Lemon. . . . His friends thought he was mad to leave his editorial position at *House and Garden* magazine in New York to take possession of a "lemon" in St. Kitts. Arthur counted on it becoming a "golden lemon." It has. Try to get him to tell you about the time he discovered booze smugglers transporting their illegal cargo across his beach. He told them they would have to cease and desist. They did and left him a case of brandy as a present! You might also drop by the Fort Thomas Hotel for a drink and meet manager Velma Schwartz, who's full of charm and information about her island.

When you roam around the capital, Basseterre, you'll most likely wander into the Palm restaurant and if you see an apparently harassed-looking

Basseterre is French for "Low Land" but means "Leeward"; nautically speaking

man directing the staff, you'll know that he's Carl Fuchs, owner and perfectionst. He also spends time at his new beach resort at Banana Bay, where, he insists, everything is run with the same kind of personal care that he gives to his restaurant.

As you stroll around town, ask anyone to direct you to Bay Front, to the Spencer–Cameron Workshop—owned by the team of Kate Spencer, originally from England, and Rosey Cameron, originally from Scotland. They'll not only tell you about their prints and paintings, all of their adopted island home, and their limited line of silk-screened yardage and cotton made-up designs, but, when there's time, they'll offer visitors tea and biscuits.

Try to catch the music of Bruce Skerritt, the leader of a five-piece band, the Quintessence, that makes the rounds of different night spots, from sophisticated hotel lounges to local spots featuring barefoot dancing on terraces splashed by ocean waves. Even though all the musicians have full-time jobs in the day and little time to practice, they make some of the best music in the Caribbean. Bruce Skerritt comes from one of the island's first families. His father, Sonny Skerritt, has a remarkable collection of photographs that dates from the late 1800s, the days of his grandfather. Both father and son have preserved the first and the finest photographs of St. Kitts. Occasionally, exhibits of their work are held on the island. Cancel any plans whenever one opens.

TOURING

Touring in St. Kitts is not an "organized" activity. In order to get the real feel of St. Kitts, you'll have to keep your eyes open to experience the country sights and you'll have to keep your ears attuned to absorb the lore of St. Kitts. Fortunately, taxi drivers here are very well versed in island history. They'll willingly fill you in on events of several centuries ago. The citizens of St. Kitts are justifiably proud that their island was the first English-speaking colony in the western hemisphere. The settlement at Old Road Town was the forerunner of the spread of Anglo culture and influence throughout the Caribbean. Frigate Bay, Brimstone Hill, Basseterre Harbour, Bloody Point, and Half Way Tree are all reminders of St. Kitts's past. Visitors who like history or things military will be able to obtain more than their fill of both.

A drive along the west and rugged east coasts, a visit to out-of-the-way coves and inlets and a stop at some of the small fishing villages are musts. The road that encircles most of St. Kitts's 68 square miles is a good one.

Cars rent for about $30 a day and are available with either left- or right-wheel drive. (Remember to stay on the left side of the road.) A moped costs $16 per day, and bicycles rent for $3.00 per hour. Minimokes go for $20 per day, gas not included. To obtain a local driver's license, visitors must present a valid U.S. driver's license and pay $4.00. The license may be obtained at the Basseterre Police Station. Take along a copy of *A Motoring Guide to St. Kitts* by Sunny Northrup for advice on places to stop and their history.

Basseterre

The island's capital is a neatly maintained melange of handsome West Indian and Georgian architecture set off by palms and nooks of garden greenery. One of your first stops should be the circus, the town's commercial center, with its wonderful Victorian-style, cast-iron clock tower, and the imposing Treasury Building. Nearby is Pall Mall, a small, pretty park occupying land once set aside for the slave market. A short stroll away (up Cayon Street and to the left) is St. George Church (Anglican), built on the

This is a typical West Indian town

ruins of a French church. The present church, rebuilt twice, once after a dev-
astating fire and then after an earthquake that shook its tower loose, dates to
the late 1600s, as do some of the graves in its yard. You'll also want to
stop by Basseterre's bustling marketplaces, bursting with local fruit, vegetables and flowers, and perhaps spend some time gazing at the ships in the
usually busy port—a regular stop for schooners from Antigua, Nevis, St.
Martin and St. Barts and for freighters from the United States, Canada and
Europe.

The Philatelic Bureau

On Bay Road in Basseterre, and a must for stamp collectors. First-day covers
and current issues are available, and arrangements can be made to receive
future issues in the mail by setting up an account.

The Chateau of M. de Poincy

Once the site of lavish entertaining and an opulent life-style, it was a splendid, three-story great house surrounded by gardens and fountains, with
sweeping views of countryside and sea. It was from here that France's
aristocratic governor, Philippe de Longvilliers de Poincy (after whom the
poinciana, or flamboyant tree, was named), ruled over French possessions in
the Caribbean for 21 years (from 1640). Today only the foundations of the
original chateau survive, but the present Fountain Estate House was built
upon them.

Bloody Point

Before any nation could claim possession of St. Kitts, the fierce and decidedly
inhospitable Carib Indians had to be subdued. To that end, French and British
forces allied themselves. Here, at Bloody Point in 1629, the rivers ran red
with the blood of about 2,000 Caribs. The massacre effectively ended island
resistance to the European colonialists.

Carib Indian Remains

These are buried beneath great stones bearing Carib inscriptions. If you're so
inclined, you can find these markers at Wingfield Estate, West Farm and Pond
Pasture.

Old Road Town

The first British settlement in the Caribbean, it was founded in 1623. You'll
spot houses here that were built over 250 years ago; you'll probably be told
about the good fishing to be had nearby, and you'll undoubtedly see local
fishermen selling their day's catches on the streets . . . just as their fathers and
fathers' fathers used to do.

Middle Island Village

Here Thomas Warner, leader of the first settlers in Old Road Town, was
buried. His tomb, in the cemetery of St. Thomas Anglican Church, is inscribed with a long and grand epitaph.

Halfway Tree Village

When the French and the British partitioned and ruled St. Kitts from 1666 to
1669, the French held the northwest and the southeast ends, and the English
held the midsection. A stately tamarind tree marked the halfway point of the
British territory.

Brimstone Hill Fortress

Called the Gibraltar of the West Indies, it is a massive 18th-century fortress built atop a 700-foot cliff by the British and named for still-lingering sulfur fumes. At the height of British power, it contained soldiers' quarters, a hospital, a cemetary, a 100,000-gallon freshwater cistern, a citadel, scores of black-iron cannon and 33 acres of battlements. It was considered impressive and impregnable—and it probably was . . . Only a lack of supplies caused the British capitulation in a famous 1782 battle that pitted 6,000 French troops against about 1,000 British troops who lacked the ammunition necessary to defend the fortress.

By the mid-1800s the proud fortress had been abandoned. Many of its guns were unceremoniously dumped into the sea; sections of its walls were carried away and used to rebuild Basseterre after the great fire of 1867. Fortunately for today's visitors, the efforts of the Society for the Restoration of Brimstone Hill have erased much past neglect and helped restore much of the fortress's past glory. The Prince of Wales Bastion, restored in 1973 and dedicated by Prince Charles, now contains a visitors' center, a souvenir shop and a restaurant. Also, the stone flooring and the walls of the citadel have been reconstructed, and by early 1982, on the anniversary of the first Brimstone Hill battle, exhibits reflecting the island's varied heritage were housed within its walls. There are French, American and Dutch rooms, rooms of African and pre-Colombian (Carib and Arawak) artifacts and a military room with an appropriate English versus French emphasis.

Mt. Misery

The island's highest (3,792-foot) peak can be ascended by intrepid hikers. The climb will take you through forests and past wild orchids. Once at the summit, you will be rewarded by the view. (Plan a full day for this expedition.)

Black Rocks

In the 1600s volcanic eruptions of the now dormant Mt. Misery deposited dramatic outcroppings of black lava rock on the eastern shore of St. Kitts. Today these strange configurations provide a majestic backdrop for picnics (including the Kittitians' annual Guy Fawkes Day feast) and serve as a favorite playground for island children who seem to tumble out of nowhere, radiating charm and exuberance. The island outlines you'll glimpse off in the distance belong to St. Barts and St. Martin.

Estridge Research Station

This station on Monkey Hill is sponsored by McGill University in Canada, the University of California at Los Angeles and Yale in the United States. Here vervet (green) monkeys are observed in an enclosed natural habitat as part of a Behavioral Science Foundation study on primal behavior. (Other monkeys, not involved in the project, come down from the hill at night to visit.) If you'd like to visit, the hours are 2:00 P.M.–6:00 P.M. on Sunday only or by special appointment (Tel. 7280).

Frigate Bay

A handle of land stretching south of Basseterre, it has pounding surf on its eastern beaches and lapping waves on its western flank. It is here that St. Kitts's hotel and condominium boom is taking place.

Inside Information

Hotels

Only a year ago St. Kitts was a quiet, little, out-of-the-mainstream island offering visitors accommodations in a scattering of small inns. Soon that era will end. Scores of architects, a battalion of bulldozers, and hundreds of construction workers are catapulting the island into the Caribbean limelight. Suddenly there are 12 *major* new hotel and condominium developments underway—representing an expansion of accommodations available to travelers from under 300 to over 3,000!

The condominiums will be available for buying *or* renting. Of these, the *Frigate Bay Beach Hotel-Condominium,* reportedly one of the best, opened some of an eventual 448 rooms) in early 1983. Other properties include the *Village du Soleil* and *Leeward Cove Condominiums.* Also, the *Hyatt* is opening 250 rooms, and the already-open *Royal St. Kitts* will add 100 rooms. All this building is clustered in the 850-acre Frigate Bay handle south of the island's capital. The plan is to transform this area into a full-facility resort complex (akin to the Hilton Head concept), while leaving the rest of the island as it is. In the coming years, your choice of lodging will depend on whether you prefer the golf, tennis and entertainment offerings of a large, sophisticated resort or the intimacy of one of the island's small, friendly, personable inns. For the time being, your options are limited to the following choices.

★★★★★ THE GOLDEN LEMON

Each room in this exquisite 12-room bayfront inn, owned by Arthur Leaman, former *House and Garden* magazine editor, is very special. In the "Paisley Room," for instance, blue and white paisley fabrics are complemented by Arthur's wonderful collection of blue and white china; the "Hibiscus Room," with canopied twin beds, is dominated by a large, beautifully-rendered painting of a hibiscus (done by a guest, Judy Lloyd of Detroit); the "Tortoise Room" is a showcase for Arthur's valuable collection of tortoise shells. Other rooms include one with an Oriental motif, another with "Lemon" accents, a pristine "White Room" and an "English Room." The inn itself was originally a great house, built in 1690 by a French settler and purchased by Mr. Leaman years ago. Three years later he brought in chef Lilian Johnson, whose inspired menus provide exactly the right counterpoint to his elegant decor. There's a pool on the grounds and, for the athletically inclined, water sports are available nearby. This is a "best bet" retreat for those who appreciate grand style. *Cost:* $190–$225, double, in season; $140–$160, off season.

This retreat is as far away as you can get on St. Kitts

★★★★ BANANA BAY BEACH

Owned by Carl Fuchs, this is the place to go if you crave seclusion. There's no disco here; no phones either; and the hotel can be reached only via a 45-minute boat ride from Basseterre. Once there, you'll find a lovely, airy nine-room hideaway. All the rooms have ocean views, some have private gardens, others private patios. Each room is dominated by a large painting by the team of Spencer and Cameron of a large island flower or fruit. All guests have instant introductions to baby Sylvester, mother donkey Potter and "aunt" Beatrix Dilly, three friendly, resident donkeys.

A light repast, packed picnic style in wicker baskets, will be provided for guests who'd like to lunch at the nearby beach pavilion. Drinks can be had at the beach bar, perched atop a rocky point of land with a view of neighboring

Nevis. Dining is in the hotel's excellent, open-air restaurant (with a banana motif—banana tablecloths, napkins). For a change of pace, water transport will be arranged to mainland restaurants. (Carl Fuchs also owns the Palm restaurant in town—one of the best.) You can wander along the 1,000-foot beach, scuba dive or snorkel, sail, join a spirited croquet, horseshoe or volleyball match or just quietly unwind, lulled by gently-splashing waves and the knowledge that you really are "away from it all." *Cost:* $185 per double American Plan, in season.

★★★★ RAWLINS PLANTATION
Near Dieppe Bay (which means rather far from town), this plantation has been in the Walwyn family almost 200 years, and the elder Walwyn was born on the plantation. Son Philip and his wife Frances are keeping up the old tradition with some accents all their own—Spencer and Cameron original watercolors in the main house. Six cottages (some of them doubles) are set on a hillside 350 feet above sea level in 25 acres, 10 acres of which are devoted to gardens that overlooking the waving sugarcane. One of the rooms, everyone's favorite, is a duplex in the sugar mill tower with a winding ship's staircase and sunken bathtub; two others are located in the gracious main house and the remainder in cottages scattered about the property. Guests visit in what was once the plantation's boiler room and dine informally in the little stone house furnished with English antiques. There's a pool on the grounds and a beach nearby. Philip Walwyn, who won the 1981 multi-hull Newport to Bermuda Race, and recently placed 3rd in his class in the '82 Route du Rhum Race, gladly takes guests (over 50% are repeat), for a Sunday sail on their 45-foot catamaran, "Skyjack," for a beach picnic and snorkel through secluded coves he's discovered. *Cost:* $215 per double MAP, in season.

★★★ THE COCKLESHELL
A neighbor of Banana Bay Beach, reachable only by a 45-minute boat ride. It also offers splendid isolation. Each of the nine rooms (some located in the main house, some in the "Foreshore Building") has a patio with a sea view (in fact, the sea laps only feet away), beds draped with mosquito netting, and Dominican straw rugs. The hotel's American owners, Laddie Hamilton and Donald Plum, plan to add batik bedspreads and curtains, but they may not be in place this winter. They certainly don't plan to change the paintings however, some over 100 years old. No matter, the place has charm and more games than a video center . . . "Kingmaker," a game of the 15th-century civil war; "Facts in Five," "Roll Around," a truly diabolical rolling pin with a metal marble which some say falls into place. Many were brought by repeat guests. (There are no phones, however—a drawback for those who must stay in touch.)

A comfy English drawing room is the site for dinner, served at a long table at which the owners preside as hosts. Breakfast and lunch are at tables with umbrellas on the terrace. Scuba diving, snorkeling and sailing are available options. *Cost:* $150 per double MAP, in season; boat ride is $10 per person (1-way) for dinner guests.

★★ FAIRVIEW INN
Three miles northwest of Basseterre, it has as its centerpiece an 18th-century great house, once occupied by the commander of the French troops, now home to Freddy and Betty Lam. The Lam's brand of warm hospitality and the inn's quiet coziness keep guests coming back year after year. Other winning qualities are panoramic views of the Caribbean and St. Kitts's lush countryside, the 30 comfortable, cottage rooms set amid gardens and blooms (the best are those in a converted stone stable), a congenial bar and good food.

There's a pool on the grounds. Arrangements can be made for tennis, golf and water sports. In the evening impromptu visits are paid by string or steel bands. *Cost:* $76–$86 per double EP, in season.

★★ OCEAN TERRACE INN

The evening view from OTI's second-floor dining terrace—of the lights of Basseterre and its harbor—makes this hotel a favorite congregating spot for both travelers and local businessmen. OTI (as it's familiarly called by all) offers 29 cheerfully-decorated rooms furnished with a tropical touch, and an array of water sports, with special emphasis on scuba diving and snorkeling. Arrangements for tennis and golf can be made. There's a pool on the grounds. *Cost:* $114–$170 per double MAP; $70–$90 double EP, in season.

a centrally located hotel

★★ THE ROYAL ST. KITTS

This was the first of the hotels to open at Frigate Bay, and it sets a tone of activity and nonstop guest events that will be echoed by the developments that follow. Designed in a country-club mode, it offers 100 rooms in two, two-story buildings nestled next to the main building called the clubhouse. Rooms are comfortable and spacious, offering views of sea, lakes, mountains and golf course. Dining is an informal affair beneath beamed, vaulted ceilings and amid spotlighted greenery. The beach is just steps away; there's a pool and a sun deck, four tennis courts, a challenging golf course, and the island's only casino (so far)—though it's a small one even by island standards. *Cost:* $195–$245 per double MAP, in season.

Restaurants

A nibble of peanuts sold on street corners in the capital, Basseterre, or a formal evening meal of local lobster prepared any of many ways by the excellent chefs in St. Kitts? The choice will be yours. For this is an island where fish are snapped from the sea to be served on your lunch or dinner table—rainbow snapper, red snapper, turtle, the local langouste, king fish—mackerel, dolphin (not the mammal, another breed entirely), even barracuda and balaho, which make a nice bouillabaisse. The fruit on your breakfast tray has come from the surrounding trees: melon, bananas, papaya, grapefruit, mangos. And at lunch or dinner, they reappear with other island-grown fruit and vegetables ripe from the hills: limes, lemons, breadfruit, the subtle christophine, breadnut, soursop, custard apple. The list is endless. Very little is imported here; almost everything on your table is island fresh, and much of it is organically grown. Many of the larger inn-hotels hold weekly buffets (check with your manager). We've rated an *expensive* dinner at about $30 per person. *Moderate* runs about $22. Downright *inexpensive* is about $15 per person!

★★★★★ GOLDEN LEMON

This an absolute must for lunch or dinner, and reservations in advance are another must. Owner Arthur Leaman collaborates with chef Lilian Johnson (born in Antigua, trained in food excellence in Curaçao, married and living for over 17 years in St. Kitts) to turn out menus that are never repeated in a span of three weeks. The cuisine is so creative that names don't really tell you what to expect. Just go, knowing that everything is fresh and that the highest standards are imposed in this special inn and restaurant. It is, however, a good half-hour drive from Basseterre, so plan to come during an around-the-island journey. *Expensive* by St. Kitts's standards; *moderate* anywhere else.

★★★★ BANANA BAY

Since this oceanside resort is owned by Carl Fuchs, who owns the Palm restaurant, it's more than worth the arrangements you'll have to make to be picked up by boat for a lunch or a dinner reservation at Banana Bay.

Transportation is part of the pre-set price. When you arrive at this beach resort, you can swim or snorkel before you sip or sup. Mr. Fuchs has transported a few of the recipes from his "Palm restaurant" to Banana Bay and although the taste is similar, the lunching ambience is more informal in this beach resort setting. Dining at night is more formal, however. Skylights open for moonlight-accented gazing. You can also dine on an open patio. The "banana" theme is carried out in table fabrics and decor, and it's simply quiet perfection. *Expensive* for lunch or dinner.

★★★★ THE GEORGIAN HOUSE
Owner Georgie Bowers has a proven track record in St. Kitts, but this is her latest venture. Originally from New York, Georgie supervises the kitchen and is the hostess. Dinner specialties include lobster thermidor; roast leg of lamb; stuffed chicken breast; and yummy desserts like guava ice cream; orange cake; or a special creme brulée. All is served on stoneware inherited from Georgie's English ancestors. There's also a house specialty, a ground-nut stew that's actually a chicken curry with all the accoutrements, including a peanut sauce. The setting is in a restored colonial house in Basseterre, with furnishing of Queen Anne reproductions, solid silver, flowers on the table and original artwork on the walls. Decor is close to perfection. *Moderate* for lunch; *expensive* for dinner.

★★★★ THE PALM RESTAURANT
Located in the heart of Basseterre, this is an oasis among the hustle and the bustle of a West Indian capital. Meander into the garden patio on the street level (enclosed by walls and tropical gardens) for a piña colada or the daily "house special" drink. Later head upstairs for lunch or dinner in Carl Fuchs's tropically-accented dining room splashed in a fresh green and white decor. Just a handful of his specialties include beef or pork sauteed in 12 spices with a special peanut sauce; a red snapper or grouper in a sauce of coconut milk; langouste Havana spiced in a Cuban-based Creole sauce. At lunch only, you can get a stateside hamburger (served, however, in Syrian bread) or a knock-wurst with sauerkraut. Owner Fuchs is so busy these days with his new property at Banana Bay, that he's hired June Mestier to be his "hostess with the mostess." *Moderate* to *expensive*.

★★★ THE OCEAN TERRACE INN
This is a favorite of both Kittians and visitors who call it the "OTI." Diners have a choice of a buffet or an à la carte menu. There's a commanding view of the harbor, the capital of Basseterre and, some nights, the lights of Nevis. Just a few of the special dishes that owners Leslie and Colin Perrera take pride in are fish cakes, langouste, plantains laced with a lime and butter sauce, breadfruit stuffed with spicy chicken. Before or after dinner, there's a choice of three bars, including the nautical Quarter Deck and the festive Carnival Bar where the Coronets Steel Orchestra band sometimes comes to play. Service, as in all of St. Kitts, is efficient and friendly, and you'll be glad you made a reservation. On the *expensive* side.

★★ THE ANCHORAGE
This is a beach restaurant that has stirred controversy, but if you're a lobster lover (of the warm-water langouste persuasion,) you'll benefit. Kittitians don't like the fact that the owners pay lobster trappers higher prices than those accepted throughout the island, but as a luncher (and this is basically a swim and lunch place), you'll benefit because you can almost always get a simply-grilled fish or a local langouste. Salads and sandwiches are also provided, but it's the lobster you'll remember along with the simple decor and the waves washing the doorstep. *Inexpensive* to *moderate*.

Also good for an informal dinner

★★ THE COCKLESHELL

This is a beachside resort that is under American management. The owners, Laddie Hamilton and Donald Plum, have taken over this property with verve and vigor. Like their neighbor at Banana Bay, they will arrange for guests to be picked up for the 20-minute powerboat spin from the capital of Basseterre. Obviously, you'll need a lunch or a dinner reservation if you're not staying at the inn so that Laddie and Donald will know when to pick you up and how many there will be for dinner at their formal Chinoiserie table where they preside as hosts and friends. The self-service bar operates on the honor system. The menu includes such Kittitian favorites as fish fresh from the sea; conch stewed, frittered or fried; langouste, when available, prepared dozens of ways; lamb and pork curries; and an occasional bit of imported beef. Low tea is served daily at 4 P.M. with tea, cake and cookies, often on the outdoor patio surrounded by bougainvillea, passion fruit, yellow bells, under an arbor of wood roses. *Moderate* to *expensive* when you consider the additional charge for the boat ride.

★★ THE FAIRVIEW INN

West Indian cuisine is noted here, served in an 18th-century great house with a French background. Owners Freddy and Betty Lam supervise the cooking. Their callaloo soup, pumpkin soup, main dishes and special Fairview papaya pie dessert are worth the time it will take you to make a reservation request and drive the short distance from town. Drinks are served in the greenhouse bar that offers a view of the Caribbean Sea and the offshore neighboring sister island of Nevis. A few of the special main dishes are pepper turtle steak; a snapper stuffed with lobster; side dishes of baked christophine or breadfruit. There's a weekly buffet, but check before you come. *Moderate* to *expensive.*

★★ VICTOR'S

"Victor," a born and bred Kittitian started out with five tables in the spring of 1981 and expanded to about 15 by 1984. Not a bad accomplishment for this man trained in some of St. Martin's finest restaurants. You will have to seek directions to find his tucked-away restaurant off Pall Mall Square in Basseterre, but it's worth it. The menu is strictly local: hot Johnny cakes with melted cheese; curried conch in a spiced Creole sauce; grilled red snapper or langouste in a secret sauce with dashes of local peppers. Of course, on certain days there's "goat water," that mixture of goat meat, spices, breadfruit and "cut spoon" (a soft dumpling) that makes a tasty stew, or steamed fish garnished with lime with butter. For dessert, count on fruit from the trees in Victor's home-grown garden, pineapple, mangos or a local pudding. The jolly waitress doing the serving is Flo, Victor's wife. *Inexpensive.*

★ FORT THOMAS HOTEL

This is a hotel that caters to groups as well as individual travelers. You might well start dinner with the "Fort Thomas Dipper," a soup with a beef-broth base, local vegetables, small dumplings and fiery spices. Then move on to a main course of grilled red snapper in a butter and lime sauce; peppered meat balls; or a broiled sirloin steak. All come with baked christophine, stewed breadfruit and crisp plantains. When it's available, local lobster is another house specialty. And what's always available is the charm and hospitality of the manager, Mrs. Velma Schwartz. *Moderate.*

Christophine is a type of island squash

BISTRO CREOLE

On Cayon Street, near Pall Mall Square in Basseterre. The menu is Creole, with local fish fresh from the sea in spicy, tomato-based sauce; a thick, very spicy pepper pot or chicken curry (West Indian style). Decor is crisp and clean done in green and white. *Inexpensive.*

THE BALLAHOO
On the second story on Bay Front, Basseterre. This is *the* in-town lunching spot ever since Peter and Marian Dupre (originally from England), edged open their doors in late 1982. Most everyone sits on the balcony: the better to people-watch as you wait for a toasted sandwich (fish filling; minced beef; cheese; tuna fish and cheese; conch) or one of the specials of the day— cobblerfish, blue parrotfish; red snapper; conch; lobster salad; fish pie, or the *special special,* a seafood hot pot that's a combination of fish, lobster and conch in a Creole sauce. The view from the balcony below is a mini-London, the Kittitian-size (but very pretty) circus, and Pretoria Gardens, with flowers and ferns. Cost is *inexpensive* to *moderate.*

Nightlife

Nightlife in St. Kitts has been limited, but, like everything that's happening on this island-on-the-move, new names will have been added to the nightlife scene by the time you arrive.

The Royal St. Kitts resort has the only *casino* in operation, but two more are under construction in the Frigate Bay condominium area. For now you can toss dice or watch the roulette wheel spin or challenge the one-armed bandits at the Royal St. Kitts.

If you're there on one of the three nights a week when Quintessence is playing, move upstairs to the Lakeside Lounge to listen to the upbeat, *disco,* international sound. The room is small, and candles provide the only light at the crowded tables; but the music and the action are fast. Try to find the Quintessence at the *Atlantic Beach Cabana.* Here you dance barefoot and carefree, and it's expected that everyone will mix and mingle in true island style. The Kittitian-style movin' and motion rock the oceanside patio where waves spash at your feet and an occasional raindrop may fall on your head. When a real rainfall begins, you run inside, and cluster with everyone else at the bar, where you'll still be able to hear the first-rate music of the Quintessence. Say hello to the leader, Bruce Skerritt. He pulled this five-piece band together, and he plays trombone, trumpet, drums and other instruments. Quintessence plays not only disco but creative music.

From Wednesdays through Saturdays, there's dancing action at the *Ocean Terrace Inn* in the Bitter End discothéque. On other nights the management makes arrangements with the Coronets Steel Orchestra, one of the Caribbean's best, to perform on the outside patio.

For the moment, that's about it. But remember, St. Kitts is an island in the spotlight, and other nightspots are bound to be open when you arrive.

Shopping

With the increase in visitors to St. Kitts this past year and the availability of hotel and condominium rentals, several boutiques have also opened. Even though shopping is not great, you will happen on some true finds, either local handicrafts or European imports. Kittitian handicrafts include embroidery done in Kittitian homes; basket work (often made by the blind); wooden furniture; a scattering of combs and bowls made from coconut shells. There are also goods from other Caribbean islands . . . Haiti's and St. Barts's are among the best. The introduction of art from the Spencer–Cameron Workshop and some boutique items imported from England and Scotland are worth more than a passing glance. Jewelry is mostly imported, as are French perfumes, but they're a few francs under the prices charged on nearby French islands! (You pay here in U.S. dollars or the local EC currency.)

On an island tour or a special trip out to the factory you're bound to discover *Caribelle Batik.* This cottage industry was started in 1976 by English-born Chris Dallow and two partners. Now over 60 people work here. The "cottage," however, is actually a 17th-century plantation great house near Old Road called Romney Manor where the batiks are created in the workshop attached to the showroom. You're welcome in both to observe or to buy. The complex batik process is explained by Chris or one of his workers in a series of steps . . . It begins in the showroom, where you'll read diagrams on the wall, continues to the actual making process in the workroom, where ladies trace designs on cotton (most of it is the special Sea-Island cotton) and then wax the parts that must be colored by a complex system (devised in Indonesia) of putting color on and leaving color off. Each piece is an individual work of art. Its value depends on the number of colors used. Designs for sale include men's, women's and children's items . . . a batik mural for your home ($100, maybe more); luxurious unisex dashikas for $35; skirts and tied tops for $35; T-shirts for about $10. Or you may choose to buy a length of cloth and create your own design. The Dallows opened a branch in Basseterre (as well as outlets in Nevis, St. Lucia and Antigua), but Caribelle Batik is still home port for serious shoppers.

The plantation is worth a trip even if you don't buy any batik — e.g. for the formal gardens

In the garden off the Palm restaurant is Martin Kreiner's *"A Slice of Lemon,"* offering sparkles and spangles well under North American and European prices. The price of 14K gold chains range from $35 to $1,008. When red or black coral, precious or semiprecious stones are added, the prices rise accordingly. Prices of perfume and cologne for men and women are surprisingly under those on neighboring French islands (their prices reflect a hidden tax levied on those départements). Although they amount to only a few dollars less, St. Kitts's prices are certainly less expensive than you would pay at home to buy (for men) Paco Rabanne; Gucci; Monsieur de Givenchy; Yves-Saint Laurent or (for women) a bottle of Opium; Chanel #5 or #19; Caléche; Shalimar; Ma Griffe; L'Interdit. A new china and crystal section has opened, offering the imported-best . . . Royal Copenhagen; Limoges china; Goebel crystal . . . even France's Gien, one-of-a-kind, handpainted plates.

You will get a very special treat when you visit Rosey Cameron and Kate Spencer at their *Spencer–Cameron Workshop* on the second story of Bay Front off the Circus. The team of Spencer and Cameron turn out personally-designed works of art; hand-colored prints of St. Kitts, Nevis, St. Barts and Antigua; plus signed lithographs, numbered to 100 editions, that sell for $15 to $30. Both artists silk-screen prints that are made into dresses (about $35); cotton shirts, tops and bikini sets: simple wraps incorporating individual designs. All their yardage comes from England's best, and it ranges in price from $35 to $70 a yard for cotton. For silk, the starting price is $25 a yard. The quality is of the highest, and keep in mind, each piece on print or canvas, is a work of art.

The *Losada Boutique* is located on Pall Mall Square, where owners Jossie and Jacques Cramer preside over their finds, many of them antiques. (M. Cramer's ancestor, A. M. Losada, was a watchmaker who worked at the site in 1843.) Their antiques mix island-finds and European imports: lamps, plates, decanters and silver- or gold-encrusted jewelry. They've added some hand-painted shirts, skirts and scarves from St. Kitts that are island specials.

The Cellar Shop in Basseterre is one of our favorites.

There are two other jewelry shops in Basseterre that are worth a look, *Higlyer* and *Kenneth Gums.*

Whatever else you buy, don't forget to pick up two special items . . . the *Motoring Guide to St. Kitts,* revised by Sunny Northrup, and a bottle of the hottest of the island *hot sauces,* the yellow or red pepper local flame. It's an acquired taste, but once acquired, it's unforgettable.

Sports

In general sports facilities in St. Kitts are not as developed as they are on some other islands. However, golfers should take heart. There's an 18-hole championship *golf* course at Frigate Bay at the Royal St. Kitts. Greens fees are $12 a round, and caddies get $3.00 per bag.

Robert Trent Jones designed it

Public *tennis* courts are available in St. Kitts. The Royal St. Kitts Hotel has four courts and The Cockleshell has one asphalt court for the use of its guests.

Beaches. The beaches are excellent. Plan on exploring more than one of them. The best? Frigate Bay, Conaree and Friars Bay. Some hotels have their own freshwater pools.

Boating, fishing and water sports can be arranged through your hotel or at the dock in Basseterre. The men of St. Kitts are known for their sailing expertise, and you'll enjoy watching them maneuvering their craft in the bustling harbor at Basseterre. During your beach strolls, be sure to keep alert for an unusual seashell to tuck into your suitcase as a souvenir.

The island's main *scuba* and *deep-sea diving* firm operates from the Ocean Terrace Inn. This is where Mike Ilkiw headquarters his Caribbean Watersports (a division of Scuba Consultants Associates in Ottawa, Canada). His partner, Robert Wagner, ususally presides over the Canadian end of the business. Their offerings range from the standard *resort scuba-diving course* (about $60 U.S.) to *full certification in scuba diving,* which takes time and money (about $150 U.S.). Discuss course offerings with Mike, and should you decide to go ahead, plan on a stay of at least six to ten days. They also offer *snorkel* and *boat excursions, beach picnics* and *moonlight cruises.* It's the kind of a thing to do when you're there.

Although *spearfishing* is legal in St. Kitts, do you really want to? If you decide to participate, you should make arrangements with your hotel chef to cook what you kill. St. Kitts Water Sports on Frigate Bay will make the arrangements as well as those for *waterskiing.*

The very British game of *cricket* is played from January to July. Annual regional tournaments are more than worth the watch.

Soccer is another local passion. The season extends from August to December. Competition features Kittitian, other Caribbean and international contestants. The stakes are high, and the players aren't friendly.

If you really want to challenge Lady Luck, there's the *casino* at the Royal St. Kitts. (Two more are on the way; they'll open when the major condominium developments are completed.)

THE HARD FACTS

Planning Ahead

Costs

The second and third most important things you'll take to St. Martin (or St. Maarten) are your proof of citizenship and your return airline ticket. The first is money . . . in any form.

St. Martin is certainly not the most expensive island in the Caribbean. But then it's not the most inexpensive. It is a *major* island of two nations, a crossroads, so to speak, to which guests come from all over the world. It has a very healthy economy based on the tourist industry. If you've just returned from a trip to Europe or the Far East, you'll call it cheap. If you're coming back from a stay with Mom and Dad in Denver, you'll clutch at your wallet.

The average high-season price in the better resort hotels is over $100 per day for a double room (European plan, no meals). Off-season prices can go down 30%–50%. Many hotels offer vacation packages at prices lower than the daily rates we've listed. Check your travel agent, airline or hotel representative to obtain the most up-to-date information. Other points to take into consideration when calculating costs: The Dutch add a 5% government tax to hotel bills, and hostelries on both sides of the island often tack on a 10%–15% service charge in lieu of tipping.

Lunch and dinner at the island's many first-rate restaurants cover a wide range of cuisine offered at a variety of prices. Fresh red snapper with white wine for two at the West Indian Tavern might be $50. A formal, excellent five-course French dinner with a fine French wine at Le Santal will run over $100 for two. We've categorized our restaurant selections as *inexpensive* ($10–$15 per person); *moderate* ($15–$25) and *expensive* ($30 and up per person).

However, both liquor and cigarettes are cheap here. Prices for these items run about the same on the French and the Dutch sides of the island.

Holidays and Special Events

Official holidays are: Good Friday; Easter Monday; Labor Day (May 1); Ascension Day; All Saint's Day (November 1); Whit Monday; Kingdom Day or Koninkrijksday (December 15); Boxing Day (December 26); New Year's

Day. Three of the biggest holidays are: St. Martin's Day (November 11); Coronation Day (April 30); and Bastille Day (July 14). All holidays are celebrated on both the French and the Dutch sides. The annual St. Maarten's Trade Winds Race is in the spring, and it gets bigger every year.

Travel Agents and Tour Operators

Major tour operators are: *French Side*—Arthur Frommer Charters; Caribbean Holidays; Adventure Tours; Cavalcade Tours; Flyfaire; GoGo Tours; and Butler Tours. *Dutch Side*—Arthur Frommer Charters; Cavalcade Tours; GWV Travel; Thompson Vacations; Tour-Dann International; Trans National Travel; Carefree David; Flyfaire, Inc.; Travel Impressions, Ltd.; and Caribbean Holidays.

Sources of Information

In the United States, contact the *St. Maarten Tourist Information Office* at 25 W. 39th St., 10018. For information in the United States on the French half of the island, contact the French West Indies Tourist Board at 610 Fifth Avenue, New York, N.Y. 10020 or The French Government Tourist Office at 9401 Wilshire Blvd., Beverly Hills, Cal. 90212. *In St. Martin,* the *St. Maarten Tourist Board* is right on the pier in Philipsburg, the capital on the Dutch side, and its representatives couldn't be more helpful.

Packing

After you've decided on a trip to St. Martin, *don't go out and buy a complete resort wardrobe.* The European-imported clothes for men, women and children are just too good to pass up buying here. By all means, take enough resort clothes, but underpack rather than overpack. And either leave room for the designer clothes you won't be able to resist buying, or pack an empty, soft-sided suitcase. Both the French and the Dutch sides of St. Martin are relaxed and informal, but no one walks around in a swimsuit unless he or she adds a cover-up. Sundresses or pants and T-shirts are the usual daywear for women; for men, it's light slacks or shorts with T-shirts. Evenings can turn surprisingly "Caribbean-formal" if you are spending a night at one of the major resorts or casinos. Women usually wear long, tropical dresses, and men may be required to wear jackets.

Documentation

U.S. and Canadian citizens need proof of citizenship (valid passport, birth certificate or voter's registration card) and a return or ongoing ticket. Visitors *landing* on the French side, do need a valid passport which is good for three months. Also, don't forget to bring (or show) a return or onward ticket.

The airport is on the Dutch side, unless you fly Air Guadeloupe from St. Barts or Guadeloupe

Getting There

American Airlines has daily, nonstop service from New York and Dallas; Pan Am returned its service in 1983, and Eastern has nonstop service from Miami and also offers connections from major U.S. cities. Sea and Sun Airlines made some splashes in January 1983 when it began New York to St. Martin service at $99 one way, but this was quickly brought more in line with the established fares. Most international passengers connect via San Juan on ALM, Prinair, Windward Islands or Eastern Airlines. Air Guadeloupe serves the French side of the island from St. Barts and Guadeloupe. Cruise ships from Miami, New York, New Orleans, and San Juan make regular calls at Philipsburg; and it's home port for Windjammer *Barefoot Cruises* on the 248-foot sailing ship *Polynesia.*

Formalities on Arrival

Customs

Casual and friendly, but lines can be long. Don't forget to keep the second half of your immigration card; it will be requested, along with a $5 departure tax, when you leave from the Dutch side, and 10 francs from the French side.

Money

The official currencies are the Netherlands Antilles florin on the Dutch side and the French franc on the French side, but the U.S. dollar is accepted everywhere. Major credit cards are also taken at most large establishments (hotels, restaurants, boutiques).

Getting into Town

Taxi is the only form of transportation available to your hotel. Although rental cars will be delivered to your hotel on request, it is not possible to pick one up at Juliana Airport (you can, however, drop it off there). All taxi fares are listed; prices have been set by the governments to the various hotels and the two capital cities on St. Martin.

Settling Down

Choosing a Hotel

Your *choice of a hotel* is strictly a personal thing. . . . Do you want golf and water sports from morning to night? The Sheraton Mullet Bay Resort, with its excellent 18-hole golf course and marina, is the answer. Do you want smaller, secluded splendor? The Oyster Pond Hotel. You really came to gamble? Maho Reef and Beach Resort; the Little Bay Beach Hotel; or head for the Seaview, which dropped a cool two million into a new casino, and has plans for future villas. Mullet Bay; St. Maarten Beach Club; or Great Bay Beach Hotel. You came to see and be seen, and money is no object? La Samanna on the French side. You want quiet, super decor and your own town house with a kitchen? Grand Case Beach Club.

There are also a number of *condominium apartments* that can be rented when their owners are away as well as quite a few fully-staffed *private homes and villas* on both sides of the island. All rent by the week or month. Three *reliable sources for information* on these: St. Maarten Rentals, N.V., "Pelican House," Beacon Hill, St. Maarten (Tel. 011–599–5–4330); St. Martin Assistance Service-Homes, 1995 New York Avenue, Huntington Station, N.Y. 17746 (Tel. 516–367–9444); and Eugenia Bedell, Caribbean Home Rentals, P.O. Box 710, Palm Beach, Fla. 33480 (Tel. 305–833–4454).

Choosing a Restaurant

There really are no bad restaurants in St. Martin. It usually comes down to what you desire to eat and what you feel your budget can afford. Prices may seem high, but don't forget that most food must be imported. We suggest booking your hotel European Plan (EP) or with breakfast (Continental Plan, CP) since eating out is one of the best vacation experiences.

Tipping

The general rule of thumb is 15%, but check your bill carefully to be sure service has not been added.

Learning to Cope

Business Hours.   Banks are open from 8:30 A.M. to 1:00 P.M., Monday through Thursday. On Fridays they add an hour in the afternoon from 4:00

P.M. to 5:00 P.M. Closed on Saturday, Sunday and official holidays. (See Shopping section for store hours.)

Electricity.   Depending on your hotel location (French or Dutch side), you may or may not need a converter and a transformer for electrical appliances. The Dutch side has 110 volt AC (60 cycle) similar to the United States; the French side is 220 volt AC (50 cycle), and a French adapter plug, converter and transformer will be needed.

Water and Drink.   All water in St. Martin is quite safe to drink; the hotels serve desalinated water. Remember that some of the tropical drinks served in the Caribbean can pack a potent punch. One-hundred-proof rum is one of the ingredients in such seemingly-innocent concoctions as Planters Punch; be careful, it can creep up on you.

and there's always good Dutch beer - Heineken or Amstel, primarily

Communications.   To telephone *St. Martin from the United States,* it's possible to direct dial. To reach the *French side,* dial 011–596 plus the number for station-to-station calls; 01–596 plus the number for person-to-person calls. For the *Dutch side:* 011–599–5 plus the number. Within St. Martin, when calling *the French side from the Dutch side,* dial 06 plus the French number. To call *the Dutch side from the French side,* dial 93 plus the Dutch number. *Information on the Dutch side* is 2211, 2277 or 2210; the number is 12 *on the French side.* Officially *mail* takes from three to ten days one way, airmail to the United States from St. Martin. Unofficially it's closer to ten days.

Language.   Everyone in *Dutch* St. Maarten *speaks English* as well as Dutch and, usually, several other languages. On the *French side,* many people speak some English, but it's helpful if you know at least a *few phrases in French.* After all, you are in France!

Medical Assistance.   There are two hospitals in St. Martin, one on each side of the island; and hotels will help any visitor needing an English-speaking doctor. There is also ambulance service for emergencies.

Getting Around
By Car
The best way to visit the island; otherwise many of the best beaches are inaccessible. Traffic moves on the right, and international road signs are observed. Avis, Lucky (National), Risdon, Holiday and other rental agencies have offices at *Juliana Airport,* in *Philipsburg* and at *major hotels.* Babi Richardson, St. Martin Auto and Hunt's Sunrise are headquartered in *Marigot.* In *Grand Case,* contact Cagan's or Esperance Car Rental. Most cars have automatic transmissions, and some are air-conditioned. Rates range from $30–$40 per day, with unlimited mileage. Gasoline is extra. Major credit cards are accepted, and foreign and international licenses are valid in St. Martin. Reservations are advised well in advance during the high season.

By Moped
Mopeds and motor bikes run about $18 per day and are available through Carter's that has offices across from Juliana and in Dutch Cul de Sac, just outside Philipsburg. Tel. 4251 or 2621.

By Taxi
A two-and-one-half-hour tour of the island by taxi costs $25 for two persons, $7.50 for each additional passenger. Such tours are best arranged through your hotel.

By Bus

Buses ply between Philipsburg, Cole Bay, Simpson's Bay, Mullet Bay, Marigot and Grand Case from 6:00 A.M. until midnight. The fare for the journey between Marigot and Philipsburg is 85¢.

ST. MARTIN/SINT MAARTEN TODAY

In 1648, a Frenchman and a Dutchman walked in opposite directions around the island, drawing the border where they met

St. Martin/Sint Maarten = One 37-square-mile island. Half French, half Dutch. Peaceful and welcoming.

If the world is in economic trouble, the word hasn't reached St. Martin. Here it's building and booming and bustling with tourists from around the globe.

Understandably so. . . . There are excellent air connections from almost everywhere; hotels to suit almost every individual desire; splendid beaches with all forms of water sports available; some of the best shopping in the entire Caribbean; nightlife that offers casinos and supperclub shows; discothéques; superb dining on both halves of this French and Dutch island; genuinely friendly people with two solid governments in back of them (French and Dutch).

This is an island where many travelers return again and again. It's also a good "jumping off" point by boat or air to the nearby, smaller islands of Saba, St. Eustatius, St. Barts, and Anguilla.

Arrival is by air at the Queen Juliana Airport on the Dutch side. Most experienced travelers coming from cold climates know the trick of carrying a lightweight ensemble and making a quick change in the plane before landing. It's worth considering since the 80°F. + temperatures that you'll be experiencing while you wait to clear customs and immigrations can make your first impression of St. Martin that of a sauna!

TOURING

Stretch. . . . And start your St. Martin day with a dash across sand that crunches beneath your toes. Dive . . . into gentle white-crested waves. Spread your beach towel or claim a beach lounge, and let the brilliant rays of the Caribbean sun soak into your being.

Stop! We know you came for a tan, but half an hour in the burning, hot Caribbean sun is all anyone should take the first day. And late morning is the perfect time to discover your chosen island. You can rent a car, a taxi with a driver, a motor bike or a scooter (the last a little dangerous because of questionable maintenance).

There aren't any museums or cathedrals on St. Martin. There isn't a sense of history or tradition. What does exist are bits of hidden history and lots of lush, tropical presence along with a seemingly-unending expanding economy . . . aided by European money and an infusion of American dollars . . . making it a commercial but highly interesting and international society. St. Martin is an island that doesn't make headlines. It just makes money and promotes for the traveler a sense of safety and security.

Many visitors begin their explorations on the Dutch side in the capital of Philipsburg. Hustle and bustle characterize the narrow, almost-nonexistent sidewalks, past or into the neighboring shops that feature goods imported from everywhere. The finest in jewelry? It's here. Cameras, stereo or recording equipment? They're here too. The latest designs from Europe? Take your pick from the countless boutiques lining Front Street that traces the harbor. Linens from China, liquor from everywhere. . . . They're all here at prices still called duty-free but which have risen considerably in the past few years.

When you see any of the many cruise ships that call on St. Martin dropping anchor, it's time to jump in your rented car or hire a taxi and head out of town. Cruise ships, though lovely to behold, mean the influx of even more people onto Philipsburg's shoulder-to-shoulder streets. Why stay when there's much more of this island to explore? You can always return when the cruise ship toots its farewell. (Most stay only a matter of hours.)

Drive the circular route around the island from the Dutch capital, Philipsburg, to the French side of St. Martin. The road climbs and hugs the coast offering a dramatic view of the neighboring islands of Saba, 'Statia and St. Barts. On a clear day, you can sometimes see St. Kitts and Nevis; and you can always see Anguilla.

According to history, it was at Cay Bay Beach that Peter Stuyvesant, the first governor of New Amsterdam (later to become New York), lost his leg in 1644 trying to wrest St. Martin back from the Spanish. This now peaceful island changed hands about 16 times between 1631 and 1816. Fort Amsterdam is in ruins now, but it's worth stopping there to reflect on the days when the English, the French, the Dutch and the Spanish played war games with these gentle islands.

The main—really the only road—takes you to Cul de Sac and reminders of the days of the big sugar, tobacco and indigo plantations of the 18th and 19th centuries. Nearby the island's oldest cemetery has faded gravestones from the 18th century, including that of Commander John Philips, the founder of Philipsburg. (It's also rumored that the ruins of the island's first synagogue are in Philipsburg in back of the West Indian Tavern, but no one knows for sure.)

After you pass Simpson Bay Lagoon with catamarans and yachts at quiet anchor, you will glimpse a famous ghost in the distance—the almost-completed but never-opened, majestic, resort, La Belle Creole at Pointe du Bluff. The dream of Claude Philippe and a consortium formed in the 1970s, it experienced financial and legal troubles. The furnishings and the fixtures were auctioned, and you'll see them in homes throughout St. Martin.

Take the turnoff at Sheraton Mullet Bay, and have a look at their 18-hole golf course and the neighboring Mediterranean-style villas of the Cupecoy Beach Club Hotel. This is also a good time for a swim-stop. Anyone can direct you to the sand dune that hides the wreck of a freighter permanently aground on a reef. You can walk through part of the rusting hull and feel the hovering ghosts.

If you haven't already photographed the signs at the French–Dutch border, this could be the time. Simple signposts proclaim "Welcome to Sint Maarten" on the Dutch side and "Bienvenue Partie Française" on the French side. That's it. You can "smuggle" all the cheese, wine and paté you desire.

You know you're in France when you reach Marigot, the capital of French St. Martin. It feels French. Two-story, faded-pastel gingerbread houses with wrought-iron balconies front the streets. The quai is alive with the sounds of the Saturday market and of the local fishermen returning with the catches of the day. Small restaurants front the quai, and there's a prosperous, purposeful attitude discernible in the people going about their daily tasks. Several of the best restaurants in St. Martin are here, and this might be the time to make a dinner reservation.

Then move on to Grand Case, a fishing village with a laissez-faire ambience and a lot of small restaurants, many "chez" . . . Rene, Max, Lolotte, which really are the homes of Rene, etc. Or lunch at the second-story Fish Pot on the ocean . . . very French Riviera with good fresh fish.

You'll pass through the village of Orleans, the earliest French town on the island. It's hard to find buildings of historical significance since the small,

Marigot is a pleasant relief from the activity of Philipsburg, a different world entirely

Grand Case is a charming little place

neat homes of today belong to owners who have kept them up without the benefit of plaques.

If you complete the circle route, you'll eventually be back in Philipsburg. Instead, take the alternate road designated by the sign that says "Oyster Pond" to one of the nicest hotels on the island. The owners welcome visitors for a drink, a meal or an afternoon at the Water Sports Center where they offer Sunfish sailing, snorkeling and windsurfing. (There is a fee for rental or lessons.)

Late afternoon . . . and now it's time for a game of golf or tennis, a snorkel expedition or relaxing moments on a private beach or patio. Your own special time of day.

Maybe you'd like to consider the "things to do" offered by the St. Maarten Tourist Board . . . beach bumming, they say. Plunging into water sports. Island hopping by flight or ferry to the nearby islands of St. Barts, Saba, 'Statia, Anguilla. Border crossing. Finally, project prowling. . . . "Visit the numerous condominiums developing on St. Martin. Choose an apartment, a parcel of land, settle down, and stay with us forever."

You just might.

Inside Information

Hotels

Smaller Hotels (on the Dutch side)

★★★★★ THE OYSTER POND HOTEL

Only 20 rooms but 20 individual rooms, each done in a striking Caribbean theme. The hotel itself is part castle and part fortress. Stone towers of natural rock herald your approach. A flag room at the entrance seems more like his majesty's entrance than a reception room. Waves splash onto a half-mile beach, and guests content themselves in beach chairs and gaze out to sea or at a Dutch flag that flutters atop a flagpole on Oyster Pond Peninsula, the closest point in all the Dutch colonies to Holland! Oyster Pond provides equipment and lessons in all water sports: snorkeling, scuba diving, sailing, waterskiing, fishing, and even the newest fad, windsurfing. There are two tennis courts on the property. *Cost:* $130–$195 per double MAP.

★★★ MARY'S BOON

Twelve rooms, each sequestered in a special Caribbean-styled home on Simpson's Bay. The showers are in breezeways, screened for privacy by thick foliage. It's almost like showering outdoors. The bar operates on the honor system, and the entire ambience is suggestive of being at a house party. Children under 16 are not invited. Dining is on a screened-in terrace over-looking the sea, surrounded by thick plants and brilliant flowers. *Cost:* $85 per single or double EP. No credit cards.

Smaller Hotels (on the French side)

★ LE PIRATE HOTEL

The casual kind of guest house you expect to find in the West Indies but seldom do. These ten, terraced rooms, a five-minute walk from Marigot, are simply furnished. The French cooking is superb, and guests are expected to turn up for breakfast or lunch in swimsuits. The heavy repeat business must mean they're doing something right! *Cost:* $125 double, MAP.

★ **PETITE PLAGE**
There are two main attractions here . . . the beach is secluded and spectacular, and you're within walking distance of the restaurants in Grand Case. The 12 apartments are very simply furnished but are more than adequate, and the cost is reasonable. *Cost:* $280–$420, EP by the week.

Larger Hotels (on the Dutch side)

★★★ **THE CUPECOY BEACH CLUB AND HOTEL**
This 129-room hotel resort is the first major property to be partly owned by a St. Maartener, Albert Fleming, and in 1983 they were still adding to two "wings" of co-op villas. The larger villas are split-levels with two and three spacious bedrooms, private sundeck, dropped living room, and kitchens with maid service. Here the feeling is luxurious and Mediterranean. An entertainment complex centers around the swimming pool and restaurants. *Cost:* $198 to $230 per double, EP; suites and one or two bedroom duplexes are also available.

a real showplace, in the best sense of the word

★★★ **LITTLE BAY BEACH HOTEL**
The oldest, large hotel in St. Maarten, it's still beautifully run and has an atmosphere all its own. The 1,000-foot sprawl of beach is the big attraction here. It spreads over a crescent bay. There are 120 rooms, most of which face the beach. The others surround the pool. There's a small Casablanca-like casino, where you expect Humphrey Bogart to appear at any moment. Meals are served indoors or out on the terrace, and occasionally there are steel-band jump-ups. The three tennis courts—lighted for night play—and a swimming pool are popular, but that spectacular beach draws the rave notices. *Cost:* $148 to $178 per double EP.

★★★ **SHERATON MULLET BAY**
L-a-r-g-e . . . 600 rooms and suites spread over 176 acres. Golfers are in heaven here. There's an excellent 18-hole course that's ranked among the best in the Caribbean. Jitneys circle the grounds, picking up guests as they go, but their timing might not be your timing. There are also 16 tennis courts; two swimming pools; a jogging course; classes in handicrafts; seven restaurants, including a Sweet Tooth ice cream parlor! The Hillside disco goes 'til dawn, which may be why the Sheraton people bill this as "the complete resort." *Cost:* $150 per double EP. $150 to $200 one-bedroom suite, double EP; $330, two-bedroom suite double EP.

★★★ **SINT MAARTEN BEACH CLUB HOTEL AND CASINO**
A five-story hotel that shares both sides of Front Street, the main shopping area of Philipsburg, and rooms on both sides look inward to flower-filled courts or outward to the ocean. Actually there are no "rooms"; instead, there are 86 beautifully-decorated suites, each with kitchenette, of one or two bedrooms named for the surrounding islands. The new restaurant and cocktail lounge opened last year, along with a casino already in full roll. Check management for a summer package that includes three nights on the French side at the Grand Case Beach Club for $299 per person; 7-nights, complete.
    In season 1984 cost: ocean front. $160 per double, EP; $140 per double, courtyard view, EP.

★★ **CARAVANSERAI HOTEL**
You can almost reach out and touch this 60-room hotel as your plane comes in for a landing. And that's about the only drawback. But most guests forgive the noise and concentrate on the beach life and the two swimming pools and

tennis courts. Dining is in an octagonal-shaped building at cliff's edge, open to waves splashing outside your window. Inside is a handful of metal sculptures by de Meyer. Many of the large sculptures in the original collection were destroyed by hurricanes of 1979. No children under 15. *Cost:* $150 per double EP. $190 per studio apartment EP. $400 for villas accommodating up to four persons.

★★ DAWN BEACH HOTEL AND VILLAS

These 155 units are called villas, but they're really well-designed studios, somewhat small, owned by absentee owners. When they're away, you can pay to play. Each has a king-size bed, two sofas and a kitchenette. By early 1984 the resort is expecting to complete a total of 254 units. The reception room is open and welcoming, with butterfly-print fabric on the walls as well as on the chairs and sofas. Beyond the balconies of the large Indonesian-styled restaurant topped by a pagoda roof is a swimming pool. A bridge over the river (or in this case, swimming pool) connects them and leads to a waterfall. The Dawn Beach, under the same management as the smaller Oyster Pond, reflects the same excellent, sophisticated taste, and the use of the Oyster Pond Marina with their water sports center is encouraged. *Cost:* $110 to $165 per double EP; $30 additional per person, MAP.

★★ HOLLAND HOUSE BEACH HOTEL

An in-town hotel in Philipsburg with 42 rooms and a rambling penthouse. It's Dutch-modern with Dutch management, genially presided over by Harry Schaminee. On weekends, the hotel has both string and steel bands, a manager's cocktail party, and a beachside barbecue. *Cost:* $110 to $130 per double, EP.

★ BELAIR BEACH HOTEL

All the suites are called "one-and-a-half" with bedroom, dining area, and kitchenette. All sport the Dutch-style furniture and have a bright Caribbean room decor. Another plus: all of the suites face the ocean: *Cost:* $220 to $240 per double, EP; $68 per additional double, MAP.

★ MAHO REEF AND BEACH RESORT

Only if you're a casino maven is this the place to be since there are year-round casino package flights. The 141 rooms are in modern decor. The casino is where the action always seems to be. Both nightly entertainment and dancing are offered. This is definitely the place to show off your new resort-wear. There are also a large swimming pool and four tennis courts. *Cost:* $120 to $174 per double, EP; suites, $205 per double, EP.

GREAT BAY BEACH HOTEL

This hotel with 225 rooms—the second largest on the island—books many conventions. About half the rooms face the ocean; the other half, landscaped grounds. There are several restaurants, several bars, and nightly entertainment in a supper club or theater-style mini-club. There is also a casino that's willing to take your money until 3 AM. *Cost:* $105 to $159 per double, EP; junior suites: $155 to $176 per double, EP.

Larger Hotels (on the French side)

★★★ GRAND CASE BEACH CLUB

Duplex two-bedroomed town houses and studio or one-bedroom apartments (49 in all), each decorated à la Palm Beach comfort . . . each with an individual decor. The club is right on the white-sand sprawl of Grand Case Beach, with gentle waves breaking offshore. The kitchenettes are the best equipped in the Caribbean, and the Acciani family stocks basics on request. It's more fun to buy from the boatmen who come in with their catches each day or to negotiate at the outdoor markets in the very French town of Grand

Case, a long walk or a short ride away. A new restaurant here, "Waves" made its own splash when it opened in 1983, and it's still riding the crest. *Cost:* $125 per studio, EP; $175, 1-bedroom, EP; $225, 2-bedroom, EP.

★ LE GALION

There's a total of 45 rooms here on the northeast coast, but the ones to request are the half that are "studios" with curtain effects separating bedrooms from sitting areas. There's an excellent beach, with one for nude bathing or sunning within strolling distance. The grounds are thick with bougainvillea and hibiscus, and there are tennis courts and a swimming pool. Several nights a week there's usually free transportation from the hotel to the casinos on the Dutch side. *Cost:* $110 to $150 per double, EP.

Somewhat secluded setting

★ PLM ST. TROPEZ BEACH HOTEL

The largest hotel on the French side, the 120-room PLM has all the amenities . . . air conditioning, patio or balcony, beach or lagoon view. All water sports are offered or, for the less energetic, a swim to the bar in the pool! There is also a tennis court, and it's an easy walk to the shops and restaurants in Marigot. At night, the small disco, Byblos, becomes very French, very St. Tropez. *Cost:* $97 to $111 per double, with American-style breakfast.

LA SAMANNA

An "in" resort that's in with everybody but us. Attitude here is unbending and unfriendly. Rooms are interesting and extremely well done in the white stucco, Mediterranean-style main house, but the most secluded and select facilities are the villas that sprawl at water's edge, to protect you from neighbors. It's always possible to dash from patio to ocean however. Drinks and dinner are served in the main house, where the decor is international perfection. At night, the bar becomes a very chic place and disco for very chic guests. One consideration may be that this is not a place to visit but to stay, and the pleasure derives from the name of fame that you carry. *Cost:* $300–$390 per double, EP; $644–$944, EP, two and three bedroom villas.

Restaurants

The official number of restaurants on the *Dutch* side of St. Maarten is over 100, but we're offering you a sampling of those tried and true where we're relatively sure the cook won't run away with the owner by the time you arrive!

Expensive means around $35 to $40 per person, without drinks; *moderate* around $25; *inexpensive* less than that.

★★★★ THE WAJANG DOLL

Front Street (Tel. 2687). One of the newest and hottest restaurants on the Dutch side of St. Maarten. One of the owners was born in Java. Authentic rijsttafel dishes. The ten tables are in a garden setting with brown and beige formally set tables, and the main room features both antique and modern Wayang puppets. Prices are surprisingly *moderate.*

★★★ ANTOINE'S

Front Street (Tel. 2964). A casually-elegant spot for lunch or dinner with an open patio overlooking the harbor. In the evening, a view of the stars and ship's lights is offered along with French and Continental fare. *Expensive.*

★★★ CAFE ROYAL

In the Royal Palm Plaza off Front Street. The word "cafe" hardly covers this major operation that imports items from Zabar's, Dean & Deluca and Balducci's in New York City. Grab the New York Times, your picnic basket and head to the beach! There's also E.A.T., where you can purchase marmalades, jams, jellies, hot sauces, from the Kittitian Kitchen on the nearby isle of St. Kitts; black peppercorns from Brazil; endless sweetnesses of Dutch chocolate and pastries from the manageress, Mrs. Ella Sluis. Cost is *moderate* to *expensive*.

★★★ CALLALOO
In a tucked-away cul-de-sac off Front Street. Currently *the* place to lunch on charbroiled steak, beef kebab, a special charbroiled chicken which is their specialty; quiche Lorraine; spinach quiche or just a thick roast beef sandwich. Cost is *moderate*.

★★★ LA GRENOUILLE
3rd Floor, Dutchman's Walk, at the head of Front Street (Tel. 2269). This informal, bayview restaurant also features French service and menu. Johnny, the cordial host, may suggest frogs legs, steak au poivre flambé in Armagnac or, in season, oysters from France. *Moderate*.

★★★ L'ESCARGOT
Front Street (Tel. 2483). A well-preserved, historic townhouse where the accent is on French and Continental cooking. Snails—served four different ways, quail with raisin sauce, caviar blinis, and duck in pineapple and banana sauce are among the specialties for lunch, dinner or late supper. *Moderate*.

★★★ WEST INDIAN TAVERN
Front Street (Tel. 2965). Food includes lobster that's lightly browned with melted butter, mayonnaise; thermidor in white wine simmered in a spicy Indian curry sauce; mornay that's gratinated in a cheshire cheese and cream sauce or cooked in white wine with grapes, shallots, etc.! Of course, there's also fresh fish and other shellfish . . . a shrimp kebab with banana, Indonesian peanut and red pepper sauce. Or perhaps you'd rather have a sirloin steak with Irish whiskey, fresh cream, and local thyme. *Moderate* to *expensive*.

Hollywood couldn't create a better Caribbean tavern

★★ CARAVANSERAI HOTEL
Maho Bay (Tel. 4218). Reservations are a must for authentic rijsttafel (Dutch for rice table), popular with local people and visitors, served every Wednesday evening. Their buffet is set up with about 35 Indonesian delicacies, some spicy, some not—beef, chicken, and shrimp curries, pork kebab with peanut sauce, pickled cucumber and other vegetable and fruit dishes. *Moderate*.

★★ CHESTERFIELDS
Great Bay Marina (Tel. 3484). A good ten-minute walk from the center of town, but it's on the modern marina, and the view of ship life is spectacular. Mermaids even "dance" on the wall murals. The atmosphere and the food are hearty and publike, with the emphasis on steaks, chops and some salads. There's also Seafood Caribbean that combines red snapper, shrimps and scallops. A special Sunday champagne brunch with steak and eggs and free-flowing bubbly bring the yachting crowd. It's open late, and the cost is *moderate*.

★★ HOLLAND HOUSE
Front Street (Tel. 2572). Informal setting overlooking a sprint of sand and ships at anchor in the busy Philipsburg harbor. Lunch usually features salads and sandwiches while dinner is a familiar blend of pepper steak; filet mignon sauced in mushrooms and cognac; lobster thermidor or possibly a red snapper meuniére. *Inexpensive* to *moderate*.

★★ PINOCCHIO'S
On the Main Square (Tel. 2166). This beachfront restaurant has three entrances, but the most unusual is through an old, arched Front Street cistern. Italian and American fare is served till the wee small hours in case you get a late-night pizza attack. *Inexpensive*.

★ PORTO FINO
Front Street. Another Italian nook right on the ocean—the place for home-made minestrone or made-to-order pizza. *Inexpensive.*

★ THE RUSTY PELICAN
Front Street (no telephone). Local fish, hamburgers and fresh salads in a nautical setting. At breakfast and lunch, small yellow sugar birds perch at the edge of your table hoping for crumbs or sugar. Happy hour, with free snacks, draws a good crowd from 5:00 PM–6:30 PM *Inexpensive.*

The *French* side of St. Martin offers about 40 restaurants, and it's hard to make a mistake in most of them. Those selected are some of our favorites, and several are among the best in the Caribbean.

Marigot

★★★★ LA CALANQUE
On the Wharf (Tel. 87–50–82). A sophisticated, formal dining experience. Jean Claude Coquin's excellent menu still lists longtime favorites—soupe de poissons (fish soup), lobster crêpes and crazy pineapple—but recipes have been added that are as creative as they are delicious. After midnight you'll begin to see young men in jazzy jeans as well as black tie wander into the bar. They're the chefs and waiters from other restaurants, and this is their meeting place. On the drawing board are plans for a complete redesign of this popular restaurant, so things may look quite different this winter. *Expensive.*

★★★★ LA VIE EN ROSE
Across from the Wharf (Tel. 87–54–42). Dine in an old townhouse, either in the very 1920s "parlor room" or outside on the tiny balconies overlooking the sparkling harbor lights. The ambience is sophisticated and international but the cuisine is definitely Gallic . . . canard, langouste, or poisson caught that morning . . . and the desserts, all made on the premises, should satisfy the most demanding gourmet's sweet tooth. *Expensive.*

★★★ CHEZ LOLOTTE
Rue de la Liberté (Tel. 87–53–38). Tropical garden setting on the sea deco-rated with fishing nets, buoys and a gazebo. The crabes farcis (stuffed land crabs), lambi à la provençale (conch provençale) and accras (codfish fritters) are memorable, as are traditional French recipes for snails, red snapper and luscious desserts. Reserve for both lunch and dinner. *Moderate.*

★★★ CHEZ RENE
Near the Lagoon Bridge (Tel. 87–52–80). Well-known for seafood and one of the island's best bouillabaisse. The menu features 15 different Caribbean fish, mostly caught by the owner himself. But the owner is originally from Bor-deaux, so his daily specialties include dishes from that region as well. *Expensive.*

★★★ LE SANTAL
Across Marigot Bridge (Tel. 87–53–48). If you decide francs are no object, you should visit this restaurant where superb classic French cuisine is pre-pared by young chef, Christian Doucet. From the moment you enter under the blue and white striped awning and sit down at your elegant pink and white table set with Christofle silver, fine crystal, silk flowers and hurricane-lamp candles, all is perfection. An elaborate four-page menu features such original Doucet creations as lacquered pineapple duck, marinated 24 hours and basted in a sauce of five fragrances. The wine list is extensive. Reserve for both lunch and dinner. *Expensive.*

★★★ MINI CLUB
Rue de la Liberté (Tel. 87–50–69). Ten years ago there were only two tables; now there are 70 and this old favorite is still growing. The latest addition is an on-the-beach "tree house" for the lavish, 35-dish, French–Creole buffet dinner held on Monday, Wednesday and Saturday evenings. *Moderate* to *expensive.*

★ LA MAISON SUR LE PORT
On the Harbor (no tel.). Especially nice for a "sundowner." As the sun sets into the sea, this spacious terrace is bathed in fabulous color, reflected from the purple and white awning floating above as well as on the walls of this old Case Creole (West Indian house). Not a gastronomic adventure, but the chef concocts eight different salads (all big enough to share) at lunch, and red snapper brochette and beef filet with bacon and tomatoes are among his dinner offerings. Open late. *Moderate.*

Grand Case

★★★★ AUBERGE GOURMANDE
Reservations must be made in person here because there is no telephone. Owner-chef Daniel Passerie's specialties are from his homeland, Burgundy. The decor of this small restaurant is French provincial; the cuisine is definitely gourmet. Open for dinner only and considered one of the best "finds" in town for moderate cost.

★★★★ LA NACELLE
Across from the Pier (Tel. 87–53–63). Charles Chevillot (the owner of New York's fashionable La Petite Ferme), continues his tradition of high-quality, fine French cuisine (some of it nouvelle cuisine), in this old gendarmerie transformed into a sophisticated, pink and white paradise. Lunch or sip an evening apéritif in the flower-filled garden under almond trees. Then dine inside, where the rustic decor features paintings and delicate silk scarves depicting colorful, hot-air balloons, each with its distinctive basket (nacelle) floating below. Reservations required for lunch and dinner. *Expensive.*

★★★ CHEZ MARTINE
Just outside of town (Tel. 87–51–59). New owners have maintained the elegant dining room decorated with velvet chairs, dark-green-and-ochre-striped walls and a lot of luxuriant plants. The interesting menu includes lobster grilled with basil, red snapper with fennel and flambéed with pastis, and such unusual appetizers as lemon stuffed with sardines in a creme fraiche sauce. Reservations are suggested both at midday and in the evening. *Moderate* to *expensive.*

★★★ HOA-MAI
(Tel. 87–56–85). A two story building in the heart of town that's a story in itself. This is "Spring Flower," St. Martin's first Vietnamese restaurant, now one of two. Authentic cuisine is served in an elegant, antique-furnished decor. Dinner only. *Expensive.*

★★★ L'HIVER
Grand Case. Very formal, very French, restaurant with classic French cuisine, new and expensive. It features Hoa Mai herself who appears nightly in ever-changing elegant costume.

★★★★ LA SAMANNA
(Tel. 87–51–22). Flower-decked terrace of the restuarant *La Samanna* in the formidable hotel of the same name. The head chef, Jean-Pierre Jury, is from Chauffailles and has several assistants. Dinner might begin with a terrine (de

langouste et mérou à la mousse de tomates or de foie gras de canard frais maison). The lunch menu offers several fish dishes (snapper, either meunière or amandine) or escalope de saumon mariné aux cives. It is also possible to have a simple salad or the lunchtime specialty, steak tartare, with a wine suggested by the maitre d'hôtel, M. Spartaco. Reservations always required. *Expensive.*

★★★ LA RHUMERIE
Colombier. The owner from Britanny, Yannic Le Moine and his wife, Francillette, have combined forces to create a Creole restaurant that is the talk of the French half of the island. It's housed in what was once a private residence between Marigot and Grand Case, and the excellent menu features poulet boucanne Creole (home-smoked chicken with baked papaya); steamed buttered cabbage hearts; conch in garden-grown herbs; curried goat; perhaps a salad of poisson coffre (a local fish). Cost is *moderate.*

★★★ SEBASTIANO
Grand Case (Tel. 87–51–87). Owners Claudio and Christine Gatto feature anitpasto al carrello . . . a pasta dish of fettuccine Sebastiano, Cannelloni all' Italiana . . . a main course of osso buco, picata al limone, fillets di orata alla livernese (red snapper with olive, capers, garlic and tomatoes), or maybe aragosta al gratin (local lobster). Cost is *moderate.*

★★★ WAVES
Perched atop a cliff at the Grand Case Beach Club in Grand Case (Tel. 87–53–90), "Waves" made waves when it opened in 1983, both for its decor and cuisine. The view is wrap-around beach by day for breakfast or lunch (dinner service until 11 P.M.). The menu features dishes such as stuffed grouper fillet à la creole; a succulently stuffed crab; curried goat or lamb; chicken breast Creole; and lobster (fresh from the sea). The wine list is extensive. Lunch or dinner are *moderate* to *expensive.*

★★ LE FISH POT
Tel. 87–50–88. A small but special place with groupings of tables inside and on an outside balcony hung over a spalshing sea. The accent here is on fish . . . fish caught that morning and prepared both Creole and French style. *Moderate* to *expensive.*

★★ RAINBOW
(Tel. 87–56–85). American David Hendrick and Dutch-born Fleur Raad built this casual terrace cafe on the beach themselves. Take a dip in the sea while waiting for your omelette and salad paysanne (a mixture of greens and vegetables). Dinnertime specialties include a good seafood brochette and the lights of Grand Case Bay. *Moderate.*

Nightlife
There are five discothéques in Philipsburg: Studio Seven in the Maho Reef Hotel; La Flirt; Hillside Disco at Sheraton Mullet Bay; Gus's Nightclub and Disco; and The Admiral's Club, but we're prejudiced and tell you to head directly for *The Admiral's Club.* Owned by Piet and Nanda Wip, who owned other discos in Europe before deciding to make St. Martin home. Their experience shows . . . The Admiral's Club could be in Paris, London or New York. It has mirrored walls, brass railings, white furniture, deep blue cushions and a floor that raises to show the "best" dancers. Two bars keep everyone swinging, and there are intermittent shows of limbo dancers, contortionists, voodoo and calypso. The sometimes-taped, sometimes-live music is the latest from the States and Europe. Hours: 10:00 P.M.–4:00 A.M.

All the large hotels have entertainment ranging from dancing to local steel bands to lounge entertainment at the *Cupecoy Beach Club and Hotel; Sheraton Mullet Bay; the Maho Reef's Studio Seven; Great Bay; Little Bay.*

The roll of the dice and the spin of the wheel are heard nightly . . . but only on the Dutch side of St. Maarten. The large hotels feature gambling . . . *Mullet Bay; Maho Reef and Beach; Little Bay Beach; Great Bay Beach; St. Maarten Beach Club.* The latest addition is a two million dollar casino at the old, now a sparkling, totally redesigned Seaview in Philipsburg.

The most popular evening pastimes on the French side? Lingering over a sunset aperitif on the harbor terrace of *La Maison sur le Port* . . . then a long, leisurely dinner at one of the many fine restaurants in Marigot or Grand Case. Much later, the more energetic might head for *Byblos,* the lively, late-night disco in the PLM St. Tropez . . . guaranteed to swing on through the night.

But the real "Evening in St. Martin" comes with a stroll along a private stretch of beach, lighted by a winking moon and a sky shot with stars scattering like slivers of the finest crystal.

Shopping

St. Martin is a shopper's treasure chest. Bring dollars. Bring florins. Bring francs. Bring credit cards. They're all accepted! The best from around-the-world—Cuban cigars; Danish stainless steel and silver; Dutch pewter and pipes; English woolens; Finnish jewelry and dinnerware; French champagne, gourmet foods, perfume, ready-to-wear and wine; Italian fashions and leather goods; Japanese cameras and electronic equipment; Scottish cashmeres and Swiss watches. It's all here. This entire island is a free port where bargain hunters can still save from 25%–40% over United States prices. The French side naturally excels in French products; the Dutch offers a better selection of Oriental imports, electronic equipment and cameras.

On the Dutch side, you can happily spend all forms of currency along Philipsburg's Front Street. On each side of this mile-long street are boutiques and more boutiques. No where else in the Caribbean is there such an abundance of designer names for men and women. Pierre Cardin, Christian Dior, Givenchy, Yves St. Laurent. It's endless.

One unquestioned favorite is *La Romana,* with two boutiques on Front Street and a branch at the Sheraton Mullet Bay Hotel. Two stories of the chicest clothes and the finest shoes and handbags imaginable from Italy and France. We'll never call them inexpensive . . . we'll just call them excellent. Their bikinis are the most unusual (and daring) this side of the Italian and French Rivieras, with bits of metal, beads and seashells, macrame. Each is a tiny work of art.

St. Trop' has two boutiques, and most of the designs are from France. Again, not inexpensive, but high-quality clothes and many "name" designers.

Finds that are now legal to bring back to the United States—as opposed to a few years ago—are the hand-embroidered linens . . . tablecloths; bedsheets and pillowcases; napkins. This beautiful work is done in the People's Republic of China and imported via Curaçao. It's all along Front Street, but three specialists in these linens are *New Amsterdam, Ram's* and *The Windmill.*

Should you decide on a few diamonds, emeralds, rubies or just a plain old gold chain or watch as your St. Martin keepsake, head to *Spritzer and Fuhrman; Little Switzerland; Le Carat; Jewels by Moritz* or *Gandelman Jewelers.* The choice is unlimited. Cameras, lenses, projectors, binoculars, tape decks, radio or stereo equipment interest you? There's an overwhelming display of makes and models at *Boolchand, Kohinoor, Taj Mahal* and *The*

St. Martin has some of the best designs in the Caribbean if you are fond of European fashions

Cellar. For items like these, it's a must to do some pre-departure homework and have your hometown discount store's price list in hand.

Looking for something guaranteed to be handcrafted in the Caribbean? Come to a full stop at *The Shipwreck Shop.* The choice includes macrame; basketware; wood carvings; Caribbean cookbooks; dolls; coral, shell and silver jewelry; steel-band records; straw hats; hand silk-screened clothing and yard goods. *Thimbles and Things,* one of the few shops of interest on Back Street, has original scenes of St. Martin and the Caribbean, designed and hand-painted on canvas by local artists for needlepointers.

Shopping Hours on the Dutch Side: 8:00 A.M.–12:00 P.M.; 2:00 P.M.–6:00 P.M., Monday-Saturday. Some larger stores *may* open on Sundays or holidays when there's a cruise ship in.

The *French side* is the place for perfumes and beauty products from France, crystal, fine jewelry and finer French clothes.

It really doesn't matter where you buy your perfume since prices are similar in all boutiques, but the largest selections are at *Vendome,* with every French scent imaginable and an equally large choice of accessories and crystal . . . check out the Lalique. It's fast becoming a valuable rarity, and even the largest stores have to order it from France over a year in advance.

Shopping in Marigot is fairly simple when you discover that most of the best boutiques are along rue de la République, rue de la Liberté and in three convenient new shopping arcades: *Port la Royale, Palais Caraibe* and the smaller *Galerie Périgourdine.* Everything is somehow much more relaxed here, browsing is encouraged and you never have to worry about overcrowding because a cruise ship is in port. It just doesn't happen on this side of the island.

Along rue de la Liberté, *Printemps,* a mini-department store where, if you don't mind picking through items not of interest, you'll find many that are (at very good prices), including cosmetics, jewelry, silk scarves and lingerie. *Shore Brothers* has its own exclusive collection of Soleiado's Provençal cotton prints that have been turned into distinctive sportswear and accessories. Upstairs, *Cannelle* offers Courreges everything . . . the whole summer and winter line . . . clothing to umbrellas. (Get some chic ski clothing early?)

In Galerie Périgourdine, just across from the Post Office, *Sandrine* features designs by Ted Lapidus, Hermani and Carel for both men and women. *Vanessa* features things for cuisine . . . Porcelaine de Paris, cheese plates and platters, breakfast sets, soufflé dishes . . . and tiny bikinis and children's clothes.

Just around the corner on rue Félix Eboue is *Le Carrousel,* which not only carries resortwear, charming children's togs and little gifts to tuck into suitcase corners, but its American owners have cleverly displayed the menus for every restuarant in French St. Martin. Decide on lunch or dinner as you shop!

Port la Royale is the largest of the new arcades. Here *Fiorucci* has the latest, wildest clothes from Europe at matching prices; *Serge and Laurence* design and make their own colorful, lightweight clothing. *La Boutique Elle* concentrates on elegant, eccentric, extravagant Italian fashions, shoes and leather bags (these sell by the armful at $60–$200). *La Bastringue* has a great variety of summerwear from Emmanuelle Khanh, Kenzo, Michel Bachot, Dorothée Bis and other quality French labels.

The *Palais Caraibe* gallery is the place for jewelry . . . *Henri Poincot's* exclusive designs—precious and semiprecious stones set in heavy 18K gold; and *Point d'Or* for smaller, less expensive bijoux. *Pomme* is a gift shop with some interesting big, soft sculpture dolls and you'll find Lanvin, Nina Ricci and Esterel costume jewelry among the ceramics and crystal at *L'Orchidee.*

Shopping hours on the French side: 9:00 A.M.–12:00 P.M. or 12:30 P.M.; 2:00 P.M.–6:00 P.M., Monday-Saturday. Stores at Port la Royal open at 3:00 P.M.

Sports
Beaches
Thirty-six perfect, seldom crowded white sand beaches . . . coves so secluded they are accessible only by boat; broad expanses reached by dirt roads off the main highway. On the French side there's a "plage naturelle" (nude beach) at Orient; Ilet de Pinel, a tiny island off French Cul de Sac, is perfect for picnics and snorkeling. It can be reached by bargaining with a passing fisherman.

Golf
Mullet Bay Beach Hotel on the Dutch side has the only course on the island . . . 18 holes plus putting green, driving range, pro shop, lessons, and locker facilities. Guests from other hotels are welcome if starting times are open (Tel. 2015). Greens fee: $12, guests; $15, nonguests. Club rental: $8 a day; $40 a week. Cart rental: $16 a day (and carts must be used).

Fishing
Albacore, amberjack, barracuda, bonito, dolphin (nothing whatsoever to do with porpoise, which is a mammal), grouper, marlin, snapper, tuna, wahoo and yellowtail are just a few of the possible candidates for catching in this part of the Caribbean. Fishing charters are available for half ($150) or a full day ($250). This price is for four passengers; usually $15 each additional person. Tackle, bait, food and an open bar are generally included. The *Lilymar* is one 33-foot cabin cruiser that can be recommended out of Marigot; and *Bonhomme Richard, The Fishing Machine, Wendy III, Natalie, Kay G* and *Lupo,* a few of the many charter boats docked in Philipsburg. For the most current information, contact your hotel, the Tourist Office, Wathey Travel, Little Pier Boat Charter Booth or Bobby's Marina in P'Burg; in Marigot, the harbor and sometimes La Calanque will be able to help.

Sailing
Most beach hotels rent Sailfish, Sunfish and Windsurfers by the hour as well as give instruction in handling these small craft. But for a small taste of what sailing's all about, try "Sight 'Sea'ing" . . . around peaceful Simpson's Bay, the Caribbean's largest lagoon . . . or out on the open sea to one of the many nearby islands. Your hotel or the Tourist Office should have a list of excursion boats and their schedules; both change frequently. The following have been reliable in the past: Day trips to St. Barts can be made on several super-sized catamarans, the Maho, or El Tigre, both of which serve liquids and light lunches, for about $40 per person. (TIP: Those who have even the slightest tendency to seasickness should take Triptone—Dramamine tends to make one too drowsy to enjoy the trip—as this channel can get choppy!) Once in Gustavia, St. Barts's capital, there's a minibus tour of the island, lunch overlooking the harbor and free time for shopping or a swim. On the return sail, the captain and the crew serve hors d'oeuvres and cocktails. Docking back in Philipsburg is about 6:00 P.M.

Larry Berkowitz's *Maison Maru* leaves the Town Pier at 9:30 A.M. daily . . . *skirts around the shore* lined with elegant hotels and private villas then puts *into Marigot* for an hour or two. A lavish buffet spread and wine are ready when passengers reboard this 57-foot catamaran . . . then it's a short sail to a swim at a secluded beach near Grand Case . . . and Rum Punches or soft drinks heading back to Philipsburg. Arrival time is generally about 5:00 P.M. Capacity: 25 passengers. Cost: $30 per person. *La Cyprae,* a 60-foot schooner, is anchored at the PLM St. Tropez on the French side. Full *day sails to*

Tintamar, Anse Marcel or Anguilla cost $45 per person with a memorable lunch and plenty of time for sunning, snorkeling or exploring these small, unspoiled islands. Shorter, half-day sails are $25 per person without lunch.

Scuba Diving and Snorkeling

The *Maho Water Sports Center* at the Sheraton Mullet Bay Hotel; *Beach Bums* at Simpson's Bay; *Water Sports Unlimited* at the St. Maarten Beach Club; *Oyster Pond Marina* at the Oyster Pond Hotel and the water center at the PLM St. Tropez all offer qualified instructors, diving trips and the latest gear. Water temperature is about 70° F., so wet suits are not needed; visibility runs from 75–100 feet. One of the biggest attractions is *The Proselyte,* a British man-o-war, which sank in 1801 on a reef just a mile offshore. Most major hotels, in addition to the sports centers, rent snorkeling equipment.

Tennis

At last count 30 courts at hotels around the island (16 at Sheraton Mullet Bay Resort alone). Fees for both guests and non-guests are $5 per hour; the most expensive fee is for courts lit for night play.

Other Water Sports

Some beachside hotels offer waterskiing ($25 per hour) and the Maho Sports Center at the Sheraton Mullet Bay Resort and Watersports Unlimited at the St. Maarten Beach Club, offer jet skiing, catamaran and trimaran day trips; Sunfish or Sailfish rentals.

Index

Admiral's Inn hotel, Antigua, 25
Admiral's Inn, restaurant, Antigua,
    32
Almond Tree restaurant, Jamaica,
    156
Altos de Chavon hotel, Santo
    Domingo, Dom. Rep., 79
Anchorage Hotel, Antigua, 30
Anchorage restaurant, St. Kitts, 237
Anguilla 6–15
    Climate, 6
    Costs, 6
    Documentation, 7
    Holidays, 6
    hotels 10–12
    Information, 7
    Money, 7
    Nightlife, 13–14
    Packing, 7
    Restaurants, 12–13
    Tipping, 7
    Shopping, 14
    Touring, 9
    Transportation, 7
Anguilla Holiday Spa hotel,
    Anguilla, 11
Antigua, 16–40
    Climate, 17
    Costs, 16
    Documentation, 18

Formalities, 18
Holidays, 17
Hotels, 25–31
Information, 17
Money, 18
Nightlife, 36
Packing, 18
Restaurants, 31–36
Settling Down, 18–19
Shopping, 36–38
Sports, 38–40
Tipping, 19
Tour Operators, 17
Touring, 21, 23–25
Transportation, 18, 20
Antigua Beach Hotel, Antigua, 28
Antoine's restaurant, St. Martin,
    251
Aquarium restaurant, Anguilla, 13
Atlantis Hotel restaurant, Barbados,
    57
Au Port restaurant, St. Barts, 215
Au Vieux Port restaurant, Guade-
    loupe, 119
Auberge de l'Anse Mitan hotel, Mar-
    tinique, 175
Auberge de la Vieille Tour hotel,
    Guadeloupe, 113
Auberge de la Vieille Tour
    restaurant, Guadeloupe, 117

261

Auberge du Grand Large hotel,
Guadeloupe, 113
Auberge du Grand Large restaurant,
Guadeloupe, 119
Auberge Gourmande restaurant, St.
Martin, 254
Autour du Rocher hotel, St. Barts,
213
Autour du Rocher restaurant, St.
Barts, 215

Bach Lien restaurant, Antigua, 35
Bagatelle Great House restaurant,
Barbados, 55
Bahia Beach Resort hotel, Samana,
Dom. Rep., 81
Bakoua Beach hotel, Martinique,
175
Ballahoo restaurant, St. Kitts, 239
Banana Bay Beach hotel, St. Kitts,
234–235
Banana Bay restaurant, St. Kitts,
236–237
Barbados, 41–59
Climate, 41
Costs, 41
Documentation, 43
Formalities, 43
Holidays, 42
Hotels, 43, 49–54
Information, 42
Map, 45
Money, 43
Nightlife, 57
Packing, 42
Restaurants, 44, 54–57
Settling Down, 43–44
Shopping, 57–58
Sports, 58–59
Tipping, 44
Tour operators, 42
Touring, 46–49
Transportation, 44, 46
Barbados Beach Village hotel, Bar-
bados, 54
Barrel Stay, 12

Barrymore Hotel, Antigua, 28
Basil's Beachbar restaurant, Musti-
que, 1
Basseterre, St. Kitts, 231–232, 233
Bayview Apartments hotel, Anguilla,
11
Beck hotel, Haiti, 136
Beefeater restaurant, Bonaire, 66
Belair Beach hotel, St. Martin,
250
Bistro Creole restaurant, St. Kitts,
238
Bistro des Amis restaurant, Bonaire,
66
Blue Horizons Cottage hotel,
Grenada, 96
Blue Mountain Inn, Jamaica, 160
Blue Waters Beach hotel, Antigua,
26
Blue Wave restaurant, Saba, 205
Bonaire, 60–71
Climate, 60
Costs, 60
Documentation, 61
Holidays, 60
Hotels, 65–66
Information, 60
Money, 61
Nightlife, 68
Packing, 61
Restaurants, 66–68
Settling Down, 61
Shopping, 69–70
Sports, 70–71
Tipping, 61
Tour Operators, 60
Touring, 63–65
Transportation, 61
Borinque Snack restaurant, Bonaire,
68
Boulangerie Rotisserie-Hediard
restaurant, St. Barts, 215
Brasserie Asserie restaurant, St.
Barts, 216
Brasserie St. Georges restaurant,
Guadeloupe, 120

Bridgetown, Barbados, 46
  museums, 46
Brother B's restaurant, Antigua, 34
Brown Sugar restaurant, Barbados,
  55
Buccaneer's Creek Club
  Mediterranee, Martinique, 176

Cafe Americas restaurant, Santo
  Domingo, Dom. Rep., 84
Cafe au Lait restaurant, Jamaica,
  159
Cafe Royal restaurant, St. Martin,
  251
Cage aux Folles, La, restaurant, Bar-
  bados, 54
Calabas Terrace restaurant, Bonaire,
  67
Calabash hotel, Grenada, 95
Calabash restaurant, Grenada, 97
Calabash restaurant, Jamaica, 157
Callalou restaurant, St. Martin, 252
Cap Haitien, Haiti, 133
Captain's Carvery restaurant, Barba-
  dos, 56
Captain's Quarters hotel, Saba, 204
Captain's Quarters restaurant, Saba,
  204
Caraibe Cat-Chez Mimi restaurant,
  Guadeloupe, 120
Caravanserai hotel, St. Martin, 249–
  250
Caravanserai Hotel restaurant, St.
  Martin, 252
Carib Inn hotel, Bonaire, 66
Casa de Campo hotel, La Romana,
  Dom. Rep., 80–81
Casanova restaurant, Jamaica, 157
Castelets restaurant, St. Barts, 214
Castle Harbour Club and Casino
  hotel, Antigua, 30
Charela Inn hotel, Jamaica, 153
Charela Inn restaurant, Jamaica, 159
Charlestown, Nevis, 188
Chateaubriand restaurant, Martini-
  que, 179

Chesterfield's restaurant, St. Martin,
  252
Chez Bach Lien restaurant, Guade-
  loupe, 117
Chez Clara restaurant, Guadeloupe,
  122
Chez Dollin-Le Crepuscule res-
  taurant, Guadeloupe, 123
Chez Francine restaurant, St. Barts,
  216
Chez François restaurant, Santo
  Domingo, Dom. Rep., 84
Chez Gerard restaurant, Haiti, 138
Chez Honore Aux Fruits de Mer res-
  taurant, Guadeloupe, 120
Chez Jacki restaurant, St. Barts,
  216
Chez Jacqueline-aux-Arcades res-
  taurant, Guadeloupe, 118
Chez Lolotte restaurant, St. Martin,
  253
Chez Lydie restaurant, Guadeloupe,
  118
Chez Mally Edjam restaurant, Marti-
  nique, 180
Chez Martine restaurant, St. Martin,
  254
Chez Odette restaurant, Guade-
  loupe, 121
Chez Paul restaurant, Guadeloupe,
  123
Chez Rene restaurant, St. Martin,
  253
Chez Robert restaurant, Jamaica,
  157
Chez Sidonie restaurant, Martinique,
  179
Chibi Chibi Terrace restaurant,
  Bonaire, 67
China Gardens restaurant, Antigua,
  35
Chinese Restaurant, Saba, 205
Cinnamon Hill and Beach Club
  hotel, Grenada, 95
Cinnamon Reef hotel, Anguilla, 11
Cliff Dwellers hotel, Nevis, 194

Cliff Dwellers restaurant, Nevis, 195–196
Club Med, Haiti, 134
Club Mediterranée hotel, Punta Cana, Dom. Rep., 82
Club Mediterranée, Caravelle, hotel, Guadeloupe, 113–114
Club Mediterranée, Fort Royal hotel, Guadeloupe, 114
Club Nautico los Charmícos, La Romana, Dom. Rep., 81
Club Nautique restaurant, Martinique, 181
Cobblers Cove hotel, Barbados, 50
Cockleshell Inn restaurant, 32
Cockleshell hotel, St. Kitts, 235
Cockleshell restaurant, St. Kitts, 238
Coconut Creek Club hotel, Barbados, 52
Coconut Cove hotel, Jamaica, 153
Coconut Cove restaurant, Jamaica, 159
Colombo's restaurant, Antigua, 32
Colony Club hotel, Barbados, 49
Copper and Lumber Store hotel, Antigua, 27
Coral Reef Club hotel, Barbados, 51
Corito Beach Cottages hotel, Anguilla, 11
Cormier Place hotel, Haiti, 135
Côté Jardin restaurant, Haiti, 138
Cotton House hotel, Mustique, 1
Couples hotel, Jamaica, 155
Courtleigh hotel, Jamaica, 153
Crane Beach hotel, Barbados, 51
Crane Beach restaurant, Barbados, 55
Cranston's Antique Inn hotel, Saba, 205
Crew restaurant, Martinique, 178
Croney's Old Manor Estate hotel, Nevis, 193
Croney's Old Manor Estate restaurant, Nevis, 194
Cul de Sac hotel, Anguilla, 10
Cul de Sac restaurant, Anguilla, 12

Cupecoy Beach Club and Hotel, St. Martin, 249
Curtain Bluff hotel, Antigua, 29
Curtain Bluff restaurant, Antigua, 31–32

D'Agostini restaurant, Santo Domingo, Dom. Rep., 83
Darcy's at Kensington Court restaurant, Antigua, 35
Dawn Beach Hotel and Villas, St. Martin, 250
Den Laman restaurant, Bonaire, 67
Désirade, Guadeloupe, 111
Diamant les Bains hotel restaurant, Martinique, 180
Diamont-Novotel hotel, Martinique, 176
Diplomat restaurant, Jamaica, 158
Dominican Republic, 72–87
    Formalities, 73
    Holidays, 72
    Hotels, 79–82
    Information, 72
    Map, 75
    Money, 73
    Nightlife, 85
    Packing, 72–73
    Restaurants, 82–85
    Settling Down, 73
    Shopping, 85–86
    Sports, 86–87
    Touring, 74–79
    Transportation, 73
Dubarry's restaurant, Antigua, 33

Eastry House hotel, Barbados, 52–53
Eden Rock hotel, St. Barts, 212
Eden Rock restaurant, St. Barts, 216
18 Carat restaurant, Antigua, 35
El Alcazar restaurant, Santo Domingo, Dom. Rep., 83
El Bodegon restaurant, Santo Domingo, Dom. Rep., 84

El Caserio restaurant, Santo
Domingo, Dom. Rep., 84
El Castillo del Mar restaurant, Santo
Domingo, Dom. Rep., 83
El Portillo hotel, Samana, Dom.
Rep., 82
El Raco restaurant, Martinique, 177–
178
El Rancho hotel, Haiti, 135
English Harbour, Antigua, 21–22,
24–25
Escale a Saigon restaurant, Guade-
loupe, 116
Extremadura restaurant, Santo
Domingo, Dom. Rep., 83

Fairview Inn hotel, St. Kitts, 235–
236
Fairview Inn restaurant, St. Kitts,
238
Falmouth Harbour Beach Apart-
ments hotel, Antigua, 28
Filao hotel, St. Barts, 212–213
Fish Trap, the, restaurant, Anguilla,
12
Flamboyant restaurant, St. Barts, 216
Flamingo Beach hotel, Bonaire, 65
Folie Plage-Chez Prudence
restaurant, Guadeloupe, 121
Foolish Fish restaurant, Barbados, 56
Fort-de-France, Martinique, 171–
172
Fort Thomas Hotel restaurant, St.
Kitts, 238
Frantel hotel, Guadeloupe, 114
Frantel hotel, Martinique, 177
Front Porch restaurant, Jamaica, 158

Galley Bay Surf Club hotel, Antigua,
26
Georgian House restaurant, Jamaica,
158
Georgian House restaurant, St. Kitts,
237
Glitter Bay hotel, Barbados, 50
Golden Lemon hotel, St. Kitts, 234

Golden Lemon restaurant, St. Kitts,
236
Golden Rock Estate hotel, Nevis,
192
Golden Rock Resort hotel, St. Eusta-
tius, 224
Golden Rock restaurant, Nevis, 196
Grand Case Beach Club hotel, St.
Martin, 250–251
Grand Hotel Oloffson, Port-au-
Prince, Haiti, 134
Great Bay Beach hotel, St. Martin,
250
Greenhouse restaurant, Barbados,
56
Greensleeves hotel, Barbados, 54
Greensleeves restaurant, Barbados,
56
Grenada, 88–100
Climate, 88
Costs, 88
Documentation, 89
Formalities, 89
Holidays, 88
Hotels, 90, 94–96
Information, 89
Map, 45
Money, 89
Nightlife, 98
Packing, 89
Restaurant, 90, 96–98
Settling Down, 90
Shopping, 98–99
Tipping, 90
Tour Operators, 88
Touring, 92–94
Transportation, 89, 91
Guadeloupe, 101–128
Climate, 101
Costs, 101
Documentation, 104
Formalities, 104
Holidays, 102
Hotels, 104, 112–115
Information, 102
Map, 103

Money, 104
Nightlife, 123–124
Packing, 103
Restaurants, 105, 115–123
Settling Down, 104–105
Shopping, 124–126
Sports, 126–128
Tipping, 105
Tour Operators, 102
Touring, 107–112
Transportation, 104, 106
Gustavia, St. Barts, 210–211

Habitat hotel, Bonaire, 66
Habitat restaurant, Bonaire, 67
Habitation Leclerc Resort and Casino hotel, Haiti, 135
Haiti, 129–143
Costs, 129
Formalities, 130
Holidays, 129
Hotels, 134–138
Information, 130
Map, 75
Money, 130
Nightlife, 140
Packing, 130
Restaurants, 131, 138–139
Settling Down, 131
Shopping, 140–141
Sports, 142
Touring, 132–134
Transportation, 130, 131
Halcyon Cove Beach Resort and Casino hotel, Antigua, 30
Halcyon Reef Resort hotel, Antigua, 31
Half Moon Bay Hotel, Antigua, 29
Half Moon Club hotel, Jamaica, 154
Half Moon Hotel Club House Grill restaurant, Jamaica, 157
Hamak hotel, Guadeloupe, 112
Harbour View restaurant, Anguilla, 13
Hedonism II hotel, Jamaica, 155–156

Hermitage hotel, Nevis, 193
Hibiscus hotel, St. Barts, 213
Hibiscus Lodge hotel, Jamaica, 154
Hoa-Mai restaurant, St. Martin, 254
Holiday Inn hotel, Guadeloupe, 114
Holland House Beach hotel, St. Martin, 250
Holland House restaurant, St. Martin, 252
Horseshoe Bay hotel, Grenada, 96
Horseshoe Bay Hotel restaurant, Grenada, 97
Hostal Nicolas de Ovando hotel, Santo Domingo, Dom. Rep., 80
Hotel Bonaire and Casino, Bonaire, 66
Hotel Bonaire and Casino-restaurant, Bonaire, 68
Hotel Santo Domingo, Santo Domingo, Dom. Rep., 80
Husavik restaurant, Nevis, 194

Ibo Beach Club hotel, Haiti, 137
Ibo Lele hotel, Haiti, 136
Il Buco restaurant, Santo Domingo, Dom. Rep., 82–83
Inn Beach Club at English Harbour, the, hotel, Antigua, 27

Jack Tar Village hotel, La Romana, Dom. Rep., 81
Jamaica, 144–164
Climate, 144
Costs, 144
Documentation, 145
Formalities, 146
Holidays, 144
Hotels, 151–156
Information, 145
Map, 148
Money, 146
Nightlife, 160–161
Packing, 145
Restaurants, 156–160
Settling Down, 146

Shopping, 161–163
Sports, 163–164
Tipping, 146
Tour Operators, 145
Touring, 148–150
Transportation, 145–146, 147
Jamaica Hill hotel, Jamaica, 152
Jamaica Hilton hotel, Jamaica, 154
Jamaica Inn hotel, Jamaica, 151
Jamaica Pegasus hotel, Jamaica, 154
Jardin de Jade restaurant, Santo
    Domingo, Dom. Rep., 83
Jolies Eaux, Les, hotel, Mustique, 1

Kaliko-Beach Club hotel, Haiti, 136
Kinam restaurant, Haiti, 139
King Arthur's restaurant, Jamaica,
    158
Kingston, Jamaica, 148–149

L'Albatros restaurant, Guadeloupe,
    115
L'Amour en Fleurs restaurant,
    Guadeloupe, 118
L'Arbre a Pain restaurant, Guade-
    loupe, 121
L'Auberge du Boukarou, Guade-
    loupe, 117
L'Escalier restaurant, Martinique,
    178
L'Escargot restaurant, St. Martin, 252
L'Etoile restaurant, St. Eustatius, 225
La Bahia restaurant, Santo Domingo,
    Dom. Rep., 83
La Baie d'Along restaurant, Martini-
    que, 179
La Belle Creole restaurant, Grenada,
    97
La Belle Epoque restaurant, Haiti,
    138
La Cage, 54
La Calanque restaurant, St. Martin,
    253
La Canne a Sucre restaurant, Guade-
    loupe, 115
La Cascade restaurant, Haiti, 138

La Chaubette restaurant, Guade-
    loupe, 117
La Cremaillere restaurant, St. Barts,
    217
La Creole-Chez Violetta restaurant,
    Guadeloupe, 117
La Factorerie restaurant, Martinique,
    181
La Grand'Voile restaurant, Martini-
    que, 177
La Grenouille restaurant, St. Martin,
    252
La Jacmelienne restaurant, Jacmel,
    Haiti, 139
La Jacmelienne sur Plage hotel,
    Haiti, 136
La Lanterne restaurant, Haiti, 138
La Louisiane restaurant, Guade-
    loupe, 119
La Maison sur le Port restaurant, St.
    Martin, 254
La Mandiana retaurant, Guadeloupe,
    121
La Marmite restaurant, Guadeloupe,
    119
La Nacelle restaurant, St. Martin,
    254
L'Ananas restaurant, St. Barts, 214
La Pecherie restaurant, Guadeloupe,
    120
La Piazzetta restaurant, Santo
    Domingo, Dom. Rep., 85
La Plantation restaurant, Guade-
    loupe, 115–116
La Posada hotel, Santo Domingo,
    Dom. Rep., 79
La Reserve-Chez Jeanne restaurant,
    Guadeloupe, 118
La Rhumerie restaurant, St. Martin,
    255
La Romana, Dom. Rep., 78
    hotels, 80–81
    nightlife, 85
La Samanna hotel, St. Martin, 251
La Samanna restaurant, St. Martin,
    254

La Vie en Rose restaurant, St. Martin, 253
La Villa Creole restaurant, Martinique, 179
Las Brisas hotel, La Romana, Dom. Rep., 81
Latitude hotel, Martinique, 177
Le Baoule restaurant, Guadeloupe, 116
Le Barbaroc restaurant, Guadeloupe, 121
Le Belvedere restaurant, Haiti, 139
Le Bistro, Antigua, 33–34
Le Bistrot restaurant, Guadeloupe, 118
Le Bitaco restaurant, Martinique, 179
Le Boucanier restaurant, Guadeloupe, 116
Le Chalet restaurant, Haiti, 138
Le Colibri restaurant, Martinique, 181
Le d'Esnambuc restaurant, Martinique, 178
Le Fish Pot restaurant, St. Martin, 255
Le Foulard restaurant, Martinique, 178
Le François restaurant, Martinique, 181
Le Galion hotel, St. Martin, 251
Le Galion restaurant, Guadeloupe, 117
Le Gourmet, Antigua, 35
Le Jardin de Jade restaurant, Martinique, 179
Le Karacoli restaurant, Guadeloupe, 122
Le Matador restaurant, Martinique, 180
Le Pelican restaurant, St. Barts, 215
Le Picardie restaurant, Haiti, 139
Le Pirate hotel, St. Martin, 248
Le Poisson d'Or-Chez Nonore restaurant, Guadeloupe, 121
Le Rond-Point restaurant, Haiti, 139

Le Santal restaurant, St. Martin, 253
Le Touloulon restaurant, Martinique, 180
Le Zagaya restaurant, Guadeloupe, 120
Les Brisants restaurant, Martinique, 181
Les Canaris restaurant, La Romana, Dom. Rep., 85
Les Cantonnais restaurant, Martinique, 179
Les Castelets hotel, St. Barts, 213
Les Filets Bleus restaurant, Martinique, 180
Les Mouillages restaurant, Guadeloupe, 122
Les Oiseaux restaurant, Guadeloupe, 119
Les Saintes, Guadeloupe, 110–111
   hotels, 111
Leyritz Plantation hotel, Martinique, 174–175
L'Hiver restaurant, St. Martin, 254
Lina restaurant, Santo Domingo, Dom. Rep., 83
Little Bay Beach hotel, St. Martin, 249
Long Bay Hotel, Antigua, 27
Longstone restaurant, Nevis, 196
Look Out restaurant, Antigua, 32

Mme. Jerco restaurant, Guadeloupe, 120
Maho Reef and Beach Resort hotel, St. Martin, 250
Maison de la Cava restaurant, Santo Domingo, Dom. Rep., 84
Malliouhana Hotel, Anguilla, 10
Malliouhana restaurant, Anguilla, 13
Manoir Alexandra restaurant, Jacmel, Haiti, 139
Manoir de Beauregard hotel, Martinique, 175
Marguerite's restaurant, Jamaica, 158

Marie Galante, Guadeloupe, 110–111
    hotels, 112
Marigot, St. Martin, 247
Marriott's Sam Lord's Castle hotel, Barbados, 51
Martinique, 165–184
    Climate, 165
    Costs, 165
    Documentation, 167
    Formalities, 167
    Holidays, 166
    Hotels, 167, 174–177
    Information, 166
    Map, 103
    Money, 167
    Nightlife, 181–182
    Packing, 166
    Restaurants, 168, 177–181
    Settling Down, 167
    Shopping, 182–183
    Sports, 183–184
    Tipping, 168
    Tour Operators, 166
    Touring, 171–174
    Transportation, 167, 169
Mary's Boon hotel, St. Martin, 248
Maurice's restaurant, Antigua, 35
Meliá Dominicana hotel, Samana, Dom. Rep., 82
Meridien hotel, Guadeloupe, 114
Méridien Martinique hotel, Martinique, 176
Merrywing Resorts hotel, Anguilla, 12
Meson de Castilla restaurant, Santo Domingo, Dom. Rep., 84
Mini Club restaurant, St. Martin, 253
Mona Lisa restaurant, Bonaire, 67
Mont Joli hotel, Haiti, 136
Montego Bay, Jamaica, 149
Montpelier hotel, Nevis, 192
Montpelier restaurant, Nevis, 195
Mooshay Bay Publick House hotel, St. Eustatius, 224

Mooshay Bay retaurant, St. Eustatius, 225
Morne Fondue restaurant, Grenada, 97
Moxon's restaurant, Jamaica, 157
Mrs. Welton Howe, at Home, restaurant, Nevis, 196
Mustique, 1–2

Nevis, 185–200
    Climate, 185
    Costs, 185
    Documentation, 185
    Formalities, 185
    Holidays, 185
    Hotels, 192–194
    Information, 185
    Map, 203
    Money, 185
    Nightlife, 197
    Packing, 185
    Restaurants, 194–197
    Settling Down, 185
    Shopping, 197–199
    Sports, 199–200
    Tour Operators, 185
    Touring, 188–192
    Transportation, 185
New Antigua Horizons hotel, Antigua, 28–29
New Kingston hotel, Jamaica, 156
Nisbet Plantation Inn hotel, Nevis, 193
Nisbet Plantation restaurant, Nevis, 194
Normandie Hotel restaurant, St. Barts, 217
Novotel Fleur d'Epeé hotel, Guadeloupe, 114

Ocean Terrace Inn hotel, St. Kitts, 236
Ocean Terrace Inn restaurant, St. Kitts, 237
Oceana hotel, Jamaica, 156
Ocho Rios, Jamaica, 149–150

Officers' Quarters Refreshments restaurant, Antigua, 34
Old Gin House hotel, St. Eustatius, 224
Old Gin House restaurant, St. Eustatius, 225
Old Yacht Club-La Brigantine restaurant, St. Barts, 215
Oloffson Montrouis hotel, Haiti, 134
Orangestad, St. Eustatius, 221
Out Island Villas hotel, Samana, Dom. Rep., 82
Oyster Pond hotel, St. Martin, 248

Palm Island, 4
Palm restaurant, St. Kitts, 237
Papillon Bar and Dining Room restaurant, Antigua, 32
Pension Craft hotel, Haiti, 137
Pension Craft restaurant, Jacmel, Haiti, 139
Peter Island, B.V.I., 2
Petit St. Vincent, 2–3
Petite Plage hotel, St. Martin, 249
Philipsburg, St. Martin, 247
Phoenicia restaurant, Haiti, 139
Pinney's Beach Hotel restaurant, Nevis, 196
Pinocchio's restaurant, St. Martin, 252
Piperade restaurant, Barbados, 55
Pirate's Cove restaurant, Jamaica, 160
Pisces restaurant, Barbados, 55
Pizzas in Paradise restaurant, Antigua, 35
Plantation Inn hotel, Jamaica, 152
Plantation restaurant, Barbados, 56
PLM-Jean Bart hotel, St. Barts, 213
PLM La Bateliére hotel, Martinique, 176
PLM Marina-Pagerie hotel, Martinique, 177
PLM St. Tropez Beach hotel, St. Martin, 251

Poi et Virginie restaurant, Martinique, 180
Pointe-à-Piétre, Guadeloupe, 115
Port Antonio, Jamaica, 150
Port-au-Prince, Haiti, 133
Port Royal, Jamaica, 149
Porto Fino restaurant, St. Martin, 253
PSV, 2
Puerto Plata, Dom. Rep., 78
  hotels, 82
  restaurants, 85
  sports, 86–87
Punta Cana, Dom. Rep.
  hotels, 82

Rainbow restaurant, St. Martin, 255
Ravine Chaude restaurant, Guadeloupe, 121
Rawlins Plantation hotel, St. Kitts, 235
Red Crab Pub restaurant, Grenada, 97
Red Snapper restaurant, Antigua, 33
Relais de la Grande Soufriere hotel, Guadeloupe, 113
Relais de la Grande Soufriere restaurant, Guadeloupe, 122
Relais de l'Empereur hotel, Haiti, 137
Relais du Moulin hotel, Guadeloupe, 113
Rendezvous Bay Hotel, Anguilla, 11
Residence Katherine Dunham (hotel), Port-au-Prince, Haiti, 135
Rest Haven restaurant, Nevis, 196
Richmond Hill Inn restaurant, Jamaica, 157
Riviera restaurant, Anguilla, 13
Roi Christophe hotel, Haiti, 137
Rookery Nook restaurant, Nevis, 196–197
Rose Hall Beach Hotel and Country Club, Jamaica, 154

Ross Point Inn hotel, Grenada, 96
Ross Point Inn restaurant, Grenada, 96–97
Rossini restaurant, Guadeloupe, 116
Rotisserie-Bertrand restaurant, St. Barts, 215
Round Hill hotel, Jamaica, 151
Royal Caribbean hotel, Jamaica, 155
Royal Haitian Hotel and Casino, Haiti, 137
Royal St. Kitts hotel, St. Kitts, 236
Rudolf's restaurant, Grenada, 97
Ruins restaurant, Jamaica, 158
Rusty Pelican restaurant, St. Martin, 253

Saba, 201–206
　Climate, 201
　Documentation, 202
　Holidays, 201
　Hotels, 204–205
　Information, 201
　Map, 203
　Nightlife, 205
　Packing, 201
　Restaurants, 205
　Settling Down, 202
　Shopping, 205–206
　Sports, 206
　Transportation, 202
St. Andrew Guest House, Jamaica, 160
St. Aubin hotel, Martinique, 175
St. Barth Beach hotel, St. Barts, 214
St. Barts, 207–218
　Costs, 207
　Documentation, 208
　Formalities, 208
　Holidays, 207
　Hotels, 209, 212–214
　Information, 208
　Map, 23
　Money, 209
　Nightlife, 217
　Restaurants, 209, 214–217

Settling Down, 209
Shopping, 217–218
Sports, 218
Tipping, 209
Touring, 211–212
Transportation, 208, 209
Villa Rentals, 214
St. Eustatius, 219–227
　Costs, 219
　Documentation, 220
　Formalities, 220
　Holidays, 219
　Hotels, 224
　Information, 219
　Map, 203
　Money, 220
　Nightlife, 226
　Packing, 220
　Restaurants, 225
　Settling Down, 220
　Shopping, 226
　Sports, 226–227
　Tipping, 221
　Tour Operators, 219
　Touring, 222–223
　Transportation, 220
St. George's, Grenada, 92–93
St. James Beach Club hotel, Barbados, 53
St. Kitts, 228–241
　Costs, 228
　Documentation, 229
　Holidays, 228
　Hotels, 234–236
　Information, 228
　Map, 203
　Money, 229
　Nightlife, 239
　Packing, 228
　Restaurants, 236–239
　Settling Down, 229
　Shopping, 239–240
　Sports, 241
　Tour Operators, 228
　Touring, 231–233
　Transportation, 229

St. Martin, 242–259
  Costs, 242
  Documentation, 243
  Formalities, 244
  Holidays, 242
  Hotels, 244, 248–251
  Information, 243
  Map, 23
  Money, 244
  Nightlife, 255–256
  Packing, 243
  Restaurants, 244, 251–255
  Settling Down, 244
  Shopping, 256–257
  Sports, 257–259
  Tipping, 244
  Tour Operators, 243
  Touring, 246–248
  Transportation, 243, 245–246
Salako hotel, Guadeloupe, 115
Samana, Dom. Rep.
  hotels, 81
Sand Dollar, The, Barbados, 55
Sandals hotel, Jamaica, 155
Sandpiper Inn hotel, Barbados, 53
Sandy Beach hotel, Barbados,
  51–52
Sandy Lane hotel, Barbados, 50
Sans Souci hotel, Jamaica, 153
Santo Domingo, Dom. Rep., 74–78
  hotels, 79–80
  restaurants, 82–83
  nightlife, 85
  shopping, 85–86
  sports, 86
Scout's Place hotel, Saba, 204
Scout's Place restaurant, Saba, 205
Sebastiano-restaurant, St. Martin,
  255
Secret Harbor hotel, Grenada, 94
Sereno Beach hotel, St. Barts, 214
Sereno Beach restaurant, St. Barts,
  216
Settlers Beach hotel, Barbados, 52
Shaw Park Beach hotel, Jamaica,
  155

Sheraton Hotel and Casino, Santo
  Domingo, Dom. Rep., 79
Sheraton Mullet Bay hotel, St. Mar-
  tin, 249
Shorty's restaurant, Antigua, 35
Sint Maarten Beach Club Hotel and
  Casino, St. Martin, 249
Skiffles Villas hotel, Anguilla, 11
Smitty's restaurant, Anguilla, 12
Sosuamar hotel, La Romana, Dom.
  Rep., 81
Southern Palms Beach Club hotel,
  Barbados, 53
Spanish Main Inn hotel, Antigua,
  29
Spanish Main Inn restaurant, Anti-
  gua, 34
Spice Island Inn, Grenada, 95
Splendid hotel, Port-au-Prince,
  Haiti, 136
Sundowner restaurant, Jamaica, 159

Taino Beach hotel, Haiti, 137
Taiwana Club restaurant, St. Barts,
  216
Talk of the Town restaurant,
  Jamaica, 159
Talk of the Town restaurant, St.
  Eustatius, 225
Terra Nova hotel, Jamaica, 153
Terra Nova restaurant, Jamaica, 159
Tiffany restaurant, Martinique, 178
Town House restaurant, Jamaica,
  157
Treasure Beach hotel, Barbados, 52
Trident Villas and Hotel, Jamaica,
  152
Trident Villas and Hotel restaurant,
  Jamaica, 156
Tropical hotel, St. Barts, 213
Tryall Golf and Beach Club hotel,
  Jamaica, 151
Tryall Gold and Beach Club res-
  taurant, Jamaica, 156
Twelve Degrees North hotel, Grena-
  da, 95

Typic Bellevue restaurant, Martinique, 178

Valley, the, Anguilla, 9
Verandah restaurant, Jamaica, 158
Vesuvio I restaurant, Santo Domingo, Dom. Rep., 84
Vesuvio II restaurant, Santo Domingo, Dom. Rep., 84
Victor's restaurant, St. Kitts, 238
Victoria hotel, Martinique, 175
Victory Restaurant and Bar, the, Antigua, 33
Villa Creole hotel, Haiti, 136
Village, the, restaurant, Antigua, 35
Village St. Jean hotel, St. Barts, 214

Wajang Doll restaurant, St. Martin, 251

Waves restaurant, St. Martin, 255
West Indian Tavern restaurant, St. Martin, 252
Witch Doctors restaurant, Barbados, 56

Xaragua hotel, Haiti, 137

Yard, The, restaurant, Antigua, 34
Young Island, 3–4

Zeezicht restaurant, Bonaire, 68
Zetland Plantation hotel, Nevis, 193–194
Zetland Plantation restaurant, Nevis, 195